A Political Economy of Canadian Broadcasting

A Political Economy of Canadian Broadcasting
Public Good versus Private Profit

David Skinner

UBCPress · Vancouver · Toronto

Printed in Canada on FSC-certified ancient-forest-free paper (100% post-consumer recycled) that is processed chlorine- and acid-free.

UBC Press is a Benetech Global Certified Accessible™ publisher. The epub version of this book meets stringent accessibility standards, ensuring it is available to people with diverse needs.

Library and Archives Canada Cataloguing in Publication

Title: A political economy of Canadian broadcasting : public good versus private
    profit / David Skinner.
Names: Skinner, David, author
Description: Includes bibliographical references and index.
Identifiers: Canadiana 20240494326 | ISBN 9780774871471 (softcover)
Subjects: LCSH: Public broadcasting – Canada – History – 20th century. |
    LCSH: Public broadcasting – Canada – History – 21st century. | LCSH: Broadcasting
    policy – Canada – History – 20th century. | LCSH: Broadcasting policy – Canada –
    History – 21st century. | LCSH: Canada – Economic conditions – 20th century. |
    LCSH: Canada – Economic conditions – 21st century.
Classification: LCC HE8689.9.C3 S57 2025b | DDC 384.54097109/04—dc23

Canada

Canada Council   Conseil des arts
for the Arts   du Canada

BRITISH COLUMBIA
ARTS COUNCIL

BRITISH
COLUMBIA

UBC Press gratefully acknowledges the financial support for our publishing program of the Government of Canada, the Canada Council for the Arts, and the British Columbia Arts Council.

This book has been published with the help of a grant from the Canadian Federation for the Humanities and Social Sciences, through the Scholarly Book Awards, using funds provided by the Social Sciences and Humanities Research Council of Canada.

UBC Press is situated on the traditional, ancestral, and unceded territory of the xʷməθkʷəy̓əm (Musqueam) people. This land has always been a place of learning for the xʷməθkʷəy̓əm, who have passed on their culture, history, and traditions for millennia, from one generation to the next.

Printed and bound in Canada
Set in Helvetica Condensed and Minion by Apex CoVantage, LLC
Copy editor: Francis Chow
Proofreader: Judith Earnshaw
Indexer: Margaret de Boer
Cover designer: JVDW Designs
Cover image: *Telecommunication Tower*, patilankur/iStock

UBC Press
The University of British Columbia
www.ubcpress.ca

To all those who have worked so hard to try to ensure that the Canadian media system might represent all the peoples living in Canada

Contents

Acknowledgments

I AM GRATEFUL to a number of persons and institutions for helping me realize this project. It began as part of my graduate studies at Concordia and Simon Fraser Universities, where Martin Allor, Maurice Charland, Michael Dorland, Liora Salter, Robert Hackett, Alison Beale, Catherine Murray, and Richard Gruneau helped set me on this path years ago. I am also indebted to a number of writers whose observations and insights helped forge the historical terrain across which this work travels. Among those are Robert Babe, Herschel Hardin, Harold Innis, Mary Jane Miller, H.V. Nelles, Frank Peers, Marc Raboy, Dallas Smythe, Serra Tinic, Mary Vipond, E. Austin Weir, and Dwayne Winseck. More recently, graduate students, research assistants, staff, faculty, and several small grants at York University – as well as a grant from the Canadian Media Research Consortium – kept it going. Specifically, Nicholas Mills, Amanda Oye, Scott Baird, and Daniela Mastrocola provided important research assistance. I would also like to thank the anonymous referees for their thoughtful comments and suggestions, and the people at UBC Press – particularly Randy Schmidt and Ann Macklem – for bringing the book to fruition. Finally, on the home front, my mother, my sister, and particularly Jennefer provided far-reaching support. Of course, any shortcomings are my own.

Abbreviations

ACA	Association of Canadian Advertisers
ACTRA	Alliance of Canadian Cinema, Television and Radio Artists
AI	artificial intelligence
AP	Associated Press
APTN	Aboriginal Peoples Television Network
AQPM	L'Association québécoise de la production médiatique
AT&T	American Telephone and Telegraph
BBC	British Broadcasting Corporation
BBG	Board of Broadcast Governors
BBM	Bureau of Broadcast Measurement
BCE	Bell Canada Enterprises
BDU	broadcast distribution undertaking
BRC	Board of Railway Commissioners
BTLR	Broadcasting and Telecommunications Legislative Review Panel
CAAA	Canadian Association of Advertising Agencies
CAB	Canadian Association of Broadcasters
CARTB	Canadian Association of Radio and Television Broadcasters
CATV	cable TV
CBC	Canadian Broadcasting Corporation
CBS	Columbia Broadcasting System
CCAU	Coalition of Canadian Audiovisual Unions
CCTA	Canadian Cable Television Association
CFDC	Canadian Film Development Corporation
CMF	Canadian Media Fund
CMPA	Canadian Media Producers Association
CNN	Cable News Network
CNR	Canadian National Railway
CP	Canadian Press
CPR	Canadian Pacific Railway
CRBC	Canadian Radio Broadcasting Commission
CRL	Canadian Radio League
CRTC	Canadian Radio-television and Telecommunications Commission
CTF	Canadian Television Fund

CTV	Canadian Television Network
CUSFTA	Canada-US Free Trade Agreement
DBS	direct broadcast satellite
DGC	Directors Guild of Canada
DOC	Department of Communications
DTH	direct-to-home [satellites]
FCC	Federal Communications Commission
FRC	Federal Radio Commission
GE	General Electric
HBO	Home Box Office
HD	high definition
HNIC	*Hockey Night in Canada*
IATSE	International Alliance of Theatrical Stage Employees, Moving Picture Technicians, Artists and Allied Crafts of the United States, Its Territories and Canada
ICT	information and communications technologies
IHAC	Information Highway Advisory Council
ILNF	Independent Local News Fund
IP	intellectual property
ISP	internet service provider
LPIF	Local Program Improvement Fund
MDS	multipoint distribution systems
NAFTA	North American Free Trade Agreement
NBC	National Broadcasting Company
NFB	National Film Board
NHL	National Hockey League
NTSC	National Television System Committee
OLMC	official language minority communities
OTA	over-the-air [broadcasters]
OTT	over-the-top [programming services]
PBS	Public Broadcasting Service
PNI	programs of national interest
PPF	Public Policy Forum
RCA	Radio Corporation of America
TVNC	Television Northern Canada
UHF	ultra-high frequency
VHF	very high frequency
VOD	video on demand
WGC	Writers Guild of Canada

A Political Economy of Canadian Broadcasting

Introduction

SINCE THE INCEPTION of broadcasting in Canada, particularly anglophone Canada, policy-makers, scholars, and activists have wrestled with the problem of foregrounding the representation of Canadian ways of life, or Canadian "culture," in broadcast programming. Yet, with every technological advance, every regulatory adjustment, the difficulties in meeting this goal seem to multiply. From the early days of radio to the contemporary environment of digital media platforms and streaming, creating broadcast programming content representing the range of ideas, values, and ways of life of the peoples living in this country has been a perennial problem. Employing a critical political economy of communication, this book situates the roots of this problem in the institutional structure of regulation. It examines the ways in which the political and economic dimensions of the system work to enable and constrain the allocation, production, distribution, and consumption of the communicative resources within it (cf. Mosco 2009, 2; Golding and Murdock 1991).

The following key questions are considered: Why is it so difficult to find programming, other than news, that represents Canadian ideas, values, and perspectives within the system? Why is it that a system that almost from its inception has been characterized as a "public service" has long been dominated by private capital and private interests? What role has the Canadian Broadcasting Corporation/Radio-Canada (CBC)[1] played in the development of the broadcasting system? If, as so often stated in federal policy studies and documents, the CBC, and public broadcasting in general, is so important to Parliament's stated objectives for the system, why is it perennially underfunded? Why can the private sector seem to always find the means to invest in mergers and acquisitions but money for Canadian programming is scarce? Why are not-for-profit organizations, and community groups that are specifically mandated to create Canadian content programming, often denied licences and privileges while the regulator perpetually struggles to pressure profit-oriented stations to meet their content requirements?

This book demonstrates that the institutional relationships deployed in broadcast regulation are derived from a historical set of relationships between the Canadian state and private capital that tend to foreground the development of private capital over other social goals, and that through time these relationships have come to be expressed in the regulatory structures and processes that give form to the broadcasting system.

Setting the development of Canadian broadcasting within the larger context of general industrial development, the book examines the growth of the system, mainly in anglophone Canada, in several historical periods ranging from the 1920s to 2023. In each of these periods, regulation is shown as working in the context of larger industrial imperatives to engender a dynamic web of relationships between the state's regulatory instruments, domestic private capital, foreign capital, and technological innovation – relationships that, taken together, produce a set of circumstances that constrain Canadian cultural expression within the system.

The Literature

Historically, the mainstream of the anglophone literature on Canadian broadcasting frames its development as a struggle between more or less rational actors competing for the representation of their interests within a system that is governed by a relatively transparent political process, scarce material resources, and dynamic technological change. Writing almost fifty years ago, E. Austin Weir (1965, 449) captures the general tenor of both the historical and contemporary literature in this vein:

> Broadcasting has been a history of struggles – between two great railway systems; between railway and telephone transmission interests; between provincial and federal authorities as to jurisdiction; between small community and large regional privately owned stations for a share of limited revenues; between the hucksters and the intellectuals; between artists demanding adequate remuneration for their talents and stations occasionally struggling to make ends meet ... between aspiring amateurs and trained professionals; between various program elements, regions and language groups seeking places in the sun as well as their share of available dollars; between bureaucracy and creativity – and, encompassing all of these, between public and private broadcasting.

Among examples of this body of work, two volumes by Frank Peers (1969, 1979) are generally acknowledged as the most thorough and rigorous, charting the history of broadcasting to 1968. Mary Vipond (1992) has examined the early development of the system prior to the establishment of public broadcasting, and Matthew Fraser (1999) focuses on more recent struggles around broadcast technology. Writers such as Margaret Prang (1965); Weir (1965); Stuart McFadyen, Colin Hoskins, and David Gillen (1980); Kenneth Dewar (1982); Paul Audley (1983); Paul Rutherford (1990), Vipond (1992); Ross Eaman (1994); Knowlton Nash (1994); Liss Jeffrey (1996); Susan Gittens (1999); and Richard Stursberg and Stephen Armstrong (2019) are just a few of those who have made more focused contributions in this area. In addition, Wade Rowland (2013, 2015) has provided two nuanced considerations of the history and plight of the CBC in this context. As well, a wide variety of MA and PhD theses add both depth and breadth to these writings (Carscallen 1966; Saunderson 1972; P. Anderson 1976; Blakely 1979), while a veritable mountain of both publicly and privately sponsored studies and inquiries develop issues and set terms for debates (e.g., [GD]* Royal Commission on Radio Broadcasting 1929; [GD] Royal Commission on the Development of the Arts, Letters and Sciences 1951; [GD] Royal Commission on Broadcasting 1957; [GD] Special Senate Committee on the Mass Media 1970a; [GD] Task Force on Broadcasting Policy 1986; [GD] Standing Committee on Canadian Heritage 2003; [GD] BTLR 2020; Nordicity 2006, 2011; [GD] CRTC 2017a; Public Policy Forum 2017; Hunter, Englehart, and Miller 2017).

There are large differences in both the sites of analysis and the research methods employed in these works. Generally, however, focusing on the broadcasting system itself, they frame the public and private sectors as antagonists, working to exert their influence in an arena that is to a large degree protected by regulation but whose parameters are dictated by a burgeoning American broadcasting industry and a scarcity of resources in the Canadian system. Consequently, they view what is perhaps the most consistent feature of the system – a growing presence of foreign programming – as the product of either consumer choice, strategic action on the part of specific interests, or forces or circumstances outside of the system's control.

The problem with this orientation is that it tends to underplay or overlook four important aspects of the system's development: (1) how transnational relations of production have not only helped determine the parameters of the field of broadcasting but also extended into the heart of its organization and development, nuancing the structure of regulation and helping finance the growth of both the public and private sectors; (2) how institutions, forged in the context of Canada's early industrial development and then deployed in the field of broadcasting, have worked together with private capital in a complex and contradictory manner to construct a common systemic response to the underinvestment or undercapitalization of the system and build a "national" broadcasting system; (3) how the structure of regulation has encouraged a division of responsibility between the public and private elements that has set the public element on the margins of the commercial system; and (4) how, both directly and

---

* All works tagged with "[GD]" are listed under "Government Documents [GD]" in the Works Cited at the end of this book.

indirectly, the public sector has subsidized the growth of private broadcasters through much of the development of the system. In highlighting and exploring these aspects of the system's development, this study differs from the existing literature in illustrating how the growing presence of foreign programming is more the product of the structure of regulation than of either successful strategic action on the part of the private sector or market forces. This is not to deny that the broadcasting system is indeed the product of social struggle. For almost a hundred years broadcast regulation has been a microcosm of the tensions and contradictions that have wracked the country as a whole. But these struggles have taken place across a field of institutions and social assumptions that, in the march of history, has played to the advantage of one often fickle and shifting interest – private capital.

A growing body of work that touches upon some of the questions animating this volume is television studies. As Bredin, Henderson, and Matheson (2011, 13) illustrate, while often drawing from a British cultural studies heritage, this work primarily examines media texts and is "marked by a multiplicity of critical methods." Here the focus is on "text and context" and the interplay between culture and its representation, including "televisual ... structures and styles, their international currency, broader institutional structures, the nature of the media industry, (and) relationships to new technologies" (Bredin, Henderson, and Matheson 2011, 15; see, for instance, Miller [1987]; Rutherford [1990]; Druick and Kotsopoulos [2008]; Bredin, Henderson, and Matheson [2011]; Mirrlees and Kispal-Kovacs [2013]). To a degree, the emergence of this work marks the success of media regulation in creating the conditions necessary for a Canadian televisual production industry, and an analytic "step forward" in "that Canadian television scholars no longer feel the need to agonize over issues of national identity or defend the role of television within the nation state" (Bredin, Henderson, and Matheson 2011, 15). As Tanner Mirrlees and Joseph Kispal-Kovacs (2013, xvii) point out, this text-centred approach is compatible with the study at hand as "the best practitioners of cultural studies are those who are firmly grounded in political economy." In this vein, rather than examine "the content of programming produced," the purpose of this book is to provide "essential economic and social context for understanding why we have the kind of television we do" (Bredin, Henderson, and Matheson 2011, 9). As Mirrlees and Kispal-Kovacs (2013, xv) observe, "US media dominance in Canada was not achieved by coercive domination, but by invitation. Canadian corporate actors have long sought to capitalize on the TV industry's proximity to the United States while maintaining a government system of subsidies and protections." Understanding the political economic dimensions of this relationship is key to understanding the practices of representation that drive Canadian media production and the content they realize.

Where this book does part company with cultural studies–inspired analyses, however, is when such work downplays or denies the importance of the political economic context in practices of representation and/or the role of televisual products in the constitution of material culture (Beaty and Sullivan 2006; Collins 1990).

Closer to the analytic take found in this volume are writers and researchers who eschew focusing on media texts to primarily examine the ways in which political and economic relationships have structured the development of the system. Like Paul Starr's (2004) book *The Creation of the Media,* this work strives to cast the development of the media in a larger historical, political economic context – only here the analysis is much more granular, focusing specifically on the Canadian broadcasting system. Marc Raboy's (1990) excellent volume *Missed Opportunities: The Story of Canada's Broadcasting Policy* illustrates how the national pretensions of the Canadian state have animated the form and direction of broadcasting policy. Other writers have also used elements of critical political economy to analyze and explain the impacts of private investment on particular sectors of the system (Babe 1979, 1990; Dewar 1982; Salter 1981, 1988; Salter and Odartey-Wellington 2008; Tinic 2005, 2009, 2010, 2015; Taras 2015; Taras and Waddell 2020; Taylor 2013, 2016). Generally, however, these writers do not address how the system as a whole works to foreground the promotion of private economic interests and marginalizes interests not directly responsible to capital. In other instances, analyses are too economically deterministic, and thereby fail to account for the often contradictory role that the state and its instruments have played in the process of development (Smythe 1981; Hardin 1985).

Focusing at the institutional level, this book attempts to bridge these gaps and point to a regulatory path that might reinvigorate public communication and particularly public broadcasting in Canada. As Raboy (1995) notes, "the history of broadcasting everywhere up to and including the present has shown that only through sustained public policy action can the medium begin to fulfill its (public service) potential." However, as we shall see, the history of broadcast regulation in Canada is also one of subordination, where the interests of public service have systematically been placed behind those of private capital. But if the goal is to reinvigorate the system, then the choice is not simply between regulation by either the market or the state. Rather, in the tumult of change and transformation that currently grips the media system, we must find new ways to foreground public goals in both regulation and practice, enlist new modes of financing production, and open new avenues of access and distribution. Getting these, however, does not mean abandoning tradition. Rather, the idea is to draw upon the strengths of the past to face the challenges of the future.

Overview of the Chapters

Chapter 1 lays the foundation for the analysis by tracing some of the key historical dimensions of the Canadian state's involvement in economic development. It shows that through the course of the nineteenth century, a number of federal institutions were developed that provided a buffer between private economic interests and the uncertainties of a largely staples-based economy, and that over time this relationship became expressed in both the general structure of regulation as well as the institutional form of specific regulatory instruments, such as the Crown corporation and the regulatory board.

Chapter 2 considers how the state's propensity to act as a buffer between private capital and the exigencies of the market informed the development of Canada's media industries in general, and broadcasting in particular. It examines how, despite some obvious differences in the form and direction of development of the newspaper, magazine, film, and broadcast industries, there is a pattern underlying state intervention and the ways in which they were all dependent upon the importation of largely American technique (e.g., technology and/or business practices; cf. Innis 1933, 34) and capital in their early formation. It also illustrates how broadcasting was differentiated from what would later become known as these other "culture" – or, more recently, "creative" – industries and set upon a unique regulatory path.

Chapters 3 and 4 focus on the development of the radio broadcasting system from 1929 to 1948. They describe how the system's growth was tied to a larger process of industrial development, and detail how the historical relationships between the state and private capital described in Chapter 1 came to frame and inform broadcast regulation. They illustrate that while the broadcasting system was envisioned within public policy as a "single system," from the outset of regulation a division of responsibility between the public and private elements began to emerge that set the public element on the commercial margins of the system, where it worked to extend the development of the broadcasting system while, at the same time, often both directly and indirectly, subsidizing the growth of the private sector.

Chapters 5 and 6 focus on the development of English television broadcasting in Canada from its inception to the enactment of the Broadcasting Act of 1968. Again, changes in the practice of broadcasting are related to a larger set of political and economic circumstances and the industrial development of the economy in general. From this perspective, some key moments in broadcast history that are characterized as lost chances for public expression can be seen as largely the product of a regulatory environment tilted in favour of private investment, rather than as simple successful strategic action on the part of private broadcasters or bureaucratic favouritism and mismanagement, as is often argued. These chapters also illustrate how the branch-plant character of the system held much stronger sway over the direction of its development than is generally acknowledged, and how, throughout the changes in technology and regulation that characterize this period, the public broadcaster continued to play a major role in both developing broadcast resources and directly and indirectly subsidizing the private sector.

Chapters 7 and 8 examine the development of English-language television from 1968 to the early 2000s. Set in the context of the ongoing capitalization and commodification of communication and culture – that is, the restructuring of cultural activity into commercial products – these chapters illustrate that although there were dramatic changes in broadcast technology and the structure of the broadcasting system during this period, broadcast regulation generally followed an established historical pattern. Private broadcasters sought to increase profits by developing economies of scale and working to minimize regulatory responsibilities, while the public broadcaster tended to focus resources on the commercial margins of the system while continuing to help capitalize it. Moreover, while the scope of regulation was expanded to include a broader range of social interests and types of broadcast programming during this period, for the most part the interests of these broadcasters were subordinated to those of private profit-driven operators.

Chapter 9 focuses on the period from the turn of the twenty-first century to the updating of the Broadcasting Act of 1991 through the legislation of the Online Streaming Act in 2023.[2] This chapter illustrates that, in the face of fragmenting markets and shrinking revenues, the Canadian Radio-television and Telecommunications Commission (CRTC) allowed private capital freer rein within the media system in general, resulting in a growing presence of foreign content and unregulated foreign media platforms and their products, escalating concentration of ownership, and increasing relief from regulatory responsibilities for private broadcasters. Meanwhile, while suffering serious financial setbacks, the CBC continued to push the margins of the media system and focus resources on producing distinctively Canadian media content.

Building on the analysis, the Conclusion suggests that perhaps the best way to encourage the production and distribution of distinctive Canadian media content is to allow the CBC and other not-for-profit elements of the system greater latitude in the ways in which they finance and organize production and distribution. Some ways in which this might be accomplished are discussed.

Some Definitions

The primary method of analysis employed here is a critical political economy of communication. It takes its focus from Vincent Mosco's (2009, 2) definition of political economy as "the study of social relations, particularly the power relations, that mutually constitute the production, distribution, and consumption of ... communicative resources." However, I add "allocation" to this formulation as the primary step in the process. At this level, the resources required for production are identified and consigned to particular social interests. To a large part, this process of allocation is the focus of this book as it traces the ways in which the Canadian state and its instruments identify and consign the resources of the Canadian broadcasting system to private, public, and community interests. In that this process of allocation impacts upon "methods of financing and organizing cultural production," as Peter Golding and Graham Murdock (1991, 15) note, it might "have traceable consequences for the range of discourses and representations within the public domain and the audience's access to them."

Other key terms employed in this book include:

- Capitalization – The process of utilizing income or assets to create the conditions for capital accumulation. Capitalization is not simply "investment," but investment that serves the purpose of creating surplus or profit from the production process.
- Commodification – "The process of transforming goods or services which are valued for their use value, e.g., food to satisfy hunger, stories for communication, into commodities which are valued for what they can earn in the market place, e.g., commercial farming to sell food, producing drama for commercial broadcasting" (Mosco 2009, 11). Commodification can take both extensive and intensive forms. Extensive commodification extends the commodity form into new areas of exploitation; e.g., the first cable systems offered a new way to distribute a number of television signals to the home for a flat fee. Intensive commodification builds upon an existing commodity form to create new commodities; e.g., cable television developed into a system that now distributes a number of different kinds of television signals that are paid for individually.
- Transnational relations of production – A situation where key elements of the production process in one country are dependent upon products or infrastructure emanating from another country. For example, to the extent that the Canadian broadcasting system has been dependent on the profits generated from American broadcast programming for financial return and investment, it might be seen as being dependent on transnational relations of production.

1

The Development Context of Canadian Communications Policy
The Economy, the State, and the Regulatory Tradition

WHILE THE DEVELOPMENT of contemporary media and media systems has its roots in the dawn of industrial society, so too some of the most decisive moments in the development of the Canadian broadcasting system occurred before the technique of broadcasting was invented, in the early development of Canadian society as institutions and organizations that would shepherd its growth were being forged in the early development of the Canadian state.

As changing patterns of political and economic organization swept across both Europe and North America, new forms of social organization took hold. Fuelled by the production and investment of surplus capital, the growth of industry gave rise to increasingly complex social relationships as both migration and urbanization stamped the geography with the spatial and temporal rhythms of industrial production. Industrial production demanded the coordination of social action across ever-increasing physical distances, as both raw materials for factory processes and foodstuffs for growing populations converged upon burgeoning urban and metropolitan centres. Industrial production also increased the schism between public and private social activities, as increasingly specialized divisions of labour reformulated definitions of family and community life. And industrial production shifted both the form and temporal patterning of social activity, as the demands of industrial time drew a distinction between work and leisure.

As Raymond Williams illustrates, it was in this context that the most visible forms of modern communications media took form. In combination with the larger diffusion of industrial social form and technique, the media developed as a "specialized means" to close the geographical and social distances created by industrial society and to serve new social interests and needs: "the press for political and economic information; the photograph for community, family and personal life; the motion picture for curiosity and entertainment; telegraphy and telephony for business information and some important personal messages" (R. Williams 1979, 22–23).

It was within this array of social forces that broadcasting was forged to "specialised means," as what began as "a set of scattered technical devices became an applied technology and then a social technology" (R. Williams 1979, 22–24). Beginning with radio, and then television, a technique that was first conceived as "wireless telephony" developed into an abstract means of sending a message from a centralized source to a widely dispersed set of relatively anonymous audience members. In this guise, harnessing electromagnetic waves to the transmission of messages is a definitively industrial technique. Its invention and adoption depended upon a broad set of factors, including a set of disparate audience members – in this instance, the private home of the nuclear family – and the industrial techniques of serial production and mass consumption.

In its early stages, the development of broadcasting was driven by equipment manufacturers who consolidated their control of the technology in an effort to derive a profit from the large-scale manufacture of transmission and receiving sets. Programming was simply an expense, a way to sell equipment. But as radio gained popularity, both governments and social interest groups began envisioning broadcasting as more than simply a way to profit from the manufacture of equipment. Its ability to bridge the gap between the newly developing urban way of life and the larger set of social circumstances that animated industrial society at large offered a means of conjoining individuals scattered in space and time and coordinating social action. Differences of opinion arose over the purposes or uses of broadcast program content, mainly regarding the comparative advantages of deploying programming to construct markets or to address non-commercial communities of interest, such as education and religion. But program production, and consequently program content, has always been dependent upon a sustaining set of economic relationships – a means of financing program production and delivery. Consequently, the history of broadcasting is largely the history of the struggle to create an economics of broadcast production, as different social interests have struggled within social, political, and geographic circumstances to find means to finance their particular vision of the technology.

In these struggles, the economics of broadcasting have been shaped and nuanced by significantly different social conditions at the national, regional, and local levels. For instance, in Britain, the physical constraints imposed by spectrum scarcity combined with the Marconi Company's lack of interest in shouldering the financial burden of program production and the political elite's distrust of "commercialism" to yield a state monopoly on radio program production and distribution (Hearst 1992; cf. Dewar 1982; Mundy 1988; Raboy 2016). Under state control, the economies of scale inherent in a limited number of broadcast channels and a densely populated listening audience were harnessed to produce a system of program production financed through receiver licence fees.

In the United States, development was led by a radio manufacturers' cartel, and programming was initially financed through profits from the sale of broadcast receiving and transmission equipment. "Toll" broadcasting, whereby time on the system was rented to program producers, was soon initiated as an additional source of revenue, and the cartel set the economies of scale inherent in the national reach of their broadcast networks to attracting audiences for commercial messages (McChesney 1993; Smulyan 1994, 100–2; Starr 2004).

While the Canadian system is sometimes characterized as a hybrid of the British and American systems, it had none of their advantages (Raboy 1990, 48). Jurisdictional disputes between the federal and provincial governments militated against the institution of a comprehensive national licensing system. Moreover, early on, radio manufacturing in Canada was consolidated on a branch-plant basis, and because signals from the equipment manufacturers' high-power American transmitters flowed freely across the border, there was little incentive for those manufacturers to invest in either program production or distribution in Canada (Vipond 1992). Without income from a licence fee or cross-subsidies from equipment manufacturers, financing presented a problem for Canadian stations and investment was largely undertaken by local businesses and educational and religious organizations (MacLennan 2005). For both technical and financial reasons, network arrangements were out of reach of these broadcasters (Weir 1965). Thus, as broadcasting took form in Canada, much of its technical infrastructure was framed by transnational relations of production that superseded domestic investment in production and distribution. As a result, what investment there was in this regard was based upon a sustaining set of economic relations constructed largely at the local level.

In the face of these problems, nationalist sentiments helped spur state intervention. From a nationalist perspective, broadcasting offered a technique for overcoming both the geographic and cultural differences that characterized the Canadian state. It offered a means of conquering space, in that it opened up an arena for public communication within which the disparate voices of Canada might, at once, both speak and be heard ([GD] Royal Commission on Radio Broadcasting 1929; Charland 1986; cf. Beale 1988).[1] In this context, state policies emerged to support a set of economic relations that would sustain both the production and distribution of broadcast programming. However, neither the rationale that legitimated intervention – a nationalist discourse that represented broadcasting as a means of conjoining a widely dispersed population – nor the chosen form of intervention – government ownership and state regulation of private undertakings – were peculiar to the field of broadcasting. Rather, these social forms were forged in Canada's early commercial and industrial development. In that process, they came to issue a particular set of relationships between the emerging Canadian state, the diverse social interests residing in this settler colonial context, and private capital.

Thus, from broadcasting's first encounter with regulation, to its representation as a technique of national import, to the institution of government ownership, to the introduction of an independent regulatory board, to the growing inter-dependence of the Canadian and American broadcast markets, the growth and structure of the broadcasting system has been nuanced and guided by institutional forms that were given shape in the larger political economic formation of the Canadian state. As these institutional conventions were carried into the formation of the broadcasting system, they not only set the development of the system on a distinctive path but also worked to bring the practice of broadcasting in concert with the larger institutional matrix of the emerging Canadian state. In this process, broadcasting developed as a micro-context of the larger process of Canada's industrial development and, through this process, it assumed a distinctive national form as a social technology that carries through to the present day.

To better understand the ways in which these regulatory forms have provided focus and direction to the development of broadcasting, we must examine their role and development in the formation of the Canadian state. For it is in this larger process of historical development that they were themselves forged to "specialised means" and their institutional character took form.

State Intervention and the Development of a Canadian Economy

To a large extent, the history of the Canadian state is the history of government intervention in the economy. Even before Confederation, the state was a central vehicle in organizing and financing the development of commercial and industrial infrastructure (Innis 1956). From both the direct and indirect financing of canals and railways to the implementation of the tariff to support the growth of industry, to the institution of monetary and competition policy, "the creation of a national economy in Canada and, even more clearly, a transcontinental economy was as much a political as an economic achievement" (Aitken 1967, 184). But located on the margins of both the British and American industrial systems, the governments of the British North American colonies, and later the Canadian government, had little control over the transnational economic currents that determined the demand for the largely staple products that were the basis of their economies. Consequently, industrial strategies were formulated in reaction to larger political economic events (cf. Tucker 1936; Bliss 1982; Albo and Jenson 1997). However, amid these diverse social and economic currents, a larger, historically evolving matrix of relationships between the state and domestic economic development emerged. To a large extent, it was by developing these institutions and the relationships they realized that a form of regulation and control was imposed over the fragmented settler and Indigenous populations that inhabited the northern half of North America.[2]

Led by the expansion of railways and a subsequent extension of the tariff to support their operation, the growth of industry in both the middle and late nineteenth century was accompanied by "a remarkable transformation in the scope and nature of governmental activity" (Curtis 1992, 104; cf. Craven and Traves 1987; Greer and Radforth 1992). At one level, these changes in the regulation of social life were symptomatic of a larger shift in the political "mode of regulation" – or "norms, habits, laws and regulating networks ... that ensure the process of accumulation" – that accompanied the process of industrialization (Harvey 1989, 122). At another level, though, they marked the emergence of a distinctive set of institutions and processes for both managing and governing development. These were some of the first efforts of the emerging state to grapple with what Harold Innis would later call the "rigidities" or obstacles that framed the development of the Canadian political economic system (Drache 1982, 37–38). In other words, they were means to help overcome the challenges of a vast geography, a thin and diverse population, and marked dependencies on other states for markets, technology, and finance capital (Resnick 1990).

Four features of this social schemata that developed between the emerging Canadian state and the social interests that it drew into its purview are described below. Through time they worked together – in a mutually constitutive manner – to form the contours of a set of productive relationships that not only helped shape the development of the Canadian economy in general, but broadcasting as well.

The State as an Economic Buffer

From the direct and indirect financing of canals and railways to the implementation of the tariff, to undertaking, granting, and regulating monopolies in transportation, communications, and other forms of industrial infrastructure, the state has always played a central role in the development of the national economy in Canada (see Innis 1956; Aitken 1967; C. Armstrong and Nelles 1986). In this process, evolving state institutions often played a particular role as both the colonial and dominion governments positioned themselves between private economic interests and the exigencies of an often volatile economy, uneven economic development, and peoples with interests incommensurate with their own. Treading a path blazed by Harold Innis (Innis 1933, 1946, 1954; cf. Drache 1995), C.B. Macpherson (1957, 200) draws the character of this relationship:

> This embrace of private enterprise and government is not at all unusual in new countries. In Canada it is the direct result of the fact that the natural resources,

abundant but scattered, have always afforded the prospect of highly profitable exploitation and could most rapidly be made profitable by concentrating on the production of a few staples for export ... This required a heavy import of capital and heavy government expenditure on railways, power developments, irrigation, land settlement and so on. To support such investment, governments have been driven to monetary and other regulatory policies to offset the swings of an economy so dependent for its revenue on the unstable demand for and prices of a few staples, and so burdened by the fixed costs of interest on its capital indebtedness.

From the Act of Union (1840) to Confederation (1867), to the institution of the National Policy (1878), one of the central motives in enlarging the structure and purview of the state was to guarantee and enhance the conditions necessary for the continued, generally private exploitation of the resources of British North America (Innis 1956; Gagne 1976; Baskerville 1992; Piva 1992). Each of these chapters in Canadian history was to a large degree animated by forces outside the boundaries of the emerging Canadian state as the governments and peoples of the region struggled to maintain their economies and interests in the face of shifting economic conditions (Innis 1956; Bliss 1982; Greer and Radforth 1992). However, as the state became increasingly embroiled in promoting and securing private capital for the purposes of economic expansion, it set the conditions for the emergence of what might be seen as a distinctly Canadian system or "regime" of accumulation, bounded on one side by state production of the conditions necessary for accumulation, and on the other by the growth of private capital and social interests (including the state itself) dependent upon those conditions for their reproduction. As Innis (1956, 229–31) illustrates, for most of the nineteenth century, the dependence of this productive system upon foreign markets, the importation of American technology or "technique," and British finance capital left Canada exposed to fluctuations in the market economy. But under the shepherding of the state and its instruments, the geography of Canada was forged into a distinctive political economic form (252–72).

Railway subsidies and tariff policies of the last quarter of the nineteenth century both broadened and deepened this relationship between the emerging state and its polity. At the end of that period, American industrial expansion began to augment British finance capital in stimulating Canadian economic growth. And, in combination with an agricultural boom on the prairies that was fuelled by the dispossession of Indigenous and Métis peoples and a wave of immigration, the outlines of a transcontinental economy came into focus (see Aitken 1967; Fowke 1967; Daschuk 2013). Throughout this expansion, however, the state was often positioned between the exigencies of economic development and private economic interests, as state institutions and policies were employed to create the conditions necessary for private accumulation and the capitalization of the Canadian landscape (Albo and Jensen 1997; Nelles 2005). In this position, the state assumed both allocative and productive responsibilities.

In combination with private interests, state institutions were employed to both mediate relationships and bridge distances between the markets of metropolitan centres and the developing hinterland. In this process, the state largely played an allocative role: defining, securing, and allocating property rights surrounding the resources under its control. Such rights were both defined and allocated not only in terms of raw productive materials such as mineral and timber rights but also more abstract kinds of resources, such as transportation and communication rights-of-way and copyright. Moreover, to support and sustain the economic relationships arising from this early process of allocation, state institutions also acted as vehicles for raising, guaranteeing, and servicing much of the capital necessary for the exploitation of these resources, especially in terms of the transportation systems that supported resource extraction. For instance, as Daniel Drache (1995, xxiv) notes, by the mid-nineteenth century public authorities had borrowed "the staggering sum" of $350 million "to pay for the first wave of railway and canal construction in Central Canada." And, later, "they borrowed more than $1 billion of foreign capital to finance the construction of the Canadian Pacific Railway and the opening of the West."

In a productive capacity, emerging state institutions also directly engaged in financing, building, and sometimes operating such economic infrastructure. Again, in these early periods, these projects usually took the form of transportation systems, such as canals and railways. Paid for with public funds, and often operated at a deficit as rates were held low to encourage traffic, these systems served as publicly subsidized linkages, or "resources," in the private, profitable exploitation of the countryside (Innis 1933, 36–37).

In neither of these guises did the state aggressively pursue productive activities that would directly generate a surplus for the public treasury. Although government ownership was sometimes envisioned as a way to increase state revenue, generally large-scale government projects were operated at a loss (Tucker 1936). Rather, capital accumulation remained the preserve of private interests, and the developing state presence served as a buffer between those interests and the exigencies of the marketplace (Easterbrook and Aitken 1956; Innis 1956, 69–71; Corry 1939, 1941).

The State's "Own Interest"

By acting as a buffer in economic development, the emerging Canadian state slowly began to develop its own political interest in this process. Driven by the political unrest of the 1830s, the Act of Union (1840) provided the legislative framework for responsible government and a general enhancement of the administrative, monetary, and fiscal powers of the colonial government. Over the next twenty years, the industrial expansion led by the railways provided impetus and form to the development of these powers (Craven and Traves 1987; McCalla 1992). As the purview and responsibilities of the colonial government increased under the pressures of this development, the project of maintaining the political economic system it realized began to force a divergence between its interests and those of the larger British imperial system.[3] Slowly, the emergent state's imperial ties were eclipsed and a distinctive, Canadian political economic system began to develop (cf. Lower 1946, 198–200).

Until the latter quarter of the nineteenth century, though, the growing powers of state institutions were exercised in a generally instrumental fashion by politicians and officials who often realized personal or commercial benefit from government legislation, loan guarantees, and subsidies (Tucker 1936; Fowke 1967; Myers 1972; Piva 1992). But as measures to build a national economy – such as the transcontinental railway, the tariff of the National Policy, and immigration policies – met with belated success in the early twentieth century, the growing rural and urban populations gave rise to a diverse set of social interests that began to exercise a complex set of demands upon these institutions (Aitken 1967, 208–9; Traves 1979).[4] With their fortunes hinging on a fickle, capitalist economy, these interests agitated for political mechanisms through which a more equitable division of social resources might be realized, and across the political and geographic terrain realized by the Canadian state "interregional, intersectoral, intra-industrial, and marked inter-class conflict prevailed on all fronts" (Traves 1979, 8). In this atmosphere, it became increasingly difficult for politicians and other members of Canada's political and economic elite to harness the state and its instruments directly to their own interests (cf. Noel, Boismenu, and Jalbert 1993). As Traves (1979, 8–9) illustrates:

> Under these circumstances the state could not be either the businessman's abject servant or his all-powerful master ... As new issues ... began to exercise the public imagination, politicians had to tread carefully between powerful corporate interests and outraged public opinion ... Throughout the period from the war to the Great Depression, as manufacturers persistently advanced their claims upon the power of the state, politicians of necessity weighed each demand in balance

against standards of national interest and public circumspection, with the latter usually determining the definition of the former. This point is crucial, for despite the ideological sympathies of the leaders and their parties at this time there was never a simple translation of economic might into political power.

Defined by specific geographic boundaries, and pressed by the demands of an increasingly large and diverse population, the Canadian state developed its own interest in development – that of "governance." In this process, the federal state and its institutions developed as a dynamic relation between both the diverse, burgeoning interests of the Canadian polity and a larger set of political and economic forces. From this position, state institutions began to focus on ensuring both the legitimacy and continuity of the political economic system of which they were a part (Curtis 1992, 106–7; cf. Foucault 1991). And, in this position, state institutions became a site of struggle as different Canadian social groups strove to realize their interests through its institutional forms.[5]

As the Canadian state entered the twentieth century, although it was often situated between the economic exigencies of the market and the diverse interests of the Canadian polity in the process of development, its interests were not simply commensurate with private capital.

Nationalism

In part, the rise of the state's own interest in economic development was given form by a "discourse of nationalism" – a meta-narrative that represented the diverse peoples and geography of Canada as a distinct political economic entity.[6] While various visions of a pan-Canadian nationalism began to emerge prior to the 1870s, as Frank Underhill (1964, 24) argues, they "lacked the basis of an effective political movement because they spoke for no particular social groups whose economic ambitions were to be furthered through the activity of a national government ... for no discontented groups who might form the basis of another Grit party ... [and] they did not speak for the most solid group of all, the French-Canadians" (24–33). However, set against the political and economic uncertainty of the early 1870s, John A. Macdonald's Conservative Party moved to articulate this sentiment with "the interests of the ambitious, dynamic, speculative or entrepreneurial business groups, who aimed to make money out of the new national community or to install themselves in the strategic positions of power within it," and a nationalist vision of Canada took form in the political arena (Brown 1966; Aitken 1967; Brewis 1968, 52).

In the face of a fragmented polity, Macdonald's government set out to "create the idea of a commonality among Canadians as a transcontinental nation rather than ... describe one already in existence" (Zeller 1987, 267). From this perspective, the disparate interests of the former colonies were for the first time represented as unified in a common economic project. At what John Thompson (1981) calls the "level of social structure," the discourse provided a linguistic schema for both constructing and legitimating state action. It positioned ideas about the cohesion and strength of the Canadian state, in particular relationships with political and economic conditions, postulating intervention as a necessary step to creating a set of social conditions that would both construct a "people" of Canada and bestow benefits upon them, as well as waylay the political and economic threats that non-intervention presented (Aitken 1967). As a practice of representation, this meta-narrative provided a way of thinking about, or "an orientation" to, the geographic terrain assembled through the political union of the colonies (Charland 1986, 198). By positing a "national interest," the government empowered the state to create a national economy – to construct a "national" mode of political and economic regulation that would sustain a regime of accumulation across a large and diverse geographic and social terrain – and thereby conjoin the provinces and territories in common cause.

While in this initial formulation Canadian nationalism was primarily an economic project, with the political and economic consolidation of the northern half of North America through the late 1870s and early 1880s, the ideological dimensions of this project were, to a degree, given material form (cf. Charland 1986). In this process, the discourse itself was legitimated and a new way of representing Canada was set in play within the political arena, and throughout Canadian history it has been articulated – both successfully and unsuccessfully – with both broad social movements and the policy process to legitimate and/or provide form to state action (cf. G. Williams 1989, 59; Foucault 1972, 220). As Bashevkin (1991, 14) argues, this discourse

> defined what would become a basic parameter of this world view for at least the next one hundred years. The ... vision of an assertive federal state that shaped economic development and, through its ties with the railway and industrial interests, functioned essentially as the architect of economic life, created a virtual identity between federal state action and national interest.

By drawing upon this idea of a single nation, the Canadian state was empowered, through time, to both allocate resources and institute particular relations of production – all in the name of a vaguely defined "national interest" (B. Anderson 2006). In this way, the discourse both legitimates and provides form to the state's own interest and the exercise of governance (Breuilly 1993).

However, the concept of nationalism has always been disputatious, as the various regional, linguistic, ethnic, and Indigenous interests that fall within the Canadian state have all struggled to advance their individual interests in this larger forum of a "national interest." In particular, for the people of Quebec, the notion of pan-Canadian nationalism has often been problematic, and for Indigenous peoples it has been a key component in their subjugation and the imposition of settler colonialism (S. Mann 2002; Daschuk 2013). Rarely, if ever, has a singular ideological vision served to unite the disparate peoples and regions of Canada in common cause or purpose. In fact, because the concept of nationalism has been deployed in so many different ways in the Canadian context, some writers speak of different Canadian "nationalisms" (cf. Bashevkin 1991, 1–38). However, I would suggest that such analytic division works to obscure the multivalent character of the broader discourse, and that its ability to cross, and in part conjoin, so many fields of activity is in fact what has allowed the term to maintain its historical currency. Hence, the point here is simply that the emergence of this "idea" of nationalism provided a conceptual space or site within which these different interests were conjoined in a struggle to press their concerns.[7]

The terms of the national economy enabled by this emergent nationalism were also somewhat paradoxical, as the tariff barrier created to forge this economy was not sensitive to the nationality of capital (Bliss 1970, 40). While the tariff provided a means of stemming the influx of foreign, mainly American, manufactured goods and encouraged the development of a national economy, it also worked to attract and encourage foreign investment in the form of American branch-plant companies that sought to profit from both the emerging Canadian market and Canada's access to British markets.[8] Driven by burgeoning capitalist enterprise in the United States, American direct investment in Canada grew rapidly under this arrangement through the late nineteenth and early twentieth centuries. By "1913 it was estimated that 450 offshoots of American companies were operating in Canada" (Bliss 1970, 97) (cf. Innis 1956, 404–5; Bliss 1970; Levitt 1970; Smythe 1981; Drache 1995).

Thus, from the outset, the project of Canadian nationalism was a project riddled in contradiction. In its initial formulation as an economic project, nationalism provided the ground for the political project of federalism to proceed amid an array of competing regional and cultural interests – particularly those of anglophone and francophone Canada. Later, though, as this branch-plant logic of national economic development encouraged increasing American investment in Canada, these changing political economic conditions would inspire a series of turns in the way the discourse was employed as a lens for interpreting these productive relations, and provoke a series of resistances to this foreign investment (Laxer 1973).

The institutional character of several common types of state action initiated to give form to this national interest in the economy is the fourth dimension of the institutional matrix we will examine.

Regulatory Instruments

As nationalism and industrialization gave rise to a complex physical and social geography, specific kinds of organizations or instruments were forged for dealing with the ensuing complexities of governing or regulating development. Two of these instruments that have played major roles in both the Canadian economy and the broadcasting system are the regulatory commission and the Crown corporation.

The institutional character of these instruments both informs and gives form to action (cf. Giddens 1984; Thompson 1981). They provide a set of material and discursive conditions "through which the accumulated conventions of the past impinge upon the actor and govern the creative production of the future" (Thompson 1981, 174). In that these policy instruments are constituted to undertake specific social and economic responsibilities, the conventions they embody provide form to a particular "institutional rationality" – a particular way (or ways) in which these institutions represent social conditions and, in turn, nuance and direct social action (cf. Mosco 1979, 2009). Consequently, set in a particular policy field, and focused by institutional imperatives other than capital accumulation, these instruments work to shape and define that field. While, as the literature illustrates, these institutions have been deployed for a wide variety of purposes, and their purpose and function in any particular sector of the economy often change through time, as we shall see in the context of both the railways and broadcasting, a key feature of their operation has been to provide form and stability to the development of capital in these fields (see Hodgetts 1973; Tupper and Doern 1981; Prichard 1983; P. Thomas and Zajcew 1993; Iacobucci and Trebilock 2012; Public Policy Forum 2016).

The Regulatory Commission

Through the second half of the nineteenth century, political and economic development was largely equated with the expansion of railways. State institutions played a central role in creating the conditions under which this expansion occurred, issuing charters, subsidies, loan guarantees, land grants, and so on. As the railways became central to the operation of the economy, they became the site of heated social struggles, particularly regarding rates. While a series of quasi-judicial bodies were created to deal with these problems through this period, amid escalating controversy over the railways' financial operation S.J. McLean, a lawyer and economist, was appointed by the federal government to study the situation in 1899. In his report, McLean argued that the railway "is not only a body organized for gain, but also a corporation occupying quasi-public position and performing public functions," and that as an economic monopoly, "the prices charged ... will be on a monopoly, not on a competitive basis" (in Baggaley 1981, 77). Consequently, he found that regulation of the railways could only "be met in one of two ways, State ownership or Commission regulation. There is no middle ground." As Carman Baggaley (1981, 77) notes, "his case for regulation was almost a restatement of the traditional textbook justification: to correct or control the improper allocation of resources caused by monopoly as a means of public interest." Thus, under conditions created by the state, the railway monopolies became key facets of production, and conflicts arose between the blocks of capital that gave them form and other economic and social interests that were dependent upon the roads. Consequently the state was pressured to institute a secondary mechanism for allocating the benefits that the railway provided, and take up the role of arbiter between these competing interests.

After some debate over the merits of public ownership of railways versus regulation, the Railway Act was amended in 1903 and the powers of railway regulation were transferred from government to the Board of Railway Commissioners (BRC). Because the BRC was composed of private individuals and/or experts rather than politicians, and because it was given a wider latitude of powers than similar organizations before it – including legislative, judicial, and executive functions – it is often considered Canada's first "independent" regulatory board or commission (Hodgetts 1973; [GD] Privy Council 1979; Baggaley 1981; C. Armstrong and Nelles 1986).

Such regulatory agencies can have far-reaching effects on "the allocation of resources, on the organization of production and consumption, and on the distribution of income" (Schultz 1982, 93). The decisions of the BRC potentially had such impacts. The rate of return on capital invested in the railways, patterns of investment along railway lines, and the incomes of those dependent upon the lines for their livelihood were all dependent upon the board's decisions. Lacking both investment capital and the capacity to undertake productive activities itself, the board focused on defining, developing, and instituting the "public interest" in the face of competing claims on railroad operation. Thus, while the board's decisions had an impact on the "organization of production and consumption," its role was generally confined to defining property rights (e.g., setting rates) and responsibilities, and dispensing privileges upon private interests, all in an environment shielded from "natural" market forces through state support of the rail system.

From this beginning the commission form has been applied to a wide range of tasks at the federal level, making it difficult to generalize its function.[9]

However, in policy fields where it has been employed to supervise productive activities, it is often argued that the commission plays a threefold function of "policing, promoting, and planning" that field (Baggaley 1981, 82).[10] In other words, playing an "adjudicative role," it works to "dispense privileges, usually amongst competing interests – and arbitrate rights" ([GD] Privy Council 1979, 110). In these capacities, the commission provides stability to capital formation, and helps ensure the maintenance and orderly growth of the field that it supervises (P. Thomas and Zajcew 1993). However, with the commission generally lacking the power to either directly raise or invest capital, this adjudicative function is performed through the allocation of perceived rights, privileges, and responsibilities within that field, with this process itself hinging upon the commission's operationalization of some broader definition or conception of the public or national interest (cf. Salter and Salter 1997, 314–15).

In Canada, the expression of this "national interest" almost immediately became focused on planning, promoting, or policing nationally based productive relationships – a practice that had significant implications for the regulation of broadcasting later in the twentieth century. Rarely noted, however, is the fact that the at least partial protection of the commission's field of operations from the larger economy is key to its operation. Creating such conditions has often been required to induce private investment and/or harness economies of scale. Thus, in the creation of these conditions, the state also constructs an economic micro-context or field that then requires regulation to ensure the smooth allocation of the "resources" created through that field's capitalization.

But while the allocative character of the commission as a policy instrument in this context has been relatively consistent through time, interpretations of its relations with the interests within its purview have not. Writers approaching the subject from a liberal economic tradition tend to stress a public interest or "market failure" interpretation, arguing that such interventions "correct the failures of the marketplace, enhance the quality of life, and ensure economic efficiency" (C. Armstrong and Nelles 1986, 187). A more critical "capture" theory has also been advanced. From this perspective, "regulatory agencies almost invariably become servants rather than masters of the industries over which they preside, and that in the rational pursuit of its long term security, business actively sought regulation to escape the travails of the market" (C. Armstrong and Nelles 1986, 188; cf. Dal Bó 2006; Croley 2007; Nowak 2022).

Building upon a structuralist vision of the state, Rianne Mahon (1980) offers a third perspective. She argues that the regulatory agency is an "unequal structure of representation" (166), which derives its character from "an issue whose resolution demands a modification of the 'rights of capital'" (161) in the larger interest of maintaining accumulation. The regulatory agency deploys its powers to ensure that competing units of capital conform to a larger "national interest" that, in turn, is constructed in the "long-term political interests of the hegemonic fraction of the dominant class" (154).

All of these interpretations are problematic, however. Public interest and market failure perspectives overlook the ways in which this instrument has functioned to both legitimate and encourage the growth of largely private capital, while capture theories subscribe to an instrumentalist vision of the state, as well as overlook the ways in which the very structure of the instrument is focused on encouraging or shepherding capital growth. Indeed, as Liora Salter and Rick Salter (1997, 313–14) point out, "of course regulatory boards and tribunals are captured. They are set in place precisely to fashion compromise; they are often created by request from industry; they establish regimes of co-management." Mahon's (1980) notion of the regulatory agency as an "unequal structure of representation" offers an improvement over these interpretations in that she illustrates that the process of regulation favours the representation of particular groups or interests. However, her reduction of the board to an expression of class forces reduces the complexity of those forces to simple class interests and thereby obscures both the wide range of social interests that might struggle for representation in regulatory decisions as well as particular interests of the Canadian state itself in the process of regulation. This formulation also forecloses on the possibilities of progressive social action in the regulatory arena – possibilities presented by the divergence of the range of interests occupying the field.

The Crown Corporation

Although government-owned corporations were created as early as the mid-1800s, these were basically administrative in structure, and their productive activities were confined to supplying and maintaining commercial and industrial infrastructure, generally in direct support of private capital (Gracey 1982). It was not until the creation of the Canadian National Railway (CNR) in 1919 that the government invented what the Privy Council ([GD] Privy Council 1979, 125) calls the "first entrepreneurial Crown-owned company – meaning a company that provided goods or services in a competitive market, or on a financially self-sustaining basis." This latter type of Crown corporation was distinguished from its predecessors in that it was structured to undertake productive activities, including the production and disposition of capital.

The path to this form of government ownership was an extension of that to the creation of the regulatory board. The allocative structure of state support for railroads imposed few checks on construction as long as it was perceived as stimulating economic growth and, consequently, garnering political support.

Coupled with economic prosperity, state support of the extensive capitalization of the system eventually led into areas where market forces were unable to support the railway's operations and contributed to an overbuilding of the railway system (Innis 1933, 48).

Fuelled by this unsubstantiated economic optimism of the federal government in the first decade of the twentieth century, and the travails of war in the second, by 1917 the debts of two of Canada's three transcontinental railroads had grown beyond the management of the private sector. After much deliberation, nationalization seemed the only way to prevent bankruptcy and the damage this would inflict on both private investors and "Canada's credit in foreign capital markets" (Easterbrook and Aitken 1956, 443).

Still, given the record of political abuses that had accompanied government supervision of such enterprises in the past, direct state ownership was not viewed as a viable option. The 1917 Royal Commission on Railways and Transportation strongly recommended that the railways should be owned by the state but "handed over to a board of trustees to control and manage on behalf of, and on account of, the people of Canada" ([GD] Royal Commission on Railways and Transportation 1917, li). From these recommendations an order-in-council constructed an independent "nonpolitical, permanent and self-perpetuating corporate entity," and over the next several years a variety of unprofitable roads were acquired by the government and entrusted to that company (Innis 1933, 49). As Anthony Perl (1994, 52) argues, however, the institution of the CNR was more than a "tentative and reluctant starting point on the road to national public enterprise." Rather, the "politics that introduced public enterprise across Canada contained a new expression of national economic sovereignty, one that was made possible by an increase in state autonomy and a strengthened state capacity that were sufficient to redirect the course of Canada's industrial development."

As a structure for the consolidation and public appropriation of private debt, the new corporation was quite a success: investors were largely protected and the railways were maintained. But, as a competitor in the marketplace, the structure of the corporation left much to be desired. First, the corporation was a loose agglomeration of what had been disjointed and competitive railway operations that were extremely difficult to coordinate as an organized, competitive whole. Second, it was saddled with a tremendous debt, a burden that it carried for decades to come. Third, because the tasks it was charged with were largely unprofitable, it was dependent on parliamentary appropriations and experienced great difficulty in securing capital for most of the 1920s and 1930s. Consequently, as Innis (1933, 58) notes, in relation to both railway markets and the advances in new transportation technologies and techniques, the CNR appeared to be subordinate to its major competitor, the Canadian Pacific Railway (CPR), and over time would "tend to become a buffer between the Canadian Pacific and the vicissitudes of railway earnings in Canada." Thus, the abilities of the CNR to compete in the marketplace or to provide an economic return for its owners were heavily circumscribed by both its structure and responsibilities.

Like the first regulatory commission, the first productive Crown corporation was born out of pragmatic necessities in the maintenance of private capital accumulation. In this instance, intervention was structured to serve private economic interests in several ways: on the one hand, safeguarding future accumulation on the parts of both private investors and the state; on the other, posing little threat to private accumulation because of disadvantages in the marketplace. Historically, however, state ownership represents more than a simple extension of the allocative rationale found in the regulatory board. Innis (1933, 80–81) provides a summary of the operational imperatives of early government ownership in this country:

> Government ownership is fundamentally a phenomenon peculiar to a new country, and an effective weapon by which the government has been able to bring together the retarded development and the possession of vast national resources, matured technique, and a market favourable to the purchasing of raw materials. It was essentially a clumsy, awkward means of attaining the end of immediate investment of tremendous sums of capital, but it was the only means of retaining a substantial share of the returns from virgin natural resources. Canada's development was essentially transcontinental. Private enterprise was not adequate to the task, although the success of government ownership has tended to obscure the paramount importance of its contributions during the early stages of capital development.

In other words, through both subsidy and direct ownership, the early Canadian state was able to extend communications, rapidly secure territory, and develop resources while deferring the cost of that development through legislative structures. With the Act of Union, Confederation, and the National Policy, the state constructed a political framework for the support and encouragement of private investment capital. State ownership, direct subsidies, and loan guarantees were the means through which this support was carried out. In effect, these institutional arrangements acted as vehicles for mortgaging the resources of the country against the future returns of the private sector. However, in the face of stilted economic growth, the emergence of a diverse set of vocal social interests, and an increasingly complex array of issues requiring national attention, public ownership took on new proportions. The Crown corporation was the result of the state's efforts to meet the exigencies of this new environment – a formal structure for financing the rapid development of resources and a further extension of the bridge between the state, private capital, and resource development. While the creation of the CNR seemingly reversed this logic in that it was created after development had taken place, its institution follows this larger pattern. As Perl (1994, 51–52) argues, "the politics that introduced public enterprise across Canada contained a new expression of national sovereignty, one that was made possible by an increase in state autonomy and a strengthened state capacity that were sufficient to redirect the course of Canada's industrial development."

While a wide range of Crown corporations were created over the next 100 years, as Edward Iacobucci and Michael Trebilcock (2012) illustrate, the economic rationale still plays a strong role in these institutions and, while many of these have not always been directly involved in rapid exploitation, like the CNR, many have played an important role in sustaining economic relationships.[11] Moreover, like the CNR, Crown corporations deployed in economic development, even those in "competitive" fields, have not generally presented a threat to private accumulation. As Chandler (1983, 209) illustrates:

> Public enterprises designed to foster economic development are not challenges to the private sector. On the contrary, they involve the use of public resources to supplement and support the private sector. The view that business is always against public enterprise is based on a misperception that intervention always poses a threat to the private sector.

Writers working from a Marxist tradition have often taken the analysis of this relationship between the state and the private sector a step further, arguing that it is a case of "private enterprise at public expense" (Whitaker 1977, 43; cf. Panitch 1977). Yet, it would appear that while many Crown corporations have worked to sustain, and even promote, the development of private capital, since the early twentieth century few have been employed to directly serve specific private interests (see C. Armstrong and Nelles 1986). Rather, following the path trodden by nineteenth-century state intervention in the economy, they have been set on the economic margins of profitable enterprise, working to sustain a larger set of productive relations – relations that are not necessarily in the direct interest of capital (or "capitals") alone.

Because of this propensity and the perception of economic inefficiency that arises from it, Crown corporations have also suffered criticism from a wide spectrum of political and economic perspectives (Hodgetts 1973; Tupper and

Doern 1981; Prichard 1983; Iacobucci and Trebilcock 2012; Public Policy Forum 2016). To some degree, these criticisms overlook the fact that at the federal level, Crown corporations have often been deployed to further the state's own agenda – the development of political and economic relationships across a particular geography. As illustrated in the history of the development of the canals and railroads, the hegemony of private capital has never been guaranteed in this process. Rather, the development of private capital in Canada has often been prodded and sustained by state intervention, and Crown corporations have often been instituted to "fill in the gaps" in this larger productive system. Either they have provided a bridge between pockets of private capital in the extensive process of capitalizing a national system or they have undertaken projects perceived to be in the "national interest" that, for one reason or another, are beyond the reach of legitimate forms of private capital. Thus, while Crown corporations have given form to a productive rationale, this rationale has not necessarily been focused on creating a profit from their operations.

While over time the particular form and character of the regulatory board and the Crown corporation has shifted within the contexts of the situations in which they have been applied and the circumstances they have encountered, tracing the historical rationales these institutions embody provides an important starting point for understanding both their historical and contemporary impacts on political economic development.[12]

2

Market, State, Culture
From Telegraphs to Broadcasting

THIS CHAPTER BUILDS on the analysis developed in Chapter 1 by exploring the early development of the telegraph, telephone, newspaper, magazine, film, and broadcasting industries. The purpose is to illustrate emergent patterns in the relationships between state intervention, private capital, and transnational relations of production in each of these sectors. While the development of each of these industries was framed and fed by American capital and technique, it was in this context that a larger pattern of relationships was established, not only between the state and private capital within each of these fields of activity but also between the fields themselves. It was also the context within which broadcasting was set on a different path from the other media industries.

Until the early twentieth century, the nationalism promoted by the federal government was largely inspired by an economic project. But as this project met with some success, a vision of a national culture began to take form, particularly in anglophone Canada. Slowly, this idea began to influence the larger nationalist project. However, the notion of culture at the core of this project was much different from the definition of the term that gained currency in the latter part of the century.

While there were a variety of competing visions of the parameters of Canadian culture through this period, the reigning view had both conservative and idealist tendencies (Tippett 1990). Here, culture was seen as a particular set of activities focused on "a general process of intellectual, spiritual, and aesthetic development," rather than a whole or "particular way of life" (R. Williams 1976, 87–93).[1] As Mary Vipond (1980, 32) put it, the period "spawned an artistic and literary nationalism more vital than anything Canada had previously seen." While, the "nationalistic" journals, associations, and societies created during this period were far from joined in a common vision of nationalist ideals, they did find a common purpose: "to create a national feeling and to focus and direct it" (44). Vipond (1980, 43–44) goes on to describe the focus of this movement mobilized by the intellectuals, writers, and artists that formed the Anglo-Canadian "intelligentsia":

To English Canadian intellectuals of the 1920s, it often seemed that the Canadian Manufacturers' Association had been far more effective in protecting and developing the nation's potential than they had; they firmly believed, however, that not only lamps and lingerie but "OPINION should be MADE IN CANADA."[2]

Because this brand of nationalist thinking focused on purely symbolic production, and accentuated primarily intellectual or aesthetic symbolic forms, it had impact only on the margins of the development of communications media, not on its industrial core. Indeed, to varying degrees, these cultural critics looked upon the commercial or popular media products that filled Canadian venues disparagingly, not simply because they were foreign but also because of their largely "mass" appeal (Whitson and Gruneau 1997).[3] Further, because of the timing of its emergence, as well as its rather stilted focus, this nascent cultural nationalism had no real impact on the development of early telecommunications industries. Similarly, it had only minimal influence over the direction taken by the newspaper, magazine, and film industries – other than to support viewing these activities as largely economic in nature. It is apparent, though, that this cultural vision did find expression in the development of broadcasting policy. In this way, the establishment of a Canadian broadcasting system as a means of developing "Canadian" perspectives in media content became a popular issue, and broadcasting was put on a very different path of development from other Canadian media of the time.

Similarly, as noted in later chapters, it is in the field of broadcasting that the relationships between the larger form of state intervention, the productive relationships it helps realize, and the character of resultant symbolic forms becomes most apparent. However, to break through the nationalist rhetoric that often surrounds Canadian communications policy and come to terms with the reasons why the broadcasting system has for so long been dominated by foreign programming, we need to examine the pattern of state intervention and the character of the growth it encouraged in Canada's communications systems, particularly in anglophone Canada.

Communication in Canada

Lines of transportation and communication generally emerge across geographical dimensions that follow patterns of trade and immigration. As Frank Underhill (1964, 3) notes, because the colonies and territories that were amalgamated in the Canadian federation "had hardly any experience of living and working together" prior to 1867, the "lines of communication of each colony ran toward the centre of the Empire in London, not toward the other colonies." But as the outlines of a political economic system began to take form in Canada under the sway of the process of late nineteenth- and early twentieth-century industrialization, new communications systems were forged along the lines of emerging social and industrial relationships.

In this process, development drew upon familiar resources. Just as the early transportation and communications systems realized in the canals and railways had borrowed heavily from American technology or technique, so did later communications systems (cf. Innis 1956). And just as much of Canadian capital formation through the early nineteenth century had been dependent upon foreign investment and transnational relations of production, so was capital development in the emerging communications systems. Through the mid to late nineteenth century, American capital began to supplant traditional British investment. The result was that new lines of communication began to coalesce around these emerging patterns of investment, drawing the young Canada ever closer into the orbit of the United States (Careless 1966, 281–83; Moffett 1972). But while in the pursuit of rapid industrialization the nationality of capital investment went largely unquestioned, fed by nationalist pretensions, the Canadian state sometimes played a strong role in shaping the development of Canada's communications systems along an east-west axis through a variety of policy mechanisms, much as it did in the development of the railways. In other instances, however, the state eschewed direct intervention in favour of less direct methods.

The result of this tangled web of relationships is that communications industries in Canada have not developed as a simple "choice between the State and the United States," as the oft-quoted Graham Spry put it with regard to broadcast development in the early 1930s (see Babe 2011). Rather, in what is now largely considered the field of communications and cultural policy, industrial development has been the product of heavy dependence upon American cultural products, American capital, and American technique.[4]

The Telegraph and the Telephone

The telegraph was the first electronic medium of the industrial age. In its early incarnations, it helped expedite railway construction by "facilitating consultation with engineers, speeding progress reports to supervisors, aiding instruction of foremen, and ordering supplies" (Babe 1990, 42). As the system developed, however, it assumed a growing role in distributing and disseminating information that coordinated political and economic action between developing urban centres.

In the realm of public communication, the telegraph fed the daily newspaper industry and forged a link between the evolving polities and markets within these new settlements and the larger web of political and industrial relations of which they were a part.[5] Fuelled by this growing market for both political and commercial information, the telegraph began to move symbols "independently of and faster than (physical) transportation" and, as the construction of telegraph lines outpaced that of railways, communications systems themselves became key vehicles in industrial growth and activity (Carey 1988, 204).[6] Profit-driven relationships drove the extension of this system, and with its capitalization the emergent Canadian state was woven even more deeply into the fabric of industrialism. The seeming dissolution of distance through electronic forms of communication brought both rural and urban Canadian communities into an increasing dependence on distant markets. Elements of self-sufficiency began to give way to specialization, and communities were subject to the abstractions of a price system within which the exchange value of goods was set by distant forces and events (Innis 1956; I. Spry 1981, 151–66; Carey 1988, 203–22).

In the 1870s, the telephone began to emerge along the trail forged by the telegraph. Because of its high cost and technical problems with voice amplification over long distances, telephony initially took form as a local communication service, serving the wealthier segments of Canadian society. However, although the telegraph and telephone services were initially separated through regulatory fiat, as innovations in both production techniques and the technology made long-distance markets increasingly viable, private telephone and telegraph interests met head-on (Babe 1990, 69, 159). After a brief struggle – and again following a pattern established in the United States – Canadian markets were segregated for these two types of service through a privately negotiated "restrictive covenant" (Babe 1990, 72–73; see also Winseck 1998, 119–22). But with the telephone, the switched systems and voice contact that characterized the technology gradually emerged as the primary electronic vehicle for individuated "point-to-point" conveyance of both business and personal information.

The emergent structure of the markets for these services followed a pattern reminiscent of the era of railway construction. Initially enabled through government charters, both the telegraph (alongside railways) and long-distance telephone service were developed through private investment.[7] Although the telegraph was initially tied to the railway, as it developed in Canada the system became heavily integrated with the US system and much of it was foreign-owned (Babe 1990, 45–53; Moffett 1972, 54–67). Later, in the wake of railway expansion around the turn of the century, telegraph ownership generally fell into Canadian hands through the railway companies. However, with the economic collapse of much of the rail system at the turn of the century, and the institution of the Canadian National Railway (CNR) in 1917, the Canadian telegraph system was rationalized to a duopoly: the privately held Canadian Pacific Railway (CPR) system and the publicly owned (and, through the railway company, publicly subsidized) Canadian National system. Thus, while private investment played a central role in development, as economic conditions changed, on the margins of the system – where what Innis might call the "rigidities of the price system" (see Drache 1982) waylaid capitalization – the system was both sustained and maintained with the aid of public funds and government ownership.

The development of the long-distance component of the emergent telephone system followed a similar pattern. In 1880, the Bell Telephone Company of Canada, a subsidiary of the American company of the same name, was granted a federal charter to establish a telephone system in Canada. While both provincial and municipal governments also routinely issued such charters within their jurisdictions, Bell's federally granted right to "construct lines along any and all public rights of way" gave the company virtual command of the long-distance market (Babe 1990, 68).[8] However, in less populated – and consequently less profitable – parts of the country, such as the prairies and rural sections of Ontario and Quebec, the company relinquished this monopoly to a mixture of private and public companies. And, where the private sector was either unwilling or unable to do so, organizations under public ownership generally financed and/or directly undertook these development responsibilities (Babe 1990, 65–149; Winseck 1998, 140–41). This pattern of development followed the strategy employed by Bell's parent company in the United States (Babe 1990, 71; cf. C. Armstrong and Nelles 1986, 60–73). Further, because the capitalization of telephone systems first developed along lines of communication that were most amenable to capital accumulation, Canadian telephone systems were more closely linked to the American system than to each other, and it was not until the 1930s, and the progressive industrialization of Canada at large, that it was possible to place a call between different regions of the country without it being routed through the United States (Moffett 1972, 61; Babe 1990; Winseck 1998, 172).

Thus, in their early development, both the telegraph and the telephone were heavily indebted to state intervention and underpinned by transnational relations of production. Restrictive charters and government subsidies set the stage for the development of both these communications systems and, as it had in railway development, government ownership extended the reach of private capital at the economic margins of the system to provide that system greater, national breadth (Babe 1990, 102–13). Moreover, as political and economic development proceeded through the late nineteenth and early twentieth centuries, as it did with railway operation, public unrest mounted over the rates charged by the largely private monopoly interests that were at the economic centres of these systems. Because Bell selectively deployed its privileges to establish and exploit telephone service only in particularly profitable areas, this company's rates and investment strategies drew particularly vehement criticism (C. Armstrong and Nelles 1986, 172–86).

Faced with growing public pressure, both telegraph companies and the federally regulated Bell system fell under the regulation of the Board of Railway Commissioners (BRC) between 1906 and 1908. Over the course of the next several decades, the shifting industrial infrastructure buffeted the economics of Canadian telecommunications markets, but, shepherded by the BRC and its successors, integrated national markets in both fields were constructed and maintained (Babe 1990). Thus, as Innis (1933, 94) points out, just as "the experience of the United States was taken over and adapted to Canadian territory" in the construction of the railways, so too that experience was employed to construct these Canadian communications systems.

The role of the federal state was limited in scope, however, particularly in the telephone industry. Where the monopoly holder of the federal charter (Bell) was loath to undertake comprehensive development, provincial and municipal governments moved to fill the gaps left in the system. This fuelled ongoing jurisdictional disputes, fragmenting regulatory control over the industry and waylaying the development of any comprehensive telecommunications policy ([GD] Department of Communications 1975; Babe 1990; Winseck 1998). Moreover, the manufacturing industries that supplied telecommunications equipment to these Canadian markets remained largely in American hands through much of the twentieth century ([GD] Restrictive Trade Practices Commission 1981; Smythe 1981, 149–51; [GD] Department of Communications 1983b, 6–10; Rens 2001). Over time, and shepherded by state regulation, Canadian capital did take root in these industries, but to a large part their development was structured between state intervention and American capital.

Consequently, while government intervention enabled relatively comprehensive telephone service through the early part of the twentieth century, both the structure and regulation of the industry were highly fragmented, stilted in development, and dependent upon both American capital and technique. Not only was this pattern of development later reflected in the broadcasting industry but it also had far-reaching implications for the way in which the broadcasting system itself developed.

Newspapers

As the rise of industry and urbanization began to alter the Canadian landscape through the late nineteenth and early twentieth centuries, the Canadian newspaper industry took on new proportions. Positioned between commercial interests and the developing home-centred, urban way of life, newspapers were at the forefront of crossing the public/private dichotomy in social life created by industrial process, and forged an initial link between serial production and mass consumption. Under these conditions, the partisan press of the nineteenth century slowly gave way to a monopolistic, commercial medium based upon advertising revenue (Rutherford 1978, 1–76; Kesterton and Bird 1995; Sotiron 1997). This shift in the means of financing production wrought a series of changes in both the form and content of the newspaper (Sotiron 1997, 17–22). In Canada, these changes were facilitated and sustained by the newspaper market's relations with both the American newspaper industry and government intervention.

As Canadian newspapers moved to consolidate their appeal to a large mass audience at the turn of the twentieth century, they became increasingly dependent upon cheap news supplied by the telegraph companies, "especially Canadian Pacific Telegraphs which furnished its clients with the 'Associated Press' world and American reports plus a Canadian news summary" (Rutherford 1978, 54). Writing in 1906, Moffett ([1906] 1972, 96) captures the character of this relationship:

> The Canadian journals are American in their whole tone, their makeup, their typography, their estimate of the value of news and their manner of presenting it. They patronize American press associations and "syndicates," and much of their matter in consequence is furnished by American writers from an American standpoint. This is the cause of incessant complaint on the part of the Canadian press itself, but the stream of news from American sources continues to flow unchecked.

In 1910, the telegraph's monopoly over news was broken in the wake of a dispute over rates that was adjudicated by the BRC. The resolution of this dispute marks an important turning point in the development of Canada's communications systems. Not only did it bring both the telegraph and long-distance telephone markets under a common regulatory regime – thereby helping to differentiate and sustain their markets – but it ended "vertical integration between publishing and telegraphs – between content and carriage." Thus, "the era of the telecommunications common carrier began" (Babe 1990, 59; see also Winseck 1998, 105–7), and a division of responsibility between the production of information and its carriage was instituted in regulation. This distinction between different kinds of communications markets slowly became entrenched in the fabric of regulation and later informed the division between telephone, broadcast, and cable TV markets. It was not until the 1980s that this political division would again come under serious question.

In the wake of the BRC's decision, publishers across the country organized the Canadian Press (CP) – which at that time was basically a holding company for the Canadian rights to the Associated Press (AP) copy. But as this organization came into being, it was immediately "wracked by the tensions endemic in an era of competitive journalism," as against the financial interests of their better staffed and financed large city counterparts, "small city and western newspapers wanted 'CP' to become a true news agency which would furnish not just the 'AP' copy but pan Canadian, British, even European information" (Rutherford 1978, 55). Over the next decade, disputes raged between these newspapers over the purposes of CP and how the huge cost of its telegraphic distribution would be shared. Economic hardship caused by the First World War exacerbated these concerns and, faced with looming bankruptcy, western publishers appealed to the federal government. As a result, in 1917, CP was granted a $50,000 annual subsidy so that it might offer greater service to the "national interest" (Nichols 1948, 124–36; see also Rutherford 1978, 54–55). Moreover, as Sotiron (1997, 100–1) points out, through the first two decades of the twentieth century, CP was not the only press organization that received government subsidy to help keep it afloat. Consequently, in its early stages of development, difficulties experienced by the private sector in creating a national news service were bridged by the state.

Disputes over the allocation of funds within CP continued, however, and politicians soon joined the fray, grumbling over the organization's monopoly on the news.[9] Finally, in the face of the subsidy's withdrawal, a 1923 Act of Parliament incorporated the Canadian Press as a non-profit co-operative corporation, wholly owned by its members. The corporate structure provided by this legislation ensured some stability in Canadian newspaper markets. It increased not only the abilities of newspaper interests to obtain preferential telegraph rates but also publishers' control of their home markets (Nichols 1948, 69). As Rutherford (1978, 52) points out, through this news co-operative, publishers

> could and did deny franchise rights to prospective newcomers on the grounds their competition would threaten the profits of existing newspapers. That made it very difficult for any entrepreneur to break into a city already served by a daily newspaper. The rationalization of the press scene during the 1920s signaled the close of the heyday of entrepreneurialism. The newspaper industry was a business like any other, wherein reigned the twin gods of Profit and Stability.

In yet another instance, a federally granted charter provided a political context that afforded private interests a degree of protection from the exigencies of the competitive marketplace and enabled the development and maintenance of a national communications service.[10] At first through subsidy, and then with legislation, state intervention provided a larger framework for the growth and stability of the newspaper industry. Moreover, through the adjudicative mechanism of the BRC, the economic rights and responsibilities of different elements of the larger system of news production were ascertained and allocated, providing stability to the overall growth of the national system (Nichols 1948, 67–69). Yet, in the wake of this institutional rationalization, Canadian newspapers remained beholden to cheap foreign news as a mainstay of their financial stability. And while this foreign news resonated with Canadian readers because the themes and issues it dealt with had currency in their ways of life – ways of life that increasingly moved to the rhythm of transnational industrial forces – to the degree that this relatively inexpensive lineage was employed to fill pages and minimize production costs, Canadian newspapers remained both dependent upon and embedded within transnational relations of production.

Magazines and Film

In the face of American industry, both the magazine and film industries had even greater difficulty establishing distinct, Canadian markets.[11] With growing industrialization through the late nineteenth century, a variety of trade, technical, and professional magazines were established in Canada. Situated in a generally small market, however, the fortunes of these publications swung on the tide of shifting patterns in industrial structure through the early part of the twentieth century (Stephenson and McNaught 1940, 271–72). The growth of periodicals designed to appeal to a more general, mass market followed a different pattern. While there had been public complaints over the overwhelming presence of American magazines and periodicals in Canada as early as the mid-nineteenth century, the proximity of the United States combined with a common language and the sparse and dispersed population of English Canada to make a national magazine market in anglophone Canada difficult to establish (Litvak and Maule 1974, 18). In combination with import duties on the raw materials for magazine production and the much larger economies of scale enjoyed by American producers, these circumstances left Canadian producers on the margins of the burgeoning market for mass circulation magazines that accompanied urbanization and the growth of industry. After the First World War, however, a range of interests began to push for state intervention in the face of this American domination.

The seemingly "salacious" character of some American mass market magazines, and the anti-imperialist sentiment expressed in others, raised the moral hackles of a number of groups. Canadian manufacturers expressed concerns that advertising in US publications was undermining the market for their products, and the rising nationalist cultural sentiment, which itself gave birth to a number of publications through the 1920s, raised the issue that US publications were sapping the development of Canada's national life (Litvak and Maule 1974, 18–23; Vipond 1989, 24–29). Despite these protests, as Mary Vipond (1989, 28) notes, Mackenzie King's Liberal government maintained that intervention "would limit competition in order to enrich Canadian publishers at the expense of Canadian consumers." Subsequently, Mackenzie King argued in the House of Commons that "thought is cosmopolitan," and refused to impose restrictions on the free flow of ideas (in Vipond 1989, 28). And while a few adjustments were made to both postal rates and duties on magazine printing materials, market relationships remained generally untouched.

With the election of the Conservatives in 1930, the attitude of the government changed. In 1931, a tariff was imposed on foreign magazines based upon their advertising content. Because the tariff was aimed at mass market magazines, educational and special interest publications continued to enjoy free entry. While the impetus behind this shift in regulation is difficult to pinpoint, Isaiah Litvak and Christopher Maule (1972, 24) note that it seems largely the result of pressure applied by "certain magazine publishers in conjunction with the Canadian Manufacturers Association" in their efforts to build an advertising market for Canadian products. The effect of the tariff was quick and decisive, and, as these authors go on to illustrate, "by 1935 the circulation of American magazines in Canada decreased by 62 percent while Canadian magazine circulation increased by 64 percent" (26). However, American magazines quickly set up branch-plant operations in Canada. These "split-run" magazines – so called because they generally employed the same editorial material as their American editions but filled the advertising space with Canadian advertising – were able to deliver advertising space at a tremendous cost advantage over their Canadian counterparts, and they became the model for future Canadian editions of American magazines.

With the Liberals' return to power, Mackenzie King reiterated that he would not restrict the free flow of ideas, and the tariff was removed in 1936 in the wake of the negotiation of a Canada-US trade agreement. Between 1935 and 1937, the value of imported US magazines more than doubled, and fifty-two magazine subsidiaries returned to the United States (Litvak and Maule 1974, 28).

While statistics for the period following the elimination of the tariff are difficult to come by, the period of intervention appears to have given impetus to the development of a national advertising market for magazines. Not only did the number of titles of Canadian magazines continue to grow through the tough economic times of the late 1930s, but both *Time* and *Reader's Digest*, as well as other American publications, spawned "Canadian" versions of their publications to take advantage of the Canadian advertising market in the early 1940s (Litvak and Maule 1974, 58; see also Stephenson and McNaught 1940, 276). Through the 1940s and 1950s, American magazines continued to capture a growing share of both magazine circulation and advertising revenue.

Consequently, seemingly under the sway of a liberal ideological concern for the "free" expression of ideas – and perhaps a larger concern for the free flow of capital – the development of the Canadian mass market magazine industry was largely dominated by American technique and capital. Just as Innis (1952, 15) observed in the context of the American newspaper industry, for Canadian magazines the "guarantee of freedom of the press ... meant an unrestricted operation of commercial forces and an impact of technology on communication tempered only by commercialism itself." Driven by the superiority of American economies of scale, the productive relationships that undergirded the industry were generally transnational in structure, and Canadian readers formed a portion of a transnational magazine market as well as an adjunct market for American manufacturers advertising in those publications. Through all of this, though, a small national market for Canadian-produced products did emerge, structured between the needs of Canadian commercial interests to develop a market for their products and Canadian magazine consumers seeking, or at least willing to purchase, products that foregrounded issues and works of particularly Canadian concern. However, as H.E. Stephenson and Carlton McNaught (1940, 277) note, "in order to compete at all with those published across the line," in both style and general content, these Canadian publishers had "to build their periodicals on much the same lines" as their American counterparts, and through the early part of the twentieth century, the hegemony of American capital and technique were pervasive within this industry.

In the face of the American industrial juggernaut, the infant Canadian feature film industry fared even less well. By the early 1920s, the Hollywood studio system had a stranglehold on film exhibition in Canada, making it virtually impossible for independent producers to have their films either distributed or exhibited across the country (Magder 1993, 19–42). As Manjunath Pendakur (1990, 87) points out, these "oppressive market conditions ... led to an enquiry under the Federal Combines Investigation Act in 1930." However, because as minister of labour Mackenzie King noted in 1910 as he shepherded the legislation forward, the law was designed to capture "the benefits which arise from large organizations of capital for the purposes of business and commerce," and weaknesses in it forestalled prosecution (92). Moreover, the federal government began actively encouraging American branch-plant production of Hollywood films in Canada in the late 1920s. Under the terms of a quota imposed on foreign films by the British Parliament in 1926, feature films made in Commonwealth countries qualified as British in origin. Hence, the Canadian Motion Picture Bureau began soliciting the production of what were called Hollywood "quota-quickies" in Canada, so that they might qualify for this exemption (Morris 1978, 175–213). While the British government revised the law to exclude Commonwealth films in 1938, largely because of this "Canadian contravention of its spirit," under the blessing of the Canadian state the feature film industry in English Canada was by this time fully integrated into transnational relations of production (Vipond 1989, 36; see also Morris 1978, 180–81). As Ted Magder (1989, 288) notes, the result was that while both workers and "interests of Canadian capital involved in the exhibition, distribution, and, quite often, production of feature films" enjoyed economic benefits under this branch-plant production regime, there was virtually no representation of Canadian perspectives in feature films during this period.

At the same time, as Magder (1993, 47–48) goes on to state, "there was no real support for the production of Canadian films," and the branch-plant structure of the industry, which followed the general logic of development promoted by the National Policy, was encouraged by the fact that in "the eyes of many, film remained a licentious form of entertainment, to be censored surely, but not to be encouraged" (see also Morris 1978). With the establishment of the National Film Board in 1939, the government set out to create its own presence in filmmaking. But while the documentary tradition established by John Grierson provided Canada with a somewhat distinctive film tradition, it did not challenge the commercial hegemony of the American industry (Magder 1993, 49–61; Morris 1978, 232–35).

Thus, framed in part by a vision of culture as the pursuit of forms of "intellectual development and refinement," through the 1920s and 1930s attempts at regulating the growth of the magazine and feature film mass media generally focused on commercial concerns. Even there, federal interest in securing a distinctive Canadian market for these products was at best divided. Indeed, it would not be until the 1960s, and the rise of a more popular vision of culture, that definitive steps to create such markets would be undertaken and American control of these industries seriously challenged. However, even then regulation would be primarily commercial in focus. At the same time, the structure of these industries would have implications for the development of broadcasting. American domination of the magazine industry, with its fascination with the star system and celebrity news, would help feed demand for US media products in Canada, while the branch-plant nature of the film industry would mean fewer resources for television production in this country when that technology developed.

Radio Broadcasting

The first radio broadcasting station was established in Canada in 1919. As what Innis would later refer to as a "space binding technique," radio broadcasting quickly attracted the attention of a diverse set of social interests (see Carey 1988, 201–30). Both commercial and amateur broadcasters took to the air – all intent upon employing the new medium to join people in common purpose, whether that purpose centred on constructing market relations or more abstract educational and religious ends (Vipond 1992, 22–24). Paralleling the experience in other industrializing countries, public interest in the medium mushroomed throughout Canada in the early 1920s, although until the 1930s its popularity was largely confined to urban centres and listeners with the means to purchase rather expensive equipment (MacLennan 2001).

From its inception, radio was viewed in a different light from other media of the day. Crossing the boundary between public and private life, it promised to unite both rural and urban households in a "common community" (Czitrom 1983, 60–88). Audiences were attracted by the novelty and apparently direct experience offered by radio. Writing in a similar vein to Raymond Williams (1979), Vipond (1992, 102) notes that as the rise of industrial forms of capitalism engendered conditions in Canadian society that were "increasingly impersonal and alienating ... the new mass medium appealed because it helped the anonymous individual feel more like a person and the mass more like a community." And while allowing the new medium to penetrate the walls of the home was perceived to have dangers for "those who ... held lofty ideals about the utility of radio in uplifting and acculturating the farm, immigrant, and working class populations" – particularly if commercial forces were allowed to dominate the medium with advertising messages and "popular" entertainment – the act of "listening in" was generally portrayed and promoted as enriching both family and community life (Vipond 1992, 24, 89, 101–3).

In the Canadian context, the technology was seen to have particular significance. As Vipond (1992, 22–23) illustrates, "the most frequently voiced hopes concerned the role radio would play in a country of Canada's large size and scattered population. Very typical of the immediate post-war period was the worry that east and west seemed to be drifting apart; radio was greeted enthusiastically as a means for counteracting that tendency to separation."[12] This perception of radio as a "space binding" medium blended with rising Canadian nationalist sentiments of the period and was key in shaping its development.

As radio broadcasting began in Canada, there was little in the way of regulation governing the practice. The federal government's powers in the telegraph field were extended to include "wireless telephony" with the Radio Telegraph Act of 1913, but these powers were intended for the technical governance of point-to-point communication, not the transmission of messages to an unknown number of anonymous recipients. Not until 1923 were the first federal broadcasting regulations implemented through the Radio Branch of the Department of Marine and Fisheries. Like earlier regulation governing point-to-point communication, these regulations assumed a simple supervisory role for the state. They specified several different types of broadcast licence, allowing for both commercial and amateur broadcast outlets, and established a fee schedule for both broadcast stations and receivers ([GD] Department of Marine and Fisheries 1923). Licensees were granted only the use of a particular wavelength, and no proprietary rights over wavelengths were extended. Moreover, in marked contrast to contemporaneous British regulatory practice, but paralleling the American development model, licences were at first granted to all who applied (Peers 1969, 16–17; Vipond 1992, 20). The assumption of a simple supervisory role by the Canadian state had far-reaching implications for the development of the Canadian system. For, as Vipond (1992, 20) notes, it meant that while many different kinds of organizations were able to access and experiment with the new technology, private enterprise, with its focus on wringing profits from its operations, "was left to set the pace and direction for the development of this new electronic medium."

Although in its development the Canadian system is sometimes portrayed as a hybrid of the British and American systems, the conditions that contextualized such development were quite different. In Britain, the physical constraints imposed by spectrum scarcity combined with the Marconi Company's lack of interest in shouldering the financial burden of program production and the political elite's distrust of "commercialism" to yield a state monopoly on radio program production and distribution (Hearst 1992; Dewar 1982; Mundy 1988). Under state control, the economies of scale inherent in a limited number of broadcast channels and a densely populated listening audience were harnessed to produce a system of program production financed through receiver licence fees. In the British context, however, centralized state control led to bourgeois patrician cultural sensibilities informing much of broadcast production (Mundy 1988, 291–92). Cast in the euphemistic guise of "uplift programs," programming was constructed to "inform, educate, and entertain" – all in the service of contributing to a "national culture" (Hearst 1992, 64; Mundy 1988, 292). Moreover, in order to ensure that British audiences stayed tuned to the British Broadcasting Corporation (BBC), "sets were made which could only receive the B.B.C." (Mundy 1988, 293n9). As Hearst (1992, 64) illustrates, the elitist, and rather authoritarian, nature of this control did not go unnoticed by committees set up to review the corporation's activities, and "the Ullswater Committee of 1936 dared to claim that its programme policy had been shaped from the outset 'by the conviction that listeners would come to appreciate that which might at first appear uninteresting or even alarming.'" Yet review committees largely endorsed the BBC's activities, and throughout the early history of broadcasting in the United Kingdom, it was neither a vehicle for the expression of popular cultural tastes nor responsive to audience input (Eaman 1994, 15–17).

In the United States, the pattern of development was somewhat different. While, as in Britain, some groups advocated that radio be employed to cultivate bourgeois values, private capital quickly developed a firm grip on radio's development (Douglas 1995, 239). Led by the investments of the Radio Corporation of America (RCA), a federally sanctioned cartel originally composed of General Electric (GE), Westinghouse, and American Telephone and Telegraph (AT&T), the growth of the system centred upon developing and maintaining markets for broadcast receiving and transmission equipment. Initially, programming was financed through the profits accrued from the sale of equipment. Increases in transmission power and the establishment of broadcast networks extended the geographic reach of these programs and provided economies of scale to this cross-subsidized form of program production.

Early on, however, in an attempt to avoid the overhead costs of program production, AT&T began renting blocks of time on its broadcast facilities to outside interests, and "toll" broadcasting was initiated as an additional source of revenue (Smulyan 1994, 100–2). To further consolidate its position in early markets, AT&T also forbade the other patent holders to utilize its lines for commercial network purposes. However, worried that public outcry over this "radio trust" would endanger its telephone monopoly, AT&T began to negotiate a withdrawal from broadcasting with RCA in 1924 (57–59). These negotiations set the broad context for much of radio's development in North America. RCA agreed to lease AT&T lines for network transmissions and, in the process, gave up experiments it had been undertaking to find alternate means of relaying signals between its stations. RCA set up a new company, the National Broadcasting Company (NBC), to control its network operations and act as a bridge between privately owned stations and its program production facilities. As Smulyan (1994, 63) illustrates, "the huge expense of renting AT&T's wires to send signals from station to station meant that programming had to be centralized both to save money and to attract advertisers needing a national audience." New York became the site of this centralized production, and the cost of wire line rental for a national service began to be financed through the sale of time to advertisers (57–59).

In this context, programming developed as a method of attracting audiences for commercial messages. This imperative had an impact on program content. "Popularity" became the hallmark of program design, as broadcasters and sponsors tailored their products to appeal to national, and later regional, audiences of widely varying tastes (Smulyan 1994, 63, 99). Independent, privately owned network affiliates were the linchpin of this system, working to maximize their income by delivering a balance of local and network-sponsored programs. To increase their revenue, these local broadcasters began to sell "spot" advertising on programs they developed, whereby advertisers had to assume only a portion of the costs of program production and none of the responsibilities. And while the local ownership of affiliates served to satisfy political concerns over monopoly ownership, this ownership pattern also served the manufacturers' interest as it maximized the sale of both transmission and receiving equipment, as well as obviated the necessity of heavy investment in broadcast markets across the country.

The rise of commercial program sponsorship sparked numerous debates over the purpose and character of broadcast programming in the United States through the 1920s and early 1930s. As the markets for both transmitters and receivers became saturated, however, commercial sponsorship or advertising gradually became entrenched as the dominant method of financing production (McChesney 1993, 289-30). Fuelled by advertising, the networks flourished, and by 1931 "NBC and CBS [Columbia Broadcasting System] accounted for nearly 70 percent of US broadcasting" (McChesney 1990, 33). In the wake of this commercial success, non-profit and non-commercial broadcasting suffered a steady and dramatic decline. Faced with a scarcity of broadcast channels, the Federal Radio Commission (FRC), "noting the nonprofit broadcasters' lack of financial and technological prowess, lowered their hours and power (to the advantage of well-capitalized private broadcasters) and thus made it that much more difficult for them to generate funds" (33). Moreover, as Robert McChesney (1990, 34) goes on to note, in an interesting ideological twist,

> the FRC equated capitalist broadcasters with "general public service" broadcasters, because their quest for profit would motivate them to provide whatever programming the market desired. In contrast, those stations that did not operate for profit and did not derive their revenues from the sale of advertising were termed "propaganda" stations, more interested in spreading their particular viewpoints than in satisfying audience needs. Hence the FRC argued that it had to favor the capitalist broadcasters, since there were not enough stations to satisfy all the "propaganda" groups; these groups would have to learn to work through the auspices of the commercial broadcasters.

These developments in the American system held great import for radio's development in Canada.

In Canada, private capital in radio markets was both weak and parochial. The manufacture of receivers and transmitters was generally controlled by the same patent holders that held a stranglehold on the industry in the United States and Britain, with Canadian partners holding a minority position in a similar "Canadian" cartel ([GD] House of Commons 1934, 181-82). While there was an investigation of this cartel under the Combines Investigation Act in 1930, with subsequent evidence of a "combine" presented to authorities, prosecution was never pursued because (1) "there had been ... a substantial reduction in the price of tubes"; (2) "the public expense would be large"; and (3) "there appeared to be no public demand for prosecution" (ibid.). Moreover, a patent agreement between this cartel and AT&T's Canadian subsidiary, Bell Telephone, separated the broadcast and telephone markets in Canada, and helped ensure that these companies maintained control of their respective Canadian markets (Vipond 1992, 28–33; Babe 1990, 201–3).

The signals from the equipment manufacturers' high-powered American transmitters flowed freely across the border. Indirectly aided by the lack of an enforceable treaty on the use of the radio spectrum between Canada and the United States, these signals often blanked out or overpowered those of the smaller Canadian stations. Consequently, as Vipond (1992, 47) notes, American interests found "no need to build stations or produce programs here ... and by the end of the decade American radio executives not only assumed but boasted that their American stations gave complete service to Canadian listeners."

Under these circumstances, private investment in Canadian broadcasting stations was generally undertaken by "small or at best mid-sized entrepreneurs and businesses." Three main types of businesses dominated this early investment: (1) newspapers, who saw the new medium as a means of promoting their papers and extending their services; (2) radio equipment retailers, who broadcast programs to create a market for receivers; and (3) "telecommunications firms, [who] were motivated to enter the field primarily to sell the radio apparatus they manufactured, or, in the case of the telephone companies, to protect their investments" (Vipond 1992, 46). Generally, these investors focused their efforts on building local listening audiences in urban centres and populous regions of the country where markets for either receivers or advertising could be found. Educational and religious organizations also took up licences, cross-subsidizing their operation with funds from other sources. Thus, as broadcasting took form in Canada, its technical infrastructure was framed by transnational relations of production, and the emergent programming pattern was local and based upon a sustaining set of economic relations constructed at the local level.

The developing Canadian system had none of the advantages of either the American or British systems. Without cross-subsidies from equipment manufacturers, or income from a licence fee, financing presented a problem for both commercial and non-commercial Canadian stations. While legislation allowed the government to pass on to broadcasters the receiver licence fees they collected, this revenue was generally employed to maintain the regulatory infrastructure and to develop techniques to overcome signal interference from both natural and "man-made" sources (Peers 1969, 27–28; Vipond 1992, 125–34). Following trends in the United States, advertising was restricted, although in Canada those restrictions were both heavier and more closely adhered to than in the United States. Both "toll" broadcasting and "direct" advertising that promoted specific products and prices were officially banned through the 1920s in the face of pressure from newspaper organizations and negative public opinion. "Indirect" advertising, however, whereby companies announced at regular intervals throughout a program that they had paid for its production, was sanctioned in 1924 and helped offset the costs of operations and programming (Department of Marine and Fisheries, in Bird 1988, 35–36). But in broadcasting's first decade, few stations were able to support their operations through this vehicle alone.

The lack of capitalization and a firm revenue base led to difficulties in financing programs. Few stations had budgets for program production. Complicating this problem was the fact that, until the late 1920s, recording techniques were generally ill adapted to broadcast purposes. Moreover, deferring to what it claimed were the wishes of the public, the government placed heavy restrictions on the use of recorded music in the evening hours, and instead encouraged the stations to produce live programs (Vipond 1992, 136–38). As Vipond (1992, 137) points out, "the resulting programming, while genuine and community-based, was nevertheless musically inferior to what could be produced from a good record collection, a factor that became increasingly important as sophisticated American stations began to set the standards for the whole continent."

Another problem was presented by the difficulty of constructing broadcast networks in Canada. In the United States, networks were employed to capture economies of scale in program production and assisted the manufacturers' cartel in maintaining its domination of the industry. In Canada, however, telegraph lines and equipment were ill suited to broadcast purposes until the late 1920s, and then the hefty transmission fees charged by the telegraphs combined with the poor capitalization of radio broadcasters to make networks all but impossible except under special circumstances (Weir 1965, 33–35). And while local telephone lines were often employed to relay live concerts and sports events to broadcast stations for transmission, as illustrated above there was no national telephone network in Canada until the early 1930s (Vipond 1992, 93).

As a result of these development factors, there were few incentives to capital investment in Canadian radio markets. Returns on investment were largely indirect, and generally confined to either promoting the sale of specific products in local markets, such as newspapers or radio receivers, or thwarting competition in existing markets for commodities such as newspaper audiences or telecommunications services (Babe 1990, 203–4). At the same time, advertising prohibitions and the fragmentation of Canadian radio audiences, caused by American broadcast signals, reduced investment incentives for Canadian commercial interests. While some efforts were made to ascertain the breadth of listenership through the 1920s, the development of Canadian radio audiences as viable commodities themselves was still some time off. Thus, as different interests struggled to forge the technology to "specialized means" in Canada through the 1920s, their avenues of action were already heavily circumscribed by foreign capital, state sanctions, and the inflexibility of entrenched commercial interests.

In this atmosphere, Canadian broadcast licences were subject to a high rate of turnover as licensees struggled to finance their operations. Some writers argue that the regulatory prohibition on the sale of broadcasting licences discouraged investment in broadcast facilities and thereby caused this financial distress (Allard 1979, 13). There is little historical evidence to support this charge, however. Rather, to ensure continuity in broadcasting service, it would appear that because of the tenuous financial circumstances of these broadcasters, licences were generally transferred between buyers and sellers without query from the Radio Branch (Vipond 1992, 122).

In these early years, the private sector was not alone in seeking commercial benefit from the practice of radio broadcasting. Both the federal and provincial levels of government also had investments in radio operations. In Manitoba, the provincial government maintained a monopoly on broadcasting in the province from 1923 to 1933. It entered the field to prevent private businesses from employing radio as a means of communication, and thereby endangering the revenues of the provincially owned telephone system. Financed through receiver licence fees that were passed on by the federal government, facility rentals and leases, and commercial income, this operation was self-supporting for most of its life (Vipond 1992, 52).

The federal government became involved in radio broadcasting indirectly, through its ownership of the Canadian National Railway, which both owned and leased a number of stations across the country. The CNR entered the field of broadcasting for several reasons: on the one hand, radio presented a ready means of promoting its service over that of its private sector rival, the Canadian Pacific Railway; on the other hand, CNR officials "made it clear that their purpose was in part to further national policy – to attract tourists and settlers to Canada, and to help in 'keeping content those who have to live in sparsely settled districts in the north and west'" (Peers 1969, 23). As part of this latter effort, the CNR is often credited with being one of the first organizations to promote broadcasting as an instrument of nationalism (24).

In its efforts to build a national broadcasting system, the CNR pioneered the technical infrastructure necessary for a national network. It was one of the first organizations to produce programming for a national audience, and it produced programs in both English and French (Weir 1965). As a subsidiary of a major corporation and Canada's first broadcasting "chain," CNR radio was able to devote considerable resources to program production, and in 1931 it was the first Canadian broadcaster to develop a dramatic series of radio plays. While much of this activity was commercially motivated, its concern with nationalist purpose in a medium that was otherwise primarily focused at a local or community level would later give practical force to the idea that broadcasting might be utilized to nationalist ends.

Because these early forays into broadcasting by state institutions were primarily motivated by larger commercial concerns rather than an avowed, mandated public purpose, they should not be viewed as forms of public broadcasting. And while politicians sometimes spoke of the nationalist potential of broadcasting, as Prime Minister Mackenzie King did in 1927 during Canada's Diamond Jubilee celebrations, the state's official interest in radio through most of the 1920s was simply one of governance, and its focus was on promoting the development of broadcasting through the orderly allocation of frequencies (Weir 1965, 35–39).

Toward the end of the decade, however, it became increasingly apparent that successful development of the system required a stronger regulatory hand. Radio broadcasting's development continued to be stunted by both poor capitalization and chaotic technical conditions. Few Canadian stations offered full daily program schedules, and broadcasters complained that commercial restrictions made it difficult, if not impossible, to carry on the service. Because of the lack of investment capital, broadcasters often shared facilities. The local orientation of broadcasters left reception of Canadian broadcast signals spotty at best, and large portions of the country, particularly rural areas, had no Canadian service at all (Peers 1969, 21).

These problems were compounded by the growing dominance of American stations and programming on the Canadian airwaves. This situation came to a head in 1926 with the total collapse of radio regulation in the United States and the indiscriminate co-optation of Canadian frequencies by American broadcasters. As control returned to the spectrum with the US Congress's passage of the Radio Act of 1927, a resurgence of private investment spurred improvements in recording and network transmission technology (Head, Sterling, and Schofield 1994, 31–49). Not only did this rationalization of the American system present stronger direct competition for Canadian broadcasters, but it increased pressure indirectly too. As US stations moved to offer longer program schedules, they developed "sustaining" programs to maintain listenership, or "audience flow," through unsponsored gaps in those schedules. In the face of this competition, Canadian stations felt they had to do the same in order to retain their audiences. However, because of their inferior financial position, the burden of offering a longer program schedule was all the more difficult and these stations began to turn to both greater commercialism and American programs to fill their schedules (Vipond 1992, 83).

Further complicating this scenario was the fact that the licensing decisions of the Radio Branch were coming under increasing public scrutiny (Peers 1969, 29–33; Raboy 1990, 21–22; Vipond 1992, 203–6). As the number of transmission licence applications exceeded the number of available frequencies, charges of favouritism and censorship began to haunt the allocative decisions made by the branch. And in 1928, when a decision to decline the renewal of a number of licences held by the International Bible Students Association sparked a national controversy over "freedom of speech on the air," the government moved to deflect growing public criticism of the broadcasting system by appointing a Royal Commission to investigate the situation (Weir 1965, 100–3).

In the face of this controversy, the Department of Marine and Fisheries prepared a report that recommended "a detailed enquiry into the existing radio situation in Canada" (in Bird 1988, 39). Several aspects of this document are of interest here. First, it identified what the government considered to be the crux of the problem, as well as a general course of action (38):

> That a substantial number of Canadian listeners at the moment appear to be more interested in programs from the United States than in those from Canadian stations ... That in the opinion of the technical officers of the Department, the remedy for the above lies in the establishment of a number of high power stations throughout the country, and a greater expenditure on programs than the present licensees appear to be prepared to undertake.

Second, it went on to offer three alternative means for alleviating these problems (Bird 1988, 38–39):

a)   the establishment of one or more groups of stations operated by private enterprise in receipt of a subsidy from the Government;
b)   the establishment and operation of stations by a government-owned and financed company;
c)   the establishment and operation of stations by provincial governments.

Finally, in delineating the mandate of the commission, it recommended that the inquiry "consider the manner in which the available channels can be most effectively used in the interests of Canadian listeners and in the national interests of Canada" (Bird 1988, 39).

These recommendations illustrate an important turning point in broadcasting policy. For despite long-standing controversies in the area, they are the first to officially define broadcasting in the national interest. As Vipond (1992, 213) points out, it set the terms of the ensuing debate and illustrated that in the federal government's eyes "the issue was not whether the government should finance Canadian broadcasting, but rather which level of government should do so, to what extent, in what manner, and with what amount of control." The recommendations went on to form the basis of an order-in-council establishing a Royal Commission on Radio Broadcasting; thus, the state began to take an active hand in shaping the development of the system.

Under the chairmanship of Sir John Aird, the Royal Commission on Radio Broadcasting (Aird Commission) conducted a series of public hearings across the country, as well as an extensive survey of broadcasting in both the United States and Europe. Both these investigations and the findings of the commission are well documented and need not be fully rehearsed here ([GD] Royal Commission on Radio Broadcasting 1929; Vipond 1992, 195–224; Peers 1969, 37–62; Raboy 1990, 22–29). What is of particular interest, however, is how the commission gave substance to Canada's "nationalist interest" in broadcasting by framing it as an instrument of nationalism. In the process, the commission set broadcasting on a very different path of development from contemporaneous national media, and set the dimensions of the social struggle over broadcast regulation in Canada for decades to come.

Although Aird was reportedly skeptical of government ownership at the outset of the inquiry, his experiences during the investigation appear to have swayed his opinion (Peers 1969, 37–44; Vipond 1992, 213–24). And while, as Mike Gasher (1998) argues, there is some question as to how united intervenors were on the question of nationalizing radio, in its report the commission states that it found public opinion unanimous on one "fundamental question – Canadian radio listeners want Canadian broadcasting," and that the "potentialities of broadcasting as an instrument of education ... providing entertainment, and of informing the public on questions of national interest" had been impressed upon them. The commission posited that "broadcasting will undoubtedly become a great force in fostering a national spirit and interpreting national citizenship," but, in the spirit of 1920s anglophone Canadian nationalism, observed that at "present the majority of programs heard are from sources outside of Canada" and that these have "a tendency to mould the minds of the young people in the home to ideals and opinions that are not Canadian" ([GD] Royal Commission on Radio Broadcasting 1929, 43).

Following the guidelines laid out by the order-in-council, the commission
went on to recommend that an independent, state-owned broadcasting company
be established and "vested with the full powers and authority of any private
enterprise, its status and duties corresponding to those of a public utility" (44).
The technical backbone of the system was to be seven high-powered broadcasting stations, with perhaps a few low-powered undertakings supplementing their
service in locales that were "ineffectively served."[13] All other stations would be
closed down. To meet jurisdictional concerns, the provinces would control the
programming of the stations in their areas.

Financing for the system would come from licence fees, indirect advertising,
and government subsidy. These recommendations reflected several concerns..
The commission was convinced that private capital was not adequate to the
task of building and programming a national system. It concluded that the
lack of a direct return from broadcasting for private investors had "tended
more and more to force too much advertising upon the listener ... [and resulted]
in the crowding of stations into urban centres and the consequent duplication
of services in such places, leaving other large populated areas ineffectively
served" (43). But, based upon the observations that only a minority of Canadians owned radios and that a high licence fee would be "burdensome to
those of limited means," the commissioners were also concerned that the public
would not support a system financed solely by licence fees or government
subsidy. Consequently, while broadcasting's "educative value" and "importance
as a medium for promoting national unity" made it appear "reasonable" to the
commission "that a proportion of the expenses should be met out of public
funds," indirect advertising provided a means of alleviating the cost of the
system to the public. The allowance of a limited form of advertising also met
the concerns of Canadian commercial interests who argued, in a vein similar
to their concerns over the magazine industry, that a ban on advertising would
leave them at a disadvantage to US companies in Canadian markets. Moreover,
just as the commission sought to ensure Canadian commercial interests access
to Canadian audiences, it allowed that audiences should have access to the
"best programs available" from foreign sources too (50). Hence, the national
broadcaster might recapture some of the audience for foreign programs by
deploying them itself. Finally, the commission underscored the importance of
maintaining Canadian control of the system by noting that the future introduction of television broadcasting held the promise of developing broadcasting
"far beyond its present state" (46).

Consequently, in the commission's eyes, the system was to be modelled along
quite different lines from either the British or American systems. Motivated by
nationalist considerations, the state was, in part, to undertake the development

of the distribution system and program production – elements that, in the United States, had been undertaken by the equipment manufacturers and other blocks of private capital. Moreover, in the national interest, the public system would extend service to less populous parts of the country and establish an economic foundation for the production of Canadian programming that all segments of the population might access, thereby offering a degree of service well beyond that provided by the private sector in the United States. In this way, the government sought to join the geographically dispersed peoples of Canada in an extended community and create a forum in which Canadian interests could be articulated and national unity strengthened. Here, the communicative space created by the technique of broadcasting was envisioned as a "means of production," in that it would be harnessed to produce a Canadian consciousness (Lefebvre 1991, 85). But although private capital was found inadequate to fashion broadcasting in this image, nationalization of the system did not exclude its participation; nor, despite the tone of the commission's report, was the pursuit of commercial revenue viewed as antithetical to nationalist purpose. As Charles Bowman, one of the commissioners, explained in a pamphlet defending the report in January 1930 (in Vipond 1992, 220–21):

> It is misleading to argue that private enterprise would be eliminated by the Radio Commission's recommendations. Wasteful competition in the building of too many stations would be eliminated, but private broadcasters would actually be furnished with better station facilities, nationally owned, than private capital could afford to build.

With the state subsidizing and holding a monopoly on the means of transmission, revenue would be focused toward program production. Both monopoly and public subsidy would lead to lower transmission fees for private program producers, leaving more money for them to invest in production. Competition would then be encouraged between program producers, as they strove both for broadcast time and to wrest audiences from American stations (G. Spry 1931, 248). As Graham Spry would later note, under this plan competition would be increased where it "is most needed, namely, between programmes" (in Vipond 1992, 236). As well, state participation would offset the propensity of the private sector to focus only on the more populous regions of the country. Consequently, the scheme advanced by the commission was not simply an empty technological vision, nor did it directly pit "public" against "private" interests, as some commentators have argued (Charland 1986; Smythe 1981, 165). Rather, nationalization was envisioned as a means of harnessing commercial interests to the public purpose of program production and distribution, and forging the interests of the listening public, private enterprise, and the Canadian state in common purpose. By joining these interests in a common enterprise, economies of scale might be constructed that would overcome the economic disadvantages presented by Canadian geography and demographics. It might then be possible for all Canadians to receive a Canadian broadcasting service, complete with both high-quality Canadian and foreign programming. In addition, commercial interests would have access to large Canadian audiences, and an outlet that guaranteed the wide dissemination of Canadian "ideals and opinions" would be created. Consequently, the interests of both the private sector and the listening public would be satisfied. Although the issue of how the quality (or, from a contemporary perspective, what we might think of as the diversity) of these programs might be judged was never addressed, the ingeniousness of this scheme, with its focus on employing an economy of scale in transmission to provide an economy of scope in productive relationships, appears to have been either ignored or downplayed by most commentators.

The model advanced by the Aird Commission did have its problems, however. Its focus on accommodating both the provincial and federal levels of government left local perspectives and interests all but shut out of policy considerations. This seeming oversight would later haunt broadcasting policy by helping underscore a division of responsibility between the privately owned local, or "community," stations as they would come to be called, and the national broadcasting service undertaken by the public broadcaster ([GD] Special Committee on Radio Broadcasting 1946, 711–12; [GD] Parliamentary Committee on Radio Broadcasting 1947b, 737).

The necessity of taking immediate action that would yield a system in which Canadian perspectives might find a voice was underscored by Bowman in another article published in the wake of the commission's report (in Peers 1969, 53):

Already the drift under private enterprise is tending toward dependence on United States sources. Contracts are being made between Canadian broadcasting agencies and the more powerful broadcasting interests of the United States. Increasing dependence upon such contracts would lead broadcasters on this continent into the same position as the motion picture industry has reached, after years of fruitless endeavour to establish Canadian dependence in the production of films.

As was the case with other Canadian media then, events in the United States formed the context for broadcasting's development in Canada, and the national interest in Canadian broadcasting took form in the face of a burgeoning

American radio empire that threatened to overwhelm yet another medium of Canadian expression. But while this threat was overtly manifest in the overwhelming presence of American programming in Canada, its roots ran much deeper. As we have seen, with only a couple of exceptions, Canadian broadcasters did not enjoy any of the corporate relationships that enabled American broadcasters to develop their market presence. Foreign control of the equipment industry forced a dissociation of the economics of program production from those of equipment manufacture, and generally precluded the possibility of Canadian stations constructing economies of scale through vertical integration or capitalization through cross-subsidization (cf. Miege 1989).[14] Similarly, the geographical distance between urban centres combined with a division of interests between telecommunications carriers and broadcasters to again preclude the possibility of economies of scale in vertical integration between production and transmission.[15] In the face of these problems, the recommendations effected a compromise between both political and economic interests that would have set radio's development apart from all other Canadian media. However, rapidly changing political and economic conditions would soon make that compromise a site of social struggle.

The government moved to quickly introduce legislation after the commission issued its report. A bill was drafted that closely followed the Aird Commission's recommendations with regard to the independence of the corporation, financial provisions, and the structure of the system (Peers 1969, 55–62; Vipond 1992, 225–26).[16] However, before this legislation could be enacted, the stock market crashed and the country sank into depression. An election ensued, and the broadcasting issue was downplayed amid more pressing economic concerns.

American Technique, Canadian Purpose

By the 1920s, the fields of the telecommunications, newspaper, magazine, and film media were largely industrial in scope and constituted through large-scale systems of serial production and mass consumption. As these industries took form in Canada, however, they all developed on the margins of American industry, where they were highly dependent upon either American capital, the economies of scale of American markets, and/or the adoption of American production "technique" (that is, American technology and modes of organizing the production process). Where these industries were apparently key to the developing industrial infrastructure, as with the telegraph and telephone, state intervention encouraged an east-west pattern of development. Where the direct industrial benefits of establishing such a pattern of development were less obvious, such as in the magazine and film industries, the state waffled on intervention. Generally, though, the content or character of the messages these media carried was not a major concern of public policy. For the telegraph and telephone, regulation generally separated content and carriage. For newspapers, a liberal concern for press freedom foreclosed upon regulation. And for the magazine and film industries, the commercial focus and popular appeal of their products left them largely discounted as cultural vehicles.

Broadcasting was treated somewhat differently. Developing a few years later, amid a growing anglophone cultural nationalism, it was envisioned as a kind of space-binding technique and began to gather currency as a means of constructing a Canadian consciousness. Spurred by growing social tensions surrounding the technique, the state moved to exert some control over the form and direction of its development. Given this impetus, broadcasting would soon be the first medium within which Canadian content was a key regulatory concern.

The striking, common feature of all of these industries, however, is their dependency upon relationships with American industry, even those that enjoyed comprehensive regulation. Whether in terms of the manufacture of equipment upon which the communicative technique was founded, as in the telegraph, telephone, and broadcast fields; in terms of cheap imported product that was incorporated into finished commodity, as in the newspaper industry; or in terms of undermining the economics of Canadian production by filling the market with comparatively inexpensive finished products, as in the magazine and film industries, American influence on their development was both pervasive and decisive. Consequently, as the development of the Canadian elements of each of these industrial fields proceeded, not only would they be without the advantage of the large economies of scale enjoyed by their foreign competitors but they also lacked the same advantages in terms of comprehensive patterns of intensive and extensive capitalization, such as vertical and horizontal integration, complex patterns of cross-subsidization, and export markets. To varying degrees, then, in each of these fields Canadian development would take place in stilted and fragmented form compared with that of American communications media. Not until the late twentieth century would political, economic, and technological forces converge to afford Canadian media such economic advantages. However, as we shall see with broadcasting in particular, even then dependence upon American capital, product, and technique would continue to be a determining feature of its development.

The CRBC and the Making of the National Radio Broadcasting System

THE STRUGGLE FOR a national broadcasting system in Canada took place in a larger context of national pressures for political and economic expansion. The 1920s witnessed a spurt of growth that had begun in the earlier part of the century but was interrupted by the First World War (Fowke 1967, 248). Fuelled by immigration and urbanization, hydroelectric power, foreign investment, and the further development of American markets for Canadian staples, this expansion is often characterized as a second wave of industrialization that swept the country (Innis 1956; G. Williams 1989, 57–58). Through this process, many of the elements of regional industrial infrastructure that had been developed earlier in the century "were integrated into large-scale systems" of industrial production (C. Armstrong and Nelles 1986, 326).

First at the municipal and provincial levels of government, and later at the federal level, state institutions shaped and sustained growth in a pattern that followed the lines of the "wheat-coal" economy given form by the National Policy (Lower 1946, 487–522; C. Armstrong and Nelles 1986). The federal referral of the railroad, telegraph, and telephone industries to the regulatory purview of the Board of Railway Commissioners (BRC) can be seen as an early manifestation of this process, as these systems became integral to coordinating the movement of goods and information in the face of increasing economic activity. And where a reliance on private capital slowed or imposed limits on development, government ownership, with its ability to obtain "low interest rates" and supply "service at cost," was harnessed to secure more rapid utilization of natural and industrial resources (Innis 1933, 78–79). These political efforts to coordinate and sustain economic development are illustrated in the wide range of legislation, regulatory boards and commissions, and Crown corporations that made their appearance through the late 1920s and 1930s. In the fields of agriculture, harbours, pensions, banking, aeronautics, unemployment insurance, and broadcasting – to name only a few – the federal state set about enhancing its powers of governance and giving form to the national interest in the Canadian economy (Hodgetts 1973, 149–51; Fowke 1967, 249–56).

The struggles of the federal state to cope with the conditions engendered by this economic expansion were complicated by both intransigence on the part of provincial governments to meet with the federal government's agenda, and later the Depression. The provinces often balked at the enhancement of federal powers, forcing a series of court battles between the two levels of government through the 1930s and the striking of the Royal Commission on Dominion-Provincial Relations (Rowell-Sirois Commission) in 1937. But while the federal government was not always successful in expanding its powers, it continued to press for control and national coordination over an expanding field of industrial activity (Fowke 1980, 249–56).

To some extent, the nationalism that gripped anglophone Canada through the 1920s can be seen as part of this larger process of political and economic expansion. Despite the fact that much of this economic growth was itself an extension of American industrial growth, economic prosperity seemed to gauge the success of Canada as a nation state (Gonick 1970, 62–63). As illustrated by the legal wrangling in the film industry, however, as American influence became more prevalent, concerns over the domination of Canadian media by American interests became more pressing.

Broadcasting developed its institutional form in these shifting social currents. Although the formulation and acceptance of the Aird Commission's recommendation of government ownership to address the problems of broadcasting seemed to signal a political shift in the treatment of the issue of communication, the event is better read as a combination of two factors: (1) the state's growing involvement in shepherding the larger process of national industrial development, and (2) the way in which broadcasting was perceived as one of a range of new "electronic" technologies that transcended the constraints of physical geography (Carey and Quirk 1988). But as the American industry tightened its grip on the Canadian radio market, it became increasingly apparent that the development of radio was weak and yielding very little benefit for a variety of Canadian interests. Coupled with the popular vision of broadcasting as a space-binding vehicle that held great promise for promoting education and national consciousness, radio's stilted economic growth left the industry ripe for intervention. As the Conservatives came to power, a number of provinces were following Manitoba's lead and moving to control the development of radio (Vipond 1992, 250–54). But neither the institution of government ownership nor the emergence of a national system was a fait accompli; both the parameters of the issue and the form of intervention were only vaguely defined as the government changed hands.

Set in this context, this chapter examines the rise of the Canadian Radio League (CRL), the enactment of the 1932 Canadian Radio Broadcasting Act, the establishment of the Canadian Radio Broadcasting Commission (CRBC), and the ways in which both the emerging broadcasting system and its nascent public element were forged to "specialized means" within the unique environment of Canada's political economy.

After Aird: The Complexities of Developing a National Radio Broadcasting System

On July 28, 1930, the Liberals lost power to the Conservatives, and fears for the fate of the Aird Commission's recommendations were raised among the supporters of public radio. Not only was the deepening Depression causing concern that new expenditures of public funds would be met unfavourably, but R.B. Bennett, the new prime minister, had close ties with the Canadian Pacific Railway, which was known to have designs on establishing a private radio monopoly.

Despite the vicissitudes of the Depression, technical improvements combined with the economies of serial production and the growing availability of electrical current to expand radio's reach. The number of radio receiver licences in Canada doubled between 1930 and 1932, and the percentage of Canadian homes with radios rose from 15 to 30 percent (Vipond 1992, 255). The act of what Mary Vipond (1992) calls "listening in" began to occupy a greater proportion of private time, and the link between centralized transmission and privatized reception was entrenched in social practice. With rising demand, radio set manufacturing in Canada was more fully consolidated on a branch-plant basis with US interests. This control precluded yet another avenue of development for the Canadian system. In the face of growing interference from foreign stations, a plan was developed to provide Canadian broadcasters with exclusive frequencies, just outside of the conventional broadcast band. However, the branch-plant industry in Canada scuttled the idea, claiming that it would raise the cost of receivers and force the industry to undertake its own research and engineering, which was then being done by laboratories at head offices in the United States ([GD] Committee on Broadcasting 1932, 125–26, 199–200, 554–65). Thus the broadcast field was narrowed and the technological parameters laid for the later struggle over the capitalization of the system.

A number of other factors strengthened the position of private capital within the system and reinforced the system's branch-plant character. Improvements in network transmission technology resulted in four stations in Toronto and Montreal regularly receiving and broadcasting US network programs, and a fifth in Calgary attempting affiliation (Peers 1969, 79). Across Canada, however, network arrangements were stifled by hefty transmission fees charged by the common carriers (Weir 1965, 90–92). Meanwhile, improvements in recording techniques spurred the use of recorded programming, just as harsh economic times forced consolidation of most of Canada's recording industry on a branch-plant basis, shared between British and American firms (Moogk 1975, 117–19). And, in the wake of the ongoing consolidation of advertising markets in the

United States, distinctions between different types of advertising and prohibitions against it were also eroded in Canada.

Together, these factors helped spur optimism regarding the profitability of the growing industry as well as a growing hostility to the complete nationalization of the system. In combination with the larger pressures forced upon the state by the Depression, this left public broadcasting with an uncertain future.

The Canadian Radio League: Building a National Vision

Faced with these conditions, Graham Spry and Alan Plaunt founded the Canadian Radio League in 1930 to lobby for public broadcasting in Canada.[1] Spry and Plaunt had strong ties with the Association of Canadian Clubs, as well as many of the other nationalist organizations founded in the 1920s. Under their shepherding, the broadcasting issue became inextricably set in a nationalist context. Spry (1931) illustrates the nationalist purposes foreseen by the CRL for the technology of broadcasting:

> Here is an agency which may be the final means of giving Canada a national public opinion, of providing a basis for public thought on a national basis ... There is no agency of human communication which could so effectively unite Canadian to Canadian, and realize the aspiration of Confederation as radio broadcasting. It is the greatest Canadianizing instrument in our hands and its cultural influence ... is equally important.

From the fall of 1930 to the spring of 1932, public debate over the issue was heated and government lobbying extensive. Amid growing opposition to nationalization of the system, much of this debate was inspired by the efforts of the CRL. The league championed the establishment of broadcasting as a "national public service," and it set out to oppose two competing plans, one led by the CPR, and the other by a consortium of private interests (J. O'Brien 1964, 107; G. Spry 1931, 247).

Initially the CRL followed the outlines of the Aird Commission's plan and advocated total nationalization (Canadian Radio League 1931). It soon modified this position, however, to allow that stations serving local markets might be privately owned or controlled by some civic authority, and locally programmed. This position gained support from some private broadcasters and helped undermine the call of the private broadcasters' association – the Canadian Association of Broadcasters (CAB) – for a privately owned system (Vipond 1992, 242–49). Like the Aird Commission, the CRL argued that financing would come through licence fees, advertising, and government subsidy. In an effort to address the popularity of American programs and the concerns of both station owners and advertisers that Canadian audiences might actually tune into the proposed network instead of the American radio networks, select programs would be obtained from foreign sources.

The CRL represented a large cross-section of Canada's political and economic elite, and the central thrust of the campaign was to offset what this group perceived would be the "narrow purposes" of the medium if solely given over to commercial concerns (G. Spry 1931, 246). But while the organization's work is sometimes represented as "an attempt on the part of cultural nationalists to distinguish sharply between high and low culture, and to delineate cultural uplift from mass entertainment," the coalition was certainly not sustained solely by such narrow cultural aspirations (Nolan 1989, 517). Joining the writers, artists, and intellectuals who had promoted the institution of vehicles of national opinion earlier in the decade were leading labour groups, professional associations, and farmers' co-operatives. And many Canadian newspapers, including the Southam and Sifton chains, provided financial and editorial support (J. O'Brien 1964, 107–33). While some members of the organization made statements deploring the mass cultural flavour of American broadcast programs and argued that the Canadian system should emulate the British system by offering educational and cultural "uplift" programs (Nolan 1989), the aims of the league's members at large were much more widely drawn. Set against the American domination of other Canadian media, the concerns voiced by the proponents of the public system centred more on the issue that the system provide a forum for the representation of a diverse set of national interests than on either the institution of a particular cultural aesthetic or ideal, or an elitist revolt against the rising tide of mass culture.[2] As Raboy (1990, 37) points out, this was a "social conception" of broadcasting and "attracted all but that sector of private enterprise which was directly interested in broadcasting industries." At the same time, however, other than in very broad terms, it is difficult to see the movement for a national broadcasting system as a definitive moment of cultural nationalism, as it is sometimes also portrayed (Bashevkin 1991, 6–9).

Rather, in the hands of the CRL, the broadcasting issue was fashioned to transcend regional, class, and, to a degree, even ethnic differences. Indeed, the populist flavour of this nationalistic movement was "irreducible to common denominators" (Snyder 1987, 3). In some ways, the coalition was a reaction against the social conditions wrought by the rapid industrial development engendered through foreign, largely American, investment, and played upon fears of growing American control over Canadian communications media – as epitomized in Graham Spry's oft-quoted rallying cry for regulation: "The State or the United States." But it was a union of interests fraught with contradiction, as many of the league's members foresaw or imagined different national implications of the technology. For instance, some members sought to promote an idealist vision of culture, while others saw radio as a vehicle for building a more popular, pan-Canadian culture. Others focused on constructing a space for national public communication and education. Some, such as newspaper companies, were concerned that radio advertising would undermine their revenues, while other Canadian commercial interests were concerned that without radio advertising they would be at a disadvantage vis-à-vis American manufacturers (J. O'Brien 1964). Thus, while pressure from this coalition would help create a national broadcasting system, that system would later be unable to either sustain the early promises that held the coalition together or accommodate the larger set of concerns that gave it form.

The Early National System: The 1932 Radio Broadcasting Act

Legislative action on the broadcasting issue was delayed by a legal challenge over the federal government's jurisdiction in the area posed by the provinces, providing a window of opportunity for the CRL to develop support and bring its forces to bear on the legislative process (Vipond 1992, 250–54). The league actively supported the federal government's case, preparing briefs and even appearing before both the Supreme Court of Canada and the Privy Council in the federal government's favour (J. O'Brien 1964, 218–26). In February 1932, based upon the principle that broadcasting, like the telegraph, was a technology that employed trans-provincial transmission, the Judicial Committee of the Privy Council placed control firmly in the hands of the federal government (in Bird 1988, 105–10). Thus, the regulation and control of broadcasting became a federal responsibility, and not simply on grounds that the radio spectrum is a scarce resource (Kaufman 1987, 4).[3] Soon after, the prime minister announced the formation of a parliamentary committee to recommend a course of action.

As the issue encountered the parliamentary process, the CRL was not the only organization arguing for government subsidy. With the financial hardship brought on by the Depression, the private, profit-motivated interests were loath to undertake further responsibilities, and "in all the schemes advanced by private interests ... it was made clear that substantial sums of public money would have to be spent to provide a national program service" (Peers 1969, 82). Thus, just as the Department of Marine and Fisheries had recommended four years earlier, it became evident that if radio were to be harnessed to any sort of nationalist purpose, the state would have to intervene.

Pressure from private broadcasters helped increasingly erode the vision of national broadcasting put forward by the Aird Commission and the Canadian Radio League as it passed through the hands of the 1932 Parliamentary

Committee on Broadcasting and into legislation.[4] The committee recommended the creation of a national service built upon a nationwide chain of high-powered stations, but it allowed stations under 100 watts to remain in private hands. Financing of this scheme would come only from advertising and licence fees, and construction of the national system and expropriation of existing stations would proceed only as funds from these sources were made available.

A last-minute attempt was made by forces both inside and outside of the government to delay legislation and push for the establishment of a regulatory commission rather than some form of government ownership. But, at Prime Minister Bennett's insistence, a bill was introduced in the House of Commons, and in May 1932 Bennett gave a speech introducing the bill to its second reading. This speech clearly outlined both the nationalist purpose and context of this legislation (in Bird 1988, 112–13). First, Bennett argued that "this country must be assured of complete control of Canadian broadcasting from Canadian sources." Without it, broadcasting "can never become a great agency for communication of matters of national concern and for the diffusion of national thoughts and ideals ... it can never be the agency by which consciousness may be fostered and sustained and national unity still further strengthened." Second, he claimed that "no other scheme than that of public ownership can ensure to the people of this country, without regard to class or place, equal enjoyment of the pleasures of radio broadcasting. Private ownership must necessarily discriminate between densely and sparsely populated areas ... Happily ... under this system there is no need for discrimination; all may be served alike." Third, he argued that "the use of the air" was a "natural resource" that must be reserved "for development for the use of the people." These policy principles, born of the broadcasting debates of the late 1920s, would become the ground over which future regulatory struggles would be fought.

The 1932 Canadian Radio Broadcasting Act and the policy instrument it constituted, the Canadian Radio Broadcasting Commission, fell short of producing the "great agency" envisioned in Bennett's speech. The commission's relations with the private sector were directed more toward regulation than eventual ownership, and its relationships with Parliament were structured more like those of a government department than an independent Crown corporation (sections 8 and 9). For instance, while the CRBC was empowered to "determine the number, location and power of stations in Canada," as well as control network broadcasting and regulate advertising, final licensing decisions remained in the hands of the minister of marine and fisheries and the acquisition of property was subject to the approval of Parliament. The commission was unable to borrow money or raise capital publicly, and it was dependent upon Parliament for releasing funds collected from licence fees – its main source of revenue.

Moreover, nowhere in the act were either Parliament's aims for broadcasting or the national purposes of broadcasting specified, leaving the commission without a clear mandate. In the area of program production and distribution, the commission had greater latitude. It was empowered to "carry on the business of broadcasting in Canada," and both "originate programmes and secure programmes from within or outside Canada." Toward distributing programs, the commission was given full power over network broadcasting and "to make operating arrangements with private stations for the broadcast of national programs." Thus, the CRBC's structure combined aspects of the government department, the regulatory board, and the Crown corporation but, in all these capacities the government reserved final control.

The creation of the CRBC is generally hailed as a victory for the proponents of public broadcasting (Hardin 1974, 294; Smythe 1981, 186), but the commission was ill equipped to mould the system to any clear public purpose. Indeed, it is sometimes noted that the architects of this legislation never intended to have the CRBC actually take over all broadcasting in Canada (Vipond 1992, 272–74). Still, state intervention did institute a particular set of relations between the state and private interests within the system – relations that would inform the growth of the system well into the development of television broadcasting.

Radio, Broadcast Regulation, and the State

Drawing upon Hugh Aitken's (1967) work, Margaret Prang (1965) claims that the institution of the CRBC is an example of "defensive expansionism" on the part of the Canadian state. She argues that the "inability or reluctance" of private investors to undertake the investment necessary to secure a Canadian presence in the broadcast realm was met by "the willingness of influential groups to use the power of the dominion government ... in the face of economic and political threats from the United States" (1). But while this characterization is commonly adopted, it is simplistic. To claim that the state was employed instrumentally, by either a political elite or private capital, overlooks the complexity of the forces that propelled the issue, as well as the ways in which particular circumstances nuanced both the process and final form of intervention.

Situated at the intersection between the burgeoning American radio empire and a range of often disputatious Canadian social and economic interests, the state certainly had an interest in exploiting the communicative space created by broadcast technology. Early in its appearance, radio broadcasting was represented as a venue within which national communication might take place, as a means of conquering "space through space" and creating a "common consciousness" among Canadians (Charland 1986, 286). This yielded a particularly powerful and seductive vision of the technology as a vehicle for overcoming the difficulties that social and physical distance presented to governing the country (L. Marx 1964; Carey and Quirk 1988, 113–41). But both the political elite and private capital were divided on the issue of intervention, and Prime Minister Bennett proceeded with legislation in the face of wide opposition from both within his own party and a diverse set of private interests (Weir 1965, 135; Peers 1969, 102; Dewar 1982). The fact that the government went ahead was probably due more to a combination of factors than the influence of any one particular interest: the idea of the technology as a potential conqueror of space, the wide range of political and economic interests that supported the cause, and the larger pressures on the federal state to impose some form of national coordination on the emerging industrial structure. Further, the facts that program production and distribution were poorly capitalized at the time, and that broadcast stations were one of the only aspects of the industry not directly controlled by foreign capital, provided the federal government room for intervention without having to mount a legal challenge.

However, this vision of bringing the country together through electronic technology did not involve the wholesale adoption of "a foreign economic and programming logic," or simply one of transmission, as others sometimes argue (Charland 1986, 209). In terms of the larger industrial infrastructure that framed broadcasting, a die had been cast that would later help mould the system in a clouded image of its American counterpart. As we have seen, however, at the time of these debates, radio advertising was still in its infancy in both the United States and Canada, and its hegemony over broadcast communication far from assured. Moreover, the state's interest in intervention was framed in terms of instituting a means of both producing and distributing Canadian programming – not simply some empty form of "technological nationalism," as critics have argued (Charland 1986). Faced with the diversity of interests that had designs on utilizing the medium, as well as issues surrounding freedom of speech, it was difficult, if not impossible, for legislators to specify the content of that programming, but its central characteristic was explicit throughout the broadcasting debates of the 1920s and 1930s – it was to be generally Canadian in nature.

But while both program production and distribution were key to this nationalist purpose, both the strength of the competing interests in the broadcasting field and the changing economic tenor of the times circumscribed the state's actions. In 1929, with the Liberal Party at the helm of government and relatively buoyant political and economic conditions, full nationalization of the system appeared possible. Three years later, conditions militated against the state's immediate expropriation of all private stations. Funds were scarce, radio was gaining popularity, and an ideological predisposition to private property precluded expropriation without "fair compensation" (J. O'Brien 1964, 289). Thus, as it had in earlier fields of state intervention, the nationalist pretensions of the state served as part of a larger mode of regulation in the emerging broadcast realm, legitimating and setting the context for state intervention but falling short of forcing the institution of a particular set of productive relationships. In other words, to paraphrase George Streeter (1986, iv), in this venue the discourse of nationalism began to shape a social system that "it failed to describe." It provided a particular discursive and ideological orientation to the system that would later provide the context for a set of events that would, in some ways, run contrary to the original motive for intervention.

The form of state intervention in this instance is of particular interest. It was not simply the product of the forces at play in the field of broadcasting, nor was it structured to simply serve the interests of private capital. Rather, a number of factors appear to have shaped it.

In the face of high overhead costs and low potential returns, private capital was unwilling to make the investment necessary to construct a broadcasting system that would deliver Canadian programming to the widely dispersed population. Moreover, the transnational relations of production within which the Canadian system was embedded were coupled with evolving Canadian regulatory divisions of responsibility in related industries, such as telegraph and telephone markets, to militate against the development of patterns of cross-subsidy or economies of scale that would aid the private sector in carrying this project forward, as had happened in the United States. Consequently, intervention to directly subsidize private interests in this regard, or provide a mechanism for raising and directing funds in this direction was necessary if a Canadian broadcasting system was to take form.

Both subsidy and direct government ownership were often proffered as solutions to economic development problems through the 1920s and 1930s. But the litany of political and economic abuses these forms of intervention had suffered "during the period of building competitive railways" combined with ideological presuppositions of the primacy of private capital to leave many people wary of their efficacy ([GD] Committee on Broadcasting 1932, 494–501). From this perspective, the state had a rather limited repertoire of instruments to call upon. Although the structure of the regulatory board was suitable for the allocative functions of broadcast regulation, such as the assignment of frequencies and the development and enforcement of rules, it was not adequate for directly investing funds at specific sites of production and fostering their growth. For such direct investment, a structure along the lines of the relatively new Crown corporation was necessary. By 1932, however, the Depression's firm grip on the national economy had led to an indictment of the supposedly extravagant spending of the CNR – Canada's premier Crown corporation – militating against the establishment of a new Crown corporation (Weir 1965, 93–97). Coupled with the ideological predispositions of the government and the lobbying efforts of those interested in the commercial prospects of broadcasting, this situation precluded the institution of a Crown corporation and the wholesale nationalization of the broadcasting system.

The hybrid structure of the CRBC was a product of these circumstances. On the one hand, it was close to government control and unable to take over private stations without the government's approval. On the other hand, the CRBC's powers of regulation gave recognition to the legitimacy of private capital within the system, while at the same time providing mechanisms for its governance. In addition, the CRBC had the ability to both raise and invest funds in specific areas to facilitate the extension of existing service. For many commentators of the time, this new organizational form of state intervention was viewed as an "experiment," a way to meld a combination of public and private ownership to a larger public purpose (Dennison 1935; Vipond 1994). Exactly how the new commission might accomplish this purpose was not clear. While the legislation left open the possibility of complete nationalization, the path of least resistance pointed the CRBC toward regulating the behaviour of the private stations while it focused on meeting an ill-defined "national interest" through program production and network construction. Moreover, and perhaps most importantly, the simple fact that the efforts of the state were focused at the national level left interests at both the regional and local levels subject to the forces of the marketplace.

The CRBC in Action

As the CRBC began operating in late 1932, it quickly became apparent that there was little consensus concerning the responsibilities that it should undertake or the direction it should follow. Informed by nationalist purpose, the commission focused its operations on three areas: program distribution, program production, and broadcast regulation. In all of these areas, however, the CRBC's activities were constrained by the peculiar political economy of the Canadian broadcasting system.

From the beginning, the commission's autonomy was severely limited by legislation, and its activities were mired in controversy. At the organizational level, the commission experienced both administrative and financial problems. The 1932 Radio Broadcasting Act placed both regulatory and administrative duties in the hands of a three-member board. Without a definitive organizational mandate or a clear division of internal responsibilities, their workload was heavy and their purposes somewhat confused. In the harsh economic climate, the government failed to pass on the full amount it collected in licence fees, leaving the commission with revenues ranging from $1,120,591 in 1932 to $1,702,965 in 1936 ([GD] CRBC 1932–36). These sums were far from the $2.5 million estimated by the Aird Commission as the annual minimum necessary to operate a national system, even without factoring in the costs of station acquisition. Moreover, the government determined and allocated the commission's budget annually, making long-range planning difficult, if not impossible, and requests for capital to build new stations were consistently refused (Weir 1965, 173–75). The CRBC's close relationship with the government, coupled with the Conservatives' apparent ambivalence toward the purposes of the public broadcaster, left the commission subject to pressures from both the party in power and a variety of commercial concerns. Partisan and hostile political interests, private broadcasters, railway companies, and newspaper concerns all left their mark on the commission and worked to subordinate its operations to the interests of private capital.

Several tasks immediately confronted the commissioners as they took up their responsibilities: staff, stations, and programming facilities had to be arranged; broadcasting regulations had to be formulated and promulgated; and new frequency allocations had to be made among private broadcasters under the terms of a new broadcast treaty with the United States. The commission also set about creating new technical standards to reduce interference and improve reception ([GD] CRBC 1932–35).

In April 1933, Parliament ratified a measure to allow the CRBC to acquire the radio properties of the CNR, reportedly at less than 40 percent of their market value.[5] In the grip of the Depression, the transfer of these assets was politically expedient and there was little opposition to the sale. The deal provided the CRBC with stations in Ottawa and Vancouver, and production facilities in Toronto and Montreal. The commission also leased stations in Toronto and Montreal, constructed a station in Chicoutimi, and, in the following year, acquired stations in Windsor and Quebec. These assets formed the core of the CRBC's facilities and, in combination with private affiliates, they were deployed to create a national network as well as six regional networks ([GD] CRBC 1934–36).

The CRBC's network structure was similar to that of its American counterparts. In practice, however, while the American networks were oriented toward commercial purposes, the commission put its network to nationalist purposes. The American companies deployed their facilities and affiliates to produce both national and regional audiences that would offer commercial sponsors a degree of flexibility in marketing their products. The CRBC, on the other hand, used its regional networks to overcome time differences and ensure that different parts of the country received national programs at the same time of day. The national network carried a "National Hour" that was broadcast to all parts of the country simultaneously ([GD] CRBC 1934–35, 9).

However, because local broadcasters had already begun to fall under the sway of the American system, the CRBC had difficulties delivering its programs at this level. Getting on air in Toronto and Montreal proved particularly vexing for the commission. With the government keeping a tight rein on the budget, leasing or buying time on existing stations was more expedient than the more costly alternative of purchasing and running a station. However, in Toronto, CFRB, the most powerful station in the area and an affiliate of an American network, was unwilling to provide airtime at a rate the commission was willing to pay. Hence, a lease agreement was struck with a lower-powered rival station whose audience share had already been depleted by CFRB. In Montreal, the two principal stations were affiliates of American networks and had no interest in cooperating with the commission. Thus the commission resorted to leasing an outdated transmitter and later purchasing its own. But even equipped with its own transmitters in these major centres, the CRBC raised the ire of the existing private broadcasters, who claimed that it was regulating its competitors and thereby had an unfair advantage over them in the market. This particular complaint dogged the public broadcaster right up to the creation of the Board of Broadcast Governors in 1958. In general, however, the development plans of the publicly owned broadcaster met with strong opposition wherever they were not commensurate with the interests of private capital.

Distribution at the national and regional levels also encountered problems. Following the recommendations of the 1932 Parliamentary Committee on Broadcasting, the CRBC quickly entered into negotiations with the railways for the telegraphic distribution of its network programming.[6] This too proved to be a difficult and expensive proposition, however. To maximize their revenues and leave room for their own possible expansion into broadcasting, telegraph companies imposed both hefty fees and restrictions on carriage contracts with the commission. Hence, the distribution contract specified that the lines could not be employed for "commercial broadcasting purposes" and that the commission agreed not to "compete with the railways in the commercial broadcasting field" (in Weir 1965, 165). These contracts formed the basis for both the national and regional networks. These commercial sanctions meant that the commission had to shoulder the full cost of network distribution, which comprised approximately 40 percent of its expenditures during its lifetime ([GD] CRBC 1932–36). This policy was not without its critics. As Thomas Allard (1979, 95) points out, to alleviate this burden the CRBC might have acted

> as a mass buyer of the lines, making use of those hours it desired for its own programs, and selling the remaining facilities at a profit to the advertisers. That arrangement would have lowered the unit cost to both the CRBC and Canadian advertisers. It would have forced the latter to pay part of the Commission's "sustaining" or non-commercial programs. Such arrangements were common in the U.S.

As Frank Peers (1969, 130–31) illustrates, however, such an arrangement had been considered and rejected by the commission in late 1932:

> It would have meant that the commission was distributing commercial programs, for which it would get little credit, and whose content it could hardly control. More than that, such an arrangement would immediately stir up opposition on the part of newspapers, who would charge that their advertisers were receiving a subsidy from the state to advertise in a rival medium.

Moreover, in the competition for advertising dollars, high-powered private stations, though they represented themselves as "local" in focus, had a distinct advantage over the commission. As Peers (1969, 131) goes on to note:

> Through a station like CFRB, Toronto – a 10,000 watt station in the richest and most heavily populated area of Canada – an advertiser could reach nearly a half of the market that a national network would bring him. Why should he put his money into a more costly program, spending a great deal more money for distribution, in return for a less satisfactory sales message. The calculation of the Aird Commission, that revenue would be available to the national network from "indirect advertising" was based on the assumption that there would be no powerful private stations in Canada. That was not the case in 1933.

While the commission appears to have had second thoughts about the line restrictions toward the end of 1933, pressure from newspapers and other vested interests forestalled any changes, and the CRBC's national network was confined to non-commercial programming until late 1935. Thus, from the outset, conflicts surrounding the generation and disposition of commercial revenue served to push the CRBC toward the commercial margins of the system.

As the Depression deepened, few sponsors could be found to assume the high cost of transmission line rental anyway, except perhaps those that wished to extend the reach of American network programming (Weir 1965, 176; Blakely 1979). Thus, although the commission prohibited private stations from instituting commercial network broadcasts without its permission, the CRBC's network monopoly did little to impede the transmission of Canadian programming by private stations, or directly impair the profits of private operators. However, the commission's inability to supply commercial programs limited the appeal of its service to private broadcasters and increased the costs of securing affiliates.

Like their American counterparts, Canadian stations found it difficult to find commercial sponsors for more than 35 percent of their broadcast schedules in the early 1930s (Barnouw 1968, 245; Nolan 1989, 502). To fill these gaps in their schedules, American network affiliates reimbursed the networks for "sustaining" programs – that is, programs designed to sustain or hold audiences through these commercial gaps – in either cash or airtime (Czitrom 1983, 80). In Canada, however, the situation was reversed. To ensure distribution, the CRBC paid the stations that comprised its basic national network to carry its programs (Charlesworth 1935, 46). In 1934–35, approximately 20 percent of the commission's budget was devoted to such payments ([GD] CRBC 1934–35, 19). Other stations were supplied with free programming. Under these terms, the commission's programs were quite popular with private stations, if for no other reason than to build and hold audiences during periods when more profitable commercial time could not be sold. The importance of these payments and programming to the economic well-being of private broadcasters and the maintenance of a "national" broadcasting system in the early 1930s is illustrated in the fact that, of the seventy-six licensed broadcast stations in Canada in 1935–36, seven were owned or leased by the commission, twenty-one were paid to carry commission programming, and fifty others carried the commission's programs ([GD] Special Committee on Broadcasting 1936, 7, 19). As we shall see, however, as more profitable commercially sponsored programming became available, the public broadcaster's programming quickly lost favour.

Producing programming with a distinctively "Canadian" flavour formed the second thrust of the CRBC's efforts. As David Walters (1960, 40–41) illustrates:

One of the CRBC's primary purposes was to produce more Canadian programs and thus stem the tide of American culture. To do this they spiced their program schedules with talks by prominent Canadians, and by visitors to Canada, and with broadcasts of special features such as the Harmsworth Trophy Race on Lake St. Clair, the National Balloon Race, and the arrival of the Italian Air Armada at Shediac N.B. in 1934. News of Canadian interest was carried on twice daily bulletins, prepared by Canadian Press ... in addition, the CRBC began the Northern Messenger Service, by which personal messages were relayed by shortwave radio to people in the far north of Canada ... How far the CRBC succeeded in Canadianizing radio can be seen from the fact that of the 7,200 radio programs broadcast by the Commission during 1934–35, 7,000 were of Canadian origin.

Programs were also exchanged with British and American networks (MacLennan 2005), although the CRBC apparently agreed to protect the markets of Canadian affiliates of American networks when broadcasting those programs.[7]

Like distribution, production was also fraught with problems for the CRBC. After distribution and administrative expenses, only about 30 percent of its budget was left for production. This drew the ire of critics, who charged that too small a proportion of the overall budget was being invested in this area (Weir 1965, 179–83). The quality of these programs also drew criticism,[8] and despite the fact that the commission brought a broadcast service based upon Canadian information and news sources, as well as Canadian talent in musical and dramatic programs, to many communities for the first time, this fare was often criticized for being of "low quality," too "popular," or too "nationalist" in character (Dennison 1935; Weir 1965; Peers 1969).[9] Moreover, under pressure from Canadian newspapers that worried about radio as a potential competitor, the CRBC did not produce its own newscasts. Instead, Canadian Press supplied the commission's stations with short news summaries that were read over the air (Nichols 1948, 258–69; Vipond 1999).

The commission's program policies also led to a much more difficult and fractious, although very Canadian, dispute. In 1933, the CRBC began broadcasting national programs in both English and French. As E. Austin Weir (1965, 149) notes, these programs "provoked a veritable flood of protests from the press and public, from the Maritimes, and particularly from Ontario and Western Canada."[10] He attributes this backlash to religious bigotry rather than a general antipathy to Quebecers. Still, pressure to separate the linguistic components of the system grew, and by 1934 the CRBC had "split its service in two and began doing separate programming in French for Quebec" (Raboy 1990, 52).[11] Thus, the nationalist pretensions of what is often thought of today as one of Canada's first cultural institutions quickly collided with the competing concepts of nationhood that characterize the Canadian federalist union.

In the regulatory realm, the CRBC drafted a range of broadcast regulations early in 1933. Most of this policing activity dealt with the technical aspects of station operations, but a few addressed program content. Among the latter were regulations that limited imported programs to less than 40 percent of the program schedule and "direct" advertising to less than 5 percent of program time ([GD] CRBC 1933). However, both these regulations had loopholes that favoured commercial interests.

The Canadian content regulation carried the following proviso: "A program of foreign origin which advertises goods manufactured in Canada, and names the address in this country where such goods are produced and distributed, shall be deemed a Canadian program" (Rule 89) ([GD] CRBC 1933). While there appears to be little or no historical record of the impetus for this regulation, pressure for its promulgation may have come from several directions: American branch-plant operations seeking to utilize programming sponsored by their head offices to promote their products sold in Canada; private, profit-oriented Canadian broadcasters seeking to minimize production costs and maximize revenue; or the regulator itself, as a means of contributing to the capitalization of the system by cross-subsidizing private operations with foreign programming. In any event, like later simultaneous program substitution rules for television, it had the effect of harnessing the popularity of foreign programs to the commercial benefit of private broadcasters ([GD] Task Force on Broadcasting Policy 1986, 459–61).

Advertising restrictions also had provisos, and in a letter to C.P. Edwards, director of radio at the Department of Marine and Fisheries, CRBC commissioner Arthur Steele stated that "advertising in the form of verses, poetry, or song" would be considered "indirect" advertising and therefore not fall within the 5 percent rule.[12]

Other restrictions of note in this set of regulations include sanctions against "programming or advertising matter containing abusive or defamatory statements ... or statements or suggestions contrary to the express purpose of any existing legislation" (Rule 90), and a prohibition on "broadcasting editorial opinions of a controversial nature" (Rule 102). Together these rules provided a basis for regulatory control over broadcast content. Rule 90 was applied to establish commercial standards and, in a move similar to one undertaken by the early Federal Communications Commission (FCC) in the United States, it was employed to limit patent medicine advertising (Charlesworth 1935, 46–47). It was also deployed to ensure that other kinds of "'ballyhoo' ... by fanatical and crank organizations calculated to give offense to large sections of the community" were "eliminated from the Canadian air" (47). In this vein, the rule was used to ensure that controversial programming such as that aired by the International Bible Students Association in 1928 would not again find its way on air and precipitate further regulatory furor. As Vipond (1994, 158–62) illustrates, these rules were also applied to controversial political broadcasts such as one sought by the Communist Party during the 1935 election campaign. While the text for this broadcast was the subject of heated debate, it was eventually aired, although heavily edited, apparently following some definition of "community standards" (161).

Vipond (1994, 153–54, 160–62) suggests that in drafting and enforcing these rules, the CRBC performed a kind of "coercive" function for the Canadian state, gently working to suppress ideas and opinions unpopular with the government of the day while at the same time trying to maintain its credibility as a non-partisan agency. Such a view is perhaps a little narrow, however, for, as we shall see, in its later incarnation as the Canadian Broadcasting Corporation, Canada's public broadcaster suffered a litany of criticism from all sides of the political spectrum for its restrictions on program content. Rather, as the shifting tide of industry wrought change at many social levels, the promulgation of such standards might be read as an effort to bring the emergent practice of broadcasting in line with what was perceived as the dominant set of social values that underpinned Canadian life. Through these rules, broadcasting took its place as part of the larger system of social governance that framed and animated Canadian society.

For the most part, the CRBC's regulatory activities were quite sensitive to the financial concerns and property rights of broadcasters. No stations were forced to disaffiliate with American networks or to carry the CRBC's programs, and all private stations were allowed to carry on business as usual. In technical matters, the commission's efforts to improve technical standards and alleviate different types of interference led to a general improvement in the broadcast environment for all broadcasters. The CRBC was key in protecting private broadcasters' frequencies from foreign incursions, and even went so far as to directly place the interests of commercial broadcasters before its own ([GD] CRBC 1934, 18). For instance, in reallocating frequencies to comply with international agreements in 1933, the commission gave up its own clear channel in Toronto so that a private station in Windsor might avoid interference from a Mexican station. When queried about this move, the commission submitted that it was "far better for the Commission's station to have this trouble than that the commercial station in Windsor which is forced to make its living should have been subject to this interference" (1934 *Proceedings*, 557, in Weir [1965, 184–85]). As Weir (1965, 182–85) notes, the commission also protected the audiences of some of its basic stations "by refusing permission to other stations in the same area to broadcast its programs." Thus, while the private stations suffered under the threat of expropriation, there was little evidence in the actions of either the government or the commission to suggest that this possibility might soon meet with fruition, or even that the possibility harmed the profits of private broadcasters. Rather, by subsidizing its operation with both free programming and payments, the CRBC played a key role in helping the majority of Canadian stations weather the tough economic climate.

Yet the private sector complained. In early 1934, a second parliamentary committee was convened to investigate broadcasting, and private broadcasters presented manifold grievances. Advertising restrictions were argued to be too onerous. The commission's stations were accused of unfair competition. Regulations controlling affiliation with American networks and creating Canadian networks were attacked. And the changes in wavelength assignment were assailed.

The stations that issued the most vociferous complaints, however, were those located in the most viable commercial markets, and the requests they placed before the committee centred on enhancing the profitability of their operations. These demands generally took one of several forms: (1) the stations wanted to increase the number of allowable commercial minutes; (2) they were already affiliates of US networks and wished to improve their abilities to garner Canadian audiences with imported programming by enhancing these agreements; (3) they wished to affiliate with US networks; and (4) they sought permission to employ more "electrical transcriptions" or recordings in their broadcasts ([GD] Committee on Broadcasting 1934). In all but one of these proposals, the net effect would have been to increase the amount of foreign programming within the system. In other words, the production of new Canadian programming, other than advertising messages, was not generally an interest of the private stations. Profit was their motive, and increasing profits was generally equated with taking advantage of the economies of scale presented by the American system and the cheap, popular programming it produced.

The report of the 1934 Committee on Broadcasting was brief and it received little attention in the House of Commons as an election call was anticipated. However, it presaged what would become a familiar pattern. On one hand, it reaffirmed the principle of national broadcasting and recommended minor technical and organizational changes. At the same time, however, it also recommended incrementally easing restrictions on private broadcasters. In the end, the only apparent change in regulation was that private stations were allowed to extend commercial time to 15 percent of their schedules, further enabling the capitalization of the system at the local level ([GD] House of Commons 1935, 3845).

Throughout the rest of its tenure, the CRBC continued to be hampered by budget restrictions, its own organizational structure, pressure and complaints from industry, and political interference (Weir 1965, 137–204; Peers 1969, 63–164). In late 1935, line contracts with the telegraph companies were renegotiated to allow the transmission of commercial programs, but before a clear position on this issue could be established, a political scandal dealt the commission a final blow. As the country entered the election campaign in the fall of 1935, the Conservative government employed the CRBC to produce and broadcast a series of partisan political broadcasts that did not identify the Conservatives as their sponsor. These broadcasts, which featured a small-town Tory armchair philosopher by the name of "Mr. Sage," extolled the virtues of the Conservatives and denigrated both Liberal Party policy and the party's leader, Mackenzie King. They enraged the Liberals and became a catalyst for wide-ranging discontent over the CRBC's organization and operations, and, upon Mackenzie King's election, a review of the commission's operation was undertaken.

Canadian Radio Broadcasting

In the wake of the "organizational, financial, and political problems" that surrounded the CRBC, the commission is often judged as a "failure" in public administration (Vipond 1994, 169–71).[13] Yet, in a number of ways the commission was quite successful in promoting the growth of a national network and exerting a degree of Canadian control over emerging broadcast technology.

Informed by nationalist purpose, the CRBC set out to create a national broadcasting system in a field that was already heavily circumscribed by the presence of American capital and technique, as well as divisions of responsibility between pockets of Canadian capital. Under these circumstances, program production in Canada was divorced from the larger set of industrial relationships that gave it form in the United States, and the commission struggled to create a set of relationships that would sustain both the production and distribution of broadcast programming at the national level. In this process, it instituted a particular set of relationships between the state and other broadcast interests – relationships that reflect the traditional structures of both the regulatory board and government ownership.

In its work as a regulator, the CRBC made rules and regulations that brought centralized management and control of technical and programming standards to a system that had been previously characterized by chaotic conditions.[14] It set technical standards and increased the technical quality of broadcasts, improving broadcast reception. It undertook allocative responsibilities, issuing controls on licences and wattage. It played a central role in establishing advertising standards. And it acted as a buffer between the government and a wide range of competing interests both within the broadcast realm and between the commercial interests in that realm and those in the carriage and advertising markets (Hodgetts 1946, 465n50). In these capacities, the commission worked to bring the practice of broadcasting in concert with both entrenched blocks of Canadian capital and a larger set of Canadian social practices. And, in this process, it created conditions for a more efficient exploitation of the radio spectrum by largely Canadian-based capital than had previously been possible.

As an instrument of government ownership, the CRBC promoted the rapid, extensive exploitation of the radio spectrum. As observed in earlier instances of government intervention, in the face of a range of market rigidities, the commission attained "the end of immediate investment ... of capital" in the spectrum and set the stage for "retaining a substantial share of the returns" from this resource for Canadians (Innis 1933, 80–81). Guided by a discourse of nationalist purpose, it harnessed revenue sources that were not dependent upon the labour process within the system (e.g., licence fees and advertising revenue from foreign programs), and directed the investment of this revenue toward aspects of the resource that the private, profit-oriented elements of the system were loath to approach. In the two areas that comprised the CRBC's greatest expenditure – program production and network construction – the financial incentives pointed profit-oriented private stations toward the use of recorded materials that, because of the hegemony of foreign capital, were largely foreign in origin; the importation of "live" foreign programs on a casual basis; or direct affiliation with US networks. But by producing and distributing Canadian radio programs on a national basis, the CRBC worked to channel development in different directions. It directly subsidized the operation of private stations by providing income and programming to stations during the tough economic times of the early 1930s.[15] Thus, through both regulatory and productive actions, the CRBC gave form and substance to this nascent system and moved to create a Canadian-based broadcasting system.

It is no surprise that, informed by a discourse of nationalist purpose, the CRBC set its operations on the commercial margins of the system. But in this role the commission did not operate in the direct service of capital accumulation, as some have claimed (Vipond 1994, 153–57). Rather, guided by the larger political system, it set out to construct a national broadcasting service. Where its operations coincided with the pecuniary interests of private operators, they cooperated with the commission and welcomed its participation. Where those operations were seen by the private sector to intrude on the private accumulation process, they were met with heavy opposition. Given its limited powers and financial resources, the commission's ability to mould the system to a larger public purpose was limited when confronted with such opposition from the private sector.

Where the interests of private broadcasters directly collided with the larger nationalist purposes of broadcasting, such as when such broadcasters pressed for the unencumbered right to construct networks based upon imported programs, they were deflected, though not without struggle. But this nationalist prerogative did not extend to station ownership and operation. The larger social consideration of private property rights surrounding the private stations' investment in plant precluded expropriation without compensation. Moreover, because this investment was based upon the productive capacity of this plant, and without access to a broadcast frequency the idle plant was virtually worthless, simply appropriating a station's frequency without adequate compensation would have amounted to expropriation, despite the regulatory sanction against proprietary rights to frequencies. Lacking the resources to purchase or build its own stations, the commission was forced to negotiate with private broadcasters for access to their frequencies in order to distribute its programs. The ensuing dependency upon the private sector worked to give the public broadcaster a direct stake in those stations' economic well-being, while at the same time the private broadcasters' growth and development hinged upon breaking that relationship.

In the harsh economic conditions of the early 1930s, gaining access to the private sector's facilities was not particularly difficult for the commission – except in instances where private operators were already extracting a greater return on their investments than the commission could afford to pay. In such markets, issues surrounding property rights forced the commission to assume a subordinate position vis-à-vis commercial broadcasters from the outset.

Thus, in the early operations of the CRBC, a pattern familiar from the history of state intervention emerged. At the organizational level, the state-owned broadcaster undertook responsibilities that were generally uneconomical or subordinate to the interests of capital. Focused on the national level and reinforced by the intransigence of private capital, the commission's operations centred on filling in the gaps of a national system left by commercial enterprise.

This national focus – one of the legacies of the Aird Commission – had an important impact upon the character of the system, as it generally left local development to the devices of private capital and profit-oriented behaviour became the hallmark of local broadcasting. Failure to envision and/or encourage the development of different kinds of broadcasters at this level – such as some sponsored by educational or community organizations – contributed to the capitalization of local stations as well as the system's further incorporation into transnational relations of production.[16] While there were exceptions, private, profit-motivated local Canadian broadcasters generally found the most cost-effective method of obtaining programs was through becoming affiliates of American networks, utilizing recorded music or obtaining electrical transcriptions – not producing programs themselves (MacLennan 2005).[17] All of these avenues generally pointed south of the border. Moreover, advertising for American network programming and other broadcast materials that spilled over the border in US magazines and other advertising vehicles increased the currency of these foreign programs in the Canadian market.

The net result of these circumstances was that the productive relationships that underpinned these local, private, profit-oriented stations had a direct effect on their representational practices. Foreign programming and recorded material were the key to profits. Only when Canadian programming was cheaper to produce than foreign programming was to purchase, or when foreign programs were unable to meet local programming demands – such as in the broadcast of local news, current affairs, weather, and political or sporting events – was there an economic incentive to produce Canadian programs. In most program categories, even Canadian network programs could not overcome the cost advantages of foreign broadcast materials. As the capitalization of the system proceeded and broadcasting markets based upon the profit motive both grew and became more competitive, this contradiction became more apparent and drove both the public broadcaster and Canadian broadcast programming to the commercial margins of the system.

In turn, this profit-motivated behaviour on the part of local broadcasters presented the CRBC with another set of pressures around the issue of commercialism. Although the entertainment programs produced by American commercial sponsors were popular with audiences on both sides of the border, there were many complaints about the announcements of commercial sponsorship inherent in their texts. In Canada, this popular distaste for commercial messages helped put considerable pressure on the CRBC, and later the CBC, to minimize commercial sponsorship of their programs. Criticisms of commercialism came from several directions. Inspired by the apparent educational and "uplift" character of BBC programs, some critics held an elitist disdain for mass cultural products in general, and commercial broadcast programs in particular (Eaman 1994, 4–22). Labour groups such as the All-Canadian Congress of Labour argued for the "complete removal of radio from the commercial sphere," apparently so that the medium might more readily serve the broader interests of the public (Raboy 1990, 53). Newspapers voiced consistent criticism over radio's encroachment on the advertising market, a concern that was skillfully exploited by the CRL in 1932 (Dewar 1982, 41–43). Finally, private, profit-oriented local broadcasters consistently complained that advertising on the public service amounted to government-subsidized competition in their markets. Consequently, as the CRBC and later the CBC sought means of financing their activities, this broad-based criticism worked to preclude commercial sponsorship. Moreover, because local private broadcasters were by definition commercial, the effects of these complaints were focused on the public broadcaster while commercial activities proceeded apace at the local level. The impact of this bifurcation in the way these two types of broadcasters were positioned in relation to commercial revenue was that the private sector was positioned to grow as commercial revenue grew, while the public sector's fortunes were subject to the whims of the political realm.

The commercial character of imported programming also helped marginalize CRBC programs. Led by nationalist concerns, programming developed by the commission often incorporated distinctively Canadian themes and issues. These programs stood in stark contrast to their popular American counterparts, which, as Peers (1969, 157) notes, focused on "creating a popular culture that was continental in scope" in order to create as large an audience as possible for commercial messages. Thus, in its home market, the commission's programs had to compete for audiences alongside foreign programs that were both better financed and constructed for wider audience appeal; consequently, they were not as popular with local broadcasters.

The pressures against commercial sponsorship on the national network exacerbated this problem and militated against the development of popular, distinctively Canadian network programs based on commercial sponsorship that might have attracted the interest of local broadcasters. Similarly, while there was an exchange of sustaining programs between the CRBC and the American networks, particularly in the area of high cultural programs, there was no commercial market for Canadian programs in the United States as there was for American programs in Canada. As the American networks were able to fill their schedules with sponsored programs, these Canadian sustaining programs were dropped (Weir 1965, 195). This cultural discount on Canadian programs would continue to haunt Canadian producers for decades to come.

Thus, squeezed between a set of transnational relations of production based in the United States, the prerogatives of Canadian private capital, and the nationalist imperative of the Canadian state, the Canadian broadcasting system was already being forged to "specialized means," and the vague outlines of a Canadian regime of accumulation were taking form in this field. Following a nationalist mandate, the public element was situating itself on what this larger set of interests defined as the commercial margins of the system, producing Canadian programming and attempting to ensure that it was available to all Canadians through a national broadcast network. Meanwhile, at the local level, private, profit-oriented stations were focused on maximizing the return on their investment by deploying programming that would attract as large an audience as possible, with the least investment.

Within this arena, the growth of the public element was circumscribed by the state's degree of willingness to invest in the system and the political strength of a range of interests that shunned commercial revenue as a means of financing public broadcasting. The growth of the private sector was limited by its ability to ward off public expropriation, the continued popularity of radio broadcast programming, and the continued supply of a cheap source of such programming. As another special parliamentary committee on broadcasting was convened in 1936 to review the broadcasting system, the fate of both these interests was in question.

4

The CBC and the Entrenchment of Canadian Broadcasting

As MACKENZIE KING and the Liberals took control of the federal government in 1935, the country was wracked by high unemployment, grain harvests were failing, and government deficits soared. Still, the worst of the Depression was over (Lower 1946, 522). In part, the downward spiral of the economy was thwarted by heavy federal intervention. The Liberals continued the path of economic reform undertaken by the Conservatives, but the national economy would not meet with a full recovery until after the Second World War.

While the Depression appeared to hinder industrial development, the widespread adoption of Keynesian economic principles, President Franklin Delano Roosevelt's New Deal in the United States, and Prime Minister R.B. Bennett's own version of the New Deal in Canada provided a public sector counterpart to the ongoing shift in industrial production. Under the sway of so-called scientific management techniques and what, following Antonio Gramsci, has been termed "Fordist" forms of production, a second wave of industrialization continued to gather force in Canada. With the onset of the Second World War, the intensification of industrial production combined with state control to give further impetus to centralized, assembly-line production, and, following the war, another round of American investment extended the tendrils of industrialism across the Canadian landscape as industry retooled for peacetime production.

This ongoing rationalization of production was accompanied by a parallel, related rationalization of the media. By helping find markets for the growing volume of products that spilled off assembly lines, media became the primary means for completing the cycle of capital. Advertising emerged as a key element of this process. Its self-conscious goal was the stimulation of mass consumption through the stimulation of demand, and it was promoted as a valuable tool for consumer education in the service of social development. US president Herbert Hoover's remarks to the 1930 meeting of the Association of National Advertisers illustrates this point:

> By the stimulants of advertising ... the lethargy of the old law of supply and demand is stirred until the advertisers have transformed cottage industries into mass production. From the large diffusion of articles and services costs are cheapened and thereby advertisers are a part of the dynamic force which creates high standards of living ... It probably required a thousand years to spread the

knowledge and application of that great human invention, the wheeled cart, and it has taken you only twenty years to make the automobile the universal tool of mankind. Incidentally you make possible the vast distribution of information, of good cheer and tribulation which comes with the morning paper, the periodical and the radio. And your contribution to them aids to sustain a great army of authors and artists who could not otherwise join in the standards of living you create. (Hoover 1930)

Radio was forged to "specialized means" within this broader set of social conditions. As the act of "listening in" found form in the rhythms and temporal dimensions of industrial life through the 1920s, the listeners it generated were slowly subsumed by the economics that drove the larger process of industrial production (McChesney 1993). As James Carey (1988, 220) notes, just as the "telegraph removed markets from the particular context in which they were historically located" and set them in common temporal interplay, radio inherited commercial techniques forged in the telephone, newspaper, and magazine industries to bridge the gap between production and consumption. In the service of industry, at first broadcasting was simply deployed to bring products to listeners – "to reach consumers in their homes" (Smulyan 1994, 92). Later, as it was rationalized to extract greater profits from the relationship it constructed, it too was seen as producing a saleable product – audiences. But, as we have seen, this commercial subsumption of radio broadcasting in both Canada and the United States was itself a contested and drawn-out process (McChesney 1993).

On the commercial side of this struggle, through the 1920s and early 1930s, the extension of commercial relationships into the broadcast realm through the sale of broadcast time was shaped by the larger pressures of the capitalist system to establish both a relatively independent means of financing station operations as well as to extract a return on investment. Because it worked to relieve station owners of having to produce programs themselves, as well as reduced the risk of investment, the practice of simply "selling time" on broadcast outlets was somewhat of a boon for them. Coverage – the geographic reach of a broadcast signal – was the broadcaster's primary concern, while both the cost of program production and the responsibility for constructing an audience out of the mass of radio owners fell to the sponsor and the advertising agency (Dygert 1939, 23).

Extending corporate reach and the commodity relation across the distance created by centralized transmission and privatized reception took longer, and required the development and refinement of techniques for constructing and detecting the presence of audience members. But developing and refining a business model for monetizing the new social relationship created by broadcasting was a struggle and the product of experimenting to find ways to make the practice self-financing (McChesney 1990, 1993; Smulyan 1994, 65–92). But with the commercial success of this experiment, both broadcast technology and programming formats were themselves forged to the specialized purpose of producing audiences of a specific size and demographic composition that could be sold to advertisers as commodities. By the mid-1930s, audience measurement techniques were established in the United States, and, by the end of the decade, advertisers were employing surveys on listening habits to target specific kinds of audiences (Dygert 1939, 30–34; McChesney 1993; Eaman 1994, 34–44). In Canada, this process developed more slowly.[1]

While the Canadian Radio Broadcasting Commission (CRBC) was helping the private sector weather the economic storm of the early 1930s, the price of radio receivers began to fall across North America, laying the ground for the expansion of the broader broadcasting market. At the same time, events in the United States were setting the Canadian agenda. While non-profit and non-commercial broadcasters enjoyed a reasonably strong presence in the US system through the mid-1920s, by 1934 less than a third of the original number remained, as a series of decisions on the part of the Federal Radio Commission (FRC) that favoured the commercial model "crystallized" advertising as the dominant means of financing growth within the system (McChesney 1990; Smulyan 1994, 125–53). Although the full commercialization of the system would take several decades to complete, the pattern for the development of radio in the United States was set by 1936.

This chapter examines the establishment of the Canadian Broadcasting Corporation (CBC). In particular, it considers the escalating pressures on both commercial and non-commercial growth that eventually led to a division between public and private purposes within the system.

The Founding of the CBC

In Canada, development of the broadcasting system continued to take a somewhat different tack from that in the United States. In the wake of the Mr. Sage scandal (see Chapter 3), with the election of the Liberals change in the structure of public broadcasting seemed imminent and extensive lobbying campaigns to influence the formation of the new public broadcaster quickly began. Through January and February 1936, a variety of interests pressed their concerns on C.D. Howe, the new minister responsible, and another Special Committee on Broadcasting was struck in March that year. Under the leadership of Alan Plaunt, the Canadian Radio League (CRL) again mustered support for the establishment of an independent corporation to undertake and oversee all aspects of broadcasting. However, because the financial stakes at play in the broadcasting arena were beginning to come into focus, the interests were more clearly defined during this round of negotiations. Represented by their various lobbying organizations, newspapers, advertisers, and private stations pressed their individual interests, which generally focused on making the system more amenable to commercial purposes. C.D. Howe took a leading role in representing the government's interest.

Generally, all parties agreed that the government had a role to play within the system, and that a public presence was necessary to ensure both program service and geographic reach. Moreover, spurred by the administrative problems that had wracked the CRBC, they agreed that a new organization should enjoy greater independence from government, perhaps, as the CRL put it, as a "public corporation, modelled on business lines" ([GD] Special Committee on Broadcasting 1936, 398). They also agreed that the administration of the system be rationalized to provide more resources and a clearer division between the government's "regulatory" and "operative" functions (Peers 1969, 177, 180; Weir 1965, 203–4; [GD] Special Committee on Broadcasting 1936, 398–673). There was disagreement, however, regarding the regulatory powers that should be given to the new public organization (J. O'Brien 1964, 356–62; Peers 1969, 175–82). And, perhaps more importantly, as Frank Peers (1969, 181) notes, there was also disagreement on the ownership:

> Where they disagreed was in the ownership of stations. The Radio League, assuming that the non-commercial programs formed the primary service, believed that the public authority must own production facilities and at least the nucleus of a distribution system. The private broadcasters, believing commercially sponsored light entertainment programs to be the primary service, felt that the government should use its funds to supplement the commercial service and provide a distribution system. But to eliminate any element of competition between public and private interests, all stations should be privately owned.

Following the pattern set by the CRBC, the private, profit-oriented interests met with those favouring a public model at the level of government ownership of a national network. Peers (1969, 179) notes that because the views advanced by the private interests "went much further in the direction of government participation in broadcasting than ... ever suggested previously," they seemed to be displaying the attitude "if you can't lick 'em, join 'em." But the history of government ownership and the changing conditions of the radio environment would suggest different motives.

Spurred by the commercial success of radio, American stations were growing in number and power at a much faster rate than those in Canada, and Canadian advertising and manufacturing interests continued to express concern that spillover American advertising would place them at a disadvantage in the marketplace ([GD] Special Committee on Broadcasting 1936, 577–81). Moreover, while private, profit-oriented interests welcomed the government's participation in subsidizing network operations and supplying sustaining programs, they also suggested that competition between the two types of programs should be avoided by "scheduling the major sustaining and major commercial broadcasts so as to avoid competition between them" (582). Thus, rather than simply capitulating to public concerns, in the face of continued and increasing competition from US stations the private sector sought government support to maintain its presence on the air and increase coverage. Indeed, for the most part, their experience with the CRBC had shown that state intervention was of benefit to their operations, not a hindrance.

In large part, the CRL's lobbying efforts on behalf of public broadcasting through this period are characterized as quite successful by both proponents and opponents of a public system (J. O'Brien 1964; Blakeley 1979, 79–82; Peers 1969, 186). The report of the Special Committee on Broadcasting reaffirmed the necessity of a government presence in broadcasting and made general recommendations for strengthening that presence. However, although the committee continued to assert that in the future all broadcasting in Canada might be taken over by the government, like the 1934 committee, it recommended that until such a project was economically feasible, "the fullest co-operation should be maintained between the Corporation and private stations" ([GD] House of Commons 1936, 335).

After considerable debate in the House of Commons, a bill was quickly drafted and in June 1936 the Canadian Broadcasting Act became law. In November, the Canadian Broadcasting Corporation assumed control of the CRBC's operations. As with the CRBC, the 1936 act charged the CBC with carrying "on a national broadcasting service within the Dominion of Canada" and granted it a variety of powers of regulation over the system, although, again, the general purposes of neither the system nor the corporation were spelled out in the legislation. In an apparent effort to rationalize the administration of the CBC, section 3 of the act provided that a board of governors "chosen to give representation to the principal geographic regions of the country" would oversee the general operation of the corporation and the system at large, while section 6 provided for the appointment of a general manager who would also assume the post of chief executive officer. In a move to clearly differentiate the purposes of the corporation from those of the private sector, governors were required to take an oath that they "would not accept or hold any other office or employment, or have any pecuniary interest, direct or indirect, individually or as a shareholder or partner, or otherwise, in broadcasting or, in the manufacture or distribution of radio apparatus" (section 3.10).

The legislation gave the CBC considerably more autonomy than the CRBC. The act constituted a relatively independent corporate body, and in addition to a variety of specific powers regarding such things as the making of contracts, the acquisition or lease of property, the employment of staff, and the right to borrow capital from government, it was granted blanket power to "do all such other things as the Corporation may deem incidental or conducive to the attainment of any objects or the exercise of any powers of the Corporation" (section 9[q]). Further, revenues from licence fees, less the cost of collection, were to be paid directly to the new corporation. But these powers, and the CBC's abilities to dispose of revenues, were circumscribed in several important areas. For instance, the CBC required the approval of the Governor-in-Council before it entered into any agreement involving expenditures in excess of $10,000 (section 10); before any "real property or private station" was "purchased, acquired, sold, exchanged or mortgaged" (section 11.1); and to authorize government loans and advances for capital works (section 17.1). Consequently, although the CBC enjoyed a greater degree of independence than its predecessor, because the ability to acquire and dispose of capital is the essence of corporate freedom, in practice the CBC's powers as a corporation were more a closely checked possibility than a real achievement.

The CBC's regulatory powers were very similar to those of the CRBC. The notion of public ownership of the system was expressed in section 11.5 of the act, which stated that "no person shall be deemed to have any proprietary right to any channel." The corporation continued to hold firm control over network operation. It could prescribe periods of time on private stations to be devoted to CBC programming, determine both the character and time devoted to advertising, and "control the character of programming" within the system (section 22). At the same time though, the act provided some recognition of the property rights of private station owners and specified that "fair and reasonable" compensation might be paid to private stations for broadcasting the corporation's programs.

The CBC's control over licensing decisions was more tightly circumscribed. While the corporation was given the power to suspend the licence of any private station not complying with its regulations for a period of up to three months, final authority over the terms and conditions of licences, as well as licence renewals and applications, remained in control of the minister responsible for the corporation, although there was allowance for a consultation process (sections 22.6, 24.1, 24.2). Thus, while the CBC was charged with the administration and regulation of the entire broadcasting system, and possessed considerably more independence than its predecessor, final authority over the private sector was somewhat cloudy.

This division of power placed heavy emphasis on the role of the government and parliamentary committees in the regulatory process. Moreover, although in theory the position of the private sector in the broadcasting system was somewhat tenuous, in practice the CBC continued to be dependent upon private stations to deliver much of its programming. In addition, the fact that the Canadian Broadcasting Act precluded expropriation without compensation gave private stations a relatively secure position within the system. Similarly, while the government refused to become directly involved in the corporation's financial affairs, it maintained strong financial control. Indeed, with final authority in many key regulatory and budgetary areas still resting with the government, the weight of political process hindered the advancement of the public sector.

CBC Service

As the CBC started up in November 1936, its officers outlined the directions in which they sought to move the system. In a radio broadcast on November 4, corporation chair Leonard W. Brockington demonstrated that nationalism continued to infuse the organization's purpose (in Peers 1969, 199):

> If the radio is not a healing and reconciling force in our national life it will have failed of its high purpose. If Canadian radio makes no lasting contribution to a better understanding between the so-called French-Canadian and the so-called English-Canadian, between the East and the West ... then we shall have faltered in our stewardship.

In the same broadcast, vice chair René Morin sketched out the general plans for the service and relations between the CBC and the private stations. He described how the corporation would focus on constructing a network of high-powered stations across the country, carry on a network service operated in the national interest rather than for profit, and allow the private sector to carry on its business subject to the CBC's control over programming (Peers 1969, 199). Further detailing the corporation's plans, in a mid-December meeting of the board of governors the general manager outlined how the corporation would work toward incorporating provincial representation in this national service by building production centres in each of the provinces. Because of the expense involved, however, general manager Gladstone Murray said in a December 22 broadcast that the Corporation would "'work through the five regions'" in the meantime (200). With the CBC focused on building this national service, private broadcasters had little reason to fear the expropriation of their local service as long as the corporation's funds remained in short supply.

Plans to put these ideas in motion were soon drawn up, complete with a request for a $500,000 capital loan. Two fifty-kilowatt transmitters were to be built in Ontario and Quebec, as well as smaller facilities in the Maritimes and Saskatchewan. It was estimated that with these measures, "good" coverage would increase from 50 percent to 75 percent of the population (Weir 1965, 209; Peers 1969, 200–8). However, this plan was not well received by the government. In correspondence with Minister of Transport C.D. Howe, the CBC's board of governors was apparently informed that the "government believes that the most important function of your board lies in the direction of building more suitable and satisfactory programs" (in Weir 1965, 209). In large part, this vision of the CBC fit with the dominant American vision of broadcast stations as mainly program distributors, but in the Canadian case, the CBC rather than the private sector would shoulder the cost of program production. Imbued with nationalist purpose, however, the CBC's board of governors was not prepared to accept such a subordinate position within the system. In his reply to Howe, Brockington pressed the plan upon the government, reinforcing it with his interpretation of the government's "declared policy on the subject of broadcasting" extracted "from the official records of the Aird Committee, House of Commons committees, and House of Commons debates" (in Peers 1969, 204).

While the ensuing struggle was resolved in favour of the broader public service model, the incident illustrates the tenuous character of public broadcasting in Canada at the time. By May 1939, however, the two fifty-kilowatt stations were complete, as well as powerful stations in Saskatchewan and the Maritimes. With these improvements, Brockington told the 1938 Standing Committee on Radio Broadcasting that its signal reached 84 percent of the population (in Weir 1965, 216). As Peers (1969, 282) notes, government ownership appears to have yielded considerably better coverage than the private networks had obtained in the United States, where, by 1939, "nearly 39 per cent of the land area ... was outside the primary service area of any radio broadcasting station during the daytime, and nearly 57 per cent at night." Moreover, within two years of operation, the CBC had doubled the government's investment in plant and increased network time from 279 hours per month to 518 hours ([GD] CBC 1939a; [GD] Standing Committee on Radio Broadcasting 1938, 79–80).

Like the CRBC, however, the CBC experienced financial difficulties. A judicious reorganization of its financial relationships enabled the corporation to appear to devote a much higher percentage of its revenue to program production than the CRBC, but it quickly became apparent that the $2 licence fee was woefully inadequate to meet financial demands.[2] Additional revenues were necessary, and the two most favoured sources were a $1 increase in the licence fee or the sale of more commercial time. Neither option was well received. Newspaper and magazine organizations were particularly critical of an increase in commercial activity, while Members of Parliament reported a tremendous number of complaints regarding a fee increase from the public at large as well as those involved in the manufacture and sale of radio equipment ([GD] Standing Committee on Radio Broadcasting 1938, 99–103). In the end, a compromise was reached whereby the licence fee was increased to $2.50 and commercial programming minimally extended, bringing down upon the corporation the ire of all groups (Peers 1969, 214–18).

The CBC was very selective in its commercial practices, however. The CRBC had begun network advertising in late 1935; the CBC continued and expanded the practice, but its commercial activities were limited by two self-imposed constraints. In partial response to criticism by private radio stations and newspapers, it set a $500,000 limit on the amount of "net" revenue it would accept through this avenue in December 1937; this limit quickly grew to 20 percent of gross revenue, however. The corporation also adopted a commercial acceptance policy, which limited the types and kinds of advertising it would accept. These measures led to the CBC's turning away of hundreds of thousands of dollars in advertising revenue annually through the 1930s and 1940s (Weir 1965, 228; Peers 1969, 226–30). Moreover, because the CBC generally envisioned itself as a national broadcaster, it accepted very little, if any, spot or local advertising, leaving this business to private broadcasters ([GD] Parliamentary Committee on Radio Broadcasting 1942, 258; Peers 1969, 286; Weir 1965, 229).

Led by this nationalist vision, national and regional network services were the focus of the CBC's activities.[3] The CBC's network policy, adopted in November 1937, was considerably different from that of its predecessor. Direct payments were phased out in favour of local broadcasters receiving a share of network advertising revenue. The country was divided into five regions, and sponsors received a cumulative 5 percent discount on station time for each region they subscribed to. If all five regions were purchased, a 25 percent discount was earned. With this formula in mind, E. Austin Weir (1965, 226–27) explains how rates were set and revenues divided:

Network station rates were set by mutual agreement with the private stations ... Stations were paid a straight one-half of their agreed network rates, and had no discounts or commissions to pay. Out of the remainder, the CBC absorbed all discounts, frequency and regional, as well as agency commissions of 15 per-cent

[sic]. When all regions were used this left the CBC slightly better than breaking even; when less than the entire network was used, the CBC made a small premium.

Weir (1965, 227) goes on to illustrate how these conditions were much more favourable than those granted by the US networks: "Under the American system, basic Canadian stations would have received only 65 per cent of what they were paid by the CBC, while supplementary stations ... would have received very little – if, indeed, anything."[4]

These seemingly generous arrangements arose as a result of a number of pressures on the CBC. First, as a national broadcaster, the corporation strove to ensure that it provided as broad coverage as possible given the available resources. But, in order to maximize coverage, the CBC had to include stations in its network whose small markets would not normally have been of interest to advertisers. Hence, to make the CBC's rates competitive with those of Canadian and American private stations, special inducements were necessary. At the same time, the CBC had to meet the revenue requirements of the local stations it included in its network. Squeezed between these interests, the ground that was lost was the CBC's profit from the network ([GD] Standing Committee on Radio Broadcasting 1938, 148–49). As the broadcasting system developed, however, the CBC's attempts to negotiate this field of interests drew increasing fire, particularly from private, commercially successful operators who viewed such rate compromises as government-subsidized competition ([GD] Parliamentary Committee on Broadcasting 1961, 43–56).

The CBC's dependence upon private affiliates led to other problems too. While the CBC offered fourteen hours of programming a day on its basic radio network in 1938, many of the private affiliates failed to pick up even half of this amount, despite supposed "reserved" time agreements ([GD] Standing Committee on Radio Broadcasting 1938, 23). Moreover, private stations often cut the CBC programs off part-way through, replacing them with their own commercial programs. As Brockington illustrated before the 1938 parliamentary committee, these problems originated from the fact that, as commercial enterprises, these stations were dependent upon advertising revenue for their survival. Hence, with the phasing out of direct payments, it was all but impossible for the CBC to expect them to accept its programming, particularly sustaining programs, if a lucrative commercial contract was available for that time ([GD] Standing Committee on Radio Broadcasting 1938, 8). As Brockington noted, "you could not expect a private station, which relies on commercials for its revenue, to take 14 hours a day. The amount varies with the arrangements that are made ... Some take three, six, and some take four" (23). Brockington used these facts to press the CBC's case for building its own high-powered regional facilities.

Despite these problems, the CBC's network service was still quite popular with many private affiliates, especially those in outlying, less populous areas. The CBC brought income and much-needed sustaining programs to these stations and, as Brockington argued, many of the private stations would not have been able to maintain their operations without the CBC's service ([GD] Standing Committee on Radio Broadcasting 1938, 23, 29, 46).

The CBC's programs were also popular with audiences, again especially in regions of the country where there was little other coverage. According to Peers (1969, 282–83), this growing popularity was driven by a number of factors: (1) a rising level of electrical interference from growing use of electrical equipment and crowding of the spectrum meant that the "average receiver did not bring in distant stations with the former clarity"; (2) by the end of the 1930s, the signals from the CBC's powerful regional stations "could be heard, even in the evenings, as easily as the American stations that had previously been so dominant"; (3) the CBC scattered some of the most popular US programming throughout its own evening schedule, thereby encouraging listenership and carrying the audience both to and through Canadian programs; (4) the CBC's own productions "began to win better reputation"; (5) regional broadcast programs, especially those in the prairies, were "enormously successful"; and (6) the CBC's officers used the radio to promote the corporation's purposes. Together, these factors bolstered and sustained government support for the CBC through the late 1930s (283).

To a large degree, the CBC built upon programming principles established by the CRBC. Networks developed to serve both regional and national purposes, and, by way of programming, they furnished "the latest market prices and information" to regional audiences as well as national music and drama programs (Weir 1965, 267–68). The differences established between the language of programming also persisted, as "after the initial unpleasant experience of the CRBC, the language question had begun to work itself out in practice through the separation of services ... [and by] 1938, [the] French language service was effectively autonomous" (Raboy 1990, 62). The CBC also advanced the principle that it was a kind of "public trustee" in the broadcast realm, and refused to sell broadcast time for the express purpose of influencing public "opinion." Rather, it "provided free access to organized groups ranging from Canadian Clubs to the Communist Party" (ibid., 64). As outlined in a 1939 CBC policy statement (CBC 1939b), in this way the corporation sought "to prevent the air from falling under the control of wealth or any one power ... [and] to bring the voice of all representative groups and bodies of opinion to the forum of the nation" (Raboy 1990, 15).[5]

The growing success of the Canadian system was directly dependent upon its relationships with the American system, however. Not only were the apparently more successful Canadian stations affiliates of the American networks but the CBC too was heavily dependent upon US programming. As Brockington testified before the 1938 standing committee, "if we paid our share of the sustaining programs that we take from the United States, having regard to population on a stations basis, for sustaining programs alone we would be paying them $600,000 a year" ([GD] Standing Committee on Radio Broadcasting 1938, 13). Considering that, for the same period, the CBC's expenditure on program production was itself in the vicinity of $600,000, this "subsidy" was key to the corporation's financial well-being (11, 13). Moreover, approximately 25 percent of the CBC's commercial revenue came from US advertisers, and more than 25 percent of its programming came from American sources (32–33, 11). Without this revenue and programming, both the CBC's popularity and its financial position would have been considerably different (Weir 1965, 278–79).[6] Affiliation agreements were not the only way by which private broadcasters directly profited from the American system, as they sometimes "journeyed south" to buy "Canadian rights on dramatized recorded shows such as *The Lone Ranger, Tarzan, The Green Hornet,* and others" (Montagnes 1941, 82). In this way, these broadcasters set the precedent for what would later become the business model for private television broadcasters.

Between 1938 and 1943, the CBC's income from radio licences almost doubled, reflecting changes in licensing patterns as well as the growing popularity of radio programs in both the United States and Canada (Malone 1962, 37). But this growing popularity also gave rise to increasing demand for advertising time, which in turn fed the revenues of private broadcasters. By the end of the 1930s, many private stations, particularly those in major urban centres, were quite profitable (Montagnes 1941). This commercial success accelerated through the period of the Second World War (Peers 1969, 346–47). In turn, growing commercial success spurred further consolidation in the marketplace as concentration of ownership was harnessed to build economies of scale (Peers 1969, 347–48, 365–68; cf. *Canadian Business* 1941). While the CBC shared in this growing prosperity and generally enjoyed good relations with the private sector during this period, the pressures from commercial growth began to put a strain on the corporation.

The Escalating Commercial Maze

From the outset, the CBC's commercial practices were highly controversial and embedded in a maze of contradictions. In large measure, these contradictions were the product of the struggle between different interests over the utilization of the emergent system for different purposes. Yet, while the CBC strove to implement a service that was, as Brockington noted, "not set up for profit," under its regulatory purview the commercial subsumption of the system proceeded apace. Riding the rising tide of radio's popularity, the growth of private, local stations accelerated, yielding greater profits that, in part, were deployed to bolster their position within the system. Thus, as the CBC worked to develop Canadian radio audiences by improving the technical conditions of broadcasting and developing sustaining programs with a Canadian flavour, the private sector worked to co-opt and/or subordinate these developments to profit-oriented purposes.

The officers of the CBC observed this process with consternation and struggled to find ways to turn private profits toward "the betterment of listening in isolated and lonely districts throughout the country" ([GD] Standing Committee on Radio Broadcasting 1938, 61). Eventually, such concerns would lead to "conditions of license" and "promises of performance" being incorporated into regulation in an attempt to redirect a portion of the profits of private broadcasters to public purposes within the communities they serve (Babe 1979, 34–37). However, complicated by disparities in income between private stations located in different markets, as well as the CBC's dependence on the government for implementing licensing decisions, no general regulations that attempted to harness the profit-motivated behaviour of private stations to the larger public purposes of the system were ever implemented by the CBC during its tenure as the regulator.

Pressures for Non-Commercial Growth

While the CBC was wrestling with the problem of redirecting the profit-motivated behaviour of private broadcasters to the public purposes of broadcasting through the late 1930s, controversy continued over the role and purpose of advertising within the system. As is often noted, the CBC's official position was that because of a shortage of income from other possible sources, it accepted advertising out of necessity ([GD] Standing Committee on Radio Broadcasting 1938, 32). However, as we saw in Chapter 3, historically the problem of commercialism was much more complicated than is commonly noted. Not only was advertising revenue an important component of the public broadcaster's income but, as in the United States, some degree of broadcast advertising was perceived as important to the promotion of Canadian business interests (Canadian Radio League 1931, 11; [GD] CBC 1946, 24–25). Indeed, during the proceedings of both the 1938 and 1939 Standing Committees on Radio Broadcasting, CBC officers claimed that the corporation had no intention of working to discontinue advertising because they perceived it to serve some sort of public purpose ([GD] Standing Committee on Radio Broadcasting 1938, 66–67; Blakeley 1979, 99–101).

Although advertising was seen as necessary to the survival of local, commercial stations and as serving a public service function, as the CBC proceeded with the development of the system at the regional and national levels, pressures continued to build for the corporation to limit its commercial activities. Newspapers and private broadcasters complained of the CBC's competition in this field, in terms of both its sale of advertising time and its use of American programs. As the CBC stepped up commercial activity, these voices became louder and more vociferous (Weir 1965, 229–32). Elitist cultural critics continued to have a general disdain for commercialism, arguing that it undermined the higher cultural and educational purposes that broadcasting might serve. And more naïve listeners, who failed to fully understand that advertising actually financed programming, continued to complain over commercial interruptions. Further complicating this scenario was the fact that as capitalization of the system proceeded at the local level, it became increasingly difficult for the CBC to persuade commercial, profit-oriented stations to carry its sustaining programs.

In combination, all these factors worked against the distribution of the CBC's sustaining programs and turned the continuous barrage of complaints over advertising against the CBC. In other words, over time, these forces pressured the CBC to develop a national, largely non-commercial broadcasting service, complete with its own local transmission facilities.

The Pressures of Commercial Growth

As local, private, profit-oriented broadcasters worked toward capitalizing their program schedules by increasing the amount of advertiser-sponsored programming they carried, the differences between this commercial programming and the programs offered by the CBC became more marked, putting further pressure on the CBC to shun commercial sponsorship.

Writ large among these differences was the fact that, as in the United States, most commercial radio programs in Canada were produced by the advertisers themselves (Stephenson and McNaught 1940, 296–97). As a result, the corporation had little control over the content of these programs to ensure that they addressed overall public and nationalist considerations. Moreover, as we have seen, in the 1930s advertisers simply sought mass audiences and radio content was generally subordinate to this broad commercial purpose. The nuances of demographics and niche marketing that later came to characterize advertising were not considerations in this early period. Thus, the relatively unbridled range of techniques employed by the private sector to attract as large an audience as possible often overshot the boundaries of what the CBC perceived to be the nationalist and higher purposes of broadcasting. This difference in purpose – one might even say, mandate – surrounding program production worked to further sharpen the distinction between commercial and sustaining programs in Canada, making it difficult for the CBC to pursue commercial revenue.

Another factor reinforcing the distinction between the CBC's programs and those of the private sector was that many of the former were simply not seen as suited to what was accepted as the commercial format of the time (Fink 1981). Plays, actuality broadcasts, symphonies, operas, speeches, educational talks from influential people – the narrative form of these programs was generally not amenable to regular interruptions by a commercial sponsor, particularly if they were broadcast "live," as was the fashion. So, despite the fact that these kinds of programs were often quite popular with audiences, as markets for radio advertising grew they lost currency among private broadcasters and were replaced by programming that was more economically efficient in attracting large audiences, as well as eliding and/or accommodating the intrusion of commercial messages (Weir 1965, 195; Eaman 1994, 68–83). Over time, as these kinds of programs were dropped from the schedules of private broadcasters in favour of commercial fare, the net effect was to put increasing pressure on the CBC to curtail its commercial practices and provide more of these non-commercial programs (Weir 1965, 303).

A final factor forcing the CBC to surrender commercial ground to the private sector was a social distinction drawn between different kinds of broadcast advertising. As illustrated earlier, spot advertising was devised by local broadcasters in the United States as a means of extracting profits from locally produced programming – such as news, weather, and other local information and entertainment broadcasts – as well as extra revenue from sponsored network programs. Generally, though, the practice was frowned upon by both advertising agencies and "big stations" through the 1930s because it was viewed as both "obnoxious to the listener" as well as a way of "stealing circulation" from network advertisers (Dygert 1939, 9–10). The CBC generally followed the received practice of shunning this form of advertising ([GD] CBC 1946, 25). However, the development of spot advertising began to separate program production from advertising at the local level. It undermined the sponsor's control over broadcast content and, to a degree, set the interests of station owners apart from individual advertisers, as stations were forced to strive to serve the interests of a variety of advertisers rather than a single sponsor. Later, this type of advertising came to dominate both commercial radio and television, primarily because it offered a way to share the burden of financing program production across a field of different advertising interests.[7] But while the CBC might have employed the scheduling flexibility of spot advertising on its national network to offset at least part of the cost of programming and/or distribution with minimal effects on program content, it would appear that the weight of social sanction against advertising in general, and this form in particular, limited this possibility.

Faced with this multiplicity of sanctions, the CBC's official position in 1938 was that commercial programming placed the corporation in a "paradox," and that its elimination was "ultimate policy." In practice, however, the CBC's attitude toward commercial programming was rather ambivalent ([GD] Standing Committee on Radio Broadcasting 1938, 33). For instance, when asked by a member of the 1938 parliamentary committee, "What real good argument is there against a certain amount of advertising on the [CBC's] programs?" Leonard Brockington replied, "At the present time I should say there was none" (32). And, when pressed on the point that the CBC's advertising practices presented unfair competition to the private stations, Brockington reminded the committee how the corporation converted this revenue to public purposes: "It is sometimes forgotten that every cent taken in by the Canadian Broadcasting Corporation is used for the building up of something for the benefit of the Canadian listener. It does not go into the profits of shareholders. It does not go to build up private operators' profits. It is held in trust for the people of Canada" (33). The CBC also used its position as "the national network" to emphasize the fact that while there was an "element of competition locally," at the national level "network business is not in competition with private stations," and that a large portion of the private stations benefited from these commercial broadcasts (98).

Thus, while it is often assumed that commercial revenue has been necessarily antithetical to the purposes of public broadcasting in Canada, in the late 1930s the reasons behind this sanction were complex and resulted from a range of social pressures. Even Brockington claimed that there were advantages to advertising. As he told the 1939 parliamentary committee (in Weir 1965, 278–79):

That commercial policy ... has proven advantageous as prophesied. It has provided a number of highly entertaining programs which many of the more favoured centres listened to before. It has established cordial relations between the Canadian Broadcasting Corporation and the great chains of the United States. It has also facilitated the procuring of a large number of sustaining programs which I think we all admit are as fine as any in the world. A second advantage has been that when time has been occupied by these commercial programs it has to some extent released time and funds for our own sustaining programs. A third advantage is that it has provided us with moderate revenue. I think that commercialism to the extent that we have allowed it has enabled us, by the additional revenue and by the release of both time and money, to improve our sustaining features.

Still, together all of the formal and informal sanctions against commercial programming worked to keep commercial sponsorship on the CBC to approximately 20 percent of broadcast time for decades to come (Weir 1965, 278).

In combination with these commercial sanctions, the ongoing process of capitalization at the local level exerted increasing pressure on the CBC, forcing it to the commercial margins of the system. Here, the CBC worked to build services and relationships – such as the extension of network services and the development of listening audiences in markets that could not support commercial service – that were seen as key to establishing a national system, but were uneconomical under the existing market regime. As capital developed within the system, in its search for new avenues of growth these services and relationships would themselves come up against the pressures of capitalization. In the interim, though, while the private stations worked at developing successful commercial strategies, the CBC's sustaining features supported their position in the market.

The capitalization of the listeners and networks produced by the CBC's services did not take long to emerge, however. Because the popularity of radio rapidly increased with both listeners and advertisers through the late 1930s and early 1940s, this period is often referred to as the "Golden Age of Radio."[8] The CBC deployed its growing revenues in this period to expand the volume of "quality, non-commercial" programs (Weir 1965, 266–73). Most private operators, however, saw the rising demand for commercial time as a lost opportunity and increased their agitation for the relaxation of commercial restrictions and the right to construct commercial networks. Faced with similar demands by advertisers, the CBC compromised on its earlier position and Brockington announced in 1939 that it would "permit temporary hook-ups subject to its control and direction" (Peers 1969, 246). Thus, unofficial commercial private networks were officially sanctioned and network service also began to feel the pressures of capitalization. But Brockington saw how the ongoing capitalization of the system undermined the position of the CBC. As he noted to the 1939 parliamentary committee, "men ... are coming before this committee who are at present making a tremendous return on any capital used ... are coming to make demands and to launch attacks on the Canadian Broadcasting Corporation in an effort to increase their profits" (247).

As private broadcasters and advertisers continued to experiment with radio broadcasting and discover successful strategies for turning it to profitable ends, sustaining programs played a diminishing role within the system (Montagnes 1941). Not only were the private sector's commercial programs increasingly successful in attracting large portions of the available listening audience, but the profits these programs produced also provided private broadcasters with capital for growth and strengthened their position within the system, making it increasingly difficult for the CBC to maintain a grip on their operations. As this occurred, interests and perspectives that were displaced by or unable to find representation within this logic of commercialism were focused on the CBC.

The Second World War: Capitalization Escalates

With the onset of the Second World War, relationships within the broadcasting system abruptly shifted. A freeze was put on the sale of transmission equipment to civilians, the CBC's construction plans were put on hold, and the corporation was moved closer to government as it assumed wartime news and propaganda responsibilities (Peers 1969, 322–65). These closer ties to government strengthened what Marc Raboy (1990, 65) refers to as the "administrative model" of public broadcasting, and precipitated a series of struggles and scandals over government control of the CBC and its program service (Peers 1969, 323–45; Raboy 1990, 65–82).[9] Perhaps the most enduring of these problems was the CBC's refusal to carry highlights of the 1942 Conservative Party convention. To the Conservatives, this refusal was evidence of political interference and, from this point on, "more influential Conservative members called for an 'impartial board' to regulate both CBC and private stations" (Peers 1969, 336). But while the CBC and the government were locked in debate over their relationship, capital's subsumption of radio again accelerated. Changes in radio news production during this period provide a case in point.

With the onset of the war, the social role of radio was greatly enhanced. It was a central vehicle for disseminating news of the war effort and it provided inexpensive distraction from the rigours of war production, disrupted family life, and rationing. For instance, as Weir (1965, 270) illustrates, news was a major component of the CBC's war programming: "At the end of 1939, news bulletins occupied 9.4 per cent of total program time, but by the autumn of 1941, this had risen to over 20 percent."[10] And as radio news gained currency, the commodity form followed.

Despite the fact that foreign news agencies sold radio news in the Canadian market in the 1930s, Canadian Press (CP) steadfastly refused to offer domestic radio news other than the free newscasts it supplied the CBC. However, as cross-ownership between newspapers and radio stations escalated through the late 1930s, this resolve began to weaken (Peers 1969, 286–87; Nichols 1948, 263–70).

To meet the demand for war news, the CBC instituted a central news bureau in 1940 and began supplying free news to private stations based upon the CP wire service – provided that these newscasts were unsponsored. Soon the CBC began to augment this service with its own wartime reports and, faced with increasing supply and demand for war news, expanded its operations in January 1941 and established five newsrooms across the country (Weir 1965, 270). Seeing this rising demand for news as a market opportunity, CP quickly expanded its service too, and in July 1941 instituted a commercial news service for private broadcasters. Because private broadcasters were able to sell commercial time surrounding the new CP service, it quickly became popular with them, and by 1948 CP was boasting that it "served 77 of the 100-odd private stations ... and provided the basic service of the CBC as well" (Nichols 1948, 267). CP also began charging the CBC, which in March 1943 began paying CP $40,000 per year for its service (Malone 1962, 42). However, although the inauguration of this commercial domestic radio news service heralded full-scale commercial sponsorship of news among private stations, the CBC again shunned the commercial impulse and delivered the news "without embellishment and free of sponsorship" – despite the fact that it was often the same news as that delivered by the private sector (Weir 1965, 270; [GD] Parliamentary Committee on Radio Broadcasting 1943, 46).

Other areas of broadcast service also met with intensified commercial pressure under the exigencies of war. As increasing demands were made on the CBC's network to "broadcast sustaining programs associated with the war effort," many requests of sponsors for commercial time went unfulfilled (Weir 1965, 233). Moreover, in an attempt to achieve the widest possible coverage, some sponsors "sought to gain an almost exclusive audience by the addition of many supplementary stations to the basic network," resulting in duplicate coverage in some areas. These events raised the concerns of the parliamentary committee of 1942. Consequently, the committee recommended that an alternative network be established to meet commercial demand and provide listeners with some program choice. While the CBC experimented with setting up an alternative, part-time network for these commercial interests that might be implemented during periods of high demand through 1941 and 1942, the arrangement "did not prove practicable, for the Corporation was never certain it could obtain time on stations when time was most needed" (234). Consequently, under increasing pressure from the government, sponsors, and private stations, the CBC instituted a second full-service national network in 1944. This largely commercial network consisted almost entirely of private stations and, in concert with other developments within the system, satisfied for a time the pecuniary interests of private broadcasters.

The Audience Commodity

While the CBC was busy attempting to negotiate the myriad contradictions that commercialism presented, the private sector was gainfully employed in turning its listeners into audiences, thereby constructing a measurable commodity that might be sold to advertisers. Following developments in the United States, Canadian broadcasters began experimenting with ways to measure their audiences through the 1930s (Eaman 1994, 49–52). But as radio's popularity increased in the early 1940s, pressure mounted for standardized procedures for measuring the size and composition of radio audiences, and the Canadian Association of Broadcasters (CAB) joined forces with the Association of Canadian Advertisers (ACA), the Canadian Association of Advertising Agencies (CAAA), and some of the larger broadcasting companies "to determine the best way of determining radio coverage." Two years later, this group recommended the establishment of a "cooperative, non-profit organization" – similar to the newspaper industry's Audit Bureau of Circulations – "to conduct (audience) surveys" (58). Shortly thereafter, the Bureau of Broadcast Measurement (BBM) was set up. As Ross Eaman (1994, 60) notes, "by the end of the 1940s, BBM had 114 broadcasting members – 80 per cent of the industry – including the CBC."

But while the information gathered by the BBM helped the private stations sell their listenership to advertisers, it was not so useful to the CBC. Surveys were focused on the major cities, where the greatest number of private stations were located and CBC audiences were smallest. In addition, measurement techniques reflected the needs of the private, profit-oriented broadcasters, who offered a more or less standardized programming format that might be depended upon to regularly produce a specific audience – not a shifting, varied program diet like the CBC's that was designed to appeal to a range of different listeners (Eaman 1994, 61, 68–83). Moreover, the data supplied by these surveys offered no illustration of what people might want to hear on the radio, only what they did listen to. Thus, while this information was key in developing markets for the services of private broadcasters and advertising agencies, it held few clues as to what kinds or types of programs audiences may have preferred. Still, the CBC subscribed to the service and by the early 1950s it provided one-quarter of the BBM's income (60).[11]

Changing Focus

By the mid-1940s, developments in the system began to relieve economic pressures for a private commercial network. Although the CBC made an effort to prevent the growth of multiple-station ownership by refusing to award new licences to existing station owners, stations began to change hands between existing owners, and concentration of ownership increased through the late 1930s and early 1940s (Peers 1969, 349–51). Similarly, in the face of sanctions against concentration of ownership, management companies contracted to run multiple stations at the same time (Montagne 1941). In combination with the increasing use of electrical transcriptions and tape recordings, these changes placed the economies of scale so long sought by private broadcasters within their grasp – without incurring the crushing burden of line charges.[12] While, as noted, information on the financial circumstances of private stations is difficult to come by, consulting Department of Transport figures the 1947 parliamentary committee ([GD] Parliamentary Committee on Radio Broadcasting 1947a, 738) noted that "from a revenue point of view the private stations seem to be in a not unhappy condition ... [and] that radio broadcasting is in most cases quite a lucrative form of private business." As television changed the economics of radio broadcasting through the 1950s, the demand for a private radio network would all but disappear. But the growing value of broadcast outlets in this atmosphere was underscored by the rising prices paid for stations that changed hands in the market, despite the sanction against licence proprietary rights over wavelengths ([GD] Parliamentary Committee on Radio Broadcasting 1947a, 407–8; Peers 1969, 367–69).

Through this increasing commercialization of the system, parliamentary committees to investigate broadcasting were struck in 1942, 1943, 1944, 1946, and 1947. Since 1939, the CAB and other representatives of the private sector had been invited to make presentations before these committees and, as they had been through the early 1930s, each committee became a forum for the struggle between the public and private elements of the system. Growing prosperity through the war years spurred the lobbying efforts of the private stations, which began calling for a separate regulatory board, following the lines of the Board of Railway Commissioners (Weir 1965, 241). As industrial production was turned to peacetime purposes at the end of the Second World War, broadcasting's popularity among both audiences and advertisers continued to grow, and so did these lobbying efforts.[13] Generally, however, parliamentary committees continued to endorse the public purposes of broadcasting and its use as a nationalist instrument. At the same time, these committee hearings also became forums for enhancing the legitimacy of the private sector (Crean 1976, 34–35).

The 1946 committee was particularly critical of the private sector. Reviewing the station logs of several of the most commercially successful private operations, it found that they appeared to be devoting too much time and effort to commercial and network activities ([GD] Special Committee on Radio Broadcasting 1946, 713). Shortly thereafter, the CBC announced that it would initiate "promises of performance" when issuing licence renewals, whereby private stations would agree to undertake particular responsibilities in exchange for the privilege of holding a broadcasting licence. Such "promises" were, however, to become great sites of struggle between the regulator and private broadcasters in years to come.

At the same time however, the 1946 committee drew a clear line between the responsibilities of the private "community" stations and those of the public broadcaster. Its report stated that "network broadcasting and nationwide coverage to the remotest parts of Canada are the functions of the national system. Service to community areas is the function of the private station. Network operation or coverage of the whole regions of the country, are not, your committee believes, the normal functions of the private radio stations" ([GD] Special Committee on Radio Broadcasting 1946, 712). While this distinction underlay the committee's rationale for more clearly defining the responsibilities of local stations, in the process it also contributed to pushing the public element further to the economic margins of the system.

As Peers (1969, 385) notes, the private stations' treatment at the hands of the 1946 committee prompted them to undertake a campaign "to persuade the public that Canada's broadcasting legislation was antiquated ... that the prevailing system threatened freedom of speech, and that under present laws the government could control all programs, and seize and operate any broadcasting station in Canada." Key among their demands was a separate regulatory board. In the face of this campaign, however, the 1947 committee remained firm in its support for both the CBC and the existing form of regulation in general, including support for both the implementation of conditions of licences for private broadcasters and measures to "foster the development and maintenance of Canadian talent" ([GD] Parliamentary Committee on Radio Broadcasting 1947b, 740). But the 1947 committee also went on to recommend a more solid footing for private stations in the system. Among its recommendations were extending the licensing period from one to three years; raising the five-kilowatt ceiling on station power; holding public hearings when considering licence applications and changes in regulations; conditionally approving multiple ownership of radio stations and ownership of stations by newspaper companies; and licensing FM stations (736–41). Applications by private stations for power increases were soon granted. As William Malone (1962, 53–56) illustrates, power increases by both

Mexican and American stations in the late 1930s and early 1940s began to encroach on channels allotted to Canada by international agreement at the Havana Conference of 1937. These incursions provided impetus to both increases in broadcast power and further licensing of private stations after the Second World War, the first of which resulted in the Toronto station CFRB being granted a power increase to 50,000 watts on its new frequency in 1947 (Peers 1969, 394–95). As a result of these increases, in many parts of the country the historical difference between the "high power" stations of the national broadcaster and the "low power" of local stations was virtually erased. Taken together, these measures underscored the legitimacy of private, profit-oriented stations within the system and began to sound the death knell for the primacy of the CBC's national network.

Toward the end of the 1940s, these events combined with other forces to put pressure on the government to further intervene in broadcasting. Peers (1969, 394) offers a summary of these forces:

> First, an authoritative answer was needed on who should regulate and control the activities of the private sector; their scope and function had to be defined or restated. Second, financial provision had to be made for the CBC; the licence fee was now clearly inadequate. The government had to decide whether to increase the fee substantially or find some other means of supporting the public system. Third, there was the new problem of television. The country, it seemed would be faced with the same kinds of difficult choices that had confronted it when radio broadcasting developed. The difference was that the pace would be faster, the costs would be greater – and the stakes would be higher.

As the economy gained speed through the late 1940s, the demand for advertising time increased with intensified industrial activity. In this environment, the regulatory division that focused the efforts of the public and private sectors at different points in the system gave the private sector a relatively clear field within which to carry out commercial expansion.[14] This division of responsibility was, to a large degree, carried into the development of television.

The Road to Television

Critics sometimes charge that the Canadian broadcasting system was founded on a "principal contradiction" between "the adoption of the BBC or the commercial model," and that this struggle over the public and private purposes of broadcasting in Canada has informed much of its growth (Smythe 1981, 159). Yet, as we have seen, this characterization provides only a pale caricature of the complex forces that underlay the system prior to the introduction of television.

With its call for provincial and federal levels of control over broadcasting, the Aird Commission set the agenda for the development of a "national" broadcasting system ([GD] Royal Commission on Radio Broadcasting 1929). This model was focused more toward ameliorating and accommodating political divisions in the country than it was to facilitating an open venue for public expression. As policy responsibility fell to the federal government, lack of comprehensive regulation at the local level left commercial forces to dictate policy and all but precluded broad public participation in the medium. At the federal level, both regulation and government ownership were steeped in, and driven by, the nationalist concerns of the Canadian state, and the public element of the system was largely structured to reflect "national" issues, concerns, ideals, and points of view – even at the regional level (Raboy 1990).[15] Through time, and under increasing political and economic pressures, the centralizing tendencies of these nationalist concerns would marginalize even regional production and its accompanying visions of Canada (J.D. Jackson 1995, 221–36).

Similarly, to argue that, under slightly different circumstances, government ownership might have offered an oasis of free public expression in a sea of industrial and commercial forces is, at best, idealist. Rather, from its inception, the system was strung in a web of industrial relationships and heavily dependent on advertising income generated from programming produced in the United States. Certainly, the CBC offered greater opportunity for the expression of a wider range of perspectives and programming than its private counterparts. But even in the corporation's most self-conscious public service moments – such as its farm and fishermen's broadcasts, replete with discussions of prices, market conditions, production techniques, and the co-operative movement – the service helped negotiate the distance between the community and the larger industrial society. In the process, these forms of public service helped incorporate Canadian staples production into transnational market relationships. By the same token, regional entertainment programs, such as radio plays and comedy programs, that reflected life in rural communities celebrated a way of life that was itself largely underwritten by its position in transnational staples markets and the larger pressures of industrialization. Popular programs, such as hockey games, as well as program scheduling and formats all reflected tastes and temporal rhythms developed in the larger context of industrial life (Whitson and Gruneau 1997, 95–97). And, just as the value of the private, profit-oriented broadcasters' service came to be increasingly measured in terms of audience size, there was growing pressure to determine the value of the CBC's service in audience numbers (Eaman 1994). The point is that radio broadcasting in Canada as a whole was a technique that was born of, and given form by, a larger process of industrialization. The development of broadcasting in Canada undoubtedly took a unique path, but its form and content were contextualized by the larger pressures of commodification and the dynamics of transnational productive relations.

The pressures of transnational capitalism put other pressures on both the CBC and its programs, although the pervasive nature of these forces is seldom recognized. Because their access to private media and other creative venues was heavily constrained by American domination of those venues, many aspiring Canadian writers, musicians, and stage performers turned to the CBC as an outlet for their work.[16] As Howard Fink (1981, 229) argues, in the face of this foreign domination of "not only Canadian theatre but magazine and book publishing and the film industry," the CBC "became the financial sustenance of and showcase for a majority of Canada's creative artists." These artists provided both scope and depth to the CBC's sustaining programs, and they often self-consciously worked to provide an alternative to American commercial programs. Similarly, these programs offered venues for developing skills and income while these artists strove to develop commercial markets for their efforts (Weir 1965, 271–75; Fink 1981, 229–30). Eventually, it would appear, many artists did develop such markets – although they were often located south of the border.

But, like many of the cultural nationalists of the early 1920s, rather than view the differences between the CBC's program fare and those of other media as at least a partial result of the domination of Canadian media markets by American producers, many commentators viewed the larger absence of a domestic market for Canadian cultural products as a product of the temperament of Canadian consumers (Miller 1987, 12). In a paper written for the Massey-Lévesque Commission, B.K. Sandwell (1951, 10) – a one-time member of the CBC's board of governors – offers an illustration of this perspective:

> One serious consequence of the unripe state of national culture is a deficiency in the ability of Canadians to formulate judgements concerning the achievements ... of their fellow citizens. The whole evaluation process among Canadians tends to await the result of an evaluation process taking place somewhere else. Recognition by New York or London is an almost indispensible [sic] preliminary to recognition by Canadians in literature, science, criticism, music and many other fields.

This perspective has always failed to take into account the fact that the Canadian media, including broadcasting, were overwhelmingly dominated by foreign capital and foreign productions and were thereby only partially accessible to Canadian "talent," Canadian artistic products, and Canadian points of view. Similarly, it has also failed to acknowledge how this evaluation process in foreign markets is itself driven by commercial imperatives as those publishers, producers, promoters, and so on also expect to profit from bringing the work of these artists to market. Nevertheless, such convictions gave impetus to the CBC's promotion of high cultural programs such as symphonies and operas, as well as the adaptation of classic literary texts to radio programming formats. These program forms were included in the CBC's schedule not only because they were being displaced by the commodification of radio programming on private stations but also because, in light of the perceived overall poor state of Canadian culture, they were viewed as "educational" as well as serving the minority tastes of the "discriminating listener" (Fink 1981, 231; Weir 1965, 274–78). In the process, the CBC helped to weave listeners into the larger ideological dimensions of European settler culture.

In the United States, this type of programming was largely displaced by the capitalization of the program schedule, and the production techniques developed in such serious radio programming were incorporated into both popular shows and commercials. In Canada, however, because commercialism was viewed as the primary villain in their disappearance – as well as generally disdained by the crustier sections of this elite audience – many of these high cultural offerings continued to be offered well into the 1960s and presented without commercial "interruption," as was the characterization of the time. These kinds of programs thus added to the financial burdens of the corporation (Fink 1981, 240; Weir 1965, 275).

Thus, framed by the domination of Canadian media markets by American capital, and at times driven by an elitist definition of culture, both the character and quality of another major facet of the CBC's programming found form. In this context, the efforts of the CBC to continue producing this kind of programming and to avoid commercial influence can themselves be seen as a product of larger pressures associated with the capitalization of the system at large. Moreover, in combination with Parliament's reluctance to raise the CBC's income, these sanctions against commercialism in general also contributed to the corporation's marginalization in the larger system, impairing its ability to adapt to changing circumstances.

The Emergence of Public and Private Purposes

Through the 1930s and 1940s, the public and private elements of the system embarked upon different paths of development. The division of responsibility imposed by regulation between network and local service provided much room for consolidation and growth on the part of the private sector. Led by nationalist purposes that were not directly responsible to the production of surplus capital, the CBC followed the lead of the CRBC and laboured on the commercial margins of the system, where it made investments in both programming and infrastructure that the private sector was either unable or loath to undertake. Through proceeds from the licence fee and advertising, these activities were, for the most part, also self-financing (Hodgetts 1946, 463). In this way, the operations of the public broadcaster continued to follow the historical pattern developed by government ownership in other sectors of the economy.

This division of responsibility within the system was given further impetus by difficulties in controlling the growth of the private sector at several levels.

First, regulatory responsibilities were divided between the CBC's board of governors and the government, making comprehensive regulation virtually impossible. Almost annual parliamentary investigations added another layer of uncertainty and confusion to regulatory direction, as these committees worked to adjudicate between the interests of the public and private sectors and often made recommendations to Parliament that allocated the resources of the system between them (Malone 1962, 42–53). Throughout this period, the private sector made slow but steady gains in the policy arena, often at the recommendation of the parliamentary committees. With rising popularity and ensuing economic rationalization, the private, profit-oriented sector dominated the system by the late 1940s.

Second, the CBC's dependence on the private sector for distributing its largely non-revenue-producing programs made it difficult to impose stiff regulations on the commercial time that constituted the lifeblood of this system, particularly as those most interested in carrying this programming were the less-profitable stations. This division between the profitable and the less profitable – between those who did not subscribe to the CBC's service and those who did – became more pronounced as the stations in the larger, generally more profitable markets were able to reinvest their profits to improve the reach of their signal, and consequently the economics of their operations.

Third, the CBC's own dependence on both foreign and commercial programming compromised its ability to impose rules on the private sector in these areas. As both broadcaster and regulator, the CBC strove to set a high standard of broadcast operation, as well as to deal fairly with the needs and concerns of its rather capricious and recalcitrant charges. Hence, as J.E. Hodgetts (1946, 465) notes, regulations were more "rigorously enforced on its own stations than on the privately owned stations." Part of the problem in this regard stemmed from the fact that the CBC had no way of knowing the true financial position of its charges. Hence, rather than jeopardize their operation, it undertook regulation with a light touch. Moreover, as we have seen, commercials themselves were not generally seen as wholly negative, particularly in terms of promoting Canadian goods and services over their American counterparts. Thus, both formulating and enforcing regulations against foreign programming and commercialism was a difficult process.

Together, these circumstances made effective regulation by the CBC difficult and, although stations were sometimes reprimanded for their activities, under the CBC no station licence was ever cancelled. Moreover, nationalist and commercial considerations both worked to constrain cultural expression. As we have seen, the CBC's national perspective was constructed at the expense of the expression of diverse cultural, regional, and local perspectives (Raboy 1990, 50–88). And, because the commercial rights of private broadcasters were implicitly allowed to foreground and constrain access to their service, issues and debates concerning freedom of speech and controversial programming were largely confined to the public sector, where, in turn, they were refracted through both nationalist concerns and political pressures (Hodgetts 1946, 461; Malone 1962, 64–82). These problems of access were compounded by the CBC board's reluctance to allow the few non-profit local broadcasters, such as universities, the right to garner commercial revenue, as well as its refusal to grant broadcast licences to the governments of Alberta, Saskatchewan, and Quebec in the late 1940s (Peers 1969, 373–77). Raboy (1990, 84–86) illustrates that the CBC was also reluctant to consider alternative forms of ownership, such as a co-operative arrangement proposed by farm organizations in Alberta in 1946. Thus, under a combination of social and commercial pressures, the range of contradictions that beset the system drove the public element to its commercial margins, where it laboured to develop Canada's broadcasting resource. Meanwhile, the private, profit-motivated element deployed economic principles and relationships generally developed in the United States to reap the benefits of Canada's industrial growth in the broadcasting system. Slowly, the public network that had been the central element of the system began to take on the more subservient role of serving minority audiences and interests, while, at the local level, private, profit-oriented broadcasting became the undisputed heir to the system.

5

Television and Early Postwar Canadian Broadcasting Policy

FOLLOWING THE SECOND World War, American assembly lines were quickly converted to producing consumer goods. In Canada, the project of reconstruction faltered in the face of a lack of investment capital and a severe balance of payments problem, but led by federal policies that encouraged foreign, mainly American, investment in both the manufacturing and resource sectors, the economy began to pick up in the late 1940s and early 1950s (Aitken 1961, 50–73). With this increasing integration of the Canadian and American economies, the new mass market industrialism that had begun to take root in the 1920s came into bloom. Just as the adaptation of American industrial technique to Canadian circumstances had led the advance of industry in Canada in the earlier period, so it continued to provide both form and substance to investment in the latter stages of this second wave. Similarly, just as American technology had formed the backbone of the Canadian radio industry in the early stages of this new industrial growth, it would also inform the development of Canadian television.

As the economy gained momentum from the late 1940s through early 1960s, labour became better organized. As Daniel Drache and Meric Gertler (1991, xlv) observe, the resultant "wage revolution was pivotal in changing the material well-being of the industrialized working class; within a generation it would transform consumption norms and enable workers to buy homes, own cars, and support mass production industries through mass consumption." As the economy advanced, the Canadian state became increasingly interventionist as it was pressed to both stimulate and manage growth across a range of different dimensions (Hodgetts 1973, 25, 151, 257). As television broadcasting took form in this period, its development reflected this larger process of economic growth and rationalization.

Tracing the development of television from the late 1940s to the enactment of the 1958 Broadcasting Act, this chapter considers how the 1949 Royal Commission on National Development in the Arts, Letters and Sciences (Massey-Lévesque Commission) and the 1955 Royal Commission on Broadcasting (Fowler Commission) sought to stamp the early development of television with a Canadian imprint as the CBC moved to cope with the burgeoning American system.

Setting the Stage for Television

Immediately following the war, the CBC quickly moved to reorganize and upgrade its radio services. But, riding the swelling wave of commercial demand, the growth of private radio quickly outdistanced its more heavily burdened public counterpart. Between 1946 and 1948, private radio's revenues grew from $10 million to over $14 million, while the CBC's income moved from $6 million to $7.5 million. During this period, the number of private stations increased by 25 percent, and by 1948 the assets of the private sector were three times those of the CBC ([GD] Royal Commission on National Development in the Arts, Letters and Sciences 1951, 281–82). As pressure grew for increases in the size of the private sector, the relative strength of the CBC's presence within the system dwindled. But just as the growth of the private sector threatened to push the CBC further to the commercial margins of the system, developments in the United States set a new agenda for the growth of Canadian broadcasting.

Television, American-Style

Eager to convert their electronics holdings to the purposes of peacetime profit-making, the RCA-NBC forces in the United States began pushing the Federal Communications Commission (FCC) for reinstatement of television licensing, which had been abruptly halted in its infancy with the outbreak of the war. In 1945, a decision was made to resume licensing, and by the summer of 1946 RCA had television sets on the market, catching CBS, its major competitor, off-guard. In early 1947, an FCC decision gave RCA-NBC a further advantage by allocating commercial channels to the very-high-frequency (VHF) band of the radio spectrum upon which its technology was based, instead of the ultra-high-frequency range where CBS's efforts were focused (Boddy 1987, 350–52). Later that year, RCA-NBC was demonstrating a crude colour version of the technology. Faced with rising interference problems, the FCC issued a freeze on television licensing in 1948, but some 100 television licences had already been issued (Barnouw 1990, 89–113).

Meanwhile, other events were taking place in the burgeoning US entertainment industry that would have tremendous import for television. In 1948, antitrust proceedings broke the big Hollywood studios' monopoly control over the feature film industry. Fearing they would no longer have markets for much of their production, the studios slashed their staffs, flooding the market with "actors, producers, directors, writers [and] technicians" (Barnouw 1990, 116). Some of these people headed for New York, where they hoped to become involved with television. Others stayed in Hollywood, where they opened small production studios and began producing episodic television series on film, such as Desilu's *I Love Lucy*, which went into production in 1951 (133–34).[1] Some of these products "went into network schedules, while others were syndicated – [that is,] sold on a station by station basis" (134).

The state of distribution technology at the time gave impetus to the popularity of these products. Videotape was not introduced in the United States until 1956. Consequently, because the telephone lines that supported radio networks could not accommodate television's broadband signal until the advent of video compression technologies in the late 1980s, and AT&T's coaxial cable network did not reach many stations in the early 1950s, the portability of "telefilms" gave them a ready market among independent television stations.

The early success of these small production houses prompted the big film studios to also enter the TV market, and by the mid-1950s Hollywood had become a major supplier for television's ravenous programming appetite. These products were also at the forefront of building foreign markets for American television programming, one of the first of which, was Canada (Barnouw 1990, 229).

Early in television's development, NBC decided to promote it as a commercial vehicle (Boddy 1987), but in the early stages of development, both the tremendous expense surrounding TV's introduction and the uncertainty over licensing standards cooled the company's commercial ardour. Equipped with technical advantage, though, NBC moved forward with its plans.

One line of attack was to promote television as the latest sales tool in finding markets for the products spilling off the assembly lines in the postwar industrial boom. Employing an argument for advertising along the same lines as President Herbert Hoover in 1930, NBC president Pat Weaver pressed this plan "in a series of speeches to manufacturers and trade groups in the early years of television: 'Advertising is to mass production what individual selling was to craft production ... The growth of our economy has reached the point where production becomes less a problem than consumption. It is no trick today ... to make great quantities of goods. Instead the trick is to sell them to people who can afford to pay for them'" (in Boddy 1987, 352). Of course, he then nominated television for this task.

A second course of action was to wrest program control from sponsors so that the network could pull as much profit as possible from its strategic position between audiences and advertisers. As William Boddy (1987, 357) illustrates, moving from single sponsorship to "participating advertising" – that is, selling the commercials surrounding a program to multiple sponsors – was a difficult struggle as sponsors were reluctant to give up program control, and the move did not gain momentum until the mid-1950s. Still, by developing programming formats based upon the study of audience demographics, the network was able to tailor "audience flow through the day and night to suit the [specific] needs of participating advertisers," thereby winning increasing commercial support for the system (358). In the process, it was able to maximize "the profitability of every moment in the program schedule" (357). Thus, "the single sponsorship form gave way to 'formula buying' on strict cost-per-thousand calculations," and "spreading network-brokered advertising insertions across the broadcast schedule made the 'modern' programming themes of audience flow, programme adjacencies and counter-programming vital to every segment of the broadcast day" (356, 357). The narrative form of television programs quickly became caught up in the attempt to pull audiences through commercial interruptions, and the whole broadcast schedule began to beat to a commercial rhythm. The quiz show scandals of the late 1950s undermined sponsor-controlled shows, finishing the process that NBC began. By 1959, the networks were deploying Hollywood telefilms to tailor the demographics they sought (Barnouw 1990, 213–18, 243–48).

In the early years of American television, attempts to capture particular types of audience members were highly generalized and usually centred on abstract categories such as "homemakers" and "children," as they had during the days of radio. In the evening, "flow" was the key, and the goal was to develop and hold as large an audience as possible through the evening rhythm of the household as children went to bed and the adults settled down for a few quiet hours before retiring themselves. The networks began to construct scheduling formats that deployed a scope of programming to yield an economy of scale through audience size. As they gained greater control of the program schedule, they fine-tuned this logic, and audience composition became an increasingly important factor. By the mid-1960s, the American television networks were generally able to command a much higher "cost-per-thousand" than their Canadian counterparts because they claimed to deliver much more specialized audiences (Firestone 1966, 117). By 1968, no American television program was sponsored by a single advertiser, and by the early 1970s, Hollywood's television products were pre-tested in an attempt to ensure that they captured the appropriate demographics (Barnouw 1990, 469–74). Consequently, as we shall see, while Canadian policy-makers were debating the place of commercialism in the new medium, the Americans were developing it into a fine art.[2]

Where it was introduced in the United States, television quickly became popular, and radio ratings experienced a quick and precipitous drop. However, what was one medium's loss was the other's gain, and, in firm control of both technologies, NBC and CBS played television and radio off against each other – financing their growing investment in one medium with their shrinking revenues from the other. In an effort to maintain the profitability of radio, programming underwent an intensive process of rationalization. Sustaining programs all but vanished from program schedules, and recorded programming made increasing inroads. Radio performers were recruited for the new medium, induced by new contractual arrangements that increased the networks' control over program production and relieved the performers of tax and administrative burdens (Barnouw 1990, 103–4). For tax purposes, programming became a capital investment and the extensive capitalization of the American broadcast industry took another step forward.

Meanwhile, both CBS and RCA also introduced new technologies toward rationalizing the radio industry and creating new markets. In 1948, they introduced the 33⅓ and 45 rpm "microgroove" phonograph records, and the battle "for sovereignty in the new disk-jockey world" was joined (Barnouw 1990, 104). These developments ushered in a whole new era in radio broadcasting, as the music recording industry became tied to radio programming formats and a popular music industry – replete with a range of diverse musical taste markets – began to take form. By 1957, radio had, in dollar terms, recovered its advertising market. However, through the mid-1960s, radio advertising remained relatively flat compared with the growth of the economy in general. On the other hand, television advertising sales exhibited strong growth and by 1963 were two and a half times those of radio (Firestone 1966, 153).

By the late 1950s, both radio and television were quickly being subsumed by processes of intensive commodification in the United States. No longer were broadcasters interested in simply selling time to advertisers or sponsors. Rather, the commercial imperative increasingly induced them to employ the least expensive programming vehicle to attract the largest possible audience of a particular demographic profile across the program schedule. For some commentators, this shift marked a turn in American television from a "Golden Age" to a "vast wasteland" as programming turned from live theatre-type productions to violent action-adventure westerns, domestic situation comedies, and police shows (Boddy 1987, 366; Barnouw 1990, 260–65).

Developing Canadian Television Policy

The development of television in Canada proceeded at a much slower pace. The CBC had neither manufacturing interests nor radio profits to propel the system into the television age. And while potential private investors watched developments south of the border with growing interest, no Canadian companies were anxious to make the necessary investment in plant and programming. The CBC advanced plans for television in early 1948, but these were dealt a serious blow when the government refused to fund them. For a time, it appeared that the government might relegate the CBC to a licensing and regulatory role in television similar to that of the FCC (Peers 1979, 10–11). Through 1948, the CBC's board of governors held several hearings on television licence applications, but the applicants most able to proceed were foreign-owned and connected to film and electronics interests (Peers 1979, 11). These affiliations raised objections from the Canadian Association of Broadcasters, and delay followed. Because the CBC was determined not to let television grow at the expense of its radio operations, and the government effectively exercised regulatory control over television's development by holding the purse strings, the CBC waited for policy direction. Meanwhile, TV signals from American border stations began to establish Canadian markets for receivers.

With an election approaching, the federal government moved to consolidate and contain a variety of social issues that had arisen and come to a head in the wake of the war. Returning servicemen seeking post-secondary education sparked a crisis in university funding, a burgeoning arts community continued to seek recognition and support from the federal government, and broadcasting required regulatory direction. In the Throne Speech of 1949, it was announced that a Royal Commission would be struck to investigate these matters. But in March, with growing pressure from both broadcasting and electronic manufacturing interests, the government announced an interim television policy prior to striking the commission.

Building upon a January request by the CBC that it be allowed to establish initial television production centres in Toronto and Montreal, the government stated that the CBC would establish stations and production facilities in these centres and that it would supply programming to stations in other parts of the country. Licences would then be awarded to private interests, on a monopoly basis, "in any city or area in Canada."[3] Funding for the public element of the project would be provided by Parliament in the form of a $4 million loan. Responsibility for network arrangements was to be placed in the hands of the CBC. Speaking in the House of Commons on March 28, 1949, Minister of National Revenue J.J. McCann stated that these plans "would provide a 'large new outlet' for the electronics industry and would eventually provide a means 'of encouraging Canadian talent, of expressing Canadian ideals, of serving the needs of the country as a whole, and of stimulating and strengthening our national life as a whole'" (Peers 1979, 17). Thus, once again, the state moved to construct a national medium of expression and ensure the presence of Canadian programming within it. But, just as it had in the early days of radio, the government sought to place the CBC in an ancillary position within this system, supplying Canadian programming to private stations that were either unwilling or unable to produce such programs themselves.

It is possible to read these developments as a self-conscious attempt on the part of the government to subordinate the public element of the broadcasting system to the interests of the private sector. But this was not necessarily the intention. Following the pattern set by radio and early American television, television broadcasting outlets were still largely perceived as program distributors. Program production was generally the responsibility of sponsors and their advertising agencies. For instance, as Frank Peers (1979, 33) notes, in 1952 "72 per cent of all sponsored network shows [in the United States] were 'outside packages.'" From the government's perspective, in the extenuating circumstances created by Canada's vast geography and dispersed population, as a program producer the CBC would serve a dual role within the system: on one hand, it would fill the role of the sponsor and finance program production; on the other hand, it would ensure that programming offered some representation of a larger set of Canadian ideas and values than commercial imperatives alone would allow. In both cases, the Crown corporation continued its historical role as a development vehicle. Yet, in the shifting currents of national politics, this was not to be the final policy design.

The Massey-Lévesque Commission

In April 1949, the Royal Commission on National Development in the Arts, Letters and Sciences (Massey-Lévesque Commission) was struck, and the CBC quietly waited for its report before allowing private stations to be built. The commission had a wide-ranging mandate and set out to investigate a field of cultural issues that had been raised by creeping industrialism (Litt 1992, 83–103). From film to the state of the arts, to university funding, to the broadcasting system – to name but a few areas under its purview – the commission spent some two years touring the country and investigating the state of Canadian "culture." Set in the deepening chill of the Cold War, it set out to fashion a defence of culture broadly based upon the British model of state-sponsored cultural institutions ([GD] Royal Commission on National Development in the Arts, Letters and Sciences 1951, 4, 274).

Both the tone of the inquiry and its ensuing report are sometimes described as "liberal humanist," at other times as "conservative" (Litt 1992, 102–3; Magder 1993, 80–82). Indeed, when viewed in hindsight, the ideological dimensions of the Royal Commission's recommendations, particularly concerning broadcasting, appear somewhat paradoxical, making them difficult to categorize. The report blatantly subscribed to an elite-centred, intellectual vision of culture, and American mass culture was clearly cast as the villain of the piece. But while the commissioners did attempt to provide a somewhat humanist counterpoint to the rationalizing forces of industry that were reaching out to subjugate Canadian society and culture, they failed to grasp how their own aesthetic concerns were derived from a class structure and division of labour that privileged the judgment of the few over that of the many.

To some extent, this perspective reflected the shifting political economic currents of the time. On the brink of being overrun by the American industrial juggernaut, conservative Canadian cultural forces allied with the fading vestiges of British Victorianism in an attempt to deploy the state as an instrument of benevolent paternalism and hold back this commercial tide (cf. Grant 1965). What this elitist perspective failed to grasp was that the political economic system that enabled this position of privilege was itself dissolving under the "revolutionizing of production," and that the "fast frozen relationships" that "venerable ideas and opinions" rested upon were soon to be "swept away" (K. Marx and Engels [1848] 1985). Still, despite the fact that the Massey-Lévesque Commission failed to establish a dominant position for its view of culture in either the broadcasting realm or Canadian society at large, it proved to be an important turning point in Canada's cultural history.

First, the commission marks the apogee of a "high" cultural vision in Canadian policy discourse, providing an important moment of legitimation for many writers, artists, and intellectuals who had long laboured to harness the power and infrastructure of the state in furthering their cultural vision. Broadcasting, of course, was part of that vision.

Second, while the Massey-Lévesque Commission's cultural prescription was not directly embraced by government, its report provided a blueprint for a vast web of cultural institutions and funding agencies. In its wake, and as funds became available from both public and private sources, the federal government spawned a series of institutions, agencies, and programs that drew upon the plans that the commission laid out, such as the National Library and the Canada Council (Litt 1992, 223–54). While many of these institutions reproduced and cultivated what might be broadly called high cultural forms, they also provided income and resources for Canadian writers, artists, filmmakers, musicians, and the like who later went on to develop projects with broader cultural appeal. Moreover, as we have seen, the elite vision of culture that framed this inquiry did enjoy some currency at the CBC and informed some of its programming practices. Bolstered by the Massey-Lévesque Commission's largely British prescription that radio has "three main functions" in any "democratic" country – "to inform; to educate; and to entertain" – this sensibility would continue to hold sway in Canadian broadcasting policy and, in a somewhat less prescriptive variation, eventually find voice in the mandate assigned to the CBC in both the 1968 and 1991 Broadcasting Acts, as well as the Online Streaming Act's update to the 1991 Broadcasting Act ([GD] Royal Commission on National Development in the Arts, Letters and Sciences 1951, 299). Thus, despite its contradictions, the Massey-Lévesque Commission helped entrench a particular ideological perspective in Canada's cultural fabric – one that would continue as an important element of the broad discourse of broadcasting policy and, at least, CBC programming decisions for decades to come.[4] Moreover, the government eventually charted a course in broadcasting policy that rather closely followed the commission's prescriptions. Hence, both the proceedings and recommendations warrant further attention.

When the Massey-Lévesque Commission convened hearings on broadcasting policy, the scenario played out much as it had before numerous parliamentary committees ([GD] Royal Commission on National Development in the Arts, Letters and Sciences 1951, 23–41; Peers 1969, 23–28; Litt 1992, 123–45). Support for the CBC was widely drawn, with a variety of educational associations and voluntary groups, as well as some labour organizations, rallying to the corporation's cause – although often for very different reasons than those officially voiced in the report (Litt 1992, 123–45). Private, profit-oriented stations argued for greater commercial freedom and an independent regulatory board. There were numerous complaints over the "Americanization" of broadcast programming, and commercials in general. The private sector was found to have spent only a small fraction of the amount of money the CBC did on Canadian programming and talent. The CBC continued to argue that it should retain control of the system but that its ability to fulfill this task was complicated by dire financial circumstances.

In its report, the commission noted that it would not "make detailed recommendations on the policy of development" because it believed these were the responsibility of the CBC's board of governors ([GD] Royal Commission on National Development in the Arts, Letters and Sciences 1951, 302). However, it maintained that "the system recommended by the Aird Commission to the nation has developed into the greatest single agency for national unity, understanding and enlightenment," and that the development of television should follow much the same course as radio, with the CBC leading and controlling the system (279, 301–13). Toward this end, the commission recommended that both the control of foreign programming and the production of Canadian programming should remain in the hands of the CBC and, building on the government's decision to include private capital in the system's development, that all private stations should be "required to serve as outlets for national programmes" (303). The commission also recommended that radio's finances be kept separate from those of television so that the quality of radio would not be sacrificed to the development of television as had apparently happened in the United States (304), and – what in the future would become a familiar refrain – that the CBC take steps to curb the "over-centralization" of program production and thereby increase the representation of the regions in its programming (298).

To finance these responsibilities, it was recommended that the capital costs of television construction be covered by federal grants and that Parliament should implement ongoing statutory grants to the corporation to meet the rising costs of broadcast production. Reinforcing the government's vision of the system, the commission envisioned the CBC as leading Canada into the television world, while the private sector was cast in the subordinate role of program distributor, offsetting the cost of development. The commission also recommended that a Royal Commission be struck to investigate broadcasting no later than three years after its report was submitted. Later, these proposals provided impetus to a greater federal commitment to television's development and more stable funding for the CBC, as well as to a Royal Commission.

But while the commission's apparent intentions were to strengthen the position of the CBC, its report also continued the course charted by the parliamentary committees of the late 1940s and recommended more latitude for private stations within the system.[5] Specifically, the commission recommended recognizing "fully the private stations as important elements of our broadcasting system" (284). Toward this end, it advocated that the licence period for private stations should be extended to five years, and that private broadcasters should be granted the right of appeal to a Federal Court in instances where they were "adversely affected by final decisions of the Board of Governors" under the terms of regulation (289). In order to avoid competition between the CBC and private broadcasters, the commission also thought that the CBC should refuse all local advertising "except in places where advertising service from private stations is not available" (290). However, because it was in the interests of Canadian business as well as to the financial benefit of the corporation, the report recommended that national advertising be continued on the CBC's networks. The commission also noted that it found no problems with cross-ownership between newspapers and radio stations. To meet with the technical requirements of network transmission, the commission again placed its faith in private capital when it noted that "our telephone and telegraph companies ... with the assurance of television network business, would provide equipment" (45). Here, one has to wonder whether the commissioners had any knowledge of the public broadcaster's past experiences with the common carriers.

Despite appearances, these recommendations to strengthen the private broadcasters' position within the system were not meant to simply bolster their commercial position or give greater play to the popular cultural products they carried. Rather, cast in terms that echoed liberal democratic ideals, these measures were offered to ensure that, as citizens, the private broadcasters were not subject to arbitrary treatment or unjust hardship at the hands of the state (289–91).[6] Moreover, despite these recommendations to strengthen the commercial side of broadcasting, and the fact that the system was besieged on all sides by transnational industrial forces, the commissioners' high cultural vision allowed them to steadfastly maintain that there was "false assumption" on the part of the private sector "that broadcasting in Canada is an industry." Rather, they argued that the Canadian broadcasting system was a "public service," and that "private stations have only been licensed because they can play a useful part in that system" (283).

Reflecting the logic of many of the cultural nationalists of the 1920s, the Massey-Lévesque Commission's elitist perspective was added to those voices that sought accommodation between the public purposes of broadcasting and private capital. In the commission's view, "true" culture existed outside of the marketplace in a realm that, seemingly, had little relation to the commercial forces that provided form and function to the more mundane elements of life. As Paul Litt (1992, 31) argues, with the state monitoring the entrance to the broadcast market, and feeding the nation a diet of what the commission saw as clearly "superior" foreign and domestic cultural products, "high culture could be dangled in front of individuals in the hope that their better instincts would prompt them to take the bait. Once they were hooked, their edification could then proceed through self-enlightenment."

However, there was a flaw in the commission's logic that seems to have eluded most commentators. By making a seemingly logical distinction between the realms of culture and commerce, the commission generally failed to grasp the dynamic, materialist relations that drove the production of cultural forms in this industrial age. Consequently, the commissioners thought it possible to harness private capital to carry their cultural vision to the country. What they overlooked was that private capital in the broadcasting arena was to a large extent dependent upon the production and dissemination of the products they abhorred. While a portion of the private sector's profits might be devoted to carrying the CBC's national program service, the processes of capitalization that drove and extended the reach of corporate capital in the broadcast realm would eventually drive the representation of its cultural vision to the margins of the system and its program schedules. Even if this general model of development was adopted – shed of elite trappings – then just as they had been in radio, the CBC's resources would be limited to the largesse of the government, and stretched between the nationalist exigencies of television's development and the profit motive of the private sector. Once again, the CBC would be pushed to the less profitable margins of the system as transnational relations of production spurred capitalization. In the end, this is largely the system that developed. Indeed, it was not television that played the Trojan horse to the vision of Canadian culture held by the Massey-Lévesque

Commission and its kind, but rather industrial capital – and to this interest they were blindly beholden.[7]

Early Growth and Capitalization of Television

While the Massey Commission was preparing its report amid a discourse of nationalist purpose, the Canadian broadcasting system was becoming further bound in transnational relations of production. Early in 1949, the government had decided to "take advantage of the advances" that had been made in television technology by the Americans (J.J. McCann, in P. Anderson 1976, 44).[8] Consequently, the American National Television System Committee (NTSC) television standard was accepted without question, and the CBC placed its initial order for transmitters with the Canadian subsidiaries of RCA and General Electric. Canadian Marconi received orders for studio equipment (Peers 1979, 19). Thus, the branch-plant electronics industry began to ride the wave of the television boom and American technique gained yet another foothold in Canada's industrial infrastructure. But, in a pattern of growth that loosely followed the Massey-Lévesque Commission's recommendations, Canada's dependence on the American system did not stop with simple technology transfer; equipped with the same pattern of "lines and frames," the Canadian system was technically prepared to become an extension of its American counterpart (Raboy 1990, 104).

The CBC began broadcasting in Toronto and Montreal in September 1952. It was estimated that by this time there were already 146,000 television sets operating in Canada – all tuned directly to US stations. Three months later, the government announced a new development policy. In the wake of recommendations from the Massey-Lévesque Commission and from the CBC itself, as well as growing pressure from the provinces, the CBC was charged with building transmission and production facilities in four more centres across the country. To facilitate regional production, Ottawa, Vancouver, Halifax, and Winnipeg would all receive publicly owned stations. Licences for stations in places other than these cities would be open to applications from the private sector, but, for the present, no two stations would be licensed in any one area. This latter provision became known as the "single station policy." Thus, in time-tested fashion, the state awarded private capital local monopolies to spur development. Supported by these monopolies, development in these areas might proceed both quickly and efficiently, thereby maximizing the potential of scarce capital resources. For the construction of the public element, Parliament was to provide a special loan. However, finding the funds to finance that loan and to maintain and operate both of these elements of the system were other matters.

In its efforts to maintain its position in the radio market, the CBC had been operating at a deficit since 1949 and meeting its rising expenses with government loans (P. Anderson 1976, 44–65). While these loans were generally later repaid, amid the federal government's postwar economic problems political pressure mounted for a new funding mechanism (44). Increasing public resistance and the rapid diffusion of television made a licence fee impracticable, and the institution of a statutory grant, as recommended by the Massey-Lévesque Commission, was politically unpopular. Hence, the government searched for another means of financing the expansion of television.

As sales of receivers took off in 1952 and early 1953, Canadian manufacturers began complaining that many people were purchasing their sets in the United States, where economies of scale brought them to market at a lower cost. To discourage this cross-border shopping and provide funds for television's development, the government imposed a 15 percent excise tax on television and radio sets and parts in April 1953. The proceeds of this tax were made available to the CBC (Peers 1979, 49; P. Anderson 1976, 62–63). Subsequently, the radio licence fee was abolished and the capital requirements of the CBC were satisfied for a time.

The sale of television sets boomed through the early 1950s, and by the end of 1955 there were nearly two million sets in use ([GD] Royal Commission on Broadcasting 1957, 317). In 1953, the government estimated that the tax would bring in an average $39 per set. Aided by this windfall, the CBC managed to show a surplus for the years 1953–56 (Peers 1979, 49, 51; P. Anderson 1976, 63).

As E. Austin Weir (1965, 417) notes, "domestic sales of television sets in Canada from 1952–1961 totalled 4,467,000 – a value of $1,250,000,000." But while the majority of these sets were apparently "made in Canada," the expected return on the excise tax is illustrative of the fact that, like radio manufacturing, much of this industry was consolidated on a branch-plant basis, with parts imported from the United States and assembly taking place in Canada. Moreover, with the average cost of maintaining and operating television and radio sets through this period estimated at $54.90 and $10.25 per annum, respectively – including depreciation, maintenance, and electricity – the electronics industry would appear to be the major direct financial beneficiary of this broadcast boom (417). In fact, using these figures, Weir goes on to illustrate that in 1961 the cash investment in receivers exceeded $250 million, while the Dominion Bureau of Statistics estimated that $103 million was spent on broadcast advertising. Hence, as Bernard Miege (1989) argues, the growth of broadcasting, like other cultural industries, is inextricably both bound in and central to the growth of industrial production technique.

Thus, in time-tested fashion, the Canadian state deployed political measures to offset the rigidities of the Canadian economy. Just as the tariff was deployed to provide capital resources for railway construction in the latter half of the nineteenth century, this excise tax provided funds for building a broadcasting system in the mid-twentieth century. In the process, a branch-plant electronics industry was also given form.

Meeting Programming Imperatives

Meeting television's ravenous appetite for programming still presented a problem. But, just as American programs had been employed in the CBC's radio schedules to offset the cost of production and improve the CBC's popularity with Canadian audiences, the corporation planned to deploy American programming in its television schedule to the same ends. To facilitate the importation of programs, Bell Telephone was contracted to construct Canada's first television microwave transmission link, running between the Buffalo television market and the CBC's Toronto facilities (Peers 1979, 22). Negotiations for programming with the American networks began in early 1952, but broke down as the CBC prepared to go on the air. Consequently, the national network went on the air without these programs, raising the ire of both private affiliates and the viewing public (31–32).

The CBC sought television programs from the US networks at the same rate it had obtained radio programs – 15 percent of the revenue received from Canadian sponsors. However, the networks were in the process of wresting control over program production from sponsors and, to maximize their returns from potential Canadian "affiliates," they wanted to sell programs to Canadian stations separately. The CBC refused to allow this. Within weeks of the CBC going on the air, the US networks agreed to negotiate, but they demanded 70 percent of the gross revenue the corporation received from its Canadian sponsors for program rights (Walters 1960, 94). After four months of negotiations, a figure of 50 percent was agreed upon (Peers 1979, 32). By acting as an intermediary between the American and Canadian markets, the CBC managed to maintain a degree of separation between them. However, this did not mean that private Canadian stations were beholden to the CBC for American programming. In a deal worked out with the corporation, private operators were given more or less exclusive Canadian rights to American syndicated programs – including Hollywood telefilms. This arrangement would soon return to haunt the CBC's operations.

Rationalizing Production: American Technique, Canadian Purpose

As in the radio field, in television the CBC began to deploy American production techniques to meet with Canadian purpose, except that it twisted the logic of what in the United States were strategies to maximize profits in order to meet its own purposes of maximizing Canadian production.

Following the lead of the American networks, the CBC too moved to wrest control of program production from commercial sponsors in the early days of television (Peers 1979, 32). However, it employed its position between advertisers and the network program schedule to a much different purpose than the American networks. It used this position to force advertising agencies to "sponsor some made-in-Canada programming if they wished to sponsor an American import" (Rutherford 1990, 62).[9] Thus, while American private networks deployed participative advertising to increase their private profits, in the hands of Canada's national public broadcaster the logic of the practice was twisted to promote the public purpose of Canadian program production (cf. Smythe 1981, 181).

Despite these efforts to wrangle sponsorship, commercial sponsors did not support the whole cost of Canadian commercial television programs in the early days of the system (Weir 1965, 295):

> Canadian advertisers generally could not pay station-and-transmission charges as well as production costs … Advertisers using Canadian productions made very substantial contributions to the national system, but with many programs [their] commercial contribution was more than equalled by the CBC itself, to cover program costs … if such [public] subventions ceased, more than 80 per cent of sponsored programs would be lost.

Because the CBC often had to pay more to distribute commercially sponsored programs than it received in ad revenue, it sometimes drew criticism that it was actually subsidizing its advertisers. This was not entirely true. The logic underlying the CBC's production and scheduling practices did not evolve simply to attract a large audience of particular demographic characteristics that could then be sold to advertisers, as it did with the American networks. Rather, for the CBC the "public interest" was always paramount. Consequently, while the US networks deployed their program schedules to construct one large audience through the evening hours, the CBC attempted to ensure that its programs served a diversity of interests – or, one might say, diverse "national" audiences. As Weir (1965, 294) notes:

> The CBC had to strive constantly with the problems of program balance, providing within its means a sensibly balanced pattern designed to give minority as well as majority interests a fair share … While popular entertainment was in demand, television had to furnish many other things that people wanted: reports on Canadian and world events; women's features; programs for fisherman, farmers, children; information and idea programs; religion and personalities of the day …

The pattern of cross-subsidization that developed out of these concerns led to popular American programs being tailored into the CBC's program schedules alongside Canadian programs not only to act as "bait" for the sponsorship of Canadian programs but also to maximize audience flow from US programs to Canadian programs. In this position, American programs were both a key source of income for the corporation as well as an important vehicle for constructing national audiences that could then be carried through to Canadian programs. As we shall see, though, as this programming strategy developed it brought the CBC into conflict with both its privately owned affiliates and cultural critics: the affiliates wanted the CBC to develop a schedule that would promote audience flow into their own "local" program schedules; the critics simply wanted less foreign programming in the CBC's program schedule.

Subsidization Fuels Growth

With the CBC pouring the proceeds of the excise tax and its commercial revenues into the system, television broadcasting in Canada grew at an extraordinary rate. Within two years, the system "ranked second in the world in the number of stations, and only Britain and the United States had more receivers" (Walters 1960, 97–98). The first private station opened in October 1953 in Sudbury, Ontario. A year and a half later, there were seven CBC stations and nineteen private stations. And by March 1958, there were eight CBC stations and thirty-six private outlets (Ellis 1979, 35). The CBC contributed substantially to this growth, and between 1952 and 1957 it pumped $170 million into the system ([GD] CBC 1959).

One of the key ways in which the CBC supported fledgling private broadcasters was through subsidizing their programming. As Weir (1965, 331) notes, "during the first three months of the life of most private stations 85 per cent of their programs were supplied by the CBC without cost to them." As stations became viable and acquired programs of their own, the CBC still "made no charge to private stations in the case of sponsored or unsponsored programs made available to them" through its network service ([GD] Royal Commission on Broadcasting 1957, 185). And when the affiliates carried the national network's sponsored programs, the CBC shared the revenue with the private stations. Still, the CBC soon began to experience a familiar problem.

Because of the high cost, the private stations produced few programs of their own ([GD] Royal Commission on Broadcasting 1957, 153). Instead, Hollywood telefims offered these stations a ready source of relatively cheap programming and, because telefims often offered greater commercial return than the service supplied by the CBC, they became a favoured product of private Canadian broadcasters. Consequently, as Weir (1965, 293) notes, CBC network service "was seldom transmitted by any private station to the public in its area." Thus, the profit motive of the private stations began to interfere with the distribution of the national network service.

As the Canadian stations went on the air, then, the Canadian television market provided both US networks and program syndicators lucrative new markets for their programs. But even in these early days of Canadian television, profits were not limited to the foreign program producers. As Rutherford (1990, 61) illustrates: "A front-page story in *The Financial Post* (17 December 1955) noted that station owners were 'riding the crest of a prosperity wave' because the demand for airtime by advertisers was apparently insatiable ... [and the] Canadian Bank of Commerce Letter of 6 June 1960 ranked broadcasting the third-best profit-maker among 140 industries in 1957" (see also [GD] Royal Commission on Broadcasting 1957, 143–57). As in the development of the radio system, however, harnessing these private profits to public purpose would prove to be a difficult proposition.

The Fowler Commission

While the CBC continued to muster a wide base of support for its role in regulating the system through the mid-1950s, that position was being increasingly questioned (Peers 1979, 55–62; Raboy 1990, 110–17). Private investment in the system was shifting relations of power between the private sector and the CBC, as well as perceptions of the relationships between those elements. As the number of private operators increased, many joined the ranks of the continuing campaign to have commercial regulations relaxed, exerting greater public pressure to remove the CBC from regulation. As well, more newspapers began to raise their voices against the CBC's powers of regulation, apparently motivated by their increasing ownership of radio stations (Peers 1969, 55–62). Moreover, as the development of television proceeded, fuelled by investment from both the public and private sectors, the developing system began to be "envisaged as a 'partnership,' in which the private stations earned their place in the system by acting as carriers of national programs in areas without CBC service" (Raboy 1990, 115). Thus, the conception of the CBC as the centre of the system continued to slowly erode.

In view of these developments, the government followed the Massey-Lévesque Commission's recommendation and struck a Royal Commission to investigate broadcasting in December 1955. The report of the Royal Commission on Broadcasting (the Fowler Commission) was issued in March 1957. Illustrating that its concerns were born of a long and noble nationalist lineage, the report noted ([GD] Royal Commission on Broadcasting 1957, 7–13):

The building of the first Canadian transcontinental railway was only the first of many devices to pull together into a nation the vast expanse of Canadian territory. In different ways but with the same purpose we created a national financial structure through the chartered banking system and we sought to build up industry and trade through a protective tariff. At a later date we developed a national air-transportation system ... The natural flow of trade, travel and ideas run north and south. We have tried to make some part, not all, run east and west. There is no doubt that we would have had cheaper air service and cheaper consumer goods if we had simply tied ourselves into the American transportation and economic system. It is equally clear that we could have cheaper radio and television service if Canadian stations became outlets of American networks. However, if the less costly method is always chosen, is it possible to have a Canadian nation at all?

Unlike the majority of the members of the Massey-Lévesque Commission, the Fowler Commission had few qualms about commercialism, stating: "We regard the commercial activities of the CBC as a proper feature of the system ... Advertising is a positive contributor to living standards and economic activity and should not be regarded as a regrettable, even deplorable, feature of our public broadcasting system" (174). To bolster commercial revenue, the Fowler Commission made numerous suggestions on how the CBC might approach commercial activities "with skill and vigour," although the point was also made that the commission was not "recommending some abandonment of basic CBC policies or the sudden expansion of its commercial activities" (185–86).

Following a nationalist logic, the commissioners were very strong on the role of the public element within the system and often praised the CBC's accomplishments. The report noted that the CBC "has accomplished much in a short time," that "it has produced programs of comparable quality and at substantially lower costs than similar programmes in the United States," and that no "mishandling in the administration of CBC finances could be found." It found "that CBC has given a good deal of tangible encouragement to Canadian creative and interpretative talent and that much of that talent was of superior quality" (68). Moreover, it was noted that the CBC had also worked to help subsidize the establishment of other community cultural resources, such as symphony orchestras. And the commission noted that while "a number of artists developed and made known by the CBC have later been lured to greener fields, particularly in the United States ... the slow drain of some of our best talent ... is [not] a valid reason to stop encouraging the development of that talent" (69). To alleviate the CBC's impending financial crisis as the proceeds of the excise tax fell, the commission recommended that Parliament finance the corporation through statutory grants, based upon a five-year budgetary period and reviewed annually.

Judged against the efforts of the CBC, private broadcasters were seen to be lacking. Generally, many were found to be "leagues away from anything resembling bankruptcy," yet they were loath to undertake public responsibilities (68, 146–54). To rectify this situation, the report recommended firmer enforcement of existing regulations and that "regulations requiring improvement in the programme content of some stations might be progressively introduced." It was also noted, however, that the CBC's job of enforcing regulations had been complicated by the fact that the corporation had no way of knowing the financial position of the private stations, and thus "the tendency has been to be lenient" (25). In light of these observations, it would seem that property rights of private broadcasters were militating against comprehensive regulation.

Although there was some division in their ranks, the private broadcasters and their association, now the Canadian Association of Radio and Television Broadcasters (CARTB), again pushed charges that the CBC was both "regulator and competitor," that "they were bound in the web of a power-hungry Corporation," and that an "independent regulatory body" should be instituted (148, 130), although, in recognition of the expense involved in program production, the CARTB shifted the position it had taken in the earlier history of the system and noted that it was not interested in undertaking network responsibilities in the current economic climate ([GD] Royal Commission on Broadcasting 1957, 153; Peers 1979, 75).

While the Fowler Commission did not agree with many of the charges of the private broadcasters, following the lines of the Massey-Lévesque Commission the commissioners did indicate that they thought it was time that "the principle of retaining private elements in our broadcasting system be placed beyond doubt" ([GD] Royal Commission on Broadcasting 1957, 144). Further, they felt that there were in fact "two public elements" in the broadcasting system: one, "an operating agency," to expedite "the national programme service"; and the other, "a board for the direction and supervision of the Canadian broadcasting system" (90–91). Under the existing structure, where the CBC performed both these functions, they felt that "some public confusion as to the nature of the relations between the governing board and the operating Corporation" had arisen and that steps should be taken to alleviate this situation (91). Toward these ends, the commission advocated the creation of a separate regulatory agency that would be responsible for all matters of regulation.

The Fowler Commission took great pains to illustrate that this agency was not the independent regulatory board long sought by the private, profit-oriented stations, but an administrative organization directly responsible for the whole system that would, among other things, act as the CBC's board of directors (130–36). Under this new agency, the CBC was to retain its control of national programming and the private sector would still, in principle, be regarded as somewhat subordinate to the national purposes of broadcasting and the CBC. Under the new structure, however, private broadcasters would be recognized as an essential part of the system, and before the new board there might be "competition between the CBC and private applicants for new licenses."

In fact, the Fowler Commission was quite keen on competition and enthusiastically advocated competition between the CBC and the private stations in both advertising markets and in applications for new licences (177). Initially, the object of this competition was envisioned as licences for "second" stations in centres that already had television service, as well as licences in areas without stations. However, the commission also tacitly acknowledged that the CBC acted as a kind of development vehicle within the system, and it noted that "the tendency will be to expect the CBC to undertake those extensions which are certain to operate at a loss" (224). The commission also maintained that the CBC should continue, and even enhance, this role it played within the system. Among the recommendations the commission made in this regard were that the CBC should continue to subsidize both the production and distribution of programming, including sponsored programs; work toward creating new programming and extending the broadcast day (178–79); provide regional services beyond the economic reach of the private sector (189); and undertake program experiments with "less immediate commercial appeal than the programme fare of the private stations" (190). Still, the commission claimed that there was "no reason why all economically attractive opportunities for new stations should be necessarily left to private enterprise" (224).

But the Fowler Commission did not want this competition to be one-sided. Consequently, throughout the report the private sector is consistently admonished to take up more programming duties in both radio and television. The report even had some programming ideas for the private stations. Illustrating a rather quaint naïveté regarding the economics that drove private broadcasting, the commission recommended that private stations produce programs that introduced "budding or amateurish" artists to local audiences. While it noted that it would be unreasonable to expect the CBC to do this, "indifferent as some of these performances might be from a purely esthetic point of view, the local audiences would likely enjoy them because the artists are part of the same community" (69). Thus, guided by an ideological vision of the Canadian broadcasting market as simply national in its dimensions, the Fowler Commission seemed to perceive this competition between the public and private elements of the system as taking place in a relatively closed national system where they would compete for audience share with programs they had produced themselves.

Further illustration that the commission did not have a firm understanding of the commercial parameters of the emergent television market can be found in some of its suggestions for increasing the CBC's commercial revenue, such as export sales of programming to the United States where, as we have seen, the emergent pattern of production focused on creating a specialized product (183). However, while some aspects of both the Fowler Commission and Massey-Lévesque Commission reports may appear to be both confused and retrograde even for their time, it must be remembered that these commissioners were struggling to make sense of sweeping and rapid change, and that caught up in this larger social process, it was almost impossible for them to realize that some of the ways in which they conceived of the system no longer had resonance with the productive relationships that underpinned it.

At the same time, in what appeared to be a considerable shift in perspective from the Massey-Lévesque Commission, the Fowler Commission sought to meld public purpose with commercial motive within the system. No longer were the private and public elements of the system to be conceived as operating in different markets at the "local" and "national" levels as they had in the development of the radio system. Rather, in those areas where their interests clashed, they might actively compete for audience share and advertising revenue. From this perspective, commercial revenue was of key importance to the welfare of the system, for it would help drive the growth of both the public and private sectors and contribute to the overall objective of the system – program production.

Although seldom acknowledged in the literature – shed of elite disdain for commercialism, and apart from the recommendation of a new regulatory agency – the Fowler Commission's recommendations were in many ways quite similar to those of the Massey-Lévesque Commission. The public sector was still to lead the development of the system and the private sector would assume greater programming responsibilities as the economics of the system were better organized. In this way, the Fowler Commission built upon the growing view that the public and private elements were partners in the development of the system (cf. Raboy 1990, 115). Supposedly, clearer regulations and stricter enforcement would ensure the private sector's compliance with the larger public objectives of the system.

At the same time, the commissioners did not embrace anything that might be termed popular culture. On the contrary, they seemed to retain the broad perspective that the system should function "to inform, to educate and to entertain," and were obviously alarmed by the growing presence of "too many disc jockey type programs" on the radio (Raboy 1990, 127; [GD] Royal Commission on Broadcasting 1957, 41). However, perhaps reflecting the business background the commissioners brought to their task, in their eyes sound commercial practice appeared to be a prerequisite to sound cultural practice. Here again, like the Massey-Lévesque Commission, the Fowler Commission showed little understanding of the underlying economic dynamics of the system and the ways in which the drive to private accumulation caused the private sector to minimize its investment in programming to maximize profits and fuel growth. Still, this apparent "failure to realize the real position of the private broadcasters" was not a simple capitulation to "unreformed and unregenerate capitalistic enterprise," as some have argued (Irving 1957, 314).

The Fowler Commission in Historical Context

Because historical processes often take place "behind the backs" of social participants, there is sometimes a tendency to read the more public and visible moments of development as new or novel. This is often the way developments in the broadcasting system after 1958 and the enactment of a new Broadcasting Act are portrayed – as though the act introduced a whole new dynamic to the system and thereby set it off on a new historical course (cf. Crean 1976, 41; Nelson, n.d.). As we shall see in Chapter 6, in some ways this is true. Generally, however, the system simply built upon long-established historical precedents. The period of industrial expansion that followed the Second World War saw enormous change in the development of the Canadian broadcasting system. Understanding these changes, and the prescriptions of those who took part in them, necessitates placing them in historical context.

Since its inception, the broad discourse of nationalist purpose that informed broadcast regulation tended to conflate public purpose with private pecuniary interest. As CBC chair Leonard Brockington had pointed out in 1938, under the guise of public purpose the CBC's broad mandate ensured that its commercial profits were reinvested in the system, while the interests of the private, profit-motivated broadcasters lay in extracting as much revenue from the system as possible. But, as we have seen, the way private interests were configured within the system by public policy obscured this difference in what might be termed "mandate" between the public and private sectors.

Throughout much of radio's development, and now with television, the private stations were indeed part of the system and responsible for carrying the national service to many parts of the country. Moreover, in the early stages of both radio and television, many of the private stations were dependent upon the CBC for their survival. In 1955, of 144 private radio stations studied, 33 operated at a loss ([GD] Royal Commission on Broadcasting 1957, 149). Of 14 television stations reviewed, 5 operated at a loss (152). For many, it would appear that carrying the CBC's service made the difference between staying in business and walking away. Consequently, there was a kind of partnership between the CBC and many private broadcasters: in exchange for income and extending the reach of the national service, the private sector provided facilities to the national broadcaster at a fraction of the cost of building its own.

Moreover the private sector did deliver a popular service and, driven by the ongoing expansion of industrial forces, there was enormous pressure from a growing array of interests to generally expand both radio and television. Through the late 1940s and early 1950s, such pressures came from a variety of sources: from the public, which wanted greater variety in programming; from advertisers who wanted more and cheaper broadcast time to sell products, particularly Canadian products; from Canadian broadcast equipment manufacturers who wanted markets for their products; from Canadian talent who wanted more outlets for their work; from private investors who wanted "a piece of the action"; from government officials who were pressured to increase investment and job opportunities; from American broadcasters who sought to build Canadian audiences and appropriate Canadian radio frequencies; and from the nationalist mandate that framed regulation of the system, which provided impetus to increasing both the scope and depth of the system in general. As the economy grew, so did these pressures. Growth could not simply be stopped.

Meeting these demands for expansion under the terms of the abstract nationalist goals prescribed for the system entailed massive investment. Given the private sector's apparent willingness to undertake aspects of such investment – as well as the fact that, ideologically, private enterprise was seen as the "natural" engine of growth – refusing the participation of private capital in the expansion of the system was neither politically nor economically expedient. Thus the state's allocation of an increasingly larger share of the broadcasting resource to private capital was driven by a wide range of historical forces. Still, in the face of both the extensive and intensive growth of capital within the system, forging the profit motive that aligned the development of capital with the nationalist objectives of the system was another matter, and it was becoming increasingly clear that the CBC was not adequate to this task. Thus, the Fowler Commission recommended bolstering control over the development of the system with a new, stronger regulatory organization.

From this perspective, the commission's suggestion of a regulatory agency was not novel to either the discourse or practice of regulation within the system. It was little more than an official recognition and formal institution of the regulatory relations that had been governing the system since its inception. As we have seen, parliamentary committees played an active role in adjudicating between the public and private elements of the system from the beginning. With the introduction of television, pressure from a variety of sources motivated the government to take closer control of the system. The Fowler Commission's recommendations simply sought to rationalize this administrative process, which had become increasingly complicated since the 1930s (cf. Hodgetts 1946).

The Fowler Commission was not alone in believing that new regulatory relationships were necessary. Amid the many controversies and pressures surrounding regulation, "a growing distaste for the regulatory role" had developed among the CBC's executive – "a distaste that was expressed frankly by CBC chairman Davidson Dunton in the Commission's hearings, and that had led in 1953 to the abandonment of the attempt to enforce provisions for Canadian content in the radio programs of the private stations" (Peers 1979, 111). New developments, such as "second" stations, would definitely place the CBC in a competitive position vis-à-vis the private sector, further complicating its role of regulator. Moreover, the CBC's growing responsibilities in administering and undertaking productive activities in the radio and television realms – as well as the seemingly impending introduction of over-the-air facsimile technology and perhaps even subscription television – all combined to exert further pressure to rationalize the regulatory process. Thus, the Fowler Commission's recommendation of a new regulatory agency might simply be read as a kind of logical extension of largely historical forces, and the result of an ongoing process of rationalization of the state apparatus in the face of extensive growth. Under similar pressures, Australia had already instituted such an agency (Hull 1962, 118–22).

Just as railway construction had led to extensive growth in the countryside that it crossed, so too the CBC's development of the broadcasting system heralded extensive development throughout the network it created. As in the development of the railway, these new broadcasting interests also began agitating for a greater share of the resources that development created. Private interests both within and surrounding the broadcasting system wanted greater control over the productive resources presented by the broadcasting system, but for broadcast regulation the trick was to keep impending development focused on the nationalist purposes of the system. Whether by default or by design, the Fowler Commission had an answer to the problem – competition – and the CBC would carry national development forward.

In the accelerated development of the television system, the CBC's role as a development vehicle was basically laid bare. Just as the Canadian National Railway carried the debt incurred by railway development earlier in the century, the CBC carried the burden of developing the television system and, by all accounts, it had done a relatively good job thus far.[10] At one level, the organizational schemata generated by the CBC's implicit mandate to both extend service and develop programming efficiently identified elements of the system that were undercapitalized and directed revenue toward their development. At another level, the organization was able to adapt to this public purpose organizational techniques such as network structures and programming formats that had been developed to further private profit. Hence, the CBC's demonstrated success at creating a national system recommended the organization to the purposes that the Fowler Commission assigned it.

The commission did not leave the CBC to meet these responsibilities empty-handed either. On the contrary, as Weir (1965, 310) notes, it forecast that the corporation would require $353,393,000 over the next six years and provided the government with a funding formula to meet those expenses. Moreover, the commission fully recognized the need to make the private sector more responsible to the public purposes of the national system. In part, these considerations motivated its recommendation of a new regulatory agency for this very purpose. The commission also made extensive recommendations as to both the authority and the powers the new agency should have, and the situations under which it should apply them, including developing regulations that would take into account the individual circumstances of stations so that those that were most profitable could be forced to carry a greater portion of the burden of the system's development ([GD] Royal Commission on Broadcasting 1957, 110–16). In this context, the commission's recommendations were both reasonable and pragmatic, and so they appeared to many (Peers 1969, 110–14). Consequently, while it might be charged with underestimating the propensity of the private sector to maximize its investments, and with overestimating the ability of the state to control such behaviour, the commission certainly did not simply capitulate to the purposes of private capital.

Many of the commission's recommendations were ultimately taken up by the government. However, while its report may have successfully negotiated the interests of its time, changing historical circumstances would soon demonstrate its weaknesses, and the general adoption of its prescriptions would signal two other important developments in the system.

While the Fowler Commission's assignment of the CBC to the unprofitable tasks of the system was simply an extension of a historical logic within the system itself, it marked a key turning point in the official discourse surrounding the CBC's place in the system. For in this formulation, the activities that the CBC had initially assumed responsibility for on its own now began to be framed in regulation as obligations. In combination with its propensity to undertake unprofitable responsibilities, slowly but surely the CBC was not only moving but now also being officially assigned to the economic margins of the system.

Second, as it had in the development of radio, the evolving nationalist focus of the regulatory framework was locking many interests out of the development of television. Under the sway of the federal state, ownership of broadcast facilities was reserved to either the public broadcaster or private capital. Thus, to have access to representation in the television realm, social interests had to negotiate the organizational interests of either the CBC or private station owners. As was illustrated in the development of radio, the all-consuming necessity to generate a profit provided a handy excuse for the private sector to legitimately narrow the scope of both the activities it undertook and the perspectives it incorporated in its programming. Consequently, as the system entered a new phase of development, pressure from interests seeking access to the system, whether to air programming or grievances or to simply find employment, would again be placed on the public broadcaster. At the same time, the CBC's own nationalist agenda would continue to determine the ways in which it represented Canada to Canadians.

Three months after the Fowler Commission's report was issued, a federal election brought the Conservatives to power after twenty-two years in opposition. They presided over a minority government until another election, in March 1958, gave them an overwhelming majority. Four months later, the Conservatives passed a new broadcasting act that roughly followed the Fowler Commission's recommendations and fulfilled the party's long-standing promise to implement a regulatory board.

6
The Emergence of the Dual System

THROUGH THE LATE 1950s and into the 1960s, American investment in Canada continued apace, accompanied by a slow but pervasive integration of the two countries' political and economic infrastructure.[1] But as C.D. Howe's branch-plant policy for postwar reconstruction came to fruition, there was a growing backlash against American domination of the Canadian economy (Bashevkin 1991, 5–28). These nationalist stirrings first found official voice in the 1956 preliminary report of the Royal Commission on Canada's Economic Prospects (Gordon Commission), and later in the populist rally that propelled Conservative Party leader John Diefenbaker to power in the late 1950s. Robin Neill (1991, 206) argues that, in large measure, these concerns generated pressure for a new national policy, as "the old one seemed no longer electable." As these pressures mounted, they focused attention on foreign ownership of Canadian industries, including the media, and calls for repatriation mounted.

Easy solutions were not at hand, however. As Easterbrook and Watkins (1980, 262) note, as "advanced industrialism, with its changed market-resource-investment alignments," gained hold on the economy, little "unity in thought or approach" could be found in the range of "Canadian economic thought" on the changes that had been wrought on the country. As Canada's political and economic infrastructure was increasingly brought under American influence, the country's nascent, Innisian-inspired intellectual tradition met with similar forces. According to Mel Watkins (1982, 17),

> the era of the Cold War saw the Americanization of the social sciences as an aspect of the Americanization of everything, and the destruction of a unified political economy appropriate to a hinterland status. Canada became, for Canadian social scientists, a "miniature replica" of the U.S., a "peaceable kingdom," America in slow motion with less of both the good and the bad. Economics, with its pretensions of fine-tuning the economy, became relevant with a vengeance when secular prosperity was thought to have been "built in."

Watkins might be accused of overplaying the influence of the staples tradition on the direction of economic thinking through the 1940s and 1950s. Still, a reified economics that forced a distinction between political and economic processes did indeed combine with economic prosperity to leave prescriptions for action sorely divided (Neill 1972, 117–22; cf. Neill 1991, 119–28, 219–23).[2] Caught between the near-necessity of American investment to the well-being of the Canadian economy at large and the isolationist tendencies of the nationalists, the Liberals vacillated on the nationalist project through the 1960s (B. Fraser 1967, 307–15).

However, as a combination of growing social tensions and increasing economic instability began to wrack the country through the late 1960s and early 1970s, the government did turn to a larger nationalist program that aimed to win back some of the ground lost to American investment (Magder 1993, 112–15).[3] This project expressed the contradictions that beset the political arena through the 1960s and earlier periods of development and, as we shall see in Chapter 7, itself came to be divided between the pursuit of nationalist cultural goals and an industrial strategy limited by the exigencies of a branch-plant economy.

Installing an independent regulatory agency at the intersection between the state and the practice of broadcasting provided the field with some insulation from events in the larger political arena, but this did not exempt it from the tensions that were already apparent, such as those between the nationalist goals of the system and private capital.

This chapter traces how the contradictions between those goals helped animate the emergence of broadcasting's dual system, composed of public and private elements.

Inside the System, 1958–68

In September 1958, a new Broadcasting Act was legislated, establishing an independent regulatory board – the Board of Broadcast Governors (BBG).[4] The new board consisted of three full-time and twelve part-time members, with the former chosen to provide provincial representation. Imbued with nationalist purpose, it was equipped with powers to police, promote, and plan the growth of a system relatively shielded from the operation of larger economic forces.

Under section 10 of the act, the BBG was charged with "ensuring the continued existence and continued operation of a national broadcasting system and the provision of a varied and comprehensive broadcasting service of a high standard that is basically Canadian in content and character." All powers of both regulation and licensing passed to the board, although new licences still required the approval of the Governor-in-Council (sections 11 and 12). Thus, the CBC would compete with private broadcasters for licences and privileges before the BBG.

The BBG's regulatory powers included all of those previously held by the CBC. The new act also provided the board with the power to require licensees to provide information regarding their "financial affairs and such other matters concerning their operation" (section 11.1[i]). Network regulation was also transferred to the BBG, and there was provision for the construction of networks by private interests, although the board retained powers over the terms and conditions of their operation (sections 13 and 11.1.g). If the board were to order the suspension of a broadcasting licence, the licensee was granted the right of appeal to the Court (section 15). In a move that reflected growing nationalist concerns, future licences were to be reserved for Canadian citizens and companies, although a provision provided protection for existing foreign licensees. While concerns persisted that the application of general rules made it difficult to harness the different market conditions of individual licensees to the national purposes of the system, this problem was not directly addressed in this legislation, other than in terms of network construction. To a large degree, however, the legislation followed the Fowler Commission's recommendations and set the stage for both the expansion of the system based upon private capital and increased regulation of private behaviour.

Within this context, the CBC was empowered to operate a national broadcasting service (sections 29–36). Against the Fowler Commission's advice, it was also given a new board of directors that was to report annually to Parliament rather than to the BBG. This divided regulatory responsibility would become problematic, although not exactly in the way foreseen by the Fowler Commission. Under this arrangement, the CBC retained its status as a relatively independent Crown corporation, but its powers remained limited. For instance, it could not acquire or dispose of property valued at over $100,000 except in relation to program material, and it had to submit both capital and operating budgets to Parliament on an annual basis (section 35). Although these provisions ensured some measure of parliamentary control over the CBC, by limiting the corporation's financial flexibility they ensured that its ability to effectively "compete" with the private sector was heavily constrained.[5]

The Emerging Regulatory Structure

As the BBG set to its task, it devised a two-pronged strategy that roughly followed the Fowler Commission's vision of the developing system. On the one hand, the BBG set out to devise regulations to ensure that programming of Canadian "content and character" had a central place on the screens of both public and private stations; on the other, it made plans to licence second stations.

To meet the larger nationalist purposes of regulation, the BBG announced that rules would be devised and applied "so as to encourage the development of production facilities, the expansion of markets for Canadian productions outside Canada, the interchange of programs of Canadian content and character among television stations in the country, the use of Canadian talent and the increase of the pool of talent available to the industry" (in Romanow 1974, 42). Moreover, explaining the board's motivation behind this expansion of the system, BBG chair Dr. Andrew Stewart later emphasized that it was undertaken with the "national interest" in mind: "the private stations should not operate on the periphery of the national broadcasting service provided by the CBC, but should be a part of a national broadcasting system; that the private stations should not operate largely on a local basis, but should make their contribution to the national purpose" (52).

Despite the apparently good intentions, the sorry saga of how the BBG's regulations and the licensing process it supervised were almost constantly subverted in practice by both the private broadcasters and the regulator itself is well documented (cf. [GD] Committee on Broadcasting [Fowler II] 1965, 45–49; Romanow 1974; Babe 1979, 141–52). However, many commentators tend to portray these events as the product of ill-conceived regulations and/or bungling or favouritism on the part of regulators (cf. Babe 1979; McFadyen, Hoskins, and Gillen 1980). In the process, these critics tend to downplay, and even overlook, the often intractable problems faced by regulation.

To a large part, the emergence of the Canadian television broadcasting system through the 1950s was the product of massive public investment. The excise tax and the commercial activities of the CBC provided much of the capital to establish the system. Private investment extended the reach of this public investment. However, as the proceeds of the excise tax dwindled, a new mechanism for generating investment capital was necessary to avoid the necessity of ever-escalating public subsidy. In 1958, this was not the only imperative, however.

As we saw in Chapter 5, with American television signals spilling across the border – and Canadian manufacturers, broadcast equipment dealers, advertising agencies, and private investors all clamoring to enlarge the system – the pressures from growth were enormous. Moreover, these private interests sought to weave the broadcasting system into the larger pattern of capitalist, industrial growth that was fuelling the economy. In this atmosphere, the pressures against simply reserving the system for non-commercial purposes were difficult to resist. However, meeting these demands while at the same time finding the means to finance the continued pursuit of the historical nationalist objectives of the system entailed a complex process of negotiation.

As the BBG took up its appointed tasks, two possible regulatory strategies were floated. One proposed the imposition on private stations of "two hours reserve time during the period 8 PM to 11 PM 'for purposes to be prescribed by the Board of Broadcast Governors'"; the other involved the imposition of a "quota" of Canadian programming on stations (Peers 1979, 219).

The first idea met with strong opposition from all of the major players in the system. Private broadcasters and the advertising agencies balked at the plan because it would mean the loss of some of the most lucrative time in the broadcast schedule. The CBC protested because it seemed to involve splitting its network schedule between both existing private licensees and the proposed new stations. Frank Peers (1979, 220) states that the negative response of the CBC's president was "surprising." But it would have broken up the corporation's developing strategy for maximizing both Canadian programming and audiences through its program schedule. Faced with this opposition, the BBG fell back on the second option, and content quotas were initiated to encourage the production and distribution of Canadian programming.

Both private broadcasters and advertising agencies also opposed this measure, but less stridently than reserved time. Initially, the BBG suggested that "the total Canadian content on any station shall not be less than 55 per cent of the total program content during any week" (in Peers 1979, 221). Research done for the Fowler Commission in 1956 had illustrated that the stations were close to this level, and since then the levels had apparently risen (Romanow 1974, 38; Peers 1979, 223).[6] But much of this domestic programming emanated from the CBC's network and, in the fragmented advertising and program markets that the second stations would herald, maintaining this level would be difficult. As a result, both the CBC and the private sector advocated lower levels. Some advertisers also protested, threatening that if such a high standard drove up "the already high cost per thousand of television," they would have to "switch into media that offered better value for money" (Peers 1979, 222; cf. Ellis 1979, 49n8). Accordingly, an initial level of 45 percent was set, with plans to raise it to 55 percent in April 1962.

As we have seen, such quotas had proven less than successful in radio. But alternatives, such as requiring licensees to devote a percentage of gross revenue to production, also had drawbacks in that a station might focus all of its revenue on one or two productions a year, leaving the rest of the program schedule to imported programs (Shea 1963, 73). So, bolstered by the Fowler Commission's confidence that vigorous regulation would bring the private sector to heel, the BBG proceeded with the quota system and attempted to draft a range of regulations that would ensure that program schedules "could not be filled with Canadian programming that required little effort to produce and which could be scheduled at low-audience periods" (Romanow 1974, 40). In this context, apart from the grumblings of the Canadian Association of Broadcasters (CAB) and the advertisers, the quotas were reasonably well met and they had the support of a number of interests, including a resurrected Canadian Radio League and the Association of Radio and Television Employees of Canada (33–34).

The BBG had to negotiate numerous difficulties in defining what actually comprised a program "basically Canadian in content and character" as specified by its proposed regulations.[7] Because of the range of considerations at play, this definition had to be extremely flexible. It had to accommodate the diverse scope of existing programming, as well as any new program ideas that might come along (cf. Shea 1963, 74). It had to enable the representation of the seemingly expanding range of social differences that characterized the peoples and regions of Canada in programs (E. Thomas 1992). Although it had already been established that broadcasters did not enjoy the same speech rights as the press, the regulations could not be too restrictive in this regard either (Vipond 1989, 171). And the regulations could not be too onerous, so that Canadian content did not become "synonymous with 'mediocre,'" as the CAB president put it (in Peers 1979, 221). In the end, such considerations steered regulation away from program content per se and led to a definition based upon the "nationality" of a range of elements employed in production. Consequently, the regulations were based upon more or less technical considerations, such as the nationality of the company financing the production, and the nationality of the people employed in production (Romanow 1974, 30–32). As long as the companies, people, and places involved in production were "Canadian," then the program would be defined as Canadian. These kinds of nationalist, technical criteria would form the basis of content regulation up to the present ([GD] CRTC, n.d.a).

Realizing that in order to maximize profits private broadcasters might attempt to schedule their Canadian programs during low viewing periods, the regulator made provisions to counteract this propensity. The percentage of Canadian content was to be calculated across specific periods of the program schedule – such as "prime time" (7 p.m. to 11 p.m.). In this way, it was hoped that private broadcasters would be bound to produce a range of Canadian programs. To ensure that they would be legally binding, these content regulations – along with provisions delimiting the content of advertising messages and political broadcasts and the number of allowable directly "commercial" minutes per hour – were incorporated in the Broadcasting Act in 1959.[8] Despite these efforts to construct a rigorous framework for regulation, however, in the shifting currents of broadcast practice enforcing these regulations proved to be another matter.

With the regulatory structure in place, the BBG set out to license "second" stations in eight of the principal cities across the country (Peers 1979, 224). Following the Fowler Commission's recommendations, these stations were to provide private sector competition to the CBC's television service, as well as work to repatriate audiences in markets where the signals of American broadcasters could be received. These stations were envisioned as forming a second national network and, in all of these centres, they were expected to be highly profitable.

Playing on the nationalist bent of this allocative process, the "contestants for these valuable rights made detailed and glowing promises to the BBG about the performance they would give" ([GD] Committee on Broadcasting [Fowler II] 1965, 225). With practised precision reminiscent of the pattern of radio licence hearings, the applicants fuelled the board's vision of a privately supported national system, complete with a range of Canadian programming (Weir 1965). As these stations began operating, another private company formed the Canadian Television Network (CTV), which took to the air after lengthy and heated negotiations with the new licensees. The program promises soon rang hollow, however.

To avoid the necessity of ever-escalating public subsidy, Canadian content regulations attempted to combine private investment with the revenue earned from broadcasts of foreign programming to advance both the construction of new facilities and the production of Canadian programs. In the process, however, these regulations ran head-on into the historical problems presented by a private, profit-motivated, competitive domestic market both underpinned and divided by transnational relations of production. The ready supply of cheap American "entertainment" programming that could be obtained for between 5 and 8 percent of its cost of production was key to the growth of both the public and private sectors ([GD] Committee on Broadcasting [Fowler II] 1965, 45). Equipped with its implicit not-for-profit public mandate, the CBC worked to convert the commercial revenue from such programs to the production of Canadian programs and the extension of broadcast service. For the private sector, though, producing domestic programs entailed a double jeopardy. Not only was Canadian programming generally much more expensive to produce than foreign programs were to purchase, but if a Canadian program was scheduled to replace an imported program – even if it drew as large an audience as the program it replaced – any return on investment would be severely reduced, if not lost altogether, unless the cost of the Canadian program was roughly equivalent to that of the imported program. These pressures are illustrated in the early programming budgets of CTV, where producers were limited to $2,500–$3,000 per half-hour show, an amount roughly similar to the cost of the rights to an American syndicated program (Rutherford 1990; Barnouw 1990, 235).

Some private producers attempted to overcome these economics by producing Canadian programs that might be sold in the US market. As we have seen, though, the commercial strategy of the US networks rested upon deploying programming tailored to produce specific, American audiences. Consequently,

American broadcasters showed little interest in what were for them foreign productions, and the owners of the private network found such productions extremely risky (cf. Rutherford 1990, 116).[9]

Given these economics, the often-noted effect of these content regulations was that they set the commercial interests of private broadcasters against the nationalist goals of the system. To maximize the return on their investments, private broadcasters were induced to invest as little as possible in Canadian productions. Content regulations did push private broadcasters toward producing some programs, but the profits generated by cheap imports, especially during prime time, pushed these efforts to the margins of those schedules. Consequently, private broadcasters quickly began to lobby the BBG to have the definition of Canadian prime time extended to the hours of 6 p.m. to midnight so that Canadian content calculations over the evening schedule could include their Canadian local and national news programs (Ellis 1979, 51).

Second Stations

As the second stations entered the market, the BBG was faced with another, more pressing problem. Many of the new licensees were mired in debt as they struggled to carve out a niche in the markets they served, and several had to undergo radical restructuring to stave off bankruptcy. Consequently, in December 1962, after licensing second stations in major centres, the BBG called a general moratorium on further licensing. When the process resumed, it was on a much more economically cautious basis, and sometimes involved shifting content regulations and relaxing limits on commercial time. It also followed a regulatory precedent set by the CBC, and refused to license new stations in areas where it appeared they would heavily erode the revenues of existing private stations (Weir 1965, 363–66; Babe 1979, 23; Ellis 1979, 53–54). In taking these measures, the BBG was often attacked for protecting private stations, but in the years immediately following the licensing of second stations, it had little choice but to follow such a policy if it was to avoid losing some of those stations altogether. Once this pattern of regulatory protection was established, however, it would prove difficult to break.

Generally, the CBC bore the brunt of this new competition, and as the second stations entered the market, the CBC's advertising revenue was reduced by 20 percent, and millions of dollars in advertising revenue that would have otherwise gone to the CBC soon began to flow to the emerging private sector (Peers 1979, 247; Rowland 2015, 43). In this way, the new stations also received an indirect economic boost from the CBC, as they were able to exploit advertising markets that it had already established. By 1963, in aggregate the second stations were showing a small profit, and by 1966 they were all profitable (Peers 1979, 224–32).

Graham Spry was particularly upset by the shift in power relations within the system heralded by these stations. As he noted in a 1961 article in the *Queen's Quarterly*, "the CBC has been outflanked, surrounded, and hemmed in to a subordinate place in the structure of Canadian broadcasting ... For private stations especially the CBC programs supplied and brought by micro-wave free of cost to the station also constitute a large and valuable form of subsidy by the taxpayers to the private owners" (G. Spry 1961, 213–14). He also identified some familiar forces at play in this process: "The CBC has been maligned, misrepresented, savaged, nagged and subject to meannesses and indignities by hostile and sometimes greedy business competitors or ill-informed politicians" (218).

Partly as a result of these shifts in patterns of growth and regulation, turmoil gripped the broadcasting system, and it was under almost constant public scrutiny from 1963 up to the enactment of a new Broadcasting Act in 1968 (*Broadcasting Act*, SC 1967–68, c 28). First, a three-member task force known as the "Troika" was struck by the newly elected Liberal government in April 1963. A Committee on Broadcasting (Fowler II), chaired by Robert Fowler, who had led the 1955 Royal Commission, followed, and reported in September 1965. Then, under the supervision of the office of the secretary of state, the government undertook the project of drafting a white paper that would eventually become the basis for the new act.

Growth and Rationalization: Divided Responsibilities

Following trends in the United States, the television system grew sharply through the late 1950s and early 1960s (Barnouw 1990, 198–99). In 1958, there were eight CBC stations and thirty-six private stations. By 1965, there were sixteen CBC stations and fifty-nine that were privately operated. Of the latter, forty-four were affiliated with the CBC and eleven with CTV (Fowler II, 8). The number of television sets in the country more than doubled between 1957 and 1965, and in 1965 92 percent of Canadian homes were considered "television households" ([GD] Committee on Broadcasting [Fowler II] 1965, 9).[10] Television advertising also experienced strong growth and, between 1958 and 1965, sales increased almost two and a half times – from $37.8 million to $91 million (Firestone 1966, 152).

Through this period, television became an increasingly important aspect of the economy. For instance, Weir (1965, 417–18) estimates that in 1961 some $425 million was spent in the television field – including expenses for maintaining television sets, advertising, and public grants (receiving set sales for that year are not included). This figure represents approximately 1.5 percent of the GNP for that year (Firestone 1966, 152). If, as the Massey-Lévesque Commission maintained, television was not an industry in 1951, a decade later it certainly was.

But this growth was not shared equally between the public and private sectors. From 1963 to 1968, the CBC's network revenues grew by 22.1 percent, while

CTV's revenues rose by 74.3 percent. In fact, the "introduction of competition from CTV was largely responsible for the slowness in the growth of the CBC revenue" ([GD] Special Senate Committee on the Mass Media 1970b, 291).[11]

Yet, the introduction of new stations did not keep up with the demand for advertising, and between 1964 and 1968 television's share of advertising revenue outpaced that of other media by 12 percent, largely because of "limited advertising supply and increasing demand for time" ([GD] Special Senate Committee on the Mass Media 1970b, 291). This rising demand for advertising time was expected to continue through the 1970s, following increasing industrial growth (Firestone 1966, 296). But, although growth was strong, it became apparent that fewer companies in Canada utilized television advertising than in the United States (Firestone 1966). This market anomaly – driven by such factors such as advertising spillover from American border broadcasters that set their sights on Canadian advertising markets, and the absence of comprehensive competition in many Canadian consumer markets – would be a continuing source of irritation to both regulators and broadcasters, as well as between the Canadian and American governments, for years to come. To some degree, it may have encouraged the protection of the private stations' advertising markets.

Delineating the CBC's Responsibilities
While the protected commercial environment afforded by regulation gave extra impetus to the growth of the private sector, it provided little solace for the CBC. In its 1959–60 annual report, the CBC voiced concern over the ways in which it was being forced to provide service in the gaps left by the private sector ([GD] CBC 1960, 9):

> The problem is one of economics ... Where economically feasible privately-owned stations are filling the gaps through the establishment of satellite stations. But in most areas, because of economics, Canadians are looking to the Corporation for service ... Because these areas can provide little or no commercial return, the Corporation must keep in mind that the operation of stations and the provision of program service represent a recurring annual cost to the public purpose.

With the growth of the private sector pushing the CBC to the commercial margins, the corporation laid out what it believed to be its purposes in the system in the following year ([GD] CBC 1961, 27; emphasis in original):

> TO BE A COMPLETE SERVICE, covering in fair proportion the whole range of programming; bringing things of interest, value, and entertainment to people of

all tastes, ages, and interests, and not concentrating on some aspects of broadcasting to the exclusion of others.

TO LINK ALL PARTS OF THE COUNTRY in two ways, (1) through the inclusion of a wide variety of national and common interests in its program services; (2) by using its physical resources to bring the national program service to as many Canadians as finances allow. Whether Canadians live in remote or heavily populated areas the national system should serve them as adequately and equitably as possible.

TO BE PREDOMINANTLY CANADIAN IN CONTENT AND CHARACTER. It should serve Canadian needs and bring Canadians in widely-separated parts of the country closer together, contributing to the development and preservation of a sense of national unity.

TO SERVE EQUITABLY the two main language groups and cultures, and the special needs of Canada's vast and various geography.

Thus, in a seemingly defensive move, the CBC provided itself with something that Parliament would not: a mandate. Thereby, it strove to differentiate its purposes from those of the private sector and provide direction to its activities. For several reasons, however, this definition of organizational purpose did not hold any answers to the CBC's problems.

First, while it built upon the historical political purposes of the national broadcasting system to provide form and focus to the corporation's activities, it also sketched the dimensions of a political project that we have seen was fraught with contradictions. As the CBC strove to serve the broadcast needs of a growing set of diverse social and geographic interests across the country, it would continue to divide its resources between a range of competing demands. Just as Canada's two main language groups and cultures had already forced a division within the corporation such that it was already essentially two systems, so too competing local, regional, and diverse cultural interests would exact increasing demands on the structure of television.

Second, while attempting to balance such interests in a national system may simply be the fate of any federal cultural institution, these organizational purposes would also encounter a more fundamental problem. For as private capital took hold of the commercial centre of the system, and began capitalizing and investing profits in those aspects of the national system from which it might expect to turn a profit, the CBC's mandate relegated the network once more to those aspects of development that provided little or no commercial return. Thus, if private capital could not be controlled through regulation and turned to uneconomical national purposes, as it carried the system forward this mandate would leave the corporation open to an increasing range of necessarily uneconomical responsibilities. Without a consistent and growing source of revenue with which to meet these responsibilities, the CBC's efforts would tend to become increasingly scattered and divided.

Contradictory Pressures and Divided Responsibilities

With the imminent arrival of free private network television, both the government and the parliamentary committees of 1959 and 1961 were hostile to the CBC's purposes, particularly its dependence on the public purse (Peers 1979, 206–7; Raboy 1990, 143–51). In 1963, budget cuts undermined its parliamentary appropriation. In that same year, the Royal Commission on Government Organization (Glassco Commission) issued a report condemning both the scattered character of the CBC's internal organization and the unclear lines of authority issued through regulation. Even those commentators who were largely sympathetic to the CBC's plight, such as the 1965 Committee on Broadcasting (Fowler II), prodded the beleaguered corporation to assume greater responsibility – recommending that it continue to expand the system into unprofitable areas while at the same time working harder to develop and provide a balanced program service to meet the diverse interests of the Canadian public. Meanwhile, faced with competition from newly licensed stations, the CBC's affiliates demanded more competitive programming ([GD] Committee on Broadcasting [Fowler II] 1965, 232–33).

Certainly, the programming utilized by the new stations and the new network offered stiff competition to the CBC's programs. The American TV shows were expensively constructed to have a broadly popular appeal, and they were equipped with a narrative structure to draw audiences through commercial breaks. In the Canadian market, they were deliberately priced at a small fraction of what it would cost to emulate similar production values in Canadian programs. They also came equipped with information regarding the kind of ratings and demographics they commanded in the American market (Barnouw 1990, 234–35). For Canadian stations, this information was a valuable sales tool for attracting advertisers, as well as a weapon to be used in constructing counter-programming strategies designed to undermine the CBC's audiences.

The new regulatory regime further complicated the CBC's problems. From the outset, the CBC refused to fully reveal budgetary and planning information to the Board of Broadcast Governors, just as it had to parliamentary committees (Peers 1969, 247–49). The BBG felt that this left it without the proper tools to carry out its own mandate, and this refusal became a serious source of friction between the two organizations. Licensing decisions surrounding second stations also became fractious. Although the CBC generally received the licences it applied for, the circumstances surrounding the process smacked of attempts by the government to influence the board's decisions in favour of political friends. In one instance, the board itself clearly subordinated the commercial interests of the corporation to those of an existing private licensee (Peers 1969, 247–61). Indeed, in the competition for licences and privileges within the system, the CBC had to struggle to protect its own interests before the board, just as it had before governments and parliamentary committees in the past.

In this regulatory process, the corporation was increasingly positioned as an independent, though somewhat privileged, interest – not as the keystone of a single, national system. Moreover, having successfully repelled the BBG's efforts to divide its programs between the two sets of private stations, the CBC again soon came into conflict with the BBG over the latter's vision of a "single" Canadian broadcasting system (Peers 1969, 257).

By 1960, professional sports programming had proven to be consistently popular with audiences on both radio and television. The 1959 Grey Cup drew a record five million viewers, second in size only to the final game of the Stanley Cup playoffs (Cavanagh 1992, 308). In 1961, John Bassett, who held interests in CFTO – Toronto's prized second station – as well as the *Toronto Telegram* and the Toronto Argonauts, purchased the television rights to both the Eastern Canadian Football League games and the Grey Cup, reportedly for twice what the CBC had paid in 1960 (309).

As the 1962 Grey Cup game approached, however, CTV could not muster enough coverage to meet its sponsor's requirements and approached the CBC to carry the game. The CBC consented, but on the condition that the broadcast be commercial-free. Frustrated, CTV asked the BBG to intervene and, viewing the game as a national event, the BBG ordered the CBC to carry the broadcast in its entirety, which the CBC still refused to do. With the game quickly approaching, heated negotiations and threats of legal action proceeded apace. In the end, the parties settled on a compromise and the CBC carried the game with "five courtesy announcements mentioning CTV's advertisers" (Peers 1979, 257).

Following this affair, the CBC president "pursued a campaign to promote the notion that the 'single system' of broadcasting was outmoded, unwieldy, confused and too complex" (Peers 1979, 257). After decades of being represented as the centre of the Canadian broadcasting system, the corporation itself was seeking to withdraw from that position. By 1965, it had no interest in returning broadcast administration to a single board, and actively advocated that the system be perceived as a "dual system" (Peers 1969, 435).

Representing itself as one of two elements within the system offered the CBC some protection from outside interests that coveted its resources, but it offered no relief from income problems. Increasing costs deepened the CBC's dependence on advertising ([GD] Committee on Broadcasting [Fowler II] 1965, 221). In turn, this raised historical concerns from both inside and outside the corporation that both service and programming standards were being compromised ([GD] Committee on Broadcasting [Fowler II] 1965, 220; Weir 1965; Peers 1979). The CBC also drew criticism from a developing lobby that wished it to obtain more of its revenue from commercial sources. These interests argued that the corporation's "cost-per-thousand" was set at a level considerably less than that of the private network, and that rates should be raised to a more competitive standard ([GD] Committee on Broadcasting [Fowler II] 1965, 221–22; Firestone 1966, 293–96). Moreover, there were recommendations that advertisers should be found for the "high cultural" programs that were now delivered unsponsored ([GD] Committee on Broadcasting [Fowler II] 1965, 222).

These suggestions for rationalizing the CBC's commercial practices struck at the heart of its commercial strategy. As we saw in Chapter 5, that strategy was not designed to simply attract a mass audience. Rather, it was constructed to draw audiences for Canadian programming across the schedule as a whole, as well as to subsidize the cost of low-audience Canadian programs. To some degree, the rates themselves reflected this pattern of cross-subsidization: advertisers paid less than market rate for time on programs with large audiences, and more for time on Canadian programs than was warranted by market conditions. There may well have been ways to maximize the return from existing advertising time, such as developing a better description of the demographics of the CBC's specialized audiences, particularly those for the high cultural programs, so that they might be specifically sold to advertisers ([GD] Committee on Broadcasting [Fowler II] 1965, 222). But maximizing the return on advertising time on the CBC was complicated by several problems: (1) the development and execution of a rather expensive research program, as the available commercial audience research services did not produce the necessary data (cf. Eaman 1994); (2) continued general disdain for commercialism evidenced by many of the producers and consumers of that programming (cf. Weir 1965, 405–10); (3) adapting the narrative formats of sustaining programs to accommodate advertising messages (cf. Miller 1987, 196); and (4) a drastic realignment of the existing commercial strategy at play. In other words, the internal schemata of the CBC's organization combined with its organizational culture and relations to the larger structure of the broadcasting system to yield a complex web of resistance to such change. Consequently, the corporation failed to fully embrace these suggestions, drawing the ire of yet another group of interests.[12]

Complicating this multitude of problems, internal strife also rocked the CBC. From the Montreal producers' strike in 1959 to the cancellation of the popular *This Hour Has Seven Days* in 1966, a litany of labour problems and programming conflicts characterized its operation. For most writers, these disputes are seen as arising from an array of problems within the organization (Weir 1965; Peers 1979). Labour disputes reflected the CBC's tight financial position. Conflicts over programming are portrayed as the product of the gap between management's view of the purpose of the corporation and that of the production staff, conflicting definitions of Canadian culture, and, in some instances, direct government interference. Taking a somewhat different tack, Marc Raboy (1990, 168) argues that these problems reflected the larger political problems of the Canadian state and were animated by "an approaching crisis for the political system that the Canadian Broadcasting Corporation had been created to serve" (cf. Weir 1965; Peers 1979). More simply, however, this general turmoil can be seen as reflecting the tensions of a thinly spread organization, responsible to a highly diverse set of interests and carrying a wide range of responsibilities.

Different but Not Exceptional

As Erik Barnouw (1990, 382–83) illustrates, the American networks also experienced intra-organizational strife during this period, particularly between management staff and the various program producers and suppliers as their different visions of the social role of a media corporation came in conflict. Within these organizations, however, this stress was tempered by the financial role of the sponsors, who by right of "financial veto" often had the final word on which projects aired or in what time slots they appeared. While the American networks were also subject to shifting political pressures, their reliance on private capital combined with a looser set of regulatory and constitutional arrangements to provide them more latitude in avoiding direct political interference (Barnouw 1990).

In Canada, the CBC's varied sources of financing combined with its nationalist mandate to provide somewhat more latitude in the range of programming it presented. At the same time, however, its professed responsibility to a wide range of interests combined with its dependence on parliamentary subsidy to subject its operation to a much wider range of demands. For instance, as we have seen, the problem of commercialism for the CBC was not generally the direct influence of profit-motivated sponsors over the content and scheduling of programs as it was in the United States; rather, it focused on the ways different interests saw commercialism as interfering with what they perceived to be the corporation's purposes. The problem of balancing these diverse interests became increasingly acute.[13] Moreover, as Raboy (1990, 175–84) illustrates, through the late 1960s the CBC's problems in meeting the diversity of demands made on it were further complicated by the federal government's initiatives to deploy it as a key tool in its effort to shore up the flagging project of federalism.

All of this was part of a context that contributed to the slow economic and political carving up of the CBC's resources. A key manifestation of this can be seen in the gradual decline of relatively expensive dramatic and musical programming in the CBC's prime-time schedule through the late 1960s (cf. Weir 1965, 388–410). In the meantime, the growing presence of private, profit-oriented broadcasters within the system offered little in the way of new programs.

The Private Network: A Clear and Present Purpose

From its inception, the structure of CTV was not conducive to the production of Canadian programming. In its initial incarnation, it was an independent private company within which the private stations owned only "23 or 24% of the stock" ([GD] Committee on Broadcasting [Fowler II] 1965, 235). It owned no production facilities of its own, "and the private affiliates, in their jealous concern that outside investors in CTV should not make a profit ... progressively made the affiliation agreements less attractive, so as to ensure that little profit was possible" (236). In 1966, on the verge of bankruptcy, the network underwent reorganization, with the largest affiliates each taking a share in its ownership. Under the new co-operative arrangement, the affiliates developed a revenue-sharing agreement whereby the affiliate shareholders received "75 percent of the net revenues earned by the network from the sale of airtime to advertisers within network reserve time, leaving 25 percent of net revenue as the operating fund of the network" to cover program and transmission expenses ([GD] Task Force on Broadcasting Policy 1986, 453). Meanwhile, program production facilities remained largely in the hands of the individual affiliates.[14]

Obviously, this arrangement was structured to deliver maximum revenue to the affiliates, not network program production. In the process, it played upon the inconsistency in the legislation that left open the question of the regulator's power to impose individual rules of operation on licensees. This corporate structure was considerably different from that of the American networks, which harnessed the economies of scale inherent in network operation to actually capitalize program production rather than the network's affiliates.[15] CTV's ownership structure and the revenue-sharing pattern it utilized became a site of struggle between the regulator and the affiliates, as well as between the affiliates themselves, as all parties began to fight over how the spoils were to be divided. In the latter years of the decade, there was apparently a brief struggle within the network offices too, as the network president advocated "producing a greater quantity of Canadian programming than was the legal minimum" (Rutherford 1990, 119). A change in management quickly quelled this internal dissension, however.

The struggle between the regulator and the network was more prolonged, however, as the network continuously worked to avoid meeting the regulator's program demands. This struggle continued well past the tenure of the BBG. It came to a head in 1980, when CTV took the regulator to court, claiming that it did not have the jurisdiction to impose comprehensive production requirements upon the network (Kaufman 1987, 50–53; Hardin 1985, 179–81). As we shall see, however, even though the regulator came away from this action with a favourable judgment, harnessing the private sector's profit motive to the unprofitable enterprise of program production remained elusive. In the meantime, the CTV affiliates set out in search of profitable avenues of investment.[16]

Program and Audience Problems

As the new network was taking form, the difference in purpose between the public and private sectors was brought into focus on television screens. As Paul Rutherford (1990, 117) illustrates, the private sector never really attempted to produce the same kind of "serious" entertainment programming as the CBC, and program expenditures were generally kept to a maximum of $2,500 to $3,000 per half-hour, roughly the same as the cost of imported programming. Yet, in the face of both declining audiences and revenues, the CBC fought the commercial impulse and delivered a program schedule that was both original and diverse. Variety, comedy, drama, public affairs, news, sports – all could be found on CBC television, although often nestled between American programs (Miller 1987; Rutherford 1990). Moreover, through the 1960s, many of the CBC's drama programs were delivered in formats that were not amenable to commercial interruption and presented as sustaining programs (Miller 1987, 196). At the same time, original work from the regional production centres did occasionally find its way to the network schedule, although rarely after the mid-1960s (Miller 1987, 325–53). For the high-brow audience, symphonies, operas, and ballets were offered, and, despite the fact that they only drew 5–10 percent of the audience, they were continued up to the end of the 1960s (Rutherford 1990, 268–69).

The benefits of these program investments were also widely disseminated. In 1963, the total revenue of the private broadcasters surpassed the income of the CBC (Raboy 1990, 162). Yet, in that same year, the CBC paid out $9.2 million for Canadian talent – three times that of the private sector (Rutherford 1990, 273). Drama critic Robert Russell noted that in 1962 CBC drama employed "more writers, directors, and actors than all other forms of professional theatre in the country put together" (in Rutherford 1990, 273). While this work alone rarely paid enough to support these workers, income from the CBC would continue to be a key source of income for many Canadians artists and performers. Moreover, the CBC also led the way in setting wage standards for technicians and other production workers, and generally settled on wage scales higher than the private sector – a practice that often led to charges of "inefficiency" from the corporation's detractors (Weir 1965, 334).

But while these programming efforts were rewarded with substantial audience shares in the 1950s and early 1960s, competition soon took a toll. In cities close to the United States, American border broadcasters cut deeply into the CBC's audiences. By 1967, the CTV network had captured 25 percent of the anglophone audience and, as we shall see, as cable TV was introduced, its offerings of American network programs also ate heavily into the CBC's audiences. By 1967, the CBC held just 50 percent of the Canadian audience, and as the number of channels multiplied, its audience share continued its downward spiral ([GD] CRTC 1979; cf. Rutherford 1990, 134–37). Set against this growing stable of American programming, particularly in anglophone Canada, the CBC never really had a chance in the competition for audiences.

A Different Logic

In its early stages of development, American television also carried wide and varied program fare. By the early 1960s, however, the popularity and economy of the formulaic serial situation comedies and dramas that were popularized by early Hollywood telefilms quickly became the mainstay of American commercial television. These serials brought both economy and continuity to television schedules as audiences were encouraged to return each week, "same time, same station," to meet with a familiar set of characters and situations. Although initially expensive to arrange, the same sets, wardrobe, cast, and crew were redeployed from week to week, leading to economies in production. The established conventions of the star system allowed the players themselves to increase these programs' currency. Moreover, the stereotypical characters and situations employed by these productions wove established popular theatrical traditions together with familiar cultural forms and situations to play upon circumstances common to many living in a modern industrial society.

The popularity of these programs extended not only across the United States but also to international audiences that were familiar with the terms and conditions of the expanding consumer society. Indeed, the cultural diversity of the United States was an ideal place to develop programs that resonated with a range of diverse tastes. Moreover, the fact that these programs had generally already generated a tidy profit before they were taken to the international market allowed their owners unlimited scope in setting the price of licence fees. Consequently, prices were set according to the individual circumstances of potential national markets, but always well below the cost of domestic production in those markets (Barnouw 1990).

Striving to differentiate itself from these formulaic American network offerings, the CBC countered with a diverse range of dramatic forms. As Mary Jane Miller (1987, 379) illustrates, "linear or complex narrative structures, expressionist, constructivist, or realist design, presentational or representational conventions were all to be found on CBC TV in its first fifteen years." As she painstakingly details in her extensive study of CBC drama, *Turn Up the Contrast,* many of these programs were not elitist in character, and while all met Canadian content guidelines, many were also explicitly Canadian. Yet, the CBC's mandate focused the corporation on tailoring these programs to different sets of interests rather than a singular approach that encompassed diverse interests, as the American programs strove for. As the CBC's program schedule deliberately focused on constructing different types of audiences from time slot to time slot through the evening, it appeared to encourage viewers whose tastes were not met by the upcoming program to switch channels. Indeed, in producing programs to meet diverse sets of audience interests one would expect such movement. But once viewers switched to another station, whether Canadian or American, they became wrapped up in a schedule of foreign programming that was deliberately devised to hold large, diverse audiences through program changes and/or capture a portion of a competitor's audience at program breaks. Thus, the CBC encountered a complex problem in scheduling its programs. Not only did it first have to pull its audiences out of this commercial maze so they might "discover" its programs, but once it turned that audience loose, it had to pull it back from a deliberately and expensively spun web of seductive programming choices.

The battle for audiences was waged not only across the television screen and around the television set tuner. As the continental broadcast industry grew through the 1970s and 1980s, potential audience members were caught in an increasing spiral of circumstances that all pointed them toward American programs. Not only did practically all of the private Canadian stations build their schedules around the most popular American programs at every available opportunity, but advertising for foreign programs spilled over the border both in and into a host of media products, including television and programming guides. As well, Canadian entertainment writers and commentators made their living publicly discussing the merits of these foreign programs. Thus, as the number of channels multiplied, even the seemingly simple task of making Canadian audience members aware of the potential Canadian choices available became increasingly difficult.

Moreover, as the CBC became swamped in a sea of competitive program choices that beat to the rhythm of hour or half-hour program intervals, it had little choice but to give up programs that did not conform to this temporal format, otherwise, it risked losing viewers who wished to switch either to or from another channel at what was, on all other available channels, a conventional break in the schedule. However, as the CBC moved to take on such a commercial format, it also encountered increasing criticism, which militated against "competing" with the American television industry on the terms that industry set for the system. As we shall see in Chapter 7, this criticism continued through the next decade as well, becoming very shrill in 1974. In the meantime, all of these circumstances worked together to present the CBC with an almost unassailable opponent. As the decades wore on and the commercial imperatives that gave form to program schedules became increasingly intense, it is surprising that the CBC managed to maintain an audience at all. The competition would only get stiffer, however.

Impending Change

As the division of responsibility between the public and private elements of the system was taking hold, the growing availability of cable television was shifting the site of the regulatory struggle. Coaxial cable was first used in the United States to improve television reception in urban centres where buildings impeded reception. Soon after, entrepreneurs in California were deploying it to deliver "pay-TV." Meanwhile, Canadian entrepreneurs set out to adapt this technology to Canadian conditions. They set their sights on capitalizing the distance between broadcaster and viewer created by the division between centralized reception and privatized transmission and, for a price, began delivering distant, generally American, signals to Canadian television markets. Although this technique appeared to present little threat to the Canadian system at the time the 1958 Broadcasting Act was enacted, and thus was outside its purview, by the early 1960s the distant signals cable TV brought to "local" markets were fragmenting audiences for programs and advertising. Despite the argument that cable TV was simply dedicated to expanding consumer choice, the threat it presented to the national network system began to demand attention ([GD] Committee on Broadcasting [Fowler II] 1965, 253–55; Firestone 1966, 277). Before cable could be brought into the regulatory fold, however, new legislation was necessary, and this concern was added to the growing list of changes to be encompassed in the legislation that was developing.

Cable was not the only new technology threatening the system with change in the mid-1960s. With the Americans' launch of the satellite Telstar I, a transatlantic satellite news broadcast was initiated and rampant speculation surrounded the broadcast applications of this new technology (Barnouw 1990, 308–15). In 1966, the Board of Broadcast Governors was presented with an application to establish a Canadian satellite corporation that would distribute programming for a proposed new television network (Babe 1990, 222). While this application was somewhat premature, it helped spur the federal government to action. In 1969, informed by a discourse of nationalism that framed the company as "'strengthening and protecting Canada's cultural heritage,'" the Telesat Canada Act gave form to Canada's own satellite venture (220).[17] However, another decade would pass before the satellites were drawn into Canada's broadcasting's infrastructure.

Meanwhile, in the United States, non-profit television was undergoing a renaissance of sorts. Educational television, which had survived the capitalization of the very-high-frequency (VHF) band through regulatory assignment to the ultra-high-frequency (UHF) range, was given a new lease on life in 1967 as "non-profit public television" and began to develop program formats to attract audiences that were disenchanted by the offerings of commercial television (Head, Sterling, and Schofield 1994, 267–71). As this public service model developed in the United States, it provided yet another yardstick for critics to measure the CBC's shortcomings.

Canadian Broadcast Production: Caught in Contradiction

Through the 1960s, a dual system of sorts did indeed emerge within the Canadian broadcasting system. Under the direction of the private sector's long-awaited independent regulatory board, the division of purpose between the CBC and the private sector – between public service and private profit-making – accelerated through the 1960s. Along one line of development, the CBC continued the struggle to convert both its sources of income and the profit-motivated behaviour of its affiliates to domestic program production and distribution. Along another line, the private network and its profit-motivated affiliates struggled to convert profits to both shareholder income and profitable investment. Meanwhile, inside each of these lines of development, or "elements" of the system, different interests struggled to realize their concerns. In the public sector, the fragmented interests of the Canadian public tossed the CBC about on a tempestuous current of competing definitions of culture and service. But while the corporation wrestled with funding problems and with the demands of its affiliates, in the private sector competing blocks of capital each sought to maximize their own interest. Straddling these two elements, the regulator strove to harness these very different behaviours to what it perceived to be the national interests of the broadcasting system as a whole.

To a remarkable extent, the struggle to produce Canadian programs at the core of this system reflected many of the same difficulties encountered by

Canadian industry at large. Canadian manufacturers had long found it difficult to produce products of a distinctly Canadian character while operating within an industrial infrastructure dependent upon transnational relations of production. As T.N. Brewis (1968, 131) observed of this larger context in 1968:

> A distinctive Canadian character can be given to products, but corporate research and engineering departments required to build in such distinctive characteristics can only do so if there is an opportunity to market substantial quantities of the products in question, in competition with well-established foreign products developed under similar expectations. The chief limitations upon any Canadian manufacturer attempting to achieve this objective [are that] ... [f]oreign tariffs prevent Canadian producers from breaking into world markets; and Canadian tariffs, by making possible the division of the Canadian market, hamper the efforts of Canadian firms to exploit the various economies of scale, including those elements of research and development which require large fixed outlays. It is not difficult to understand why firms producing small quantities of a wide range of product lines will rely upon designs provided at low cost by parent firms, or through licensing arrangements. It is the circumstances that maintain such structural conditions that must bear the responsibility for the consequent restraint on development of distinctive characteristics and products.

While the cultural character of broadcast products added another dimension to these structural conditions, the transnational relations of production underlying the broadcast system posed a similar set of problems for Canadian broadcast producers.

As we have seen, in the United States, the capital-intensive project of developing programs designed to attract audiences consisting of middle-class American consumers militated against the CBC's marketing its wares in that venue. While some of the CBC's more expensive drama programs found outlets in Britain and other European countries, the Canadian character of other programs worked against their currency in those markets. These circumstances did not completely preclude foreign sales, but in the international market all comers had to find their place alongside the glut of cheap, popular American programs. Accordingly, export markets offered no great source of income for Canadian producers.

Meanwhile, in the Canadian domestic market, the system's dependency on foreign programming to finance production resulted in similar constraints. For the CBC, licensing agreements with foreign producers provided it with popular programming around which it built audiences (markets) for its own line of distinctive Canadian products. These agreements also provided revenue to cross-subsidize Canadian production. Still, both commercial sanctions and the continued fragmentation of the Canadian broadcast market restricted the corporation's avenues of growth, making it increasingly dependent upon state subsidy to meet its objectives.

As for the private sector, these same export problems combined with the ongoing division of the market by new entrants – including cable TV – to prevent development of the necessary economies of scale for large-scale program production to fill the various elements of their own product line. Meanwhile, the ready supply of American entertainment programming acquired through licensing agreements enabled private broadcasters to generate revenue for growth and profit, as well as for cross-subsidizing the development and capitalization of particular niches of their domestic program schedules.

But the Canadian system's dependence on foreign broadcast products introduced it to a set of what Harold Innis might have called "rigidities," whereby the expression of Canadian perspectives in programming became a function of the economic success of foreign products in Canadian markets. Within this logic, growth and financial success were dependent upon the very products the system was supposed to eliminate. In the short term, state subsidy of the CBC worked to ameliorate this contradiction (cf. Innis 1956, 150; Neill 1991, 201). In the longer term, however, the absence of a viable export market for Canadian broadcast products capped the growth potential for Canadian products.

In the meantime, the historically established division of labour between the two elements of the Canadian system would continue to develop under these structural conditions for decades: the public element would continue the struggle to convert revenue to the nationally defined public purposes of the system; the private element would strive to convert its revenue to increasing profits. Within this system, the growth of the public sector hinged upon continued state subsidy and balancing of the national interests it served against the need for commercial revenue. For the profit-oriented stations, growth hinged on extracting as much surplus as possible from scheduling foreign programs and then investing this surplus in profitable ventures. Straddling these interests, the regulator would need very different strategies to convert each of these elements to what it perceived were the national purposes of the system. In 1968, new broadcast legislation aimed to provide the regulatory power to do that.

The 1968 Broadcasting Act

After a slow and arduous passage through the House of Commons and its committees, a new broadcasting act was proclaimed on April 1, 1968.[18] Generally, it followed the lines of its predecessor and offered only incremental changes in the larger process of regulation. In substance, though, the 1968 act was considerably more comprehensive than any previous legislation, and, for the first time, the nationalist goals of the system were enunciated. In addition, the act contained a mandate for the CBC.

For instance, section 2(c) stated that the system "should be effectively owned and controlled by Canadians so as to safeguard, enrich and strengthen the cultural, political, and economic fabric of Canada." But while the act stated that the broadcast undertakings within the system constituted a "single system," two elements were defined: a "national broadcasting service" and a "private element." Following the lines set out in the CBC's self-proclaimed mandate, the public broadcaster was charged with the presentation of "a whole range of programming," extension of service to "all parts of Canada," "contributing to the flow and exchange of cultural and regional information and entertainment," and contributing "to the development of national unity and provid[ing] for a continuing expression of Canadian identity" (section 2[g]). The private sector, on the other hand, was given the more modest responsibilities of establishing a program service that would provide "reasonable and balanced opportunity for the expression of differing views ... of high standard ... [and] using predominantly Canadian creative and other resources" (section 2 [d]).

In its original form, the act clearly placed the interests of the national broadcaster over those of the private sector, but under pressure from the Conservatives the wording was changed to defer both of these interests to the larger "public interest." Still, in the case of conflict between the two elements, "paramount consideration" was to be given to the "objectives of the national broadcasting service" (section 2[h]) (Raboy 1990, 179). Moreover, while there had originally been provision for a five-year funding formula for the CBC, by the time the legislation reached the House annual appropriations were still the rule.

The powers of the new regulator – the Canadian Radio-Television and Telecommunications Commission (CRTC) – were much greater than the BBG's. The commission was given power to bring cable under its control, as well as establish the terms and conditions of licences (Babe 1979, 29–39; Kaufman 1987). Thus, while regulations might be promulgated that applied to all undertakings within the system, the regulator was finally given official power to formulate regulations to meet the individual circumstances of licensees. Under these terms, regulation might be comprehensive yet flexible – conditions that had hitherto eluded legislation. The commission's relations with Parliament were also clearly defined. The Governor-in-Council could issue specific direction regarding the classes of applicants that might hold licences, and refer back to the commission decisions that, "in his opinion, the Commission failed to consider adequately" (sections 22 and 23). Thus, the commission was indeed relatively independent from Parliament – a relationship that would soon lead to controversy.

With this legislation, the dual economic systems that had underwritten broadcasting policy at its inception and driven development of the system for more than thirty years were enshrined in regulation. Similarly, reflecting both its historical position within the system as well as the political tenor of the times, the CBC was defined as a "national" broadcaster – not a "public" broadcaster. Moreover, the CBC's seemingly new mandate also reflected the difficulties in forging private capital to the larger interest of public communication, and left the corporation with the larger purpose of constructing programming that reflected the diversity of interests that comprised Canada's different communities, while at the same time attempting to bind these interests to the larger national purposes of unity and expression of a Canadian identity. Thus, the "dual system" rose to meet the changing circumstances of the 1970s.

Division

Under the guise of nationalism, the capitalization of the Canadian television broadcasting system proceeded along avenues of growth both framed and animated by transnational relations of production through the 1960s. In the process, the system was divided against itself, as the very programming that regulation sought to marginalize within the system began to, ironically, marginalize Canadian expression. Indeed, if, as the second Fowler Commission ([GD] Committee on Broadcasting [Fowler II] 1965, 3) put it, "the only thing that really matters in broadcasting is program content; all the rest is housekeeping," then the housekeeper created by the 1958 Broadcasting Act – the BBG – couldn't seem to handle the job. The BBG certainly was not "captured" by the private sector, and even the most ardent supporters of the CBC and the public system generally recognized some place for private capital within the system (cf. Peers 1979; Raboy 1990). From a nationalist perspective, private capital was viewed as one interest among many in a system of "formally free and equal legal subjects," and the failure of the system to meet the objectives set out for it was viewed as a series of "missed opportunities" engendered by bureaucratic fumbling and regulatory inefficiency (Jessop 2021, 164; Raboy 1990, 230). All of this tended to overlook the fact that while Canadian private capital was beholden to the larger state infrastructure for its very existence, its interests were not always commensurate with the national interest. However, neither was the BBG simply a class instrument. The problem was more a question of ideology: private capital was simply viewed widely as the somewhat "natural" engine of economic growth.

Constrained by budget and focused by mandate, the CBC had proven it could not be an effective competitor with the private sector. It set its activities on the edges of the system, improving its reach in terms of both distribution and the production of programming. Indeed, as former CBC chair Leonard W. Brockington had noted some thirty years earlier, the purposes of the public and private sectors were in many ways antithetical. The former returned investment to the people of Canada, the latter to private shareholders – in some cases, shareholders who weren't even Canadians. Yet, while the productive relationships that animated the growth and activities of the private sector were not conducive to producing any great quantity of programming that represented the character and diversity of Canadian life, set between the advertising and electronics industries the private stations and their network were central to myriad industrial relationships that underpinned Canadian life. Program choice spurred television set sales, increased viewership drove the advertising market, and television advertising spurred consumption in general – at least so the cycle appeared. Attempting to cut the transnational relations of production underpinning the advertising industry and harness the revenue it produced to national purpose would form a major focus of the next stage of regulation, as emerging cable markets fragmented audiences for both programs and advertising messages, and gave impetus to the perception that a lack of advertising revenue was impeding the production of Canadian programming.

Meanwhile, as much of the regulatory attention was focused on the emerging television market, in radio markets the CBC was pushed to the far edges of the commercial system through the 1960s. Increased licensing on both the AM and FM frequencies foregrounded the American popular music format throughout the system and, as national advertisers moved to television, CBC radio all but abandoned commercial broadcasting despite the urgings of various public and private studies ([GD] Committee on Broadcasting [Fowler II] 1965). Once again, American technique set the stage for economic development in Canada, and, following a programming logic developed in the United States, private, profit-oriented Canadian radio broadcasting stitched itself to the margins of the American recording industry. To fill the gaps left in the system by its fleeing affiliates, the CBC deployed a network of small regional stations and retransmitters. By the turn of the decade, its direct impact on the revenue of the private sector was minimal, and by the mid-1970s it was out of advertising altogether. Still, on occasion, the private sector complained that the corporation was an unfair competitor because it existed on the largesse of the state and undercut the private sector's audience share.

So, as private capital gained hold of the system, it struggled to forge the relationships that broadcasting constructed for the purpose of creating a privately appropriated surplus. Where that interest met with the interests of the state, an alliance was created; where these interests collided, capital rebelled. By the end of the 1960s, private capital had clearly demonstrated two aspects of its character in the Canadian broadcasting system: first, it was single-mindedly tenacious; second, it was a fair-weather patriot. Over the next fifty years, the characters of both the public and private elements of the system would change considerably, as new technologies were introduced and new kinds of broadcast organizations were instituted to meet changing circumstances and demands. But, even in the face of these shifts, the public and private elements would follow much the same paths as they had always followed. Private broadcasting continued its attempt to capitalize only those elements of the system that presented a potential for profit, while the public sector continued to pursue the more ephemeral goals of extending service and program production into areas where capital was loath to tread.

7
The Capitalization of Canadian Communication and Culture

By THE LATE 1960s, the postwar boom that had signalled rapid industrialization across the Western world had begun to wane, and a massive shift in both the structure of the economy and the role of media and communication within it was on the horizon. As Michael Storper and Alan Scott (1986) note, "the very success of the boom was creating market conditions which were starting to undercut its further advance. Markets were already becoming saturated and industrial overcapacity was pervasive." The effects were stilted growth and a series of "multiple recessions and recoveries, with the recessions becoming each time more severe, and the recoveries more shallow in terms of employment, personal income, and profitability increases" (4). On the margins of the American economy, Canada was particularly vulnerable to these volatile conditions, and through the 1960s increasing state intervention sought to provide relief from tempestuous bouts of inflation and recession (Bliss 1982, 35–38). In the mid-1970s, the crisis reached global proportions, and by the mid-1980s, "restructuring" became the byword of politics and the focus of public policy.

As David Harvey (1989) illustrates, at the heart of the problem were a series of "rigidities" that constrained the temporal and spatial dimensions of the flow of capital. Long-term and large-scale fixed capital investment, combined with heavily entrenched labour markets and increasingly onerous financial commitments on the part of state institutions, stifled investment and the movement of capital in heavily industrialized centres. But just as capital's growth under the centralized Fordist regime of production focused on crossing geographic distance and bringing spatial relations under a common temporal rhythm, so too the move to ameliorating the problems the regime faced focused on first shattering the rigidities that constrained those relations, and then reconstituting them in extended and intensified form (Harvey 1989, 142–72).

In slow, halting fashion, this reshaping and revitalizing of the accumulation process took place on several dimensions. At the transnational level, capital sought to reduce the costs of production by seeking out and exploiting social conditions that were amenable to its purposes across vast geographic space. Countries of what was once termed the "Third World" were renamed "Newly industrialized countries," as production processes were reconstituted across transnational dimensions that exploited differences in wages, government regulation, and market demand. In this context, trade agreements became the hallmark of political process.

On the home front, rationalizing production processes by reducing overhead and labour costs was another dimension of this change. Automation, deregulation, dismantled labour legislation, and privatization were touted by governments as the sacrifices that had to be made in deindustrializing countries to remain competitive in this shifting environment. Across a third dimension, technology was deployed to traverse the social divides between work and leisure and between production and consumption to reregulate and capitalize social life in the service of reducing costs and more closely targeting consumers.

In this atmosphere, new productive relations in several sectors of the economy increasingly hinged on systems of flexible accumulation, whereby relations of production were stretched across geographic and social space, seeking to join distant units of production and consumption in the larger process of accumulation ([GD] Royal Commission on the Economic Union and Development Prospects for Canada 1985). Here goods might be produced in one part of the world and sold in another, taking advantage of disparities in such things as wages and labour and environmental regulations. Realizing profits, however, required closing the distance between the time the goods were produced and the time they were consumed in distant markets – in other words, the expeditious completion of the cycle of capital. Thus, seemingly compressing space by shortening the time necessary to accomplish tasks within it became the key to exploiting these new productive relationships and what Karl Marx called the "annihilation of space by time" became the unspoken creed upon which this new political economic order was founded.

At the technological centre of these economic shifts were new communications technologies. Increasingly sophisticated telecommunications networks incorporated satellite transmission to, in the vernacular of the day, "wire" the globe, while the microchip handled the complex processing and switching tasks. Not only did the high-tech electronics industries offer new avenues of economic growth and employment in the face of widespread deindustrialization in the Global North, but these technologies also offered the vehicle for coordinating and controlling processes of investment, production, and consumption – across both physical and social distance – literally at the speed of light (Castells 2000; Sassen 1991). In Innis's terms, the technology carried a "hyper" space bias and offered a means by which producers might be linked to both suppliers and consumers located across the globe, issuing increasing control over the cycle of capital.

Within these new electronic distribution systems, information took on the form of a resource – a vehicle key to planning, promoting, and undertaking production and consumption at all levels of social life (Schiller 1988, 27–41). At this level, the production and exchange of information offered a new field of economic development – the basis for a new economy that might take form around the slowly depleting industrial infrastructure. Sound, images, text – all became resources upon which new and/or intensified commodity relations could be founded. Copyright formed the legal infrastructure for new property relations and market transactions increasingly began to form the arena within which information was exchanged (Babe 1988; [GD] IHAC 1997).

This chapter examines the Canadian state's early responses to these shifts in the transnational political economy. It considers some of the ways in which the state and its instruments helped set the ground for the increasing participation of investment capital in the communications industries, particularly broadcasting, as well as the pressures these policies put on the CBC.

The Evolving Communications Infrastructure and Canadian Policy

Largely driven by efforts to seek strategic advantage under the ideological sway of the Cold War, the American military-industrial complex invested heavily in developing domestic and international communications technologies through the 1960s (Matheson and Walker 1970). In the midst of these efforts, apparent civilian spinoffs abounded as new cable, satellite, and computer technologies were set on a collision course with existing telecommunications systems. This fuelled visions of new integrated, broadband communication networks that would "carry voice, computer and television signals all on the same wire" and revolutionize both work and leisure (Streeter 1986, 125).

By the late 1960s, these "wired-city" forecasts and scenarios were a favoured topic of both think tanks and popular futurologists throughout the United States. As the postwar boom began to wane through the late 1960s and early 1970s, however, the development and application of these technologies shifted to focus largely on manufacturing and other industrial processes, and the direct benefits to consumer households that they had promised – such as home shopping, home-delivered educational services, video on demand, and regular polling of public choice and preference – faded to the future. In the meantime, however, by 1972, cable television technology, with its capacity to carry high volumes of broadband signals was receiving preferential treatment at the hands of the Federal Communications Commission (FCC), and through the mid to late 1970s cable and satellite were forged into a partnership that would change the face of broadcasting (Head, Sterling, and Schofield 1994; Streeter 1986, 136–46).

Set in the shadow of the American empire, the Canadian economy in general, and communications and media systems in particular, were slowly drawn into this new political economic regime.

The Canadian Response: Communication and Culture

By the end of the 1960s, political economic events on the world stage were beginning to shape Canadian public policy, and technological developments in the United States were driving similar shifts in Canada. As we saw in Chapter 6, cable in particular was beginning to undermine the market and regulatory distinctions that had characterized the long-standing division between broadcasting and telecommunications. But the peculiarities of the Canadian political system set a distinctive course for policy development. On a broad front, growing Anglo-nationalist sentiment combined with increasingly unstable economic conditions to engender a political climate within which the nationality of capital appeared increasingly important. Gaining control of the economy seemed to necessitate Canadian-based industry. Thus, the industrial imperatives that had broadly followed lines set by the National Policy in the late nineteenth century began to shift. No longer could American branch-plants be relied upon to act in the Canadian national interest. As the wired world began to take form in the United States, the Canadian state set out to create its own national system: a system that would meet the needs of Canadians and, like radio and television in the past, electronically stitch the vast geography into a common social fabric. At the same time, though, rising social discontent, particularly in Quebec, illustrated that the new nationalist project could not simply be technological or economic in focus, and the development of a common set of symbols, ideas, and perspectives drew the government's attention. A new flag, bilingualism and multiculturalism, centennial celebrations, and Canada's "own" industries became political projects of the time. Among the policy directions taken during this period, two stand out for our purposes: communication and culture.

Communications Policy

In 1969, the federal government established the Department of Communications (DOC), and under its direction a Canadian version of the emerging high-technology communications system was pursued. In this process, the government followed the Canadian state's traditional strategy of attempting to forge private capital to national purpose, bridging gaps in the productive infrastructure through a range of policy vehicles (Bliss 1982, 38). Key components of this structure, like the new satellite company, Telesat Canada, were to be Canadian-owned.[1] In large measure, however, these new communications projects were economic in nature, and the focus was on establishing Canadian relations of production to carry them forward – not on the qualitative character of the information that the system might eventually carry.

By 1971, all of the technological components necessary for what was trumpeted in the early 1980s as the "convergence" of communications technologies were envisioned within the field of communications policy ([GD] Department of Communications 1971; Lyman 1983, 21). As innovations in semiconductor, digital, and optical technologies accelerated under competition between competing blocks of transnational corporate capital, the technological character of these components would change, as would the role of both the Canadian government and industry in their development (Lyman 1983, 3–8). Yet, in broad outline, the integrated communication systems heralded in the early 1970s bore a striking resemblance to the information systems that emerged several decades later. But, with the economy in the grip of recession in the early 1980s, as this system came into focus, putting these plans into action would prove difficult.

Having developed on the margins of the American industry and under the protective hand of regulation, the Canadian telecommunications industry was regionally based, and highly concentrated ([GD] Restrictive Trade Practices Commission 1981; Babe 1990). Moreover, regulatory jurisdiction in the field was divided, not only between different levels of government but also between different government departments. Consequently, as the federal government moved toward development of an integrated, national communications policy, it encountered a series of setbacks in orienting both state interests and private capital to the task.

In part, this problem was the product of the structure of Canadian industry itself. For instance, from the inception of Canada's satellite system, the telephone companies were suspicious of the ways in which it might work to replace the terrestrial systems they had in place, and thereby undermine their revenue base (Babe 1990, 225–28). Thus, they were reluctant to participate in the deployment of the system and worked to force a regulatory situation under which Telesat's capacity remained underutilized. In the face of these efforts, the system remained mired in debt through the 1970s and early 1980s. Although the Canadian Radio-television and Telecommunications Commission (CRTC) was able to force some change in the structure of the system's operations through the mid-1980s, in 1991 the federal government's divestment of its shares in the satellite agency resulted in even closer control by telephone interests. Similarly, issues of federal-provincial jurisdiction, particularly in the case of Quebec, threw up a number of roadblocks to developing a comprehensive federal policy (Raboy 1990, 184–272).[2]

Still, by the early 1980s the outlines of a seemingly coordinated culture and communications policy began to appear and, with communications increasingly under the sway of economic imperatives, this drew the field of cultural policy ever closer to the realm of industrial development ([GD] Department of Communications 1983b).

Steps to Consolidate Canadian Cultural Markets

As this larger industrial strategy took form, broadcasting, as well as other Canadian media systems, were put on a different path of development. In an effort to mend the increasingly fractious relationship between anglophone and francophone Canadians, after taking office in 1963 the Liberals struck the Royal Commission on Bilingualism and Biculturalism, signalling the direction this strategy would take. "Culture," broadly defined, would become the field for constructing a common national vision; increased federal funding and coordination of the public and private elements of that field would provide the vehicle. By 1965, "the Secretary of State had taken on administration of ... [t]he Canada Council, the CBC, the Board of Broadcast Governors, the NFB, the National Gallery, the National Museum, the National Library and Public Archives, [t]he Centennial Commission and the Queen's Printer" (Magder 1993, 118). Beginning in the mid-1960s, a series of somewhat tentative measures were taken to carry this project forward.

Framed by the ongoing concern over American domination of Canadian industry in general, the federal strategy built upon the traditional pattern of deploying state intervention to establish a national economic base for cultural production (Bliss 1982, 34–35, 38). However, rather than simply subsidize the production of largely high cultural forms as had been suggested by the Massey-Lévesque Commission, the emphasis was on creating relations of production based upon Canadian private capital. Thus, the broad commodification of the realm of Canadian culture became the target of public policy.

These measures targeted a number of media industries and included a range of policy instruments. For instance, in the periodical industry the mid-1960s saw amendments to the Income Tax Act and the Customs Tariff, as well as a slight adjustment to the postal subsidy. All these measures were designed to improve the profitability of Canadian-owned magazines (Litvak and Maule 1974, 64–78). Prohibitions in this legislation against deducting advertising expenses in foreign publications for tax purposes also guaranteed Canadian ownership in the newspaper industry and, later, the repatriation of advertising from American border broadcasters that set their sights on Canadian advertising markets (Berlin 1990). In the film industry, the Canadian Film Development Corporation (CFDC) was established to provide capital for feature film production, although the funding base was small and the legislation did not preclude funding of co-productions with the American majors (Magder 1993, 121–32). And, as we shall see, in 1968, under cabinet direction, steps were taken to repatriate the ownership of broadcast outlets. Thus, as capital burgeoned in the wake of postwar industrial growth, the federal government moved to provide political form to a range of emerging media industries.[3] These measures would be the subject of trade disputes with the United States over the next several decades (Berlin 1990), but through the 1970s and 1980s, this logic of developing and maintaining distinct Canadian markets for cultural products would gain momentum, as the Canadian government struggled to deploy protected Canadian markets as springboards for developing products that might later be exported to foreign markets.

As the state moved to establish these Canadian units of production, it did not directly initiate any new direction or innovative forms of cultural expression. Rather, these policies simply built upon existing market definitions to create Canadian versions of largely American popular cultural products. To some extent, the logic of these interventions followed what economists commonly call import substitution, whereby domestic manufacturing industries are encouraged to develop products behind protective tariffs or other barriers to market entry along lines similar to those foreign products the barriers are designed to exclude. This logic encouraged the growth of popular media products not only for the Canadian market but, in some instances, also for export markets.

Radio broadcast regulation followed a similar logic. In the mid-1970s, Canadian content regulations were created in an effort to harness private broadcasters to national purpose by bolstering the Canadian recording industry. Here, musical programming formats that mimicked those deployed in the American market were coupled with Canadian content quotas, and laid across local Canadian radio markets, to ensure that Canadian listeners had diversity in programming as well as Canadian versions of these musical "genres" (Berland 1994). As a result, the regulations helped promote the growth of a seemingly independent Canadian music industry whose products were readily adaptable to the larger, flexible structure of the transnational recorded music industry (Berland and Straw 1994).

As this process of capitalizing Canada's cultural industries began to take form, it spurred increasing concentration of ownership, and that began to draw public attention. Within communications policy, consolidated Canadian ownership offered the opportunity to develop monopoly markets that encouraged economies of scale and ultimately research and development opportunities ([GD] Department of Communications 1983b, 8). The historical relationship between Bell Canada and Northern Telecom – a company that, before its eventual spectacular downfall, would go on to become an international superstar in the evolving telecommunications market – provides a case in point. In the cultural field, however, concentration of ownership and the centralized management of resources it entailed had the added effect of narrowing the range of perspectives and program choices available in the media marketplace. Consequently, in 1969, in the midst of the development of policies that encouraged Canadian ownership, the Senate Special Committee on Mass Media, chaired by Senator Keith Davey, was struck to investigate "the impact and influence" of "ownership and control" of the mass media ([GD] Senate Special Committee on Mass Media 1970a).

Although frank and thoughtful, the Davey report never really questioned the place of private capital in the media field. In fact, the later enactment of Bill C-58 and the subsequent strengthening of Canadian private capital that it engendered are often attributed to the Davey report's recommendations (Vipond 1992, 63–65). Yet, while the report was laying the ground for bolstering private capital in media markets, it also made careful note of the escalating trend to concentration, and issued a litany of complaints over the fact that private media outlets of all stripes put the pursuit of profit over their supposedly more public responsibilities. To encourage greater responsibility in this direction, there were recommendations for all players, although, given that these media were generally under private ownership, some of the report's strongest admonitions were addressed to those who had the least control over the product: journalists, the government, and the public ([GD] Senate Special Committee on Mass Media 1970a, 4, 255–60).

A decade later, increasing concentration of ownership in the newspaper industry spurred the establishment of the Royal Commission on Newspapers (Kent Commission). The commission recommended legislation to help maintain diversity of perspectives in the daily newspaper industry and media in general ([GD] Royal Commission on Newspapers 1981). Cross-media ownership was seen as a particular concern because of its propensity to encourage the sharing of editorial resources. However, draft legislation never garnered enough support to make it through Parliament, and the only regulation that was implemented was a 1982 cabinet directive by the Liberal government to the CRTC instructing it "to deny new broadcasting licences or renewals to applicants who owned daily newspapers in the same market. This directive, however, allowed for exceptions 'in the public interest'; in the course of its enactment – until its withdrawal by the Mulroney government – this exception was applied to nearly every case heard by the Commission" (J. Jackson 1999).

Thus, as corporate capital came to inhabit a growing portion of what was perceived as the public sphere of communication, the state's representatives were again at odds over how to discipline private property to public purpose. The contradiction they met was that – similar to social media of the twenty-first century – the seeming public space that facilitated communication was not simply inhabited by private capital; it was also created by capital. Consequently, growth and development of the media industries was somewhat dependent on allowing capital a free hand to find ways to foster that growth. But rather than offer the possibility of diverse opportunities for public expression and reflection upon the conditions of social life, these media industries were now increasingly focused on a single purpose, the creation of private profits.

Caught at the centre of this struggle were the shifting, diverse interests of the Canadian public – in all of its local, regional, national, Indigenous, ethnic, linguistic, gendered, and racialized forms. As Canada's premier cultural institution, in this context the CBC was increasingly the focus of this public alienation.

The Cable Conundrum

Having established a beachhead within the broadcasting system, through the late 1960s and 1970s cable straddled the emerging fields of communications and cultural policy, where it acted as a lightning rod for all of the political and economic tensions of the time. Set between developing satellite and computer terminal technologies, cable's high-capacity switched network capabilities promised to be the keystone of a system that would draw consumer households into the fold of the impending information revolution ([GD] Department of Communications 1971, 190). Whole new electronics industries might be built on developing the hardware that would give form to the system, while the channel capacity cable offered promised a whole new range of broadcast and information services. Conceived as a direct information pipeline into the consumer households of an information economy, the cable system offered the epitome of "flexibility" in the rising regime of flexible accumulation (16).[4] For those interests feeling increasingly disenfranchised by the existing broadcast system, it presented myriad new venues of representation. But, as Robert Babe (1990, 209) notes, bringing cable into the regulatory fold "as a broadcasting-receiving undertaking" in 1968 sent sparks flying: "first, from traditional broadcasters threatened by increased competition, second from levels of government squabbling over jurisdiction, and finally from telephone companies eyeing cable as a latent competitor." For telecommunications companies, cable's common carrier capabilities – such as two-way data transmission – posed a particular threat ([GD] Senate Special Committee on Mass Media 1970a, 213–23; B. Jeffrey 1980). And for Quebec, cable appeared as a means of instituting its own comprehensive "national" media system.[5]

But whatever direction it might go, developing the potential of this new technology was a daunting task. As cable entered the regulatory arena, Canada's cable system generally consisted of a highly diverse set of small local companies with little investment in anything other than wire. It would be many years before this seeming industry would be ready to assume any of the larger services or responsibilities the various pundits, policy-makers, and visionaries of the time envisaged for it. Within the broadcasting system, however, cable did present a clear threat to the established logic of regulation.

Until cable's appearance, markets had been increasingly defined by the physical reach of broadcast signals. By fragmenting local broadcast audiences with imported signals, cable shattered the carefully cultivated dimensions of those markets, and undermined the larger regulatory strategy of providing local licensees a firm revenue base with local advertising markets. Here, then, if left to develop outside the purview of broadcast regulation, cable threatened to dash all hope of developing the economies of scale necessary for program production. Because it largely involved rebroadcasting signals emanating from other markets, it also raised a host of copyright issues at both the national and international levels. Consequently, despite the fact that it would be several decades before the potential foreseen for cable systems in the 1960s was actually developed on any scale, these systems were the harbingers of both the promise and problems of the information millennium.

1968–80: The Rise (and Demise) of Comprehensive Broadcast Regulation

As we have seen, under the purview of the Board of Broadcast Governors, broadcasting developed as a relatively distinct policy field through the 1960s. It would continue to do so for a time under the 1968 Broadcasting Act. The growth of the system from the legislation of the 1968 Broadcasting Act to the promulgation of the 1991 Broadcasting Act[6] is well documented in a number of sources and need not be fully rehearsed here.[7] What is not well illustrated in this literature, however, are the dimensions of growth that we have concentrated on thus far: (1) how the structure of regulation and the assumptions it carried encouraged a particular division of responsibility within the system and drove the public element to its commercial margins; and (2) how the growth of the system, particularly after 1980, was shaped by the imperatives of the new post-Fordist economy and the demands it placed upon the Canadian state.

The years 1968–76 are generally seen as a period of close management by the CRTC, as it worked to consolidate Canadian ownership of the broadcasting system and rationalize the relationships between cable companies, television broadcasters, and the CBC, so that each might make more focused contributions to the growth and character of the system. Regulation sheltered the field from the pressures of the larger economic environment, as the CRTC struggled to bring an increasingly complex set of circumstances under regulatory control. It pursued this task along several dimensions, all of which built upon established or already emerging principles within the system.[8] This project met with mixed success, however.

First, under the guidance of an order-in-council, new licences and licence renewals were issued only to companies under Canadian ownership. Despite protests and legal maneuverings by the private sector, the CRTC was largely successful in this project. But while this move gave it more control over companies' operations and helped guarantee that operators might be responsible to the overall public goals of the system, ownership regulations also contributed to increasing concentration of media ownership.

As a second line of attack, new Canadian content regulations attempted to close the loopholes of earlier versions. Despite the CRTC's greater powers, these efforts met with much the same problems encountered by the BBG and, in the end, left the peak viewing hours filled with American programming (Babe 1979, 141–48). Efforts to promote program production followed the familiar pattern. Where aspects of the program schedule could be turned to profitable enterprise, such as in news production, the private sector willingly invested in Canadian programming. Generally, however, Canadian programs were low-budget and easily produced, such as "public affairs and interviews, panel and game shows, music and sports" (144). Although, the private sector did undertake a few co-productions with independent producers, these were designed for international markets and were "virtually indistinguishable from American programs" (144).

Despite these ongoing problems, the CRTC continued its efforts to channel commercial benefits to Canadian units of production. In 1972, it set guidelines to ensure that "at least 50 percent of the total cost" of co-productions and co-ventures "were spent on 'Canadian participation'" (143). At the request of the Standing Senate Committee on Transport and Communications, the commission introduced content regulations for commercials in 1975 (143). As noted above, it also took aim at the American border broadcasters and requested that the government amend the Income Tax Act so that advertising expenditures with broadcasters not under Canadian ownership would not be eligible for tax deduction. Also, to protect advertising markets for local broadcasters, the CRTC began to prescribe geographic boundaries within which stations might solicit advertising. Thus, to a large degree, the CRTC simply carried the historical logic of regulation forward, protecting the revenues of private broadcasters while continuing the attempt to force compliance with content regulations. In an increasingly competitive environment, however, the focus of this protection began to shift. Whereas through the 1950s and 1960s protective measures were largely focused at the local level, through the 1970s they took on a more national flavour and attempted to more clearly delineate the Canadian from the American market so that more commercial revenue could be wrung from the system.[9] At the same time, there were the first attempts to forge common production arrangements between the Canadian and American markets (Babe 1979).

On a third front, the CRTC moved to make cable systems responsible to the larger purposes of the system.[10] Carriage rules were imposed to limit the import of distant signals and foreground the signals of the CBC, local stations, and provincial educational broadcasters. While the carriage of American signals was initially limited to "one commercial and one non-commercial" channel, under pressure from both the public and industry three US signals – one from each of the big American networks – were allowed by 1971 (Babe 1979, 71; 1990, 210–11). In cases where the system carried Canadian and American stations offering the same programming, substitution rules were imposed under which the cable operator was required to replace the commercials on the foreign station with those from the Canadian signal. These "simultaneous program substitution" rules triggered court action by American stations, but in 1977 the Supreme Court of Canada ruled that such regulations were within the CRTC's jurisdiction (Babe 1979, 161–62; Berlin 1990). With these efforts, the commission again moved to define the new broadcast "space" created by cable in terms of the productive dimensions of a Canadian market. As is often noted, however, because the substitution rules encouraged broadcasters to match their program schedules with those of the American networks to maximize audience reach and advertising revenue, to a large degree they actually worked to discourage the viewing of Canadian programming during peak viewing hours.

In response to pressure from other interests, the CRTC also created and introduced new types of broadcast licences during this period. Cable operators were directed to provide, equip, and staff a community access channel to encourage local participation in program production and programming pertaining to local events and information (Goldberg 1989). Provincial governments were issued licences for "educational" purposes, and the CRTC also approved applications for community radio stations, which were generally run on a co-operative basis (Kozolanka 2012; Skinner 2012; Raboy 1990, 237–38). But despite the fact that these stations' programming was generally by definition "Canadian," like the CBC their interests were generally subordinated to private capital within the larger system. For instance, they were not allowed to solicit advertising, signal strength and reach were limited compared with private broadcasters operating in their areas, and access channels were kept under the control of the cable operators (see [GD] CRTC 2000b).

A fourth dimension of the CRTC's strategy was to increase Canadian programming by issuing new licences to privately financed companies. As the commission noted in 1971, further productive capacity was necessary within the system to prevent it from simply becoming a "technically sophisticated distribution system for imported programs" (in Raboy 1990, 215). Following an allocative rationale, the CRTC worked toward this end by licensing six independent stations in the period 1968–76. Among the hopes of the commission was that through these measures a "third, English-language television service would thereby evolve" (Babe 1979, 148). This was not to be the case. Rather, within two years of beginning operation, two of the licensees that held the greatest promise – CITY-TV and the Global Television Network – were on the verge of bankruptcy, victims of their own ambitious production plans (87–193). After restructuring, both stations fell into the familiar mode of offering popular American programming through peak viewing hours and making minimal investment in Canadian programs. Moreover, while the new licensees increased audiences of Canadian stations in general with the increased American programming they brought to the system, overall viewing time of Canadian programming suffered a slight decrease (149).

These failures also had more far-reaching implications for the system. As new licensees turned to purchasing American programming to fill their program schedules, the ensuing competition for American programs reportedly drove up their price for all Canadian buyers by as much as 30–40 percent (Babe 1979). Consequently, like the BBG, as the CRTC set out to increase Canadian programming choice, its inability to directly raise and allocate capital ran headlong into the rigidities of the national system, whereby private capital's dependence on foreign programming foreclosed on the abilities of these new licensees to produce Canadian programs.

Finally, a fifth avenue of action pursued by the CRTC was an attempt to make the CBC more responsible to its mandate. Early in its tenure, the CRTC began envisioning the CBC as a key player in preparing the system "'to compete with the rest of the world'" (in Raboy 1990, 214). The CBC's 1974 network licence renewal hearings gave the CRTC a venue for disciplining the corporation to this vision.

The CRTC received 305 briefs in the hearing, most of which argued that the CBC did not adequately serve the interests of the public (Babe 1979, 112–13; Raboy 1990, 228–34). Regional and local interests claimed that there was not enough program consultation or production at these levels. Representatives from "northern and native" groups as well as "'ethnic' organizations" argued that the CBC was "failing to reflect the multicultural and multilingual character of Canada in its programming" (Raboy 1990, 229). Advertising in general drew the usual criticism. Women's groups complained of the representation of women in programming and commercials. Other groups argued that audience size should not be as important a consideration as the spectrum of interests a program attracted. The Canadian Labour Congress argued that while the CBC should in fact strive for a large, diversified "'national' audience ... it doesn't have to be a mass audience'" (in Raboy 1990, 231). Graham Spry appeared to argue for stable funding for the corporation (ibid., 230).

The CRTC's decision ([GD] CRTC 1974b) broadly reflected all of these concerns. It argued that "despite the need for the CBC to continue to provide a 'popular' service" it should guard against "considering the audience as a 'mass'" (in Raboy 1990, 233). The commission claimed that the CBC's programming practices reflected "'an exaggerated concern with the American way of doing things'" and that the prime-time schedule should contain more Canadian programming (in Babe 1979, 11).

Here, it would appear, the CRTC did not adequately recognize the CBC's programming strategy. Through the early 1970s, the CBC continued to deploy the principles of balance and audience flow to "combine popular imported programs, information programs, and programs of specialized appeal in a way that will maximize the audiences for each" (in Babe 1979, 107). As we have seen, to some extent, this practice was designed to develop a kind of mass "Canadian" audience, but it was undertaken with considerably different intention than the "flow" strategy practised by the private broadcasters and American networks, which focused on maximizing audiences for advertisers. At the opening of the hearings, the CBC representatives touted this strategy as increasingly important in the face of the further fragmentation of Canadian broadcast audiences caused by cable (Raboy 1990, 229). No one seemed to agree, however.

The CRTC also took the opportunity to admonish the general industrial character of North American program production and the mass marketing strategies that underlay scheduling practices in general, arguing that these imperatives "impose on their audiences a limited number of expeditious and lucrative formulas instead of enlarging the possibilities of viewer choice" (in Babe 1979, 145).

Given the tone and tenor of this hearing, it would appear that the CBC once again became a lightning rod for many of the interests that felt disenfranchised by the larger commercialization of the system. As in the past, though, the CBC was responsive to these regulatory criticisms. Generally, it moved to raise levels of Canadian content and cut back on advertising revenue. With these moves, its advertising revenue fell from 21.9 percent of total income in 1969–70 to 16.7 percent in 1975–76 (Babe 1979, 103).

Through the late 1970s and early 1980s, the CRTC kept up the pressure and the CBC responded. But as has already been demonstrated in the larger history of the system, by admonishing the CBC to undertake greater responsibilities, the CRTC was largely preaching to the converted. Moreover, in meting out their criticisms, many of the corporation's detractors again displayed an inadequate knowledge of the CBC's operations. By the time of the 1974 licence hearings, the CBC had already taken steps to meet many of the concerns. For instance, it had already made a concerted effort to undertake regional programming, and steps to "Canadianize" the prime-time schedule were taken in 1968 (Babe 1979, 111). From the period 1969–74, the CBC had shifted the programming mix in its prime-time schedule from being predominantly American to being 72.1 percent Canadian in a "representative winter week" (Babe 1979, 108). It still refused advertising for news programs and voluntarily removed ads from children's programs. In 1967, it moved to take television to remote communities through its "Frontier Coverage Plan." In 1973, the CBC became Telesat's first broadcast customer and began introducing "live" television to the North, pioneering the delivery of television via satellite; in 1974, it sped up extension of service through its "Accelerated Coverage Plan."[11]

As we have also seen, the CBC was keenly aware of its responsibilities to serve the diverse interests of Canadians, and attempted to incorporate these interests into its programming through a variety of measures, including its preoccupation with meeting the multi-faceted criteria of "balance" and a variety of audience research measures (McKay 1976; Eaman 1994). As Stuart McFadyen, Colin Hoskins, and David Gillen (1980, 261) illustrate, despite critics' charges that CBC programming through the 1970s was "virtually indistinguishable from that of the private broadcasters ... CBC does, in line with its mandate, provide a better overall balance of programming and more diversity than the Canadian private networks or groupings." Also, throughout this period, the CBC continued to spend a much higher percentage of income on program production than the private sector, and continued to be Canada's largest "patron of the arts" (Babe 1979, 110). And while its efforts to anticipate and meet all of the diverse demands placed upon it often fell short of expectations, to a large extent these shortcomings were a product of the conditions for which it was created – a lack of revenue within the system and the attempt to construct a national perspective through broadcast technology.

As the 1970s continued to unfold, the CRTC generally managed the system along well-established lines and continued to focus on constructing conditions for capital growth within the system. As the private sector continued to expand, audiences continued to fragment and the CBC's overall audience share fell. Under regulatory protection, the private sector was generally profitable – in some cases extraordinarily so (McFadyen, Hoskins, and Gillen 1980, 255). The greatest profits continued to accrue to the affiliates of the CTV network, with companies holding four of those affiliates accounting for 40 percent of the industry's profits, and the top ten television groups – again generally the CTV affiliates – accounting for 65 percent of those profits (248). Harnessing these profits to program production proved another matter. Between 1968 and 1979, the amount of Canadian programming the CTV network scheduled from 8 p.m. to 10:30 p.m. fell from 22.8 percent to 5.7 percent ([GD] CRTC 1979, 48). Throughout this period, the CRTC's vociferous attacks on the CBC's apparently "commercial" programming activities were almost directly related to its inability to control the private network's programming. At the same time, the CBC's declining audience share seemed to correspond with its greater Canadian content.

In 1979, the CRTC issued a *Special Report on Broadcasting in Canada* ([GD] CRTC 1979), reviewing the system's development over the previous decade. The report illustrated that in the face of greater program choice throughout this period, the CBC network's overall audience share for Canadian programming "declined from about 18 per cent to something slightly less than 13 per cent" (100). Thus, as Canadian content on the network went up, the overall audience for such programming decreased. Whether this loss was simply the result of increased fragmentation or other factors, such as changes in scheduling practices that fractured audience flow, is not clear. What the report does illustrate is that between 1967 and 1976, the overall audience share of Canadian English-language programming remained relatively steady at 29 percent (99). However, within this percentage, the viewing of news and information programming rose from 12.5 to 16.8 percent, with the gain largely shifting to private stations (100). Throughout these years, the private stations also generally increased foreign programming in the peak viewing hours, drawing audiences away from the CBC network stations (Audley 1983, 260, 266). Consequently, as audiences migrated to the foreign programs on these stations it would appear that they did flow through to the private stations' news programs. Similarly, although there is not enough information to support the assertion, it is possible that as the CBC broke up its balance of American and Canadian programming within its schedule, audiences migrated to the foreign programming offerings on the private and American stations, thereby decreasing the network's overall audience for Canadian programming – much as the corporation's executive feared.

The CRTC also experienced problems controlling the cable sector. While the industry was responsive to regulations that could be "enforced by the Commission," it was "much less responsive ... to regulatory policies in areas where the Commission's jurisdiction [was] in doubt" (Babe 1979, 134). Similarly, as Babe (1979, 157–68) illustrates, while the CRTC generally provided cable companies wide latitude in setting rates – seemingly in the hope that profits would be reinvested in cable systems – as with television broadcasters, inducing those companies to convert those profits to the larger public purposes of broadcasting was another matter.

While the private elements of the system were generally enjoying profit levels well above other Canadian industries, the CBC delivered "more balanced and diversified" Canadian program schedules than its private counterparts and, despite a shrinking overall audience share, generally attracted a much larger percentage of its audience through Canadian programs than the private sector (Babe 1979, 101; McFadyen, Hoskins, and Gillen 1980, 261). Throughout the 1970s, however, the CBC's total share of revenue within the system declined significantly, and its parliamentary appropriations were vulnerable to shifting political and economic tides (Audley 1983, 279). Consequently, as the CBC was both pushed by the regulator and pulled by its own mandate to ever-increasing responsibility, it was spread ever more thinly across the commercial margins of the system. One of the obvious symptoms of this financial crisis was that dramatic programming almost completely faded from the CBC between 1977 and 1982 (Miller 1987, 381–82).

Regulatory Ineptitude or Systemic Imperatives?

By the late 1970s, there was a growing critique of the CRTC's regulation of both broadcasters and cable companies (Babe 1979; McFadyen, Hoskins, and Gillen 1980). Accusations that the CRTC had been "captured" by industry and that it condoned "license trafficking" were common, and a host of suggestions for improving both its performance and that of its charges were advanced. Yet, as we have seen, the CRTC was in a difficult position. With the system under both internal and external technological assault, the growth of Canadian program production was imperative if the system was to meet with the national objectives Parliament laid out for it. But lacking either investment capital and/or control over the CBC's budget, there was little the commission could do other than exercise its allocative powers. To encourage investment, the private broadcasters had to be profitable. But once the profit motive was unleashed within the system, forcing them to invest their profits in what they perceived as an unprofitable activity proved difficult at best. Various other regulatory schemes – such as auctioning licences, rate-of-return regulation, or fixing percentages of revenue to be devoted to "public purpose" – all had their drawbacks, particularly in a shifting transnational technological context that was largely outside the purview of the regulator. Similarly, depreciating the market value of broadcast outlets through some form of regulatory fiat and/or directly imposing a cap on profits might deter private investment.[12] Perhaps most importantly, though, caught up in the nationalist rhetoric that has framed the broadcasting discourse, critics sometimes overlook both the central role that private capital played in the larger development of broadcasting, as well as the role of broadcasting in the economy at large. With parliamentary approval, the growth of the system had become increasingly dependent upon private capital since the 1930s (Audley 1983, 280).[13] Moreover, despite the downturn in traditional economic sectors during the 1970s, broadcasting continued to record a strong economic performance ([GD] Department of Communications 1983b). From a policy point of view, it would probably have appeared to be almost foolhardy to discourage this strong economic performance by what would have been framed as excessive regulation at a time when many other industries were failing ([GD] Department of Communications 1973b). All of this is to say that during this period, the CRTC simply followed the path that both the shifting transnational political economy and Parliament laid out for it, and struggled with the consequences.

Cable regulation was another matter. Once a regulatory schema had been devised to contain the threat cable TV presented to broadcasters, other considerations worked against a firm hand in rate regulation. During the early 1970s, the imperatives that were incubating in the field of communications policy began casting a shadow on the field of broadcasting. In 1973, the Department of Communications published *Proposals for a Communications Policy for Canada* ([GD] Department of Communications 1973b), portending dramatic change for both the fields of communications and broadcasting. The document noted that the "regulatory link between transportation and communication is no longer of special importance," and that in a time of "very rapid technological change," there was a need to move away from "ad hoc" forms of profit regulation such as "rate of return" and toward more flexible forms of performance "surveillance" (19). In this shifting environment, a new regulatory framework seemed to be required. Developments in telecommunications, satellites, computers, and cable TV appeared to need central coordination so that cable TV systems might develop their potential in terms of "remote-access data processing and information-based services," and conflicts between these developing systems and those of existing telecommunications companies could be "reconciled to the greatest advantage of the public" (20–21). Toward these ends, the department recommended the institution of a single regulatory agency to oversee development. In 1974, the CRTC published new criteria for determining cable rates ([GD] CRTC 1974a). Among these were "additions to or improvements in service," such as "new forms of local origination services ... the improvement of technical quality beyond minimum requirements ... [and] the introduction of converter service." With these changes, it appeared that cable was being prepared to become more than a simple broadcast delivery vehicle.

In 1975, the CRTC was assigned responsibility for telecommunications regulation, and in 1976 it took over the field. As is often noted, from this point on the commission began to take a less active hand and a more supervisory role in regulation ([GD] Task Force on Broadcasting Policy 1986, 177). But while this stance was generally dictated by a growing regulatory burden, it also met with the larger concerns of the Department of Communications.

As these events unfolded, pressures south of the border that would soon impact Canadian cable systems were building. In 1975, Time Inc. launched the first satellite-to-cable pay service in the United States – Home Box Office (HBO), a twenty-four-hour subscription movie channel. A year later, Ted Turner's WTBS (Atlanta) followed suit, offering cable companies a satellite-delivered, advertising-sponsored channel for ten cents per subscriber (Head, Sterling, and Schofield 1994, 79). As well as capitalizing on the economies of scale that satellite broadcasting offered, the channel capacity of these services began to provide cable operators and satellite companies economies of scope as they ushered in a new era in commercial broadcast strategy.

Services such as HBO eschewed the traditional commercial strategy of attempting to harness a large audience of diverse interests, and began to seek audiences of "special interest" (Head, Sterling, and Schofield 1994, 248–50). In this way, these satellite broadcasters began the intensive capitalization of specific program genres or categories, and also introduced new types of programming. Following in the footsteps of HBO, Turner launched the Cable News Network (CNN). Music video and all-sports satellite-to-cable networks quickly followed, as well as networks devoted to "cultural," "family," and "educational" programming. While most of these services were initially financed solely through subscriptions, many soon carried advertising too. And some, like the music video services, were essentially pure product advertising. Thus, the age of narrowcasting was born, and the varied interests of consumers were supposedly directly catered to through a market mechanism. Later, as the technology improved, satellite broadcasters would begin directly targeting consumers with subscription direct broadcast satellite (DBS) services. In the meantime, as these American satellite networks went on the air, their broadcast footprints bled into Canada and posed a new threat to national broadcast markets.

Crisis and Change

During the late 1970s, the economy continued to falter, and the DOC continued its efforts to jump-start Canada's "information revolution" by stimulating prospective information industries. To fill the gap in domestic computer technology, research into Telidon, an interactive videotex system was funded ([GD] Department of Communications 1973a; Gillies 1990). To spur the development of the cable system, increasing pressure was applied to the CRTC to introduce pay-television. The commission was recalcitrant, however. While a series of hearings on the service were held through the decade, the commission argued that no public demand was found for the service, and the propensity of cable to fragment audiences was seen as a threat to the existing system ([GD] CRTC 1978). This intransigence on the part of the commission was an ongoing source of irritation to the DOC and sparked a series of moves to have the Broadcasting Act revised to allow the government to issue broad policy directives to the agency ([GD] Department of Communications 1975; [GD] Federal Cultural Policy Review Committee 1982).

By the end of the decade, however, the situation began to shift. In 1979, the Consultative Committee on the Implications of Telecommunications for Canadian Sovereignty (Clyne Committee) sounded the alarm on aligning the diverse and fragmented interests of Canada's communications environment with the common purpose of economic growth ([GD] Consultative Committee on the Implications of Telecommunications for Canadian Sovereignty 1979). At the heart of the report was the idea that "the rich countries in the world today are those that exploited the industrial revolution in the nineteenth century; the rich countries of the future will be those that exploit the information revolution to their best advantage" (B. Jeffrey 1980, 15). A number of key concerns, framed as central to Canadian sovereignty, were highlighted, including the need to regulate cable companies as both broadcast receivers and telecommunications carriers; the introduction of pay-TV; legislation controlling the trans-border data flow; creation of Canadian-based data banks; maximizing the utilization of communications satellites; and a new Telecommunications Act. The report added to the pressures on government to address burgeoning communications issues.

Increasing border spillover from US satellite broadcasters added further pressure. Throughout the North, and increasingly in urban locations, Canadians began purchasing satellite dishes to directly receive American broadcast signals ([GD] CRTC 1980). In 1980, government reorganization shifted the secretary of state's cultural responsibilities to the DOC. With this move, the industrial imperatives so long simmering behind and around broadcasting policy quickly came to the fore. In April 1981, the CRTC issued a call for pay-TV licence applications, and less than a year later a range of national and regional applicants were licensed (Raboy 1990, 276; Woodrow and Woodside 1982). Interestingly, proposals from non-profit operators were shunted aside, and all of the new licensees were firmly set in private hands and informed by the profit motive. Of particular note was a proposal by the CBC to develop a second television network on cable. As Wade Rowland (2015, 45–46) notes, the new service would "be non-commercial and feature regionally sourced programming to national audiences, along with programs from the provincial education channels." Rebroadcasting programming from around the country to a national audience, "they would address under-served specialized audiences for content such as science and technology, business and the economy, culture and the arts. They would provide a venue for experimental new productions, and would air some quality programming purchased from abroad ... They were to be partly financed by a small additional levy on subscriber's monthly bills." Borrowing from the private sector's economic playbook, here the CBC was at the forefront of the economic logic that would over the next forty years come to characterize the system, as private media companies would work to assemble a stable of properties across which they might rebroadcast and cross-promote programs in order to increase the size of audiences for those programs. However, in the face of objections from both private television companies and cable operators, the CRTC refused to license the service.

Marc Raboy (1990, 277–79) argues that given the history of difficulties involved in harnessing private capital to the public purposes of broadcasting, all the government and the regulator had to do to resist further adoption of the American television model was "say 'no'" to private capital and adopt one or more of the not-for-profit proposals. He goes on to note that, "incredibly, American style pay-television was adopted amid waves of rhetoric about serving Canadian national objectives" (279). As we have seen, however, in the face of the larger historical circumstances and the promise of cable TV to play a major role in the impending information revolution, saying "no" was not an option as it would have derailed this larger industrial vision. Moreover, the CRTC had already noted in 1978 that only private capital appeared to have the "flexibility" required to deal with the rigours of introducing these services ([GD] CRTC 1978, 40). Indeed, given the inability of the CBC to borrow substantial amounts of money without cabinet approval, the private sector did appear to be more flexible in terms of its investment capabilities.

Given the traditional over-optimism of all parties for the Canadian system to sustain new private services, it was not a complete surprise that the new pay-TV licensees soon ran into severe financial problems ([GD] CRTC 1978, 38). In the face of impending bankruptcies, the new pay-TV system quickly underwent reorganization, complete with rollbacks on Canadian content requirements. Similarly, with its largely "Canadian" program offerings, the Cancom satellite network also experienced trouble attracting subscribers, so it too was granted an increase in the carriage of American programming.

Meanwhile another federal government inquiry added its voice to the calls for the commercialization of culture. In 1980, the Federal Cultural Policy Review Committee (Applebaum-Hébert Committee) was struck to "pick up the threads of cultural enquiry" where the Massey-Lévesque Commission had left off ([GD] Federal Cultural Policy Review Committee 1982, 5). However, while also decidedly liberal in focus, the inquiry bore little of the elitism of its predecessor. By framing cultural products as examples of "merit goods" in the context of a "market failure" that denied them their "proper share of resources and ... incomes," the committee's report unequivocally linked culture with the economy (65–68). Here, the role of the state and its instruments was to encourage domestic cultural activity and help service minority tastes. Prescriptions for the National Film Board (NFB) and the CBC were a case in point. It was recommended that the NFB abandon production and become a centre for research and training in film and video production (264). With the exception of news programming, the CBC too should abandon all in-house production and acquire its "television program materials from independent producers" (292). Increasing local television coverage was seen as particularly important. But this was framed as the purview of private broadcasters, to be undertaken with the advertising revenue they would gain from the CBC's withdrawal from television programming (303). The committee also saw a greater role for the cable community channels, financed by a 10 percent levy on cable fees (303). Thus as the system was poised for expansion under private capital, the public broadcaster was once again relegated to a supporting role.

Generally, however, the committee's recommendations for the CBC were tinged with contradiction. On one hand, the committee condemned the CBC's sale of advertising as undermining "the CBC of a more distinctive character" because it leads to "a search for larger audiences" (278). Yet, the committee also praised CBC Radio for its rising audience share (279) and admonished English television for "losing audience support" (280). Hence, the committee's position on audience size was not entirely clear and appeared to hinge on whether the programming in question was supported by advertising.

Culture and Communication

In 1983, the Department of Communications published a series of papers that sketched out the dimensions of an emerging strategy to situate Canada's culture and communication industries as part of a larger, transnational system of production, as well as details of how broadcasting in general, and the CBC in particular, fit into its larger industrial strategy. The broad strategy was laid out in *Culture and Communications: Key Elements of Canada's Economic Future* ([GD] Department of Communications 1983b), a brief submitted to the Royal Commission on the Economic Union and Development Prospects for Canada (Macdonald Commission). The Macdonald Commission was the crucible within which Canada's industrial strategy to meet the shifting political economic conditions was formed. While it spanned the transition from Pierre Trudeau's Liberal government to Brian Mulroney's Conservative one, the neoliberal tenor of its recommendations was reflected in two key directions for policy development that it laid out: "a free trade agreement with the United States" and a reliance on "market forces over state intervention as the appropriate means through which to generate incentives in the economy, from which growth will follow" ([GD] Royal Commission on the Economic Union and Development Prospects for Canada 1985, 66).

The DOC's submission illustrates that the department was prepared to at least partially embrace these principles. Within this document, culture is clearly framed as an industry, although the document represents the field as consisting of two types of activity, "commercial" and "non-commercial." The brief also unequivocally links the development of both the cultural field and information technology with the deindustrialization of traditional manufacturing industries. It deploys a host of figures to illustrate the growing importance of culture and information industries in creating employment and contributing to Canada's GNP over the previous decade ([GD] Department of Communications 1983b, 29–37). Shifting from the nationalist vision of the early 1970s, however, the brief goes on to note that because of the stilted character of Canadian capital and the research and development expenditures required to build a comprehensive information infrastructure, Canada could not hope to be a full competitor in the development of the technology (11–12). Hence, it was necessary to "rethink its approach to industrial support in this area" (13).

Consequently, the brief recommended that trade barriers be forsworn so that Canada might have access to the "most advanced equipment in the world," and that industrial efforts focus on deploying the domestic market as a set of "seedbeds" within which products might be developed that could then be exported to "niche" markets in the larger transnational marketplace – in the case of telecommunications technologies, particularly for components in larger information and telecommunications systems (11–12). Looking back on Northern Telecom's success in developing digital switching equipment for which it was later able to corner world markets, the DOC put the advantage of Canadian monopoly ownership in this broader transnational market in this way: "in 1971 Northern Telecom decided to establish a separate R&D organization to develop new products, Bell Northern Research ... This was only possible, however, because of the ... fact that they enjoyed unrestricted access to a captive monopoly market" (8). As the brief goes on to note, with this "assured Canadian market," the company was able to sustain the costs of quickly developing a digital switch, which it was then able to sell in the United States. Based upon this export success, the company went on to become the "world's largest producer of fully digital switching systems" (8). Thus, in the emerging communications environment of the early 1980s, the DOC envisaged the fractured blocks of Canadian capital that formed the communications industries as specialized yet flexible producers in the global market for information systems.

The new broadcasting policy that sprung out of the broader framework lent itself more to the commercial side of culture ([GD] Department of Communications 1983c, 15). After more than a decade of sitting on the cusp of industrial development, the new policy framed cable as the "cornerstone" of a new system that would help "sweep Canada into the information age" (Babe 1990, 212). Key to this shift was the planned introduction of a range of new cable services that would provide the programming necessary to draw audiences into the system. Important to this project was a new pool of capital provided by the Canadian Film Development Corporation (CFDC) that would help seed program production – the Broadcast Program Development Fund.

The fund – later renamed Telefilm – came on-stream in 1983 and was immediately successful in stimulating independent production. It provided a new outlet for both film and television producers alike, as they geared their products for the opportunities the new broadcast environment offered. For the first eighteen months of the fund's operation, over 75 percent of the monies provided by broadcasters came from the CBC. Faced with budget cuts, however, the corporation froze its participation in the fund in September 1984, and production stalled ([GD] Task Force on Broadcasting Policy 1986, 365). A key problem was the reluctance of the private sector to utilize the fund. Under its terms, financing for up to 30 percent of the cost of projects might be arranged, but foreign programming still provided a much better return on investment. Consequently, as in the 1960s, when they did participate in productions, private broadcasters were reluctant to contribute any more than the price they paid for Canadian licence fees for American programs. At this time, that equivalent appears to have been about 15 or 16 percent of the cost of these new Canadian products ([GD] Task Force on the Economic Status of Television 1991). As noted in the 1991 report of the Task Force on the Economic Status of Television, "English-language television broadcasters have a financial incentive to purchase 'six-pointers' – programs that garner only six points on Telefilm's scale of 10" (126). While they generally contained little content that was readily recognized as "Canadian," they qualified as Canadian content under CRTC regulations and could be procured at about the same cost per play as US programs" (126). Simultaneous program substitution complicated this scenario. While it captured much-needed revenue for the system, it ensured that the most lucrative elements of the private broadcasters' program schedule were filled with American network programs. Until Canadian programs could yield the same revenue as these American programs, they would remain on the margins of this schedule ([GD] Task Force on Broadcasting Policy 1986, 367; Ellis 1992, 167).

However, butting up against the budget restrictions of the private broadcasters, through the 1980s independent producers proved to be highly entrepreneurial. Caught between public and private television broadcasters, and foreign – often American – markets, they began to cobble together complex licensing and co-production agreements (Audley 1983, 289). As technological developments gave rise to an increasing range of broadcast delivery vehicles in both domestic and foreign markets, deals might be arranged such that, in some cases, "a Canadian broadcaster may pay as little as 10% of the budget" for such programs, while as much as 50 percent might come from the American in the deal (Ellis 1992, 137). By 1992, this flexible financing strategy was so successful that it would lead to a "glut" of "Canadian" programs on the market, driving licence fees down (136). For the most part, however, there was little that was recognizably Canadian in their content. Consequently, once again the Canadian state was drawing on a familiar development strategy and, against a backdrop of American economies of scale and other economic advantages, utilizing a Crown corporation to extend the reach of Canadian private capital in the pursuit of social and economic objectives. The recognition of independent producers as a key component of the broadcasting system also signalled the establishment of another interest with a claim to the resources that the system might generate. Over the next several decades, the CRTC and regulation in general would move to help capitalize this emerging sector.

Meanwhile, by increasing the range of consumer choices within the Canadian system, especially through extended cable services, the new cable-based broadcasting strategy was envisioned as serving several purposes at once: (1) it would head off the threat presented by a growing range of American satellite broadcasters by pulling Canadian viewers into the system and containing them there; (2) it would provide both a delivery vehicle and a catalyst for the wide range of programming and non-programming services that were heralded as "soon to be available" as the information revolution gripped the Canadian economy; and (3) the new investment in plant required by cable companies and consumers would be a boon to Canada's nascent high-technology industries (Babe 1990, 212). Meeting the emerging logic of the larger information economy, much of this programming was to be offered on discretionary cable tiers and delivered on a pay or transactional basis. Thus, the traditional technological divide between centralized transmission and privatized reception was to be bridged by the capitalization of the gap between production and consumption, whereby new technology would be deployed to provide consumers a choice in the expanding spectrum of services provided by the burgeoning information economy.

The CBC was allotted a key position within this system ([GD] Department of Communications 1983a). In the new "multi-channel broadcasting environment ... the Canadian broadcasting system as a whole, rather than the CBC [would] provide a balanced and comprehensive programming service." The CBC was to provide a Canadian programming service that would "complement" that of the private sector and help spur program production. Toward this end, its Canadian content targets were raised to 80 percent during peak viewing times, to be met over five years. Faced with growing pressure from both independent producers and policy-makers, the CBC was to contract 50 percent of its programming from private producers within five years – excluding news, public affairs, and sports. Here then, as a Crown corporation, the CBC was once again charged with pursuing another facet of the role of development vehicle in an effort to support the capitalization of the emerging production industry. At the same time, however, with the corporation's increased reliance on the private sector, both its financial independence and ability to choose the direction of program development were circumscribed.

In this emerging environment, the regulator would again fall back to a more supervisory role within the system, allowing private capital the flexibility necessary to establish itself within this new territory. Thus, plans for the Canadian road to the information age were laid. Cable would serve as a central rail in the new electronic system leading to the untapped Canadian information hinterland, and the broadcasting system would play a central role in capitalizing and building it. And just as the Canadian state, in concert with private capital, discovered ways to adapt the Canadian telecommunications industry to the new transnational environment in the late 1970s and early 1980s, it hit upon a similar strategy for broadcasting. As federal economic priorities took new direction, the broadcasting market was deployed to develop and then act as a springboard for Canadian broadcast products into the transnational marketplace (Audley 1983, 289). Once again, state intervention worked to shape the industry to meet the changing economic circumstances of the emerging economy. The strategy that developed was flexible, in that the broadcasting system offered a market within which a wide scope of products could be developed. Because it provided a range of products at a much lower cost than either of these producers could obtain in their own markets alone, the strategy also met the economic concerns of domestic and transnational producers alike (Gittens 1999, 166–68; Tinic 2005). The conditions that enabled broadcast production – a skilled workforce, readily available production equipment, and tax incentives – were equally adaptable to film production, and so Canada also became a hotbed of transnational or "runaway" film production, which helped to cross-subsidize the production of broadcast products (Elmer and Gasher 2005). The problem was, and still remains, that the new market had difficulty generating "distinctive" Canadian programming. Indeed, the price of market success is often the cleansing or removal of distinctively Canadian elements in the representations these products deploy (cf. Lorimer 1996; Magder 1993, 1996; Tinic 2005). In turn, this direction of development put increasing pressure on the CBC to offer a distinctive alternative to the growing range of transnational Canadian broadcast products.

8

The Rise of the Transactional Audience

DURING THE 1980s and 1990s, the political economic forces that had been simmering in the late 1970s came bubbling to the fore. In an effort to revive the economy at the end of the postwar boom, supply-side economics became the order of the day, and both industry and labour were disciplined to this emerging economic regime. As Thomas Pikkety (2014, 98) notes, in Britain and the United States Margaret Thatcher and Ronald Reagan "promised 'to roll back the welfare state' ... and thus return to pure nineteenth century capitalism." Thatcher's Conservatives came to power in 1979. Privatization was high on the agenda as government-owned companies such as British Gas, British Aerospace, British Steel, and water and electricity utilities were sold off. Labour unions came under attack, and the BBC's media dominance was challenged. In the United States, with Reagan's election in 1980, "Reaganomics" – which sought to reduce government spending, taxes, and regulation in general, as well as tighten the money supply – became the economic mantra. And in 1984, the election of the Progressive Conservative Party under Brian Mulroney signalled that conservative forces had gained control of Canada's restructuring.

In this context, neoliberalism became the guiding ideology of the time. As Harvey (2005, 2) illustrates, such a perspective posits that "human well-being can best be advanced by liberating individual entrepreneurial freedoms and skills within a framework characterized by strong private property rights, free markets, and free trade." In a speech to the Economic Club of New York soon after his election, Mulroney indicated that this was the direction in which his government would lead the country. "Canada is open for business," he declared, as he called for "closer ties and more trade with the United States" (in Kristof 1984). Mulroney served two terms as prime minister (1984–93) and under his leadership the nationalist concerns that had underpinned federal economic policy in the previous decade were swept aside in favour of market-based imperatives. He opened the country to foreign investment, eliminated the National Energy Program, transformed the Foreign Investment Review Agency into Investment Canada, brought in the Canada-US Free Trade Agreement (CUSFTA), and negotiated the North American Free Trade Agreement (NAFTA). Several of the country's key Crown corporations – including Air Canada, Petro-Canada, and the Canadian National Railway – were set on the path to privatization. As Dwayne Winseck (1995) notes, the privatization of telecommunications firms was also a key project of both the federal and provincial levels of government during this period. Most importantly, however, much of the branch-plant economy that had been the hallmark of the Canadian economy was dismantled in favour of further integration with the US economy (R. Blake 2007).[1] As Serra Tinic (2009) points out, "in their embrace of neo-liberalism and globalization, governments around the world are increasingly reluctant to invest in sectors that have long been considered vital components of the cultural and political life of the nation-state." Canada was not an exception to this rule.

As we saw in Chapter 7, enhanced trade with the United States had been recommended by the Royal Commission on the Economic Union and Development Prospects for Canada. The commission was appointed by Trudeau's Liberal government in 1982 and reported to Mulroney's Progressive Conservatives in 1985. Led by John Turner, however, the Liberal opposition strongly opposed the Mulroney trade deal with the United States.

This chapter explores how this context of reregulation, characterized by the cutting back of the social and political responsibilities of both private capital and the state, shaped both emerging information and communications technologies and public broadcasting (Sauvageau 1998).

Culture, National Unity, and Free Trade

Following the 1980 Quebec referendum, national unity and its related constitutional issues remained high on the federal political agenda. In this context, media and what, amid the ongoing commodification of culture and communication, were increasingly seen as Canadian cultural industries – broadcasting, film, book publishing, periodical publishing, and sound recording – were perceived as important vehicles for the communication of culture in the political life of the country. As the Department of Communications' publication *Vital Links: Canadian Cultural Industries* put it, "inextricably our culture and our life as a nation are intertwined" ([GD] Department of Communications 1987, 7). Here, cultural nationalism appeared to be ascendant as economic nationalism was undermined by CUSFTA. However, as *Vital Links* went on to point out, "seventy-six percent of books sold in Canada are imported, 97 percent of theatrical screen time goes to imported films, 89 percent of earnings in the sound-recording industry accrues to 12 foreign-controlled firms that principally market imported popular music, and, despite decades of effort to regulate broadcasting, over 90 percent of dramatic television presentations are non-Canadian in origin" (11). Nevertheless, despite political hand-wringing, subsidies and supports for Canadian cultural producers were buffeted by fickle winds on the home front. As trade talks with the United States advanced through the mid-1980s, there appeared to be a relatively broad consensus that culture should be protected. However, as James Pitsula (2007, 363) points out, "when the Mulroney government tried to have it both ways – pro-free market and pro-Canadian culture – it became enmeshed in a mass of inconsistencies." This led to dissension within the government as different ministers argued different sides of the issue.

In the end, that ambivalence was reflected in the trade agreements the government negotiated. As Vincent Mosco (1990, 49) notes, supporters of CUSFTA "cite Article 2005 (1): 'Cultural industries are exempt from the provisions of this Agreement.' But just one clause down in Article 2005 (2), the Agreement qualifies the exemption by permitting a Party to take 'measures of equivalent commercial effect in response to actions that would have been inconsistent with this Agreement.' In other words, if one Party believes that the other is unfairly subsidizing an industry, including culture, it can retaliate by raising duties in some other area."

More importantly, however, framing "culture" as simply one section or piece of the larger agreement is misleading. As Mosco (1990, 48) argues, "the FTA is more than a treaty that arguably applies to cultural industries. Its provisions promote major changes in political culture, particularly by advancing the harmonization of Canada's political values with the neo-Conservative agenda of the Reagan-Bush era. In essence the agreement is not just about culture, it is culture." He points to a number of provisions in this regard, including the agreement's "American cultural redefinition of a crown corporation" as a "*monopoly*" (emphasis in original). As he notes (and as we have seen), "Canada has built its communications systems on a foundation of crown corporations or public enterprises empowered to advance national or provincial goals. At the national level, the CBC, the National Film Board, Telefilm Canada, and others have prompted Canadian cultural expressions that extend well beyond the cultural sphere" (49). Similarly, as above, by agreeing that "if one Party believes that the other is unfairly subsidizing an industry, including culture, it can retaliate by raising duties in some other area, 'Canada has accepted the American definition of culture: a commodity to be bought and sold for profit'" (Cameron 1988, xvi, in Mosco 1990, 49). While the commodification of culture was well underway before these trade agreements, they mark an important point in the erosion of federal efforts to maintain Canadian cultural expression. Although there would be instances when NAFTA would help further the interests of American capital in Canadian media markets, technologies given form by the larger restructuring of the postwar economy, combined with the impetus to the industrialization of culture accompanying that restructuring, would exert more direct pressure toward the commodification of culture and the capitalization of media industries (L. Jeffrey 1996, 214; [GD] Standing Committee on Canadian Heritage 1995).

The Transactional Audience on the Rise: Pay and Specialty Networks

As the Mulroney government assumed the levers of power in Parliament in 1984, the Canadian Radio-television and Telecommunications Commission (CRTC) continued to implement the vision of the broadcasting system crafted by the previous Liberal government. In what would become an ongoing series of licensing hearings to add new pay and specialty services to the cable system, two Canadian offerings were licensed – a sports network (TSN) and a music video service (MuchMusic). At the same time, to help build demand for the new pay-TV system, cable companies were also authorized to import a range of US satellite services. In another instance of import substitution, the idea was that cable companies would package these American services with Canadian offerings to increase the attraction of pay-TV to Canadian audiences and, as new Canadian services came on stream, they would replace the American services. However, as the American services established Canadian audiences, the new Canadian service providers strove to mimic their programming as best they could in order to capture and retain those audiences. Consequently, to a large degree, Canadian pay-TV services developed as clones of their American counterparts (Rowland 2015, 49).

With the introduction of these new cable services, the channel capacity that had lain dormant for years finally began to be utilized. New levels or "tiers" of service were introduced, and each apportioned a consumer entry fee. Under such a strategy, it was argued, audiences long held hostage by commercial program schedules designed to appeal to a range of tastes (but in the process appealing to none in particular) might be finally freed. It was to be the triumph of the market over the tyranny of technique as new technology finally "solved" the problems of consumer choice posed by centralized transmission and privatized reception. The possibilities seemed endless, as long as people could, and would, pay.

Toward a New Broadcasting Act

Under growing pressure for new legislation to meet the shifting technological conditions, the Task Force on Broadcasting Policy (Caplan-Sauvageau) was appointed in April 1985 to make recommendations on "an industrial and cultural strategy to govern the future evolution of the Canadian broadcasting system." In the spirit of the new economic imperatives driving public policy, the task force's terms of reference noted that the strategy should take "full account of the overall social and economic goals of the government ... including the need for fiscal restraint [and] increased reliance on private sector initiatives" ([GD] Task Force on Broadcasting Policy 1986, 703). The ensuing inquiry became the backdrop to the enactment of a new Broadcasting Act in 1991.

In the context of a broader austerity program, the newly elected Conservative government cut the CBC's $906 million budget by $85 million in 1984, resulting in program cancellations and layoffs (CBC News 1984; [GD] CBC 1985). Still, in partnership with the private sector and other federal and provincial bodies, the CBC's submission to the task force outlined an ambitious plan for "Canadianizing the Spectrum" ([GD] CBC 1985, 25). Ideas included were the elimination of American commercial programs on the English network; a stronger regional presence; partnerships to support a "children's channel," a "commercially supported Canadian TV channel in the United States," and a revivified proposal for a "second CBC TV channel to showcase programs of the regions, provincial broadcasting organizations, and independent program producers" (90–91). Building on the fact that the CBC "provides more journalistic programming than any other national network in the western world" (23), an all-news channel, similar to the US-based CNN, was also proposed (34–35). The document also highlighted the corporation's ongoing economic challenges, such as the difficulties that single-year financing presented for planning purposes (78), its lack of a short-term borrowing capacity (79), and the necessity for funds to make the switch from "analogue to digital technology" (87). At the same time, the CBC also took the opportunity to defend itself against detractors, arguing that it was more efficient in terms of the cost of the services it provided than both the Public Broadcasting Service (PBS) in the United States and the BBC in Britain (105).

Reporting in 1986, the Task Force on Broadcasting Policy set out a comprehensive vision for the system and its role in social and cultural life. With its report coming in at over 700 pages, it neatly summarized its findings ([GD] Task Force on Broadcasting Policy 1986, 691):

> The problems are clear enough: inadequate Canadian programming; inadequate high quality programming; insufficient performance programming by the private sector in English Canada, insufficient attention paid to information and public affairs programming in the private sector in Quebec; and a general reluctance to give priority to the social goals of the broadcasting system.
>
> The reasons for these problems are equally clear: the public sector, which must be the chief purveyor of quality Canadian programming, is inadequately scaled and funded; the private sector, which should complement the public sector at least to the extent of contributing to the fulfilment of the social objectives of the Broadcasting Act, is not contributing enough.

Fighting the neoliberal tide, the task force sought to strike a balance between public policy goals and commercial interests. An important element of the strategy was to increase the scope and size of the public elements represented in the system. Some work in this direction was already underway when the task force was formed. For example, building on policy directions taken in the previous decade, the federal government announced the Northern and Native Access Program in 1983, and the CRTC formulated new regulations in the areas of community and multicultural broadcasting in 1985 ([GD] CRTC 1985a, 1985b; Spiller and Smiley 1986; E. Thomas 1992; F. Fraser 1994).The task force built upon and suggested ways to further animate these efforts.

In this regard, similar to Applebaum-Hébert, community broadcasting, complementing the public and private sectors, was seen as "an essential third sector of broadcasting" ([GD] Task Force on Broadcasting Policy 1986, 491). Exactly how these operations would be financed, however, remained somewhat murky, and while some degree of advertising was envisioned as acceptable, commercial revenue was largely seen as the preserve of the private sector, particularly in areas where commercial stations operated (502). Consequently, even in this vision of the system, private broadcasters were given freer rein than their not-for-profit counterparts.

A greater role for multicultural broadcasting was also envisioned, and concerns over the depiction of cultural minorities in programming and their employment in the broadcasting industry were voiced (535–39). In keeping with the regulatory propensity to have the CBC forge new ground within the system, the report recommended that the "CBC should establish a policy of multiculturalism and cultural programming objectives throughout the Corporation, similar to those developed for English radio" (536).

The task force also sought to "recognize the special needs of the more than 500,000 status Indian, non-status Indian, Metis, and Inuit" (515). Here the sometimes controversial role the CBC played in bringing service to the North was also noted. One Indigenous leader was quoted as saying about the CBC's 1974 Accelerated Coverage Plan: "The introduction of television has meant the last refuge of Inuit culture, the home, has been invaded by an outside culture" (515). Still, as the task force noted, promises in 1981 by Cancom, the private-sector satellite service in the North, to provide a "video uplink suitable for native produced programming and to substitute up to 10 hours per week of native produced television programming" had gone unfulfilled (516). Consequently, the task force recommended that the Broadcasting Act "should affirm the right of native peoples to broadcasting services in aboriginal languages," with two caveats: "where numbers warrant and to the extent public funds permit" (519). At the same time, it noted that the CBC did play an important role in both providing programming in Indigenous languages and acting as a vehicle for distributing programming made by independent

Indigenous producers, and recommended that "as a national cultural priority, the provision of native-language services should clearly be a part of the mandate of the national public broadcaster" (520). Thus, the CBC was again singled out as a key vehicle for advancing the cultural goals of the system. As for financing the CBC, the task force recommended that its parliamentary appropriation "should be calculated and publicly announced to cover the same period as [the] network licenses" (328).

Once again, however, the public broadcaster's role was also seen as circumscribed by the economics of the system at large. The task force noted that the "threat" of American television to the Canadian broadcasting system is "when it discourages self-expression by leaving few financial incentives for domestic production," and it is in countering that threat "where the CBC has a role to play" (272). In meeting this role, the task force recommended that the CBC "be allowed to develop new specialty channels" (286). It was somewhat circumspect in how this might be implemented, however, and rejected the CBC's idea of providing a multiplicity of channels in the growing spectrum of television offerings (351). In the end, it recommended only that the public broadcaster be allowed to develop an all-news channel, to be financed by both advertising and a "pass-through" charge to cable subscribers (303). Thus, once again, the possibilities of utilizing such channels to develop economies of scale and scope, which would later be exploited by the private sector, were foreclosed. Instead, the task force recommended the establishment of a second public non-commercial service, called "TV Canada in English and Tele-Canada in French," to help serve the "legitimate minority needs" of "those of the regions, those of children and youth, [and] those with a preference for arts programming and documentaries" (351).

Finally, while supportive of the CBC's mandate, the task force was sensitive to the possibility that the corporation might be directly drawn into national unity debates, and recommended shifting the focus of the organization's mandate from contributing to "the development of national unity" to helping develop "national consciousness" ([GD] Task Force on Broadcasting Policy 1986, 285; Sears 1990).

In the end, many of the task force's recommendations ran counter to the government's concerns for restraint and were ignored. As well, some of the nuances of its broadened social vision for broadcasting fell victim to the infighting and compromise of the parliamentary process (Raboy 1990, 327–33). Still, important elements of that vision did find their way into the new Broadcasting Act.

Meanwhile, amid charges of profiteering on the part of the cable companies, pay-TV penetration rates were lower than anticipated. To help guarantee the financial success of pay-TV, as eleven new services came on stream in 1987, their Canadian content requirements were lowered and the sports and music services were moved from the optional tier to basic service. A number of new services were also added to basic service, including a CBC English-language all-news channel, Newsworld. New financing arrangements were implemented, with some specialty channels receiving a mandatory subscription fee levied on cable subscribers. A storm of protest ensued as these fees were imposed upon cable companies and their subscribers. As Marc Raboy (1990, 321) illustrates, Newsworld triggered perhaps the greatest public debate as cable companies objected to being forced to carry the channel, private news producers fought for a piece of the action, and "francophone public opinion was outraged at the CBC's proposal to create a new 'national' service in English only." In the end, cabinet referred the Newsworld licensing decision back to the CRTC (*Globe and Mail* 1988). After heated negotiations, a deal was struck and Newsworld was launched in July 1989. It was financed by both advertising and a mandatory subscription fee, and the CBC was not allowed to transfer revenue between Newsworld and the main corporate body; it could, however, share resources such as personnel and programming.

The 1991 Broadcasting Act

New broadcasting legislation was introduced in 1988 but died on the Order Paper when an election was called. It was reintroduced when the Progressive Conservatives were returned to power, and a new Broadcasting Act was passed in 1991.[2]

The 1991 act built upon the 1968 act to set out a wide range of social and cultural goals for both the system in general and its different parts (section 3.1[b]). Set against the rising tide of commercial and industrial imperatives that framed public policy at the time, it calls upon a discourse of cultural nationalism to define broadcasting as a "public service essential to the maintenance and enhancement of national identity and cultural sovereignty," and, like the 1968 act, it charges the system with a broad purpose: to "serve to safeguard, enrich and strengthen the cultural, political, social and economic fabric of Canada" (section 3.1[d][i]). It expands the definition of the components of the system to include not only public and private elements but also a community element (section 3.1[b]). Building on the 1983 policy initiative to promote independent production, it also specifies that the system should include "a significant contribution from the Canadian independent production sector" (section 3.1[i][v]). The act also recognizes the importance of Aboriginal (section 3.1[o]) and educational broadcasting (section 3.1[h][iii]). Among other changes were a new responsibility for all elements of the system to provide a wide range of programming incorporating Canadian perspectives on the world (section 3.1[d][ii]).

The CBC's mandate was further elaborated and expanded to include specific reference to the character of programming it carries, including reflection of "the multicultural and multiracial nature of Canada" (section 3.1[m][viii]). And, as recommended by the Task Force on Broadcasting Policy, the clause holding the CBC responsible for promoting "national unity" was removed ([GD] Task Force on Broadcasting Policy 1986, 285). In its place, the now "national public broadcaster " was charged with delivering programming "essential to the maintenance and enhancement of national identity and cultural sovereignty" (Broadcasting Act, section 3.1[b]). While the amount of money that the CBC might borrow was increased, its ability to either borrow money or purchase or dispose of property was still heavily circumscribed (Part III, section 48[1] and [2]).

As for the CRTC, to avoid conflicts of purpose that had characterized the relationship between the government and the CRTC surrounding the introduction of pay-TV, the government provided itself with the power to "issue to the Commission directions of general applications on broad policy matters" (section 7.1). The objectives of the CRTC (section 5.2[a][2]) were also extended to ensure that regulation might be "readily adaptable to scientific and technological change"; "does not inhibit the development of information technologies and their application or the delivery of resultant services to Canadians" (section 5.2[f]); and "is sensitive to the administrative burden that, as a consequence of such regulation and supervision, may be imposed on persons carrying on broadcasting undertakings." Here, then, the technological purview of the CRTC was extended, but at the same time, its powers were somewhat muted in terms of its control over private capital and information technology. These would prove to be important signposts in the directions the CRTC would take in the coming years.

Competition and Consolidation

As the new Broadcasting Act moved through Parliament, a Task Force on the Economic Status of Television (Girard-Peters) was appointed to study the economic circumstances of the television system ([GD] Task Force on the Economic Status of Television 1991). The task force found a quickly deteriorating situation, with "massive entry of new players" driving "more intense competition for advertising" (23) and higher prices for foreign programming (37). In this context, both private and public television were "laboring under increasingly difficult economic conditions" (21). As the report notes, for private television, "net profits before taxes suffered an annual decrease of 19.4% between 1985 and 1989 and profits after taxes went from 10.7% in 1985 down to 4% in 1989, an annual drop of 22%" (21). These financial conditions "in part created the environment for [increasing] industry consolidation" (25). On the English side, the Canadian Association of Broadcasters claimed that consolidation was "primarily motivated by the need to increase effective bargaining power with US program suppliers and augment Canadian program and financing production capacity." On the French side, "consolidation has linked cable and conventional television to expand revenue opportunities and augment Canadian program financing and production capacity." However, because of the costs of these acquisitions, "presumed economies of scale ... [did] not always ensue." The report went on to warn that "if these trends continue unchecked broadcasters may seek to increase the size of their holdings in other industries or develop non-program services to complement their over-the-air general interest services. In any case the industry will need to rely on a flexible regulatory and policy structure enabling it to devise a business response to these trends" (30).

For the CBC, public funding steadily declined as a percentage of operating income from 1986 to 1990. While this loss of income was offset by increased advertising sales, the corporation was not able to maintain its operations, and in 1990 announced a "closing of television production at eleven regional and local stations, resulting in the layoff of 1,100 employees." The Girard-Peters task force was particularly concerned with the way in which the CBC dealt with this shortfall, stating that it "firmly believes that there were many other areas where the CBC could have trimmed its expenses without reducing services" (29). No evidence to back up this assertion was presented, however. As for ameliorating the corporation's concerns over income, like so many inquiries and studies before it, the task force recommended that "the CBC should receive adequate, ongoing, and stable funding to fulfill its mandate" (28).

The Girard-Peters report spawned a series of meetings and studies seeking to develop a new economic strategy for television. Building on the CBC's submission to the 1986 Task Force on Broadcasting Policy, one proposal focused on developing a satellite channel to market Canadian programming internationally ([GD] Task Force on the Economic Status of Television 1991, 111–24), although it was noted that due to the dependence of private broadcasters on American programming, the CBC would have to supply much of the material for such a channel. With direct broadcast satellites (DBS) looming on the horizon, it would not be long before the private sector was granted the regulatory conditions necessary for reorganization, together with new options for revenue growth. The CBC would not be as fortunate.

Here the uneven way in which the shifting conditions of the system impact the public and private sectors is readily apparent. In the face of weakening economic conditions, private sector consolidation and relaxation of regulatory conditions are seen as necessary and generally inevitable, despite the fact that consolidations necessarily end up yielding less broadcast programming and/or fewer services as reorganization strives to create and exploit new economies of scale. Given that it has been consistently denied the opportunity to offer other services, the public broadcaster, on the other hand, is unable to "grow" its way out of financial crises. At the same time, faced with stagnant or diminishing parliamentary funding, it is chastised for taking either of the only avenues available to it to meet the shortfalls: limiting services or increasing advertising revenue.

Television Northern Canada

Meanwhile, spurred by the recognition of the importance of Aboriginal broadcasting in the new Broadcasting Act, in October 1991 the CRTC approved the application of a group of Aboriginal and Northern broadcasters for a television network serving northern Canada – Television Northern Canada (TVNC) (Roth 2005, 187; see also Raboy 1990, 344–45). In the wake of the failure of both Cancom and the CBC to provide a television service that focused specifically on the needs of the people of northern Canada, as the CRTC noted, the new not-for-profit network was designed to "serve northern Canada for the purpose of broadcasting cultural, social, political and educational programming for the primary benefit of aboriginal people in the North." Supported in part by government loans and grants, TVNC was initially to "provide 100 hours per week of programming in as many as 12 languages or dialects to 94 transmitters spanning five time-zones" ([GD] CRTC 1991b). TVNC would lay the groundwork for the development of a national Aboriginal network.

Recalibrating Regulation

With the threat of a range of new technologies – particularly direct-to-home satellites (DTH), with their inexpensive, pizza-sized delivery dishes – looming on the horizon, the CRTC undertook a review of the system. It identified "three intersecting environmental forces" as pushing change on the system: "changing technology, increasing competition," and, drawing on the neoliberal zeitgeist of the time, the "new consumer." The central technology driving this shift was characterized as the "digital revolution," which was seen as giving rise to a host of new "programming services and concepts" that might be delivered interchangeably through "cable, over-the-air broadcasting, satellite and MDS (multipoint distribution systems) transmission." In turn, the greater choice and customization of services heralded by this new technology was framed as "serving to produce a new consumer environment and consciousness ... [that would] transform the captive subscriber into the discriminating consumer."

The CRTC concluded that in the swiftly changing technological environment, protectionist measures to control foreign competition "would only prove counterproductive and impractical"; instead, the focus should be on direct competition by "aggressive encouragement [of] the production and distribution of more and better Canadian programming" ([GD] CRTC 1993, 4).

Interestingly, in its initial consideration of DTH satellites, the CRTC decided to exempt the service from regulation, and it was only after a 1995 order-in-council[3] directing the commission to bring such distributors under the wing of regulation that it did so (J. Anderson 2016, 178–79).

In this context, the CRTC called for the development of new Canadian specialty, pay-TV, and pay-per-view channels, as well as the creation of a new production fund with contributions from newly licensed DTH and MDS services ([GD] CRTC 1996). With this move, competition between "broadcast distribution undertakings" (BDUs) was introduced and cable was displaced as the central distribution vehicle within the system ([GD] CRTC 1997). At the same time, the threat that foreign satellite signals presented to the system was averted, and all BDUs, including DTH distributors, were made responsible to the larger purposes of the system. With the introduction of these new types of broadcasters, the traditional over-the-air (OTA) broadcasters began to be referred to as conventional broadcasters ([GD] CRTC 2017b).

But just as Canadian sovereignty – albeit in a newly emerging commercial form – seemed to be once again restored to the system, a new threat was quickly taking shape. In the United States, Vice President Al Gore was touting plans for an "information superhighway" rising out of the impending digital revolution. Not to be left behind, the newly elected Liberal government used the January 1994 Throne Speech to announce its commitment to develop a strategy for a Canadian "Information Highway" ([GD] CRTC 1995a; [GD] IHAC 1997).

Following along the lines recommended in the report of the Task Force on the Economic Status of Television, key among the new policy directions underpinning this initiative was a 1996 Convergence Policy Statement that broke the sixty-year-old regulatory tradition of keeping telecommunications and broadcasting markets separate ([GD] Industry Canada 1996; see also Winseck 1998). Central to the strategy was creating a policy environment that would allow capital more flexibility and encourage competition between what had been seen as different industrial sectors. The policy set the terms for the entry of telecommunications and broadcasting companies into each other's markets. Cable and telecommunications companies would be able to compete on each other's turf, and telecommunications companies would be able to provide broadcast programming services as long as the broadcast licence was held by a structurally separate entity. The policy also noted that in the emerging environment, there was still "a need for greater clarity with respect to the services to be included or excluded from the definition of broadcast programs" ([GD] Industry Canada 1996). It would be several years before these policy changes took form within the broadcasting system, but when they did, they heralded a sea change in its structure.

Meanwhile, conventional OTA broadcasters pointed to rising corporate debt and depleting revenues in a call for relaxation of their regulatory burden as pay-per-view, pay-TV, and discretionary cable and satellite services attracted increasing audience shares (L. Jeffrey 1996). Subsequently, in a move to further relax the regulatory environment, "in the 1994 license renewal decisions for local broadcasters, the CRTC offered private broadcasters a choice of regulatory mechanisms – content quotas or proportion of program spending in specific target program areas" (L. Jeffrey 1996, 250; [GD] CRTC 1995b). In concert with Telefilm and ever-entrepreneurial independent producers, these regulations began to boost private broadcasters' participation in production. Through co-productions between American networks and Canadian broadcast companies arranged by these producers, programs such as CTV's *Due South* began appearing on both US and Canadian broadcast schedules at the same time. In terms of content, such programs were not distinctively Canadian, but they met Canadian broadcasting content regulations and at the same time captured the benefits of simultaneous program substitution rules for Canadian broadcasters ([GD] Department of Canadian Heritage 1996, 224–26). They were thus able to sidestep the "cultural discount" of distinctively Canadian programs, marking to some degree a convergence of Canadian and American program markets (Tinic 2005).

Despite these machinations, the CBC continued to dominate the scheduling of Canadian programming through the early 1990s. As Tony Manera, CBC president from 1992 to 1995, points out:

> For the 1992–93 broadcast year, in the peak viewing hours of 7 to 11 p.m., the CBC's English Television schedule was 85 percent Canadian; for CTV the figure was 24 percent and for Global 25 percent. During the same time slot, Radio-Canada was 84 percent Canadian, while private networks TVA and Television Quatre Saisons trailed at 59 percent and 50 percent respectively. During the 1994–95 season, between 7 and 11 p.m., CTV carried only one hour per week of Canadian news and information programming, W5. Global did no better, with its one-hour Canwest/Global Showcase. During the same period, CBC English Television carried ten Canadian information programs: Prime Time News, Sunday Report, Venture, Contact with Hana Gartner, The 5th Estate, Man Alive, Market Place, Witness, The Nature of Things, and The Human Race. (Manera 1996, 21)

Deregulatory forces were also gripping the telecommunications sector. In 1992, the CRTC opened up long distance telephone markets to competition. As the Broadcasting and Telecommunications Legislative Review Panel would note some years later, "the implications of the CRTC's decision were enormous: over the next decades, new players entered the telecommunications market, challenging the dominance of the telephone companies and seeking access to their networks and services. Canadians saw growth not only in long-distance telephone competition but also in competition based on wireless and broadband technologies" ([GD] BTLR 2020, 62).

In an attempt to keep up with shifting technologies, a new Telecommunications Act was enacted in 1993.[4] Despite the fact that at this point in history broadcasting and telecommunications were treated as separate industries, under the terms of the act telecommunications was defined as "the emission, transmission or reception of intelligence by any wire cable, radio, optical or other electromagnetic system, or any similar system." Consequently, in formal terms under this definition, both broadcasting and the emerging internet might be seen as forms of telecommunication. Underpinned by a nationalist vision like the 1991 Broadcasting Act, the Telecommunications Act detailed key social objectives for the telecommunications system, such as "(a) to facilitate the orderly development throughout Canada of a telecommunications system that serves to safeguard, enrich and strengthen the social and economic fabric of Canada and its regions," and "(d) to promote the ownership and control of Canadian carriers by Canadians." At the same time, however, the neoliberal tenor of the time is infused in the legislation. For instance, as Objective (f) specifies, regulation should "foster increased reliance on market forces for the provision of telecommunications services and to ensure that regulation, where required, is efficient and effective." Here, social objectives provide the system with a national focus but also frame market forces as the key driver within it. As Winseck (1995) argues, this legislation reflects "a 'power shift' towards the subordination of the public interest to private, commercial interests," and "a prioritizing" of larger social values such as the "universality" of service "over commercial values"; it also marks "the transformation of regulation from social policy to industrial policy." He goes on to note that "the losers of this 'power shift' will be labour unions, public interest groups, and the general public as government and industry officials continue to conflate their discourse of democracy and communication with the imperatives of industrial policy."

Return of the Liberals: One Step Forward, Two Steps Back

The Liberals were returned to power in 1993 under Jean Chrétien. In retrospect, the Mulroney government's cultural legacy was mixed at best. In broadcasting, boosts to the Telefilm budget seemed to fuel an approximately 30 percent increase in prime-time viewing of Canadian programming (Pitsula 2007, 370). The Mulroney government clashed repeatedly with CBC president Pierre Juneau, a Liberal appointee, and a cut of about 10 percent from the CBC's 1991–92 budget resulted in the closing of eleven stations and the loss of 160 programs, dramatically reducing regional news and public affairs programming and closing regional drama production (Tinic 2005, 65; Nash 1994, 450–76; *Maclean's* 1990). Theatrical screen time for Canadian films remained relatively unchanged (Pitsula 2007, 370), and an attempt to repatriate elements of book publishing failed to shift the branch-plant character of the industry (367–68). In 1985, the Mulroney government also revoked the previous Liberal government's 1982 instruction to the CRTC to deny broadcasting licences to companies that owned daily newspapers in the same market (J. Jackson 1999).[5]

Despite voicing concerns about increased trade during the election campaign, the Liberals, shortly after taking office, signed an agreement to extend CUSFTA, to include Mexico (NAFTA), that had been negotiated by the previous government. Faced with a global recession and high interest rates, the Liberals inherited a government mired in debt. Consequently, despite promises of a softer economic touch, the Liberals generally continued down the largely neoliberal path of government restraint taken by the Mulroney government, and Finance Minister Paul Martin set in motion some of the most severe cuts ever to public spending in his 1995 budget.[6] This move quickly put Ottawa back in the black, but the apparent fiscal success was underpinned by cutbacks to a wide range of policy fields, including broadcasting.

The Liberals also inherited government restructuring. In a move that was seen at the time as an attempt to separate cultural and economic concerns, many of the responsibilities of the Department of Communications (DOC) were transferred to the newly created Department of Canadian Heritage just prior to the election. Telecommunications, apart from broadcasting, went to a newly created Department of Industry in 1995. In the face of what soon became the convergence of the broadcasting and telecommunications sectors, coupled with the emerging information and communication technologies (ICTs) that straddled these policy streams, this separation would hinder coordinated policy action for years to come (Barney 2004; [GD] Innovation, Science and Economic Development Canada 2020).

Pay-TV Takes Hold
With the increasing number of satellite and pay-TV services, audience fragmentation accelerated during the 1990s. Although the CBC and over-the-air stations were all carried on the growing cable and satellite distribution services, the growing number of channel options saw the English CBC's share fall from

12.9 percent in 1993 to 7.1 percent in 2003. The share of conventional stations fell from 44.1 percent to 35.1 percent, and the new discretionary channels rose from 6.2 percent to 16.4 percent during the same period ([GD] CRTC 2004, 47). In this context, the fragmenting market continued to undermine the profitability of television,[7] and private operators continued to cope with these events by reassembling audiences across different broadcast properties through mergers and acquisitions (Hatton 2002). Owning new discretionary channels offered opportunities for private broadcasters to both cross-promote and rebroadcast programming, but the CRTC continued to refuse the CBC's request to develop discretionary channels where it might accomplish similar ends. All told, the CRTC turned down eight such applications by the CBC between 1989 and 1999 ([GD] Standing Committee on Canadian Heritage 2003, 595).

Pressure from the private sector and the CRTC also worked to limit the CBC's actions in terms of the channels it did have. In October 1997, Baton Broadcasting and the Canadian Association of Broadcasters complained to the CRTC that, in contravention of the CBC's licensing agreement, it was airing the comedy programs *This Hour Has 22 Minutes* and *Air Farce* on CBC News-world. As Tinic (2005, 125) illustrates, these programs, initially aired on the main network, were attracting audiences of a million or more "in their second airing on CBC Newsworld ... and [t]heir scheduling coincided with the rerun hour of American syndicated programming on the private stations ... thus drawing audiences away from the commercial broadcasters." The CBC countered the private broadcasters' "grievance by stating that since both programs were satires of news and current affairs they did not violate the 'news only' licensing requirement of Newsworld." As Tinic (2005, 26) goes on to point out, despite overwhelming public support for the CBC's position, the CRTC ruled that such programs were not "a suitable component of a specialty news service such as CBC Newsworld," and ordered them removed. Interestingly, in 2005 the CRTC allowed Bell Globemedia to add sports-related film and comedy programming to the schedules of its English and French specialty sports channels (G. O'Brien 2005).

As the system was extended under the hand of private capital, the public sector experienced other setbacks. As the Liberals worked to reduce the federal deficit during the 1990s, the CBC again suffered a series of budget cuts. Measured in constant dollars, its parliamentary allocation fell from a high of $1.031 billion in 1992–93 to a low of $691 million in 1997–98 (Ménard [2013] 2016, 7). A 1995 cut led then CBC president Tony Manera to resign rather than preside over the ensuing corporate restructuring. As Tinic (2005, 182n7) illustrates, "between December 1996 and May 1997 there were several high-profile grass-roots campaigns organized to protest continuing funding cuts to the CBC." These protests went unheeded by government, however, and by 1998 the CBC's full-time staff was reduced to half its 1984 level (Friends of Canadian Media 2001). To a large degree, these cuts impacted regional and local programming as the CBC withdrew from smaller centres into Montreal and Toronto ([GD] Standing Committee on Canadian Heritage 2003, 203–7). Thus, the ambitious plans of the mid-1980s for increasing the corporation's regional presence were largely shelved.

In the midst of the Liberals' deficit reduction efforts, the minister of heritage struck the Mandate Review Committee to provide a "fundamental review of its support to, and mandates of, the CBC, NFB, and Telefilm Canada ... at a time of great financial and technological challenge" ([GD] Department of Canadian Heritage 1996, xi).The committee noted that the CBC seemed to be drawing away from its public broadcasting mandate: "on the English side, viewers have been offered a significant increase in the volume of sports, more emphasis on popular drama and variety, and continued emphasis on using the late afternoon period for syndicated American entertainment – instead of programming more suited to young, after school viewers" (71). While the committee's concerns with Radio-Canada were somewhat different, the commercial impetus to become more "entertaining" was noted and criticized there as well (72–73). In the face of an apparent slide to more popular programming, the committee's general recommendations focused on keeping up "television news and current affairs in local communities across the country," continuing the "tradition of thoughtful, long form documentaries," and "drama that reflects the rhythms of daily life in this country" (75, 78). More specifically, it recommended that the corporation provide a "high quality alternative ... in the areas of 'news and current affairs journalism ... distinctively Canadian drama, in arts and science, in children's programming ... unique Canadian comedy and variety programming'" (100). Other recommendations included abandoning American commercial programming, dramatically reducing emphasis on sports, and "phas[ing] out commercial advertising activities" (101). Interestingly, these recommendations did not entail any changes to the CBC's existing mandate. Rather, the committee focused on how the corporation was apparently operationalizing its mandate, and generally admonished it to move further into areas underserved by the private sector. Here, then, the committee might be seen as playing to the logic of the Crown corporation as a development vehicle.

Two other recommendations were more explicit. While recognizing that the "CBC already has a significant presence on the Internet," the Mandate Review Committee believed "that the CBC must be able to experiment with new media, and, over time assume a leadership role as a content provider in this field." Consequently, in its only legislative recommendation regarding the corporation's mandate, it proposed that the wording in the Broadcasting Act be changed "to ensure that it allows the CBC to become a content provider in new and emerging media" (123). Similarly, following up on the logic employed in 1983 when the government tasked the CBC with developing the independent production sector, the committee also recommended that "the majority of its programming (outside of news, current affairs, and sports) should be produced by the independent production community" (102). This latter recommendation was somewhat puzzling, however, given the committee's earlier observation that "for compelling economic reasons, an increasing amount of Canadian independent production is now being produced primarily for the American market and for American audiences ... If we want to create an indigenous Canadian drama industry that reflects the rhythms of daily life in this country, it is increasingly clear that most of that responsibility will have to fall on the CBC and Telefilm" (77–78). How the contradiction between these two goals might be resolved was not immediately clear.

To pay for these changes, the committee recommended a levy on "all distributors of electronic communications," including "cable, direct to home satellite companies, and other communications services such as telephone companies" (141). However, the levy was never implemented and funds to expedite the committee's recommendations were never forthcoming. While the CBC experienced some financial relief in the form of increases to its parliamentary appropriation in the short term, budget cuts continued into the new millennium.

Meanwhile, not-for-profit television came under attack on another front, when in 1997 community television was sacrificed to the larger commercial purposes of the system. In return for increased contributions to program production funds such as the Broadcast Fund, the CRTC ruled that cable companies would no longer be required to provide a community channel ([GD] Standing Committee on Canadian Heritage 2003, 333–41). In light of the companies' ownership of growing stables of specialty channels that as a condition of licence were required to air Canadian programming, this gave those companies a way to directly profit from the fund rather than sink it into a venture that offered no direct economic return.

Soldiering On

With the growing number of pay and specialty TV channels – or "discretionary services," as they would come to be known, covering topics from history to science and sports to nature – being launched, it seemed as though the scope of the CBC's once-singular responsibilities was, to a degree, reapportioned among new players in the system.[8] In the face of these changes the corporation floated a repositioning strategy in the early 1990s that would have strengthened its representation of regional issues and concerns (at the time, a noticeable gap in the system), as well as create some economies through centralization. But the plan was cut off at the knees when the CRTC refused to allow the CBC to solicit "local" advertising for "regional" service ([GD] CRTC 1991a; Raboy 1996). At the time, this was seen as necessary to ensure the private sector's continued production of local programming, particularly news. As we shall see, however, in the coming decade shifting advertising markets would drive private broadcasters out of these broadcast markets anyway (Robertson 2009).

In the meantime, the CBC stayed its traditional course, squeezing efficiencies where possible as it continued to increase Canadian content in the wake of cuts, and throughout the 1990s it remained the largest single source of Canadian television programming. For instance, it continued to devote a much higher percentage of its income to program production than the private sector, and in the early 1990s it accounted for 42 percent of spending on Canadian programming while receiving only 20 percent of the system's total revenue (Raboy 1996, 194–95). Moreover, the CBC contributed 25 percent more to the production of Canadian programming than private broadcasters, and it continued to attract a much higher percentage of its audience through Canadian programming (L. Jeffrey 1996, 226–27). Between 1991 and 1997, English-language CBC stations and affiliates increased the amount of Canadian drama in the 7 p.m. to 11 p.m. peak viewing window by four hours per week, compared with an increase of approximately thirty minutes per week by private broadcasters over the same period ([GD] CRTC 1999c).

In 1995, the CBC announced that it was going to "Canadianize" prime time, and by 2000–01, on the English side, 90 percent of programming during peak viewing hours (7 p.m. to 11 p.m.) consisted of Canadian content, while the private conventional stations averaged less than 25 percent. On the French side, Canadian programming averaged 88 percent, while the private French networks averaged about 50 percent between them. Moreover, during peak viewing hours, 93 percent of viewing time on CBC's English television was devoted to Canadian content, while on the private conventional networks it accounted for less than 15 percent ([GD] Standing Committee on Canadian Heritage 2003, 190).

Despite its financial difficulties, the CBC continued its efforts to expand the dimensions of broadcasting service and began pioneering work on the emerging internet. Its relationship with online technologies had its roots in its involvement with teletext and Telidon in the early 1980s (Gorbould n.d.). In 1990, it began to quietly experiment with digital audio broadcasting, and in 1993 the first CBC radio programs were made available on the internet (Patrick and Whelan 1996). In 1994 CBC radio launched its first website, followed by a CBC television site in 1995, and the launch of Galaxie, a service that offered thirty digital audio music channels in 1997 (Patrick, Black, and Whalen 1996).

Echoing the Mandate Review Committee, and drawing upon the historical role of the CBC in developing new media technologies in Canada, the Information Highway Advisory Council (IHAC) pointed to the special role public agencies like the CBC might play in developing content for the emerging digital world ([GD] IHAC 1997, 67). And in 1998, CBC president Perrin Beatty identified new media as "a core function of the national public broadcaster" (in O'Neill 2006, 182–83). At the heart of the strategy he laid out was a goal "to create a critical mass of content and services to ensure that Canadians can never be relegated to a back corner of the web." That same year CBC News Online was integrated with CBC Radio, Television, and Newsworld into a single site, complete with text, video, and audio content ([GD] CBC 1998). Beatty's commitment was underscored the following year when the CBC announced that it would invest 2 percent of its budget to create "a strong Internet beachhead in both official languages" and a place for "Canada in a medium where Canadian voices risk being submerged" ([GD] CBC 1999). Consequently, while the CBC was further marginalized within the system during the 1980s and 1990s in terms of regulation, funding, and audience share, it identified a role for itself in the emerging internet and moved toward being both a key source and a driver of Canadian media expression in that venue. This investment was not well received by private media operators, who questioned the advisability of allowing the public broadcaster to expand into areas where they themselves were beginning to move (Saunders 1999; Whyte 1999).

Private Sector "Success"

For private broadcasters, media policy through the 1990s continued to emphasize market liberalization. Amid increasing competition and escalating concentration of ownership, the CRTC called for a review of private television policy in May 1998 ([GD] CRTC 1998). In the public notice outlining the findings of this review, the CRTC declared Canadian broadcasting to be a "success" ([GD] CRTC 1999c). Despite falling profits in some markets, operators remained healthy overall, with "1997 PBIT [profit before interest and taxes] margin(s) at 15.6% for conventional television and at 17.4% for pay and specialty television." Recognizing that this financial success was at least in part the product of mergers and acquisitions, the commission went on to note that "in both English- and French-language markets, ownership groups [grew] in size ... [and] resulted in efficiencies and synergies which should provide increased investment in Canadian programming and a greater likelihood of the export of that programming." Moreover, recognizing that cross-promotion of content was of increasing importance to ownership groups, the commission changed the definition of "advertising material" to exempt all promotions of Canadian feature films and other Canadian programs, thereby increasing the number of allowable commercial minutes.

But while the commission essentially endorsed increasing concentration of ownership, it also went on to specify forms that it found to be of concern. For instance, it stated that it would "continue its current policy which generally permits ownership of no more than one over-the-air television station in one language in a given market," and that, in instances "where a broadcasting licensee owns or has acquired a production company, either in whole or in part, the Commission will expect the licensee to address the issues arising from vertical integration." In the commission's words, "this policy ensures the diversity of voices in a given market." Given that, historically, the profit motive has pointed private broadcasters in a similar direction in terms of both the demographics they try to capture and the imported programming they use to do so, it is not clear what form of diversity the commission thought it was promoting. Moreover, despite the seeming financial strength noted above, the policy also set out what the commission called "a more flexible policy framework" for Canadian content, increasing the range of programming that qualified as "priority programming" and removing programming spending caps. The commission also provided added flexibility to its definition of Canadian content, allowing private broadcasters 125 percent credit for every hour of Canadian drama aired during peak viewing hours that met with six to nine Canadian Audio-Visual Certification Office (CAVCO) points and 150 percent credit for every hour that met with ten CAVCO points ([GD] CRTC 1999c).[9]

As Antonia Zerbisias (2005), media critic for the *Toronto Star* noted, one of the worst things about these changes was that they gave "networks the 'flexibility' to run cheap infotainment and reality TV instead of labour intensive drama." And that is what private broadcasters did, taking advantage of the change in regulations to run "reality shows" as "long form documentary" and using "regional programs (like cooking shows) and entertainment magazines" to meet their quotas for priority programs (CCAU 2002; MacDonald 2002). Moreover, as pointed out by the Coalition of Canadian Audiovisual Unions (CCAU), the new regulations further incentivized the production of cheap "generic" programming, with little or no Canadian cultural representation (CCAU 2002):

> While the new policy maintained a 150% time credit incentive for 10-out-of-10 drama ... it eroded this incentive by introducing a new 125% incentive for six-out-of-10 drama – "industrial" or generic drama driven by sales to the U.S. market. With license fees from U.S. cable channels in their financing structure, these series can be offered to Canadian broadcasters much more cheaply than an indigenous drama ($100,000 an hour compared with $250,000 an hour).

In the face of these changes in regulation, the production of Canadian drama fell by over 50 percent between 1999 and 2002 (CCAU 2002). Consequently, as the broadcasting system expanded in the hands of private capital through the 1990s, conventional television broadcasters were granted a series of concessions to incentivize them to maintain their already low levels of Canadian programming. At the same time, faced with a series of budget cuts during this period, the CBC doubled down on its commitment to Canadian programming.

Aboriginal Peoples Television Network (APTN)

Building on the success of TVNC, the Aboriginal Peoples Television Network (APTN) was launched in September 1999. Financed largely through a mandatory $0.15 subscription fee from cable and satellite providers, in 2002 "it received $15.8 million in subscription fees," $2.1 million from the Department of Canadian Heritage, and a further $4 million through advertising and other sources, for total revenues of nearly $22 million ([GD] Standing Committee on Canadian Heritage 2003, 226). As a condition of licence, it was required to devote not less than 90 percent of the broadcast year and not less than 90 percent of the evening broadcast period to Canadian programs. The CRTC also noted that "APTN committed to broadcast programming that 'will reflect an appropriate balance among the needs of all Aboriginal people, including First Nations, Inuit and Metis' and is relevant to all regions of the country. The schedule will include 30 hours of programming in Aboriginal languages each week, with up to 15 different Aboriginal languages being used ... APTN also made a commitment to offer a minimum of 18 hours of French-language programming each week beginning in the first year of operation" ([GD] CRTC 1999a). The Canadian Cable Television Association (CCTA) – the cable operators' largest lobby organization – strongly objected to the channel receiving mandatory service, instead arguing that it should be licensed as a regular specialty pay-TV service. In the end, however, the mandatory designation prevailed (Roth 2005, 202–3). While the establishment of the new network was a victory for the representation of First Nations and Métis peoples, apart from very marginally increasing the price of service for BDU's, the very large commitment to Canadian content and specific language commitments posed no threat to the revenues of BDUs or private broadcasters.

Into the New Century: The Internet

In May 1999, as the private sector digested the new Convergence Policy and the CRTC's vision of acceptable forms of concentration of ownership, the CRTC announced that it would not regulate the internet. In its public notice on new media ([GD] CRTC 1999b), the CRTC concluded that the internet was not subject to either the Telecommunications Act or the Broadcast Act, and for those services that did fall under the legal definition of broadcasting – digital audio and audiovisual signals – "the Commission has concluded that regulation is not necessary to achieve the objectives of the Broadcasting Act." The CRTC reported that, in terms of Canadian content, an estimated 5 percent of the world's websites were Canadian, and it determined that new media had no detrimental impact on radio or television advertising markets. It went on to note that websites specializing in "offensive and illegal content," such as pornography and hate messages, were already covered by the Criminal Code of Canada. In a self-serving comment tinged with unconscious prescience, Michael McCabe of the Canadian Association of Broadcasters was quoted as saying that "radio and television broadcasting had 'enormous costs' that the internet industry did not," but that the CRTC "can always ease regulations for the traditional broadcasters ... So that if they find themselves facing direct competition from the internet, it will be on a more level playing field" ([GD] CBC 2019b). In time, this decision would unleash a whole new set of pressures on the system at large, and the CBC in particular, as advertising dollars began to shift to new media, and foreign digital streaming services further fragmented Canadian audiences – much in the same way that cable and satellite broadcasting had done decades earlier.

While the CRTC was downplaying the impact the internet might have on the broadcasting system, media content began to slip through the fingers of traditional providers. In June 1999, the recording industry was disrupted as Napster provided a means for people to share music files across the internet. A few months later, television broadcasting came under attack as Toronto upstart iCraveTV began retransmitting the signals of Canadian and American TV stations on the internet. The company claimed that as long as they were prepared to pay a fee for the right to rebroadcast the signal, what they were doing was perfectly legal. Under a wave of lawsuits, however, it shut down a few months later (Evans 2000). But as high-speed internet became increasingly available in the first few years of the new century, webcasting, or "streaming," as it would later become known, was anticipated to rise dramatically (Tuck 2000).

Convergence

In the year 2000, three major cross-media ownership deals built on the 1996 Convergence Policy and the 1999 ownership pronouncement to radically alter the Canadian mediascape. Canwest Global Communications, owner of the Global Television Network, purchased the Southam newspaper group and a 50-percent share in the *National Post*, one of Canada's two national newspapers, from Hollinger Corporation. Bell Canada Enterprises (BCE), Canada's largest telecommunications company, purchased the Canadian Television Network (CTV), the country's largest private television network, and then struck an alliance with Thomson Newspapers, publisher of the *Globe and Mail,* Canada's principal national daily newspaper, to form Bell Globemedia. In Quebec, Quebecor, one of Canada's largest newspaper groups, purchased Videotron, the largest cable service provider in Quebec, and the private French-language television network TVA. Taken together, these deals represented a massive increase in the concentration of media ownership, particularly in terms of cross-media ownership.

These early steps toward convergence were only the first in what would be a long struggle to craft corporate ownership structures that might capitalize on the peculiar political economy of Canadian media markets. As Winseck (2022) well illustrates, by 2019 five heavily integrated media conglomerates dominated what he terms the Canadian "media network economy." The forces shaping that corporate consolidation were complex and include shifting advertising practices and fragmenting audiences brought on by specialty and pay-TV channels; advertising markets shifting from local and regional to national focus; and the migration of advertising dollars from television and newspapers to the internet ([GD] Standing Committee on Canadian Heritage 2003, 13–14). For our purposes, the key features of the history of the system between this first major iteration of corporate media convergence and its contemporary form are the ways in which the larger political economy helped shape the growth of the CBC and other not-for-profit broadcasters.

Shifting Political and Economic Currents

The first CRTC decision of the new millennium focused on licence renewal for CBC English-language television and radio. While all licences were renewed, the CRTC's recommendations in its decision were particularly telling regarding the forces at play within the system at the time and the commission's perspective on the CBC's role within that shifting environment. Following up on the CBC's own commitments to develop more regional and local programming, the CRTC underscored its concern that the corporation move in that direction. As the decision states, "the Commission considers that it is absolutely necessary for the CBC to increase the amount of programming in the peak time schedule that is reflective of all parts of Canada" ([GD] CRTC 2000a). The decision went on to specify a number of ways in which the commission thought the corporation should accomplish this goal. On another front, the CRTC told the CBC that it **expects** [emphasis in original] the CBC to fulfill its commitments with respect to televised sports made at the hearing," specifically, a "decrease of 120 hours in professional sports programming" and an "increase of 60 hours per year in amateur sports programming." The commission also admonished the public broadcaster "to fulfill its commitment to feature more music/dance and variety programming." At the same time, the CRTC condemned the CBC's practice of scheduling "non-Canadian 'blockbuster' movies in peak time," stating that "the only reason for scheduling such programs ... is to maximize rating and advertising revenue. This is not an adequate rationale for the use of the most valuable time in the public broadcaster's schedule."

In this decision, the CRTC can be seen as exercising its allocative powers to move the CBC away from lucrative advertising markets and into areas underserved by private investment – that is, to withdraw from professional sports and "blockbuster" films and produce more regional programming. At the same time, however, in keeping with its mandate, the CBC had already recognized that there was a paucity of local and regional programming outside of major centres and signalled that it was willing to move in those directions. However, in the face of the devastating budget cuts the corporation had suffered during the late 1990s, money for investing in such programming was at a premium. But the CRTC appeared to have little sympathy or concern for the financial position of the CBC, and instead moved to foreclose on two of the lucrative forms of programming it had. At the same time, there was no concern for how the CBC might fill the programming gaps left by dropping those programs.

Further, the CRTC's concern over the CBC's scheduling of "blockbuster" films ignored the value that these films might have brought to the CBC in terms of helping repatriate dwindling audiences, as well as the opportunities they presented for promoting and showcasing the CBC's other programming. Indeed, these were strategies employed by private broadcasters at the time. Moreover, there was no recognition that even with these films the CBC was still scheduling more Canadian programming in this time period than private broadcasters.

But there was another twist to the commission's concerns over the foreign films. Interestingly, it was not all non-Canadian films that raised the ire of the commission, but only those that seemed to have the most commercial appeal. As the commission noted:

The licensee shall not broadcast in the peak viewing period (7 p.m. to 11 p.m.) any non-Canadian feature film ... that was:

- Theatrically released in Canada within two years from the date the film is broadcast by the licensee or,
- Listed within the top 100 films of Variety magazine's list of top grossing films in the United States and Canada, within the 10-year period preceding the date the film is broadcast by the licensee. ([GD] CRTC 2000a)

Here, then, the CRTC is limiting the CBC's access only to the more commercially viable non-Canadian films, rather than non-Canadian films in general.

Meanwhile, the CBC continued to innovate on the emerging internet, and in 2000 launched Radio 3 – an online music archive directed toward youth and consisting of, among other content, user-created and uploaded music by Canadian musicians. Originally envisioned as an FM channel aimed at a youth audience in the mid-1990s, it was pared back to an online offering due to budget cuts. By 2005, it had won thirty international awards and was attracting nearly two million unique visitors each month (O'Neill 2006, 188).

The Lincoln Committee

In the face of accelerating technological change, in 2003 the Standing Committee on Canadian Heritage launched a sweeping review of the regulation of the broadcasting system. Known as the Lincoln Committee after its chair, Clifford Lincoln, this committee had broad terms of reference that set the committee on a path to examine "the state of the Canadian broadcasting system and how successful it has been in meeting the objectives of the Broadcasting Act of 1991" ([GD] Standing Committee on Canadian Heritage 2003, 642). In this context, the goal of the inquiry was to "determine whether the Act remains an effective instrument for the CRTC to deal with the challenges facing the broadcasting industry and its stakeholders." While nationalism was not explicitly mentioned in the committee's report, cultural sovereignty was a major theme, as evidenced in its title, *Our Cultural Sovereignty: The Second Century of Canadian Broadcasting*. The report also noted that "even with the advent of the Internet ... broadcasting remains the principal vehicle for communicating about culture and identity" (18). Hence, while discourse of cultural nationalism was not immediately foregrounded, it framed the inquiry. The report spanned more than 600 pages and provided an overview of the different aspects of the system and the issues and challenges facing it. The private, public, and community elements; northern and Aboriginal broadcasting; educational and non-profit broadcasters – all were profiled and their situations examined. Fighting against the neoliberal tide that continued to push market solutions to social and cultural issues, the committee gave serious consideration to how each of these stakeholders might, as section 3(d)(i) of the 1991 Broadcasting Act specifies, "serve to safeguard, enrich and strengthen the cultural, political, social and economic fabric of Canada." Among the issues considered were ownership, copyright, foreign ownership, and the digital transition. All in all, the committee made over ninety recommendations.

For our purposes, the Lincoln Committee had some familiar concerns: (1) ongoing corporate concentration, particularly the threats to diversity of media content that recent and ongoing escalations in cross-media ownership presented; (2) declining local and regional media coverage by both the private and public sectors; (3) audience fragmentation and declining advertising dollars; (4) difficulties in getting private broadcasters to invest in Canadian production; and (5) chronic underfunding of the CBC and other not-for-profit broadcasters.

The report noted that over the last decade, income for private broadcasters was "volatile ... ranging from profits of $635 million in 1998 to losses before taxes of $51.9 million in 2001" ([GD] Standing Committee on Canadian Heritage 2003, 255). Despite the fact that the growing media conglomerates were composed of "structurally separate" entities, it was becoming increasingly difficult to tell how that separation was realized. For instance, as one witness from the independent production sector told the committee (263):

> In the past, a broadcaster would typically obtain rights to show a film or series, for instance, over several years for a certain number of plays with some guarantees of promotion. Now they may want to pay the same fees but ask or demand that their sister channels share the right to broadcast such programs as well for an unlimited number of plays without offering any additional moneys and with limited publicity guarantees.

But while tracing how costs are allocated and profits realized in such a web of corporate relationships was a difficult exercise, the cost advantage of foreign over domestic programming remained clear: "Even after subsidies and advertising revenues are taken into consideration, an English-language broadcaster averages a net loss of about $125,000 for each hour of Canadian drama, and a net profit of about $275,000 for each hour of American made drama" (136). American programs also continued to receive the benefit of advertising that spilled over to the Canadian market through print, television, radio, and the Web. However, because of their lower cost and greater popularity, some profits might be made from Canadian drama in French markets.

In the face of these economics, the report illustrates how, despite recent budget cuts, once again the CBC was the largest single source of Canadian television programming within the system. On the English side, 90 percent of programming during peak viewing hours (7 p.m. to 11 p.m.) in 2000–01 was Canadian content, while the private stations averaged less than 25 percent. On the French side, Canadian programming averaged 88 percent, while the private French networks averaged about 50 percent between them. Moreover, during peak viewing hours, 93 percent of viewing time on CBC's English television was devoted to Canadian content while on the private conventional networks, it accounted for less than 15 percent. On the private French networks, the percentage was considerably higher, and averaged about 50 percent between them. However, Radio-Canada still led the way with 93 percent of viewing time devoted to Canadian programming (190). Here we can see the outlines of a familiar historical pattern, as the CBC continues to consistently outperform the private sector in terms of the production and scheduling of Canadian programming.

The report also illustrates how recent audience fragmentation hit the CBC hard. Its share of the national English audience fell from 16.4 percent in 1985–86 to a low of 6.6 percent in 1999–2000, and then made a 12 percent recovery to 7.5 percent in 2001–02.[10] On the French side, the audience share fell from 31.7 percent in 1985–86 to 14.5 percent in 2001–02 (189).

Some of the committee's most trenchant criticism was reserved for the CRTC (591):

> First, the Commission seems to have created a great deal of confusion in the area of community broadcasting. Second, it seems to have arbitrarily changed definitions of priority programming in such a way that local news and prime-time drama have been reduced in importance. Third, recent decisions on cross-media ownership transactions have endorsed corporate concentration. Fourth, the CRTC seems to have lost sight of its cultural objectives.

Here, the committee seemed to recognize that in the exercise of the CRTC's allocative rationale private capital was taking centre stage, and it wanted to restore some balance to the CRTC's decisions. The committee was also critical of the relationship between the CRTC and the CBC. There were particular concerns that the CRTC felt that it was within its purview to issue direction to the CBC regarding the kinds of programs that it should produce and air, as it had done during the 1999 licence review. Similarly, the committee noted that in the previous ten years, the CRTC had denied the CBC's application for eight new television licences, and that it could not "understand why the Corporation was denied these services by the CRTC. Indeed, cable and satellite subscription fees would have supported all of these services; as such, the Corporation would not have required any increase in its parliamentary appropriation." As a result, the committee specifically recommended that "the CRTC's regulatory supervision of the CBC be limited to the approval of new licence applications" (595).

As for the CBC, the report succinctly outlined a number of questions that haunted the corporation: "The conundrum [is] clear – how does one situate a publicly funded broadcaster in an era of increasing choice and fragmented audiences? What is its role? What should its mandate be? What should it be doing? Can it still be justified? And how should it be funded?" (208). The committee was particularly impressed by "the scope, quality, and quantity of new media services the Corporation [had] developed." It noted that "it was clear that [such] initiatives ... are an appropriate and cost effective use of the Corporation's revenues to reach a wider and younger audience. Moreover the Committee was strongly persuaded ... that the future of communications ... will be dependent on cross platform strategies in which online content is used to supplement radio and television programming." Consequently, the committee recommended "that for greater clarity the Broadcasting Act be amended to recognize the value of new media services as a complementary element for the CBC's overall programming strategy" (218).

The committee's recommendations were particularly supportive of the CBC but also sought to help clarify its place in the system. Specifying public broadcasting as an "essential instrument" in the system, the committee asked "that the government direct the CRTC to interpret the Broadcasting Act accordingly" (625). "Increased and stable multi-year funding" was also recommended. For its part, the CBC was asked to "deliver a strategic plan to Parliament within one year" that would detail "how it would fulfill its public service mandate to ... a) deliver local and regional programming; b) meet its Canadian programming objectives; c) deliver new media programming initiatives" (624). In other words, while the committee was keen on securing public broadcasting's position within the system, it also appeared to see the CBC's place as on the margins of private capital working to support and develop services that were marginal or outside the scope of the private sector.

Moving to help solidify the position of not-for-profit broadcasters was also part of the committee's agenda. Visibility to potential viewers, similar to what would come to be known as "discoverability," was a key concern for a number of not-for-profit broadcasters. As a representative from APTN told the committee, while the network was granted mandatory carriage, the placement of its channel in the larger lineup meant that many potential audience members were not aware of its existence. As he noted, "channel placement ... would unlock many doors for us" (245).

Channel placement for not-for-profit or "public service" broadcasters was also a key concern for Bill Roberts, president of Vision TV. Roberts defined public service broadcasters as those that provide "programming to meet a public policy goal. It is typically guided by a mandate to address the public interest, rather than by the need to deliver a return on shareholder investment" (Roberts 2001, 75). At the hearing, Roberts went on to propose that BDUs be required to provide a must-carry "green space" or "foundation tier" within their systems where such broadcasters would be easily available. As the committee noted, "the rationale for such a move is that 'public service' broadcasters require carriage on low-price high penetration tiers ... to remain economically viable, [otherwise t]here may be little hope of their survival in an 'a la carte' universe, in which subscribers pick and pay for programming on a channel by channel basis" ([GD] Standing Committee on Canadian Heritage 2003, 245). But whatever currency the proposal might have had appears to have been curtailed when the CBC refused to participate in it (Taras and Waddell 2020, 66). CBC president Robert Rabinovitch stated: "I am not opposed to Vision and APTN and others trying to create what they call a 'green space.' We are a green space, and will continue to be a green space. I think we should be handled quite differently from those specific specialty channels" ([GD] Standing Committee on Canadian Heritage 2003, 246–47).

While the proposal for a green space was not forwarded, the committee made number of recommendations to strengthen not-for-profit and community broadcasting, including steps for bolstering their funding and making them more visible and accessible on BDUs. For instance, there were recommendations that "the CRTC permit the national distribution of English and French provincial broadcasters" (Recommendation 7.6); that the Broadcasting Act be amended to recognize not-for-profit broadcasters as an integral part of the Canadian broadcasting system; and that the "CRTC be directed to ensure that audiences have fair access to not-for-profit public broadcasters on broadcast distribution undertakings" (625–26). Also in terms of distribution, the committee recommended that the government "investigate the feasibility of creating new digital channels for the distribution of the best of Canada's community, local and regional programming to Canadians" (628). The committee was also particularly "very frustrated by the absence of data on community television and is dismayed that virtually no information exists on what happens as a result of cable company expenditures (approximately $75 to $80 million) in support of community television each year" (368).

The committee also wanted to recognize the special place that not-for-profit broadcasters held within the system, and recommended that the Broadcasting Act "be amended to recognize not-for-profit public broadcasters as an integral part of the Canadian broadcasting system" (626). Here, then, like the 1986 Task Force on Broadcasting Policy, the committee stands out as envisioning not-for-profits as having an important role to play in contribution to the larger public objectives of the system and wanting to ensure that they have a real foothold in the larger mediascape.

As for private broadcasters, the committee was concerned about impacts that escalating cross-media ownership might have on their abilities to deliver on their obligations, particularly the production of news. In this regard, there were recommendations for the CRTC to "issue a clear and unequivocal policy statement concerning cross-media ownership before 30 June 2004," and, until that time, to "postpone all decisions concerning the awarding of new broadcast licenses where cross media ownership is involved." The committee also recommended that "the CRTC be directed to strengthen its policies on the separation of news room activities in cross media ownership situations to ensure that editorial independence is upheld" (631).

In 2005, a sixty-page federal government response to the committee and some other smaller recent inquiries provided a relatively comprehensive response to the committee's recommendations, complete with plans for action in areas where the government felt that was warranted ([GD] Standing Committee on Canadian Heritage 2005). For instance, concerns about the CBC's financial situation were addressed through the provision of an additional $60 million grant for the 2005–06 fiscal year and a promise to set aside monies in the Canadian Television Fund for the CBC's express use (8–9). The government also noted that it believed "that the CBC can play a leadership role in the transition to digital television," and invited the corporation to "submit a fully developed plan for its transition to digital, including HDTV, encompassing both its transmission infrastructure and production costs" (25). However, the government also noted that under the terms of the Broadcasting Act, the CRTC was required to provide some supervision of the CBC, and that limiting the CRTC's powers in that regard "would impede it from fully exercising its mandate to regulate and supervise the Canadian broadcasting system, as set out in the Broadcasting Act, and, in particular, from achieving the cultural objectives set out in the Act relating to the CBC" (30). There were also promises of support for other not-for-profit broadcasters (12–13).

But while both the committee and the government of the day appeared sympathetic to the purposes of public media writ large, a June 2006 report sponsored by the CBC and issued by the media consulting firm Nordicity revealed a disturbing trend in the treatment of the CBC. At $33 per "inhabitant," Canada had the third-lowest level of public funding among eighteen Western countries – not even half of the $80 per inhabitant average for those countries (Nordicity 2006, 7–8). And not only was the CBC poorly treated by international standards, but Nordicity (2006, 4) also found that between 1996 and 2004 "federal government spending on other culture (excluding the CBC) grew by 39%," while "government support for the CBC (including direct and indirect support) dropped by 9%." Over the same period " indirect support," meaning revenues accruing from tax measures such as simultaneous program substitution and Bill C-58, grew between 31 and 41 percent (Nordicity 2006, 4).

Whether the Liberals might provide further support for public broadcasting became a moot point as the levers of power soon slipped out of their reach. In a summer election in 2004 with Paul Martin as leader, the Liberals lost their majority. Elections in 2006 and 2008 saw Stephen Harper's Conservatives win minorities, and another election in 2011 gave them a majority.

Stepping into the New Millennium

The last twenty years of the twentieth century were wracked by political and economic upheaval as governments wrestled with the fallout of the end of the postwar boom. Neoliberalism took hold as the dominant ideology and governments moved to deregulate markets, shrink the dimensions of state intervention, and clear budget deficits. Information and communications technologies (ICTs) played a key role in this restructuring as they were deployed to reshape both national and transnational political economies.

In Canada, trade deals that blurred the boundaries between the Canadian and American economies, coupled with political friction between the federal and Quebec governments, undermined the discourse of nationalism that had helped frame and drive federal policy for several decades. The nationalist discourse that had traditionally underpinned media policy shifted to focus instead on cultural sovereignty. At the same time, ICTs helped drive an increasing array of media delivery vehicles and choices. As audience members began to pay directly for media consumption, subscription revenue began to replace advertising revenue within the broadcasting system, and the transactional media audience took form.

The development of new ICTs also drove the convergence of telecommunications and broadcasting technologies, and new corporate forms that crossed the traditional divide between telecommunications and broadcasting markets began to take shape. For private broadcasters, the competitive pressures brought on by shifting technologies helped relax regulatory burdens and propel consolidations. Here, the promise of new economies of scale and scope offset the impact of fragmenting audiences on traditional media. However, the CBC was blocked from these opportunities by regulatory fiat.

Government austerity severely undermined the CBC budgets under both Conservative and Liberal governments. But, as private capital retreated from its traditional responsibilities, the corporation was admonished by both government inquiries and the CRTC to fill the growing gaps in traditional media coverage. At the same time, driven by mandate rather than profit, the CBC strove to deliver Canadian programs and services that reached beyond those offered by the private sector. Still, despite deteriorating financial support, the corporation was criticized for its pursuit of advertising and the carriage of popular Canadian programming.

9
Plus ça change

WHEN THE LIBERALS led by Jean Chrétien won the 1993 election, conservative power in Parliament was fractured as the Progressive Conservative Party was reduced to two seats and the Reform Party, a fiscal and socially conservative party based in western Canada, became the dominant conservative party in the House of Commons. But in the 2003 election, led by Stephen Harper, conservatives came together under the banner of the Conservative Party of Canada and helped hold the Liberals to a minority government. Harper's Conservatives won minorities in the 2006 and 2008 elections, and finally formed a majority government in 2011. However, as the dropping of the "Progressive" descriptor from the party's name suggests, this Conservative Party was of a different stripe from its predecessors. Undergirded by a western populism, the new party had both fiscal and social conservative dimensions (Gergin 2011; Linnitt 2014; Ibbitson 2015). As Ruth Mann (2016, 15) notes, this perspective

> charges states with the task of doing whatever they can do, given prevailing contingencies, to unencumber the market and the private property rights, implicitly of global corporations, upon which the market depends. Specific to this is the task of dismantling established institutions, powers and narratives associated with twentieth century efforts to make a space for social justice, and a rewriting of political culture to accommodate this dismantling.

While the Liberals were not kind to the Canadian Broadcasting Corporation under Jean Chrétien and Paul Martin, the Conservatives were worse (Taras and Waddell 2020, 58–64). They attacked the corporation in their fundraising letters, ruthlessly cut its budget, stacked its board of directors with party faithful, and charged the corporation with having a Liberal bias. Perhaps the only saving grace for the CBC was that polls seemed to indicate that Canadians on the whole – many of whom claimed to be Conservatives – supported the corporation (Taras and Waddell 2020, 59; Canadian Press 2014).

This chapter tracks how, as political, economic, and technological conditions continue to shift, the CBC continues to follow its historical path.

Falling Profits, Growing Pressure
As the Conservatives moved to consolidate power, traditional media markets came under increasing pressure. In 2003, roughly 32 percent of the daily newspaper industry's income came from classified advertising. By 2012, it was about

12 percent as websites specializing in selling cars, real estate, and household goods increasingly drew away that business (Reinan 2014; News Media Canada 2022). As revenues shrank and digital media gained popularity, newspapers increasingly moved online. Meanwhile, fuelled by satellite broadcasters, pay and specialty TV services continued to fragment television markets. And through the second decade of the new century, platforms such as Google and Facebook grabbed an increasing share of advertising revenues, while streaming services such as Netflix grabbed both audience share and subscription revenue. These circumstances drove escalating concentration of ownership, as media companies strove to create economies of scope and scale. In this context, local media production increasingly became an unsustainable expense (Public Policy Forum 2017; Watson 2018).

Outside of large city centres, the shrinking number of local private media outlets put more pressure on the CBC to provide coverage in those areas. But as the CBC moved to meet Canadians online, it faced growing pressures from the private sector. Against this backdrop, in the first decade of the twenty-first century, both the Standing Senate Committee on Transport and Communications and the Standing Committee on Canadian Heritage (Lincoln Committee) held investigations that touched upon relations between the public and private sectors.

Two Committees

Following closely on the heels of the Lincoln Committee's report on the broadcasting system as a whole ([GD] Standing Committee on Canadian Heritage 2003), the Standing Senate Committee chose to focus specifically on the news media. Its report noted that "the widespread availability and use of the Internet" was radically altering the ways in which people accessed news. "Consumer markets for all forms of news media have fragmented dramatically in recent years, triggering a widespread struggle for economic viability among Canada's major media firms. Media mergers, sales, re-mergers, and divestitures of broadcast and print media holdings have been the most striking coping strategies" ([GD] Standing Senate Committee on Transport and Communications 2006, 3). The committee saw this escalating concentration of ownership as a clear threat to the diversity of media in general, particularly news media. More specifically, it felt that the Canadian Radio-television and Telecommunications Commission's loosening of regulations had undermined the production of local television and radio news by private broadcasters.

As for the CBC, the Senate committee observed that the corporation's audience shares had generally "witnessed dramatic declines ... [but that] national news and information programming ... has maintained an audience share competitive with those of private broadcasters" (20). However, this was not seen as a positive thing, as budget cuts had pushed the corporation away from its core mandate and led to cuts in local and regional news (21–22). The committee thought that a new, more focused mandate should be developed. And, in the face of complaints from private broadcasters, its message was clear: "Public broadcasters should complement, not compete with, private broadcasters" (36). In particular, echoing the CRTC's recommendation in the 2000 English-language licence renewal, "the CBC should leave coverage of professional sports and the Olympics to the private sector" (36). Interestingly, this recommendation was made despite the fact that CBC president and CEO Robert Rabinovitch told the committee that the impact of losing *Hockey Night in Canada* would be "millions in lost revenue, as well as 400 hours of content" and that, if that were to happen, the CBC would "have to seriously re-evaluate almost everything about [its] English television" (Dixon 2006). The committee recommended that, once a new mandate for the CBC was in place, "the government should make a commitment to provide the realistic and stable funding on a long-term basis." In another nod to the private sector, however, it also stated that "this funding should be sufficient to allow the CBC to remove advertising from its television services" ([GD] Standing Senate Committee on Transport and Communications 2006, 35).

Like the Lincoln Committee, the Standing Senate Committee also had concerns about the CRTC's overstepping of its power in the governance of the CBC, and recommended that the CBC board of directors include people who have had experience as working journalists, broadcasters, or program developers and that "appointments to the Board of Directors be reviewed by an appropriate parliamentary committee" (38).

Among the Standing Senate Committee on Transport and Communications' wide-ranging recommendations for supporting news media and journalism were suggestions for strengthening community broadcasters. But it noted that these broadcasters were "discouraged from competing with incumbent licence holders in any meaningful way, and are all subject to a number of restrictions (e.g., low power signals) that limit their reach" (32). Consequently, the committee recommended that "the CRTC revise its community television and radio regulations to ensure that ... a diversity of news and information programming is available through these services" (33).

In 2007, the Standing Committee on Canadian Heritage set out to review the CBC's mandate. Reporting in 2008, like the recent Standing Senate Committee on Transport and Communications, it was largely supportive of the corporation. But also like the Standing Senate Committee, it was clear that the CBC should be an "alternative to the private networks," with greater focus at the local and regional levels ([GD] Standing Committee on Canadian Heritage 2008, 21,

25–26). Similar to the ways in which the CBC had played a leading role in the development of radio and television, this Standing Committee on Canadian Heritage saw the CBC taking a lead in developing new media content. It noted that the CBC already had one of the most visited websites in Canada (57), but was also concerned about the CBC's financial situation and pointed out that in 2007 the corporation's budget was "roughly a third less, in constant dollars, than it was 10 years ago" (110). Referencing the Nordicity Group's (2006) study, it recommended that "CBC/Radio-Canada's core funding be increased to an amount equivalent to at least $40 per capita" ([GD] Standing Committee on Canadian Heritage 2008, 113).

The Heritage Committee was also concerned about the broadcasting system's transition to digital technology and how, with their screens filled with almost 100 percent high-definition (HD) US programming, private broadcasters were "giving new life to concerns over the influence of US programming on Canadian viewing habits" (75). Here again, with its efforts to provide Canadian HD programming, the CBC was seen as leading the way in the Canadian context of this emerging technology, but how the corporation might finance a full transition, particularly in terms of converting transmitters, was uncertain (79). The CBC told the committee that, given the cost, not all over-the-air (OTA) transmitters would be converted to digital, and that some small and rural communities would have their service discontinued. A number of citizens and organizations expressed dismay at how this move would impact the principle of universal service (86). But while the committee made a number of recommendations on minimizing the impact of conversion, how these recommendations might be paid for remained unclear (87, 95).

In large part, the recommendations these two committees followed reflected a path well worn by previous inquiries. While the CBC was admonished not to duplicate the services offered by the private sector, it was also encouraged to both fill in gaps in the system left by the private sector's retreat from unprofitable markets – in this instance, primarily local and regional news programming – and stake new ground in the context of emerging technology. Once again, the responsibilities and directions of growth laid out by those investigating the CBC were generally activities that the corporation had already identified as important to pursue; however, the abilities of the corporation to meet these perceived obligations were severely circumscribed by budget constraints – constraints that were bolstered by admonitions to forgo commercial revenue that might otherwise go to the private sector.

Interestingly, these admonitions that the CBC focus its efforts at the local and regional levels brought regulatory prescriptions almost full circle from the early days of radio and television when they pointed the corporation toward providing national services.

While the Standing Senate Committee was examining the shifting dimensions of the media system, the CRTC was considering ways of offsetting the impact of those changes on conventional television broadcasters. In the wake of fragmenting advertising markets and shrinking revenues, conventional private broadcasters were agitating for ways to alleviate the financial pressures they were facing ([GD] CRTC 2007). Their share of advertising revenue was in a downward spiral, falling from 79.4 percent in 1997 to 64.4 percent in 2002, to 55.9 percent in 2007 ([GD] Statistics Canada 2008). This fall in income closely followed a shift in viewing patterns, as from "1998/99 and 2004/05, Canadian pay and specialty services increased their share of viewing from 23% to 35.8%, while the viewing share for conventional television services decreased from 47.2% to 41.4%." High on the list of the CRTC's concerns was the fact that despite this falling audience, because of the revenue garnered from the American programming that dominated their schedules, "OTA television broadcasters accounted for approximately $1.2 billion of spending on Canadian programming, or 57% of the $2.1 billion spent on Canadian programming by all Canadian licensees, in 2005–2006" ([GD] CRTC 2007). Consequently, the CRTC saw supporting conventional broadcasters as important to maintaining the television production industry. In this context, two ideas advanced by broadcasters were explored. The first was a "subscriber fee for the carriage of local OTA stations by BDUs [broadcast distribution undertakings]." The CBC argued it should also be entitled to the proceeds of such a fee to "ensure it can continue to fulfil its regulatory obligations." The second idea was to remove restrictions on advertising, including regulations applying to product placement, virtual advertising, and limits on the number of commercial minutes allowed per hour of broadcast time.

After reviewing the broadcasters' finances, the CRTC found that despite declining revenues in 2006, they still had an average profit before interest and taxes (PBIT) of 10 percent on the English side and 11 percent on the French side over the period 2002–06, so the short-term drop in profitability did not seem an immediate concern. At the same time, the CRTC was worried that introducing a fee for OTA signals might undermine the revenues of pay and specialty services, some of which were in precarious financial situations. Consequently, it did not support that idea. This would not be the last of fee-for-carriage, however. Broadcasters did have some success in relaxing the advertising regulations. The commission granted the removal of "non-traditional advertising (product placement, virtual ads) from the calculation of the maximum number of advertising minutes that may be broadcast," and "instituted a stepped removal of restrictions on commercial time, with the total elimination of such rules by September 2009" ([GD] CRTC 2007). The CRTC did express some displeasure with the broadcasters, however, noting that since elimination of program expenditure requirements in the 1999 Television Policy, "Canadian programming expenditures by English-language OTA broadcasters decreased from 50% to 40% of total programming expenditures." But addressing this concern would have to wait until a future hearing.

Given the ongoing strictures against advertising on the CBC, the relaxation of commercial regulations was much more likely to benefit the private sector than the corporation. Consequently, Our Public Airwaves, an Ottawa-based advocacy group for public broadcasting, admonished the CRTC for failing "to distinguish the needs of private broadcasters and the CBC" (Beltrame 2007). The CBC also took issue with the decision, noting that increasing advertising time provided private broadcasters an incentive to schedule more American programming and that "over the longer term, the net result will be fewer opportunities for Canadian stories to be told" (Sorensen 2007). Independent community television broadcasters were not included in the relaxation of advertising rules either, once again underscoring their subordination to private capital.

On another front, the CRTC also took the opportunity to push OTA broadcasters along the path toward converting their operations to digital, and set the shutdown date for analog television transmission at August 31, 2011.

The Canadian Television Fund Mutiny

Meanwhile, in January 2007, cable companies Shaw Communications and Videotron withheld their payments to the Canadian Television Fund (CTF). As Jim Shaw, CEO of Shaw Communications, put it, the fund "has become nothing more than a means of subsidizing ... television programming that few watch and has no commercial or exportable value." He was also upset about the CBC's share in the fund, arguing that "the CBC already receives $1.2 Billion from Canadian taxpayers" and the corporation's access to the fund "should be ended immediately" (McMurdy 2007). Videotron CEO Pierre Peladeau raised similar concerns (Quebecor 2007). In a statement clarifying the CBC's relationship to the fund, Rabinovitch noted that "the government of Canada has set aside 37 per cent of the fund – not for CBC/Radio-Canada – but for independent producers who make programs for broadcast on CBC or Radio-Canada Television" (*CBC News* 2007b). Moreover, as Richard Stursberg, executive vice president of English television for the CBC, pointed out, while about "50% of the drama money available" on the English side of the fund ends up in productions aired on the CBC, they have " two thirds of the audiences for English Canadian drama programs. [So in] that sense, it is a more efficient utilization of the money" ([GD] Standing Senate Committee on Transport and Communications 2007).[1]

Following these complaints, the government issued an order-in-council requesting the CRTC to investigate the matter. The CRTC recommended that the Television Fund be restructured into two streams: one for the private sector, and the other for the CBC, educational broadcasters, and other not-for-profit broadcasters ([GD] CRTC 2008c). Funding for the private sector would come from the funds they contributed, while funds for the public sector would come from the funding contributed by the Department of Canadian Heritage. As the CRTC noted, the changes would probably result in a $12 million dollar shortfall on the public side, which would largely be absorbed by public and not-for-profit broadcasters other than the CBC. To help offset the shortfall, the CRTC proposed that the Aboriginal Peoples Television Network (APTN) might access two-thirds of its funding from the private side. However, this still left the smaller public sector and not-for-profit broadcasters with a $10 million shortfall.

After further review, in April 2009 Conservative heritage minister James Moore announced the creation of the Canadian Media Fund (CMF) through a merger of the Canadian Television Fund and the Canadian New Media Fund. While the CMF was not divided into private and public sections – reportedly in a move to encourage "competition among all players" – Moore said the government would end the "guaranteed funding envelope for CBC/Radio-Canada and provincial educational broadcasters" (*CBC News* 2009b). Thus, while in this process efforts to divide the resources of the supposed "single system" into public and private parts were derailed, once again the predisposition of the administrative elements of the system to subordinate the interests of the public element to those of private capital was evident.

Diversity of Voices

Meanwhile two major deals fuelled escalating concentration of ownership within the broadcasting system. Bell Globemedia – owner of the twenty-one-station CTV network, twenty-one specialty channels, and the *Globe and Mail* newspaper – purchased CHUM, which operated twelve local television stations, twenty-one specialty channels, and thirty-three radio stations (*CBC News* 2006a). Cuts to both staff and programming quickly followed (*CBC News* 2006b). In the other transaction, Canwest Global Communications – owner of the Global Television Network and the country's largest chain of daily newspapers – partnered with US investment bank Goldman Sachs to purchase Alliance Atlantis. Alliance Atlantis was a major media production and distribution company that owned thirteen specialty channels as well as an extensive library of film and television properties. Apart from concerns about concentration of ownership, the deal also raised concerns over foreign ownership and the ownership of the company's

$2.5 billion film and television library – much of it financed by Canadian tax-payers (*CBC News* 2007a; MacDonald 2007).

Soon after these consolidations, the CRTC announced that it would "hold a public hearing to review its approach to ownership consolidation and other issues related to the diversity of voices in Canada." It reported on its findings in January 2008 ([GD] CRTC 2008a).[2] Here, an analysis of thirty-one representative markets made public by the CRTC illustrated that in all but the smallest markets studied by the commission, "the three elements (public, private, and community) are available and, within the private element, there is a variety of ownership in the local media." The commission went on to specify both a number of areas where it felt a reasonable diversity of voices were already being heard – such as in ethnic and Aboriginal broadcasting sectors, as well as areas that required further study, such as "onscreen reflection of diversity" and community broadcasting. Here, the CRTC seemed to largely depend on the 1991 Broadcasting Act for defining the possible range of voices within the system.

The CRTC went on to specify a set of general ownership principles designed to maintain a diversity of voices in broadcast markets. While maintaining an existing rule that "permits ownership, by one person, of no more than one conventional television station in one language in a given market," it went on to specify that as a general rule "no one person": (1) may own or control "a local radio station, a local television station and a local newspaper serving the same market"; (2) may control "more than 45% of the total [national] television audience share"; (3) may "effectively control the delivery of programming services in ... [a particular] market"; and (4) addressing concerns over vertical integration, private OTA operators must acquire "75% of priority programming, or 6 hours per week" from independent producers ([GD] CRTC 2008a).

In the face of continuing pressures to consolidate, these rules would help fix the outlines of growing Canadian media conglomerates over at least the next fifteen years. They also helped guarantee that the CBC would continue to face pressure at both the local and regional levels as, with ongoing consolidations, the private sector continued to abandon unprofitable markets.

Great Recession

In late 2007, a crash in the US housing market precipitated by the liberalization of rules surrounding mortgage lending sent shockwaves through the world financial system. Thanks to stricter regulation, Canada fared better than the United States, but recession gripped the economy until the spring of 2009, fuelling a federal government deficit, hammering advertising markets, and reverberating through the already stressed media system. As the economy began to slow, the CRTC held hearings in January 2008 to consider the shifting structure of the broadcasting system ([GD] CRTC 2008b). Key issues at play were access to carriage and the ongoing economic problems of conventional private broadcasters.

In a preface to its decision, the commission noted that it had based its findings on a particular set of principles, including "relying on market forces wherever possible," and recognizing "the increasing autonomy of audiences and consumers, providing them with the greatest possible choice of services at affordable prices." The CRTC also noted that, in the face of "new media and the rapid evolution of related digital technologies ... the Canadian broadcasting system [needs] to be regulated in a more flexible way," and that "regulation be as targeted as possible and impose the least burdensome constraints." Clearly, the principles of neoliberalism were becoming firmly entrenched in the fabric of regulation ([GD] CRTC 2008b).

The evolving structure of the system reflected these principles. At this point in time, six broadcast distribution undertakings (BDUs) accounted for over 90 percent of all cable and direct-to-home (DTH) subscribers ([GD] CRTC 2008b). In terms of programming, two companies controlled over 60 percent of all viewing to Canadian services and stations and, for French-language television, "the two largest companies account for over 55% of all viewing to Canadian services and stations." In this context, access to carriage was a major concern for the rapidly growing number of program services, which included public and private OTA stations, pay and specialty services, video-on-demand, and Aboriginal, educational, and community broadcasters. But while some changes were made to the way programming services were packaged, in keeping with concerns for "flexibility" existing rules were either maintained or relaxed in ways that favoured the BDUs. Carriage on DTH services was of particular concern to the CBC. Because of the limited number of signals it was technically able to carry, and the growing demand for HD services, DTH services were required to carry fewer conventional signals than their terrestrial counterparts. This impacted the ability of the CBC to deliver its local signals to audiences via satellite outside of major centres. The corporation explains this concern ([GD] CBC 2010; author's translation):

> Out-of-market signals shift the audience from the local television station to the out-of-market signals. The result is that local advertisers are not willing to pay as much for advertising at the local station, while at the same time advertisers at out-of-market stations will not pay more for the additional audience. The end result is lower ad revenue.

Given the limited capacity of DTH providers, however, little was done in this regard.

In the face of the ongoing economic problems experienced by local stations, conventional broadcasters used this hearing to continue to push for "fee for carriage." But the CRTC was not convinced by their arguments. As the commission noted, private broadcasters had shied away from spending in local markets in favour of more profitable investments, including increased spending on foreign programming. But while the commission recognized that "this strategy may make sense from a business point of view, since stations in smaller markets are on average not profitable," the broadcasters did not provide any financial information regarding things such as "recent major acquisitions, nor the basis for financing those initiatives or the impact of those initiatives on profitability." Nor was there any "commitment given by OTA broadcasters that any fee the Commission might grant would be utilized in improving Canadian programming or, if it would be so utilized, how the monies might be spent" ([GD] CRTC 2008b).

Although a general subsidy for conventional broadcasters was not sanctioned, encouraging investment in local programming was on the agenda. To bolster the viability of the stations in smaller markets, the CRTC established a Local Program Improvement Fund (LPIF) for non-metropolitan markets. For private broadcasters, it stated that "although all categories of local programming will qualify for LPIF funding, the Commission considers that priority should be given to local news and public affairs programs." The CBC was also given access to the new fund, "as long as [it] broadcast[s] original local news programming." Hence for the public broadcaster, the conditions were somewhat more restrictive. Community broadcasters were excluded altogether. Like the rejected fee-for-carriage proposal, the fund was to be financed by a small surcharge to BDUs (ibid.).

There were two dissenting opinions from CRTC commissioners, one from Peter Menzies and the other from Michel Morin. Menzies was concerned that because the lack of investment in local programming could be traced to the cost of acquisitions, the fund "means that consumers are subsidizing private-sector expansion." Morin argued that the LPIF was poorly targeted and should have been focused directly on the production of news and made available to community television. Neither of them thought the CBC should have access to it, largely because, as Morin put it, "by allowing the CBC to benefit from the LPIF ... the CRTC is reneging on the very principles it established last June in its report on the CTF. Under this new philosophy of the CRTC ... funds contributed by private distribution undertakings were to be earmarked for private broadcasting undertakings" (ibid.).

Uneven Relations of Power

Reviewing this decision and the other regulatory recommendations of the first few years of the new millennium, the uneven relations of power manifested through the structure of regulation are once again evident. For the private sector, centralizing resources is seen as a somewhat regrettable but sound business decision – one that is to a degree rewarded, as Menzies points out, by the fact that the broadcasters can turn to the CRTC to help finance programming when budget shortfalls arise as a product of those acquisitions. However, when the CBC is faced with shrinking budgets and resorts to a similar centralizing strategy, it is roundly criticized by the CRTC, parliamentary committees, and private broadcasters (Canadian Press 2005), despite the fact that it consistently commissions and schedules more Canadian programming than private broadcasters. Indeed, there is a consistent historical pattern: as the private sector reduces expenditures and/or scheduling of Canadian programming, the CBC moves in the opposite direction as budgets permit. However, when new resources do become available within the system, such as the LPIF, there is pressure to exclude the CBC from accessing them.

As for the CBC's funding, while there was sustained pressure and uncertainty over the parliamentary appropriation, there was also consistent pressure from politicians and the private sector to cut back on advertising sales and lucrative sports programming. Consequently, major portions of the corporation's income were consistently under attack, raising uncertainty around even short-range year-to-year planning. Moreover, as Morin pointed out, with the CTF regulations an overt principle appeared to be emerging that "funds contributed by private distribution undertakings were to be earmarked for use by private broadcasting undertakings." This ran counter to the grain of the 1991 Broadcasting Act, which specifies that the broadcasting system is a "single system" (section 3.[2]). To some degree, the resources generated by the private sector are the product of regulations such as licensing, Canadian ownership regulations, and so on that comprise the system at large. Specifying that the resources generated by the private sector under the cover of regulation seemingly all "belong" to the private sector diminishes that sector's responsibility to the larger system and further restricts the income possibilities for public and not-for-profit broadcasters.

The Recession Bites

In 2009, the effects of the recession bit into the system. Advertising sales for television broadcasters fell "8.4%, to $3.1 billion, the first drop in 15 years." Profit margins for conventional television were particularly hard-hit, falling from 11.2 percent in 2005 to –5.7 percent in 2009. In dollar terms, profits fell from $4.8

million (PBIT) in 2008 to a loss of $113.4 million in 2009, the first losses in thirty years. At the same time, advertising revenues were only 47 percent of the sector's total revenue, falling from almost 60 percent ten years earlier. Meanwhile, as a group, pay and specialty channels continued to perform well, with their profit margin rising from 22.1 percent in 2008 to 23.5 percent in 2009, the fifth consecutive year that margin was in excess of 20 percent ([GD] Statistics Canada 2010). In a memo to employees, CTV CEO Ivan Fecan stated: "We believe the only solution to the crisis in conventional [television] is fee for carriage" (in Surridge 2009). Exacerbating the situation, about one-third of private local stations were still unable to secure carriage on satellite DTH systems, foreclosing on their viewership as those BDUs gained subscribers, particularly in Quebec ([GD] CRTC March 2010a).

As the recession took hold, advertising sales plummeted at the CBC. While they were anticipated to recover in the coming years, in January 2009 the corporation made a formal request to the government for a bridge loan to cover the shortfall. But without explanation the Conservative government refused the request and, reportedly, when CBC president Hubert Lacroix asked to speak to Prime Minister Harper about the situation, the prime minister did not respond (Stursberg 2012, 238). In the face of this refusal, Lacroix announced that the CBC was planning to raise $125 million, largely by selling some stations and leasing them back (Quill 2009; *CBC News* 2009a). In the end, 800 jobs were cut after a budget shortfall of $171 million in 2009–10. Regional and local news and public affairs in both anglophone and francophone markets were among the cuts. As Richard Stursberg noted, the government's refusal to help did not seem related to the popularity of the public broadcaster: "The irony is, we are in financial trouble when we're doing better than we've ever done before ... More than 20 million Canadians tune in to CBC Radio, CBC-TV, and CBC.ca every week, he said." In Parliament, opposition parties charged that the cuts were "strictly ideological," and "accused the Tories of using the economic downturn as an excuse to gut the CBC" (*CBC News* 2009a).

As Serra Tinic (2010) notes, the recession met the CBC and conventional private broadcasters on uneven ground. For private broadcasters, elements of the crisis were to a degree of their own making, the product of increased spending on foreign programming and debt accumulated from expanding corporate holdings ([GD] CRTC 2010a; Tinic 2010, 194). But with the recession adding weight to their financial problems, the crisis may have been "the perfect 'crisotunity' for the private broadcasters to attain long sought after objectives" (Tinic 2010, 194).

With the recession eating away at conventional broadcasters' revenues, the government issued an order-in-council in September 2009 requesting that the

CRTC revisit the value-for-signal debate ([GD] CRTC 2010a). Escalating concentration of ownership also spurred the CRTC to revisit its television licensing
practices, so it ran the decision on the value-for-signal (also known as "fee-for-
carriage") question together with developing a new policy for licensing the
newly created television groups ([GD] CRTC 2010b).

In that hearing, television broadcasters won a number of regulatory concessions ([GD] CRTC 2010a). These included (1) the flexibility to attribute 100
percent of their Canadian content expenditures to any other qualifying specialty
service, or to conventional television services, within the same (corporate) group
(conventional broadcasters would be allowed to transfer a maximum of 25
percent of their requirements); (2) replacing the Canadian content exhibition
requirement with an expenditure requirement; and (3) rolling back of the
requirement that 60 percent of the broadcast year be devoted to Canadian
programming to 50 percent. At the same time, the CRTC noted that there was
a "continuing need for regulatory support for key genres of Canadian programming," and that its 1999 decision to remove spending caps on Canadian content
may have been responsible for "a decline in the number of Canadian drama
productions as well as a sharp rise in the proportion of expenditures devoted
to non-Canadian programming." Hence, it sought to re-establish minimum
spending caps on Canadian programming of at least 30 percent of gross annual
revenues. To help ensure the production of what had been designated as "priority programming," the commission created a new programming category,
"programs of national interest" (PNI), consisting of drama, comedy, award
shows, and some children's programming. Ownership groups' PNI expenditure
was pegged to be "at least 5% of gross revenues over the licence term." Perhaps
most importantly, however, the CRTC recommended the creation of a value-
for-signal regime whereby BDUs would pay broadcasters for the content they
distributed. However, the CRTC stopped short of setting the value of the broadcasters' signals. Instead, they specified that a signal's value should be negotiated
between the broadcaster and the BDU. This proposed mechanism raised the
issue of whether the CRTC was venturing into the field of copyright law and
thereby exceeding its powers. In the face of conflicting legal opinions in this
regard, the issue was referred to the Federal Court of Appeal.

Returning to Tinic's (2010) point, the crisis did seem to present private broadcasters with an opportunity. While re-establishing minimum spending caps on
Canadian programming might be seen as increasing their regulatory burden,
as the CRTC noted at the time, the figure of 30 percent was chosen because it
did not impose "additional obligations on the groups beyond their recent historical expenditures." Hence, the regulatory changes laid out in this decision
generally translated into economic gains over the private broadcasters' pre-1999

obligations. For the CBC, however, there was no equivalent relief despite the fact that they faced similar market circumstances as private broadcasters. Without a stable of specialty channels, shifting expenditure requirements between broadcast properties was not possible, and reducing the exhibition of Canadian programming was antithetical to the corporation's mission. Perhaps most importantly, the CBC was not included in the value-for-signal decision. As the decision headed for the courts, Lacroix lamented that the "CBC invests more in Canadian programming than all of the other broadcasters combined. Denying us the same rights held by every other broadcaster in this country means that this supposed solution will not apply to over half of the Canadian content produced and aired in this country – over $650 million last year alone'" (*CBC News* 2010).

The New Media Exemption Revisited

By 2009, the broadcasting environment was in the grip of fast-breaking changes as Facebook, Twitter, and YouTube presented myriad new ways for people to engage with content created by both users and traditional media. BDUs offered video on demand (VOD), breaking up network schedules and services that offered film television programs, and podcasts "on demand" over the internet were multiplying (Stursberg 2012). In the face of these developments, the CRTC revisited its New Media Exemption Order ([GD] CRTC 2009a).

While the commission found that regulatory "exemptions for new media broadcasting continue[d] to be appropriate," the hearing raised a number of issues that were key to the development of the larger media system. Intervenors suggested that just as BDUs had been made responsible to the overall objectives of the system through contributions to production funds, so too internet service providers (ISPs) might be brought into the fold of broadcast regulation by having them contribute to a new media production fund. The CRTC ruled that new funding was "neither necessary nor appropriate" at the time, but it was concerned whether other forms of broadcast-related regulation – such as measuring the kinds of content broadcasters carry and curtailing their abilities to provide preferential access to some content over others – might be applied to ISPs. Having this kind of data would be a first step toward developing a regulatory framework for new media content. Consequently, the commission referred the question of whether ISPs are "broadcasting undertakings when they provide access to the broadcasting content" to the Federal Court of Appeal.

The court ruled that because ISPs have no control over the content they carry, they are not subject to the Broadcasting Act. In turn, because of concern that the decision would foreclose on new modes of financing Canadian content, the Alliance of Canadian Cinema, Television and Radio Artists (ACTRA), the

Canadian Media Producers Association (CMPA), the Directors Guild of Canada (DGC), and the Writers Guild of Canada (WGC) appealed that decision to the Supreme Court of Canada (R. Armstrong 2016, 185).

Another important concern that arose during this hearing – and one familiar to public service media – was in order "to ensure a Canadian presence in an environment of seemingly limitless content, Canadian content must be favourably placed and visible among service provider content offerings." The commission noted that it was too early to enact "specific measures" in this regard. However, this issue of "discoverability," or how Canadian media products might be found in the ever-growing sea of available media products, would soon return to the regulatory agenda.[3]

Meanwhile, the emerging environment presented particular challenges to the CBC. Programs were no longer tethered to certain platforms and, without a stable of media properties across which it might distribute programs, the CBC was at a disadvantage in terms of maximizing audiences for its programs. As CTV CEO Ivan Fecan rationalized Bell's 2010 takeover of his company: "In today's digital age, it is extremely important to be part of a vertically integrated company that can take advantage of video delivered on multiple screens" (Bell 2010). It also had implications for the kinds of content the corporation might produce. With the CBC freed from the strictures of creating content for particular time slots, the question was what kinds of content, or what genres of content, the corporation might focus on creating (Stursberg 2012, 286).[4] At the same time, because most programming other than news was co-produced, the corporation's ability to exploit broadcast rights across this range of delivery platforms was also an issue.

How the CBC might meet the challenges and opportunities presented by this new technological environment were dependent on the resources available to it, but the corporation was trapped between a regulatory environment that tended to foreclose on allowing it opportunities for innovation and a hostile federal government.

Over-the-Top (OTT)

As the second decade of the new millennium dawned, trends that had begun to emerge in the first continued to coalesce. After recovering slightly from the recession in 2008, advertising revenues for conventional broadcasters began a slow slide from a high of $2.344 billion in 2011 to $1.988 billion in 2015, and to $1.481 billion in 2020 (News Media Canada 2022). Daily newspaper advertising revenue dropped more precipitously, from $2.216 billion in 2011, to $1.424 billion in 2015, to $530 million in 2020. At the same time, internet advertising grew from $2.674 billion in 2011, to $4.604 billion in 2015, to $9.624 billion in 2020. As Dwayne Winseck (2021b) argues, it would be a mistake to claim that these figures represent a simple transfer of advertising revenue from traditional media to new media, but during the decade, Google and Facebook quickly emerged as the dominant players in online advertising. This shift in advertising revenue stepped up pressure on the CBC, as hard-pressed private media coveted both the corporation's online revenue and its audiences.

As advertising revenues for traditional media shrank, efforts to develop new avenues for financing content faltered. In September 2012, the Supreme Court ruled that ISPs did not fall under the definition "broadcasting undertaking," and were therefore not subject to the Broadcasting Act (R. Armstrong 2016, 261). Shortly thereafter, the court also ruled that the value-for-signal regime proposed by the CRTC conflicted with the Copyright Act and was therefore outside of the CRTC's jurisdiction to impose upon broadcast players (Lexpert 2013). Thus, two potential avenues to bolster flagging revenues for broadcasters were foreclosed upon.

Meanwhile, in September 2010, Netflix arrived in Canada. In its first year, the content streaming company had revenues rivalling Canadian pay-TV services Movie Network and Movie Central; in two years, the company had 1.34 million subscribers (Rimock 2013). In the beginning, Netflix's business model simply relied on reruns of others' content. But soon it was producing its own original content based upon audience preferences gleaned from the data it gathered from its quickly growing pool of transnational subscribers. Using this information, it married the logic of episodic television with transnational film production and apparently developed a means of creating guaranteed audience hits (Carr 2013). At the same time, it also became a major transnational distributor of film and television products. While, as many had feared, Netflix did not drive traditional TV and BDUs out of the market, it did further fragment audiences and contribute to cable and satellite "cord cutting." Of particular concern to critics, however, were the facts that not only were internet services like Netflix exempt from sales tax but, unlike other players, they made no contributions to the larger purposes and objectives of the broadcasting system (J. Anderson 2016).

In the face of rising concerns from both broadcasters and program producers over the possible impacts that such unregulated programming delivered directly to consumers over the internet might have on the broadcasting system, the CRTC held a fact-finding exercise on the impacts of "over-the-top (OTT) programming services" on the broadcasting system. Here, the commission noted that "the defining feature of what have been termed 'over-the-top services'" is "Internet access to programming independent of a facility or network dedicated to its delivery (via, for example, cable or satellite)." But while stakeholders identified a range of possible impacts on the existing system, in the end the CRTC noted that despite calls "for the imposition of regulatory obligations on OTT providers," it would not consider any changes to existing regulations ([GD]

CRTC 2011). As new foreign OTT players came on stream and their impacts upon the system became more apparent, calls for regulation would grow.

Meanwhile, in the wake of a budget scandal, Stephen Harper's Conservative minority government lost a confidence vote in Parliament in March 2011, setting the stage for a May 2011 election. In that election, the Conservatives managed to win the majority that had eluded them in the 2006 and 2008 elections. Thus equipped, they laid plans for their first budget as a majority government.

A Strategic Plan

Meanwhile, in preparation for a licence renewal hearing that was originally scheduled for September 2011, the CBC unveiled a five-year strategic plan. The plan noted that in the 2009–10 broadcast year, CBC English television's prime-time share was the highest in five years, surpassing some of its private-sector rivals. Television Radio-Canada continued to attract 20 percent of francophone prime-time viewing ([GD] CBC 2011b, 3). The CBC's internet sites were among the most popular in Canada, with more than seven million visitors a month. And both AM and FM radio enjoyed particularly strong performance (11).

Building on these strengths and reflecting the recommendations of both the CRTC and parliamentary committees, the corporation promised to expand local and regional programming (26), and both new radio and innovative online services at the local level were promised (24–26). Contrary to the recommendations of the CRTC and parliamentary committees, however, the plan also called for developing a "multi-media sports strategy" and creating and launching a "best of class website for CBCSports.ca" (24). Charts illustrating the corporation to be a leader in digital services, but only a minor player in the field of specialty services, were included (30). For instance, in 2010, while revenue from specialty channels accounted for almost 50 percent or more of the revenue of private broadcasters, only 10 percent of the CBC's revenue was acquired from this source. Hence, to provide more scope to their offerings, the plan noted that most of the corporation's investments would focus on "strengthening our leadership in digital services" (30). Key projects in this regard were digital-only news operations serving the Hamilton, Waterloo, Kamloops, London, and Saskatoon markets (Alzner 2012; [GD] CBC 2012a).

The CBC also noted how the recession had helped recast the structure of the broadcasting system ([GD] CBC 2011b, 8):

> Those elements of the system relying on subscription revenue (cable and satellite BDUs, specialty channels) were almost immune from the effects of the recession, while those sectors dependent on advertising revenue (conventional TV broadcasters, private radio) were the hardest hit. In 2009–2010, television

distributors reported over $1.7 billion in profits. Conventional TV broadcasters, on the other hand, had combined losses of nearly $300 million. TV subscription revenue actually increased in 2009, while the advertising revenue of conventional TV broadcasters dropped by more than 8 per cent.

In this context, the plan notes, the CBC is "now the only national broadcaster not owned by a cable or satellite company." Not only did this lack of diversification leave the market-dependent elements of the CBC's income in a more vulnerable position than that of its private competitors, but, as the plan goes on to state, "we can expect more pressure on the cost of our key sports properties as these conglomerates seek attractive Canadian content for their specialty services." In the face of escalating foreign OTT offerings, the document also voiced concern over Canadians' abilities to "access to a diverse range of Canadian content in the new environment" ([GD] CBC 2011a, 18).

A number of risks to the strategic plan were also noted, such as the loss of the $60 million one-time funding for programming, a possible 5–10 percent cut in the parliamentary appropriation in the 2012 budget, and the possible loss of the Local Program Improvement Fund ($37 million) (36–37). In an apparent show of optimism, however, the corporation launched an internet radio platform – CBC Music – showcasing Canadian artists in February 2012.

Budget Blues Meet the Licence Renewal
In March 2012, the federal government presented its budget. Amid large cuts to the public service, the CBC's budget was cut by 10 percent. The licence hearing was delayed while the corporation assessed the impact on its plans ([GD] CBC 2012b).

When the licence hearings did get underway, the CBC argued that the corporation should enjoy more regulatory flexibility, as had been granted to the private sector in 2009 ([GD] CRTC 2013a). Key among such requests were a proposal to begin national advertising on the CBC's FM networks, relaxing quotas on children's programming, and loosening PNI exhibition requirements, similar to what the private sector had been granted in 2011 (R. Armstrong 2016, 109). The advertising proposal drew particular ire from both private radio broadcasters and Radio 2 fans and intervenors expressed concerns that any loosening to the PNI commitments would have serious consequences for both the types of programming aired by the corporation and its commitment to independent producers. And a number of private broadcasters were concerned that additional spending on digital media would come at the expense of traditional services.

Whether the CBC left the licence renewal process with more flexible terms of regulation is difficult to assess. One thing that was clear, however, was that while financial and technological pressures pressed upon the corporation, a wide range of interests all sought to put their stamp on the character of its operations.

Perhaps more important, however, was the impact that the Conservatives' budget cuts had on the organization. Over the next several years more than 650 jobs were lost; news bureaus in Africa and Latin America were closed; in-house documentary production, once a hallmark of the organization, was cut; and over 175 hours of television programming were cancelled. Plans for expanding specialty channels were also cancelled. CBC Bold was put up for sale. The corporation also noted that it would "cancel the planned launch of a kids digital TV channel and Radio-Canada," and would no longer pursue a digital sports TV channel ([GD] CBC 2012b). Stations in Sydney and Saskatoon were also closed. Of the new digital-only news operations announced in the strategic plan, only the one in Hamilton went ahead as planned. The cuts also impacted the CBC's digital transition as the budget cuts finalized the shutdown of 600 transmitters, leaving 27 digital OTA transmitters in larger markets (Taylor 2013, 138). The CBC also said that it would lease "significant square footage in the Canadian Broadcasting Centre in Toronto ... [and] sell some of its buildings to become tenants in more efficient and less-costly premises" ([GD] CBC 2012b).

Besides squeezing the CBC financially, the Conservative government continued to stack its board of directors with party loyalists (Taras and Waddell 2020, 62). Similarly, Hubert Lacroix, who served as the CBC president and CEO from 2008 to 2018, was a Conservative appointee who, as David Taras and Christopher Waddell (2020, 62) put it, "instead of ... represent[ing] the interests of the corporation to the government ... represent[ed] the government to the corporation" (see also Saulnier 2015). And while, as we have seen, private media in anglophone Canada was not kind to the CBC, in Quebec it was even worse during this period as Quebecor, the largest media company in that province, mustered its resources to launch a series of attacks against Radio-Canada, "filing hundreds of requests over several years for details of CBC spending, from which it hoped it could generate stories it could inflate into scandals" (Taras and Waddell 2020, 62).

A New CRTC Chair

The Conservatives appointed long-time civil servant Jean-Pierre Blais as chair of the CRTC in June 2012. In what seemed to be an unprecedented move to influence the direction of the commission, Minister of Heritage James Moore laid out the government's "objectives for broadcast and telecommunication regulation" under Blais in a mandate letter (Moore 2012; Winseck 2014). Consistent with larger government priorities, the letter emphasized consumer concerns and market considerations. Over the next five years, Blais would refract the Conservatives' brand of neoliberalism through the lens of the commission's decisions (Raj 2013; Morin 2017).

One of Blais's first moves was to phase out the LPIF, effectively cutting another $40 million from the CBC's budget and exacerbating the crisis in local programming. With much fanfare, the CRTC then announced a major review of television, called Let's Talk TV. Set in three stages, ostensibly the primary goal of the process was to help ensure that "the Canadian television system delivers compelling and diverse programming in an age of digital technology marked by an abundance of channels and on-demand content" ([GD] CRTC 2013b). None too subtly signalling one of the outcomes it was looking for from these hearings, the government issued an order-in-council to the CRTC requesting a report on "how the ability of Canadian consumers to subscribe to pay and specialty television services on a service-by-service basis can be maximized in a manner that most appropriately furthers the broadcasting policy for Canada" ([GD] CRTC 2014). The future of OTT services within the system was also high on the agenda. While the government signalled that it was not in favour of taxing internet-based video services, Facebook and Google dampened the proceedings by rejecting the commission's jurisdiction over their operations (Pedwell 2014; Davis and King 2017). And while concerns over the future of local television, particularly local news, were voiced early on, the commission promised to address these in the final hearing of the process.

The hearings spawned a series of controversial decisions that generally gave market forces more play within the system. Daytime Canadian content quotas for conventional broadcasters were eliminated, and quotas for specialty channels were streamlined. Genre protection for specialty channels was phased out, with exclusive rights to particular types of programming being eliminated. Access rights for discretionary services were also eliminated, making it more difficult for services not owned by BDUs to find distribution. The necessity of establishing general terms of trade between program producers and broadcasters was also eliminated, providing broadcasters more flexibility in bargaining with producers ([GD] CRTC 2015a). Enacting these decisions would have to wait until television licence renewals, several years down the road. But as they came into effect, private broadcasters were definitively given more play within the system, including a halving of the minimum annual PNI expenditure to 5 percent from 9–10 percent of income ([GD] CRTC 2017a).

Following the government's admonitions, a series of regulations promoting "consumer choice" were also enacted (Danks 2015). Key among these were rules that (1) BDUs must offer customers a $25 per month "skinny basic" service package consisting of the major conventional and not-for-profit broadcasters;

(2) BDUs must offer customers the ability to individually pick the program services they want rather than be forced to pick program packages curated by service providers; and (3) Super Bowl ads would no longer be subject to simultaneous program substitution rules ([GD] CRTC 2015b). Program producers and BDUs loudly objected to these changes. A report commissioned by ACTRA, the Canadian Media Guild, the Directors Guild of Canada, Friends of Canadian Broadcasting, and Unifor predicted that breaking up program packages could result in the loss of 4,000 jobs and $600 million in the broadcasting sector by 2020 (Nordicity and Miller 2015).

The BDUs put up stiff resistance to implementing both skinny basic and pick-and-pay product offerings, and designed the program packages such that they provided little savings over original offerings (Harris 2016a, 2016b). Bell Canada, which held exclusive rights to the Super Bowl games in Canada, challenged the CRTC's prohibition on substituting the American ads with Canadian counterparts in court. (A 2019 Supreme Court of Canada decision overturned an initial ruling that upheld the CRTC decision [Canadian Press 2019b].)

The final stage of the Let's Talk TV hearings focused on a review of local and community television policy. From the outset, this hearing appeared oddly structured, bringing what the 1991 Broadcasting Act characterizes as two different elements of the system together in the same hearing. On the one hand, the local news operations owned by BDUs and independent private operators argued for increased support for local programming. On the other hand, community television broadcasters repeated long-standing concerns that BDUs were stifling their access to both facilities and funds that should be available to them under the terms of current regulation. The rationale for the odd juxtaposition of the two interests became clear, however, when, in its decision, the CRTC chose to go against the recommendations of myriad government studies and investigations over the last several decades and sacrifice community television in order to prop up private broadcasters.

Characterizing local media markets as having "many media sources on television and radio, as well as online and in print, that provide community reflection," the CRTC authorized BDUs to redirect all of the funds currently earmarked for community television in large markets to local news. In smaller markets, 50 percent of those funds might be reallocated ([GD] CRTC 2016). Cutbacks to community TV operations by BDUs quickly ensued (Faguy 2017). To bolster the independent, largely small market broadcasters that did not have access to these freed-up BDU funds, the commission instituted a new Independent Local News Fund (ILNF). The CBC was excluded from accessing the new fund because, the commission said, "evidence from this proceeding [illustrated] … that the CBC is meeting its mandate" with its current funding ([GD] CRTC 2016).

The CBC

Arguably, the flurry of decisions arising from Let's Talk TV had greater impact on private broadcasters than on the CBC. However, by denying the corporation access to the new funding stream for local news and leaving it as the only conventional broadcaster responsible for daytime Canadian content, Let's Talk TV did contribute to further marginalizing the corporation within the system. Moreover, while the CBC was guaranteed slots in basic service packages, the elimination of access rights opened up the possibility that the CBC's documentary channel and French-language specialty channel ICI ARTV could be dropped by BDUs ([GD] CBC 2014a). Also, the removal of genre protection meant that these services might face direct competition. But as the hearings wound on, the CBC suffered a blow from another source.

In late 2013, the long-time threat of losing its premier sports franchise finally materialized as Rogers Communications struck a $5.2 billion deal to take over *Hockey Night in Canada (HNIC)*. Under the public broadcaster's management since the early days of radio, professional hockey had grown to command highly valuable audiences. But coupled with the promise of greater profits from new media markets, the broadcast rights to those games grew beyond the financial reach of the corporation (Shoalts 2014). Consequently, just as happened with professional football, another field of programming that the CBC had nurtured and developed was effectively spun off to the private sector for further exploitation.

While there was much speculation that a better bargain might have been struck, under the terms of the deal the CBC would continue carrying some games for years to come and thereby evade the need to find new programming to fill in the gaps left in its program schedule. But the advertising revenue would flow to Rogers, and in wake of its loss the CBC's advertising revenue fell from a high of $491.19 million in 2014 to $ 249.92 in 2016 (Statista 2022). Advertising in hockey broadcasts was not the only potential loss here because, as one reporter put it, "the CBC's advertising sales people, many of whom were laid off in the wake of losing the NHL [National Hockey League] rights, can no longer strong-arm sponsors into buying time on lower-rated shows as the cost of getting on Hockey Night" (Shoalts 2014). Moreover, as Taras and Waddell (2020, 101) point out, by "turning over all editorial control to HNIC to Rogers, the CBC was now a participant in promoting not only the NHL … but also Rogers and its corporate interest."

A New Plan

Faced with both the Conservatives' budget cuts of 2012 and the loss of NHL advertising revenue, the CBC released a new strategic plan in 2014. Titled *Strategy 2020: A Space for Us All,* it outlined directions for development in the face of shrinking resources. The central focus of the strategy was to shift "resource allocation" from conventional television and radio platforms to digital platforms, particularly mobile digital platforms. Along the way, goals included reducing real estate holdings by 50 percent, reducing the workforce by 1,500–2,000 jobs, or approximately 25 percent, and eliminating remaining in-house television production except news and current affairs. Here then, the focus was on distribution, on meeting Canadians on emerging mobile and digital platforms – as the document puts it, a shift from being a "producer to multiplatform broadcaster" ([GD] CBC 2014b, 9).

The plan drew the ire of critics on several fronts (Kiefel 2014; Vlessing 2014). In a scathing critique, University of Calgary professor Gregory Taylor (2016) argues that it would be a mistake to abandon traditional broadcasting as it remains "the dominant tool to reach mass audiences and will provide a significant forum for public information and debate for the foreseeable future" (349). Quoting 2013 statistics from the Television Bureau of Canada, Taylor illustrates that "94% of Canada's population is still connected to television through a broadcast distributor or by OTA signals"; hence, he argues, the "mobile sector, while increasingly significant, simply does not engage citizens at anywhere near the numbers of conventional broadcasting" (358). He also points out that, given that the CBC had been withdrawing from in-house production for some years, it was somewhat misleading for the corporation to claim that it was now eschewing such production. All in all, he states that "the national public broadcaster is enthusiastically embracing a post broadcasting era when there is ample evidence that broadcasting is alive and well" (357).

Focusing more specifically on the way the plan prioritized distribution over production, nine former CBC executives and members of the board of directors wrote a pointed letter to the current chair of the board, all of whose members had been appointed by Stephen Harper's Conservative government. It stated: "It appears that the board has forgotten that the board members are trustees of a statutory mandate based on the maintenance of a capacity within the corporation to broadcast, inform and certainly to create." Furthermore, "for decades, CBC/Radio-Canada has contributed to a national awareness of the different facets of our national 'tissue' by representing our cultural diversity through a capacity to create and support this diversity. We believe that with the most recent cuts, the mandate of the CBC is in peril. To suggest that replacing a capacity to produce with social media is dodging the issue; to eliminate the creative potential of the CBC is to sacrifice one of its raisons d'être" (Houpt 2014).

Friends of Canadian Broadcasting (2014) also took issue with the CBC's plans, framing them as "burning the furniture to heat the house." Calling president Hubert Lacroix "the Harper Government's best weapon for the institution's destruction," it stated that the corporation's current plans would leave it "as little more than a commissioner and scheduler, seeking to broker deals between parties who create content and others who operate digital delivery systems."

Indeed, as has been noted, partnering with private sector producers necessitates giving up some degree of creative control as the private partner may strive to focus the end product toward what it believes is in its best economic interests. With entertainment products, this might mean watering down distinctively Canadian content to allow for wider appeal to international markets, but it can have even more profound consequences for documentary programs as producers weigh the potential impact of their subject matter against future funding possibilities. Thus, partnering with private producers to create content can make it difficult for the public sector to differentiate itself from the private commercial sector.

A Change of Government

In October 2015, a new Liberal government took office. After years of budget cuts under the Conservatives, the Liberals promised to increase the CBC's appropriation by over 10 percent annually.[5] Despite this promise of new funding, however, critics charged that CBC executives were going ahead with planned cuts to staff and services, and CBC unions called for the resignation of Harper-era appointees Lacroix and the board of directors (Tencer 2015). Soon after, the government also announced that the Department of Canadian Heritage would undertake a public consultation, called Canadian Content in a Digital World, to develop a digital policy for the cultural – or, as they were now being called, "creative" – industries ([GD] Department of Canadian Heritage 2017).

Meanwhile, in the wake of the Conservatives' election loss, Stephen Harper resigned as leader. As the race for a new leader heated up, candidates began openly calling for dismantling the CBC. As Kelly Leitch, one of the leadership hopefuls put it, "the CBC doesn't need to be reformed, it needs to be dismantled ... For Canadian democracy to thrive, we need to hear from the different voices in the press ... So long as the CBC continues to distort the market by consuming advertising revenues and having its operations underwritten by the taxpayer, the market is uncompetitive" (Canadian Press 2016). Over the next few years, such rhetoric would become standard fare among Conservative leadership hopefuls (Naylor 2021).

The CBC's submission to the Department of Canadian Heritage consultation noted that it drew upon the central themes of its 2016 strategic plan and was "centred around four priority areas: Digital Innovation; Contributing to a Shared National Consciousness and Identity; Creating Quality Canadian Content; and Promoting Canada to the World" ([GD] CBC 2017b, 5). While the first three areas are readily identifiable as drawing from *A Space for Us All* ([GD] CBC 2014b), the fourth, Promoting Canada to the World, appeared to be a somewhat new responsibility the CBC had identified for itself. Given the ways in which technology was erasing borders in the broadcast world, and how private broadcasters' dependence on foreign programming for their financial well-being made them unlikely champions of Canadian content in the transnational market, promoting Canadian content internationally looked like it might well fit with the CBC's historical mandate of extending the reach of the Canadian broadcasting system.[6]

Bolstered by the promised boost in funding, CBC's brief to the consultation struck a more optimistic chord in terms of the corporation's contributions to program production than the 2016 strategic plan. While not stating a return to in-house production, the CBC did promise to "create, produce, and partner with Canadian cultural entrepreneurs to offer more quality content than ever before" ([GD] CBC 2017b, 27). At the same time, responding to concerns over growing gaps in local broadcasting services and differentiating itself from the private sector, it also promised that the CBC would be "more local than ever before" (12). Drawing on the 1991 Broadcasting Act's reframing of the nationalist purpose of public broadcasting, it also promised a continuing role in contributing to a shared national consciousness and identity as "an enabler of social cohesion" through "unparalleled access to information and programming that reflects a diversity of voices and perspectives" (27).

The document also clearly lays out how the "business model and cultural policy framework in which CBC/Radio-Canada operates and carries out its public mandate is profoundly and irrevocably broken" (14). The problematic dimensions of the framework included in that description were (1) declining advertising revenues; (2) OTT subscriptions outpacing those of subscription TV and subscription revenues in general; (3) declining BDU revenues resulting from cord cutting and pick-and-pay policies, which, in turn, were contributing to declining contributions to production funds (14–17); (4) declining government investment in culture and broadcasting since the early 1990s (24).

Echoing observations made by various industry observers since at least 2010, the document stated: "We now have two different realities in Canada: traditional broadcasters that are closely regulated and that contribute to the Canadian content production industry, and new media entrants that operate without those restrictions and contribute nothing to the funding of the Canadian cultural sector" (19). As was also noted, in the face of declining advertising revenue, the corporation was at a disadvantage vis-à-vis the private sector in that, unlike "vertically integrated broadcasting distribution companies," it did not have "other sources of revenue" to "mitigate the impact of these changes" (17). Still, despite being outflanked on all sides, statistics were provided to illustrate how among conventional broadcasters, the CBC was far and away the largest investor in, and scheduler of, Canadian programming (18).

Charting a path to the future, the document pointed to how, since the late 1990s, the BBC had played a central role in providing "a strong foundation for Britain's creative economy," and recommended that the CBC might play a similar role in Canada (19–24). To help accomplish that goal, the CBC also floated the idea of going advertisement-free (14–17). The cost of exiting advertising was pegged at $318 million – $253 million to replace lost conventional, specialty, and digital advertising revenue, plus $105 million for content to replace advertising time, less $40 million in cost saved from procuring ads (31). The proposal would see funding rise from $34 per capita in 2017 to $46. To help avoid political interference and provide stability, it would be linked to a five-year licence period and to inflation. Given the increasing pressures the organization faced from both the loss of NHL advertising and mounting pressure from newspapers and others over digital advertising, the pitch to go ad-free was not entirely surprising. At the same time, responding to concerns over growing gaps in local broadcasting services, it also promised that the CBC would be "more local than ever before" (12).

After extensive consultations, the Department of Canadian Heritage issued its report, *Creative Canada: A Policy Framework* ([GD] Department of Canadian Heritage 2017). The report promised a wide range of supports for the cultural sector, including increasing the federal contribution to the Canadian Media Fund to offset declining BDU contributions, a review of copyright, a new periodical fund to help support local news, and support for Indigenous creators. The report reaffirmed the CBC's place within the system and appealed to the idea that, in large part, the founding principles of public broadcasting in Canada – programming and distribution – still drove its operations:

> The expectations for CBC/Radio-Canada are high, but reflect what Canadians expect: a CBC/Radio-Canada that showcases the best of Canada to the world; that reflects the country's diversity, including Indigenous cultures, on multiple platforms, from coast to coast to coast; and that continues to provide an essential local service to Canadians in all regions of the country, and in both official languages. ([GD] Department of Canadian Heritage 2017, 32)

However, *Creative Canada* also noted that "there is general agreement, regardless of which camp, that the CBC/Radio-Canada should not be competing with private sector broadcasters, specifically for content and advertising revenues" ([GD] Department of Canadian Heritage 2017, 31).

Although increased support for the CBC was promised, no immediate steps to alleviate the problems and inequities identified in the corporation's submission were proposed. Instead, the development of steps to "strengthen the future of Canadian media and Canadian content creation" was deferred to a review of the Broadcasting and Telecommunications Acts announced with the 2017 federal budget. The same review was also earmarked to serve as a forum for "renewing" the mandate of the CBC. Reforms to the appointment process for the CBC board of directors were also announced, although the prime minister retained the power to appoint the chair of the board of directors and the president and CEO.

Regarding OTT, the report noted: "We have made it clear that we will not impose new taxes on online services that will increase the cost of these services to Canadians. Affordability and access to online services are important to Canadians." Instead, the report also noted that the government would work to build partnerships with transnational platforms to provide space and opportunity for promoting Canadian cultural products and perspectives. Perhaps the most controversial of these was a deal with Netflix to spend $500 million over the next five years in Canada ([GD] Department of Canadian Heritage 2017). As Taras and Waddell (2020) note, compared with regulations applied to domestic broadcasters, the "deal" seemed to be "largely a one way street," and the review offered no tangible remedy for the inequities between Canadian broadcasters and their OTT competitors, such as adhering to content regulations, contributing to production funds, or paying Goods and Services Tax (GST) and/or Provincial Sales Tax (PST). Criticism of the Netflix deal and of Canadian Heritage Minister Mélanie Joly was strong and swift, particularly in her home province of Quebec, where Netflix made only a minimal promise of investment. Joly was shuffled out of her Canadian Heritage position within a year of delivering the new policy framework.

Under Attack

While the CBC waited for the mandate review promised in *Creative Canada*, attacks from the private sector continued. With more than 14.8 million views of CBC.ca in 2015–16, and more than 3 million views of Radio-Canada's digital offerings in Quebec during the same period, the CBC was the online leader in Canada ([GD] CBC 2017b). But at the 2016 hearings of the Standing Committee on Canadian Heritage, representatives of the Canadian Newspaper

Association complained that the CBC competed with newspapers for digital advertising revenue. Philip Crawley, publisher and CEO of the *Globe and Mail,* said that the corporation was their main competitor in the digital ad space, with almost twice as many unique monthly visitors as the *Globe and Mail*. However, as Hubert Lacroix noted in a letter to the committee, only $25 million, or 10 percent, of the CBC's advertising revenue was derived from digital advertising. Other witnesses called for the CBC to make its news available to others through a Creative Commons licence that would effectively allow other organizations to publish news produced by the CBC free of charge. While not wholeheartedly endorsing the suggestions of the private sector, the committee did recommend that the "CBC/Radio-Canada prioritize the production and dissemination of locally reflective news," and that the corporation "eliminate advertising from its digital news platforms" ([GD] Standing Committee on Canadian Heritage 2017).

While the Standing Committee on Canadian Heritage was deliberating, co-sponsored by the federal government and the Public Policy Forum (PPF), a panel of news industry experts was investigating the news business in Canada. The PPF report, *The Shattered Mirror,* was published in January 2017 (Public Policy Forum 2017). Recommendations largely focused on the larger structure and practices of the industry (82–99). Suggestions for reorienting the CBC's news practices and subordinating them to those of the private sector figured prominently in this context. It was recommended that the corporation give up digital advertising and pay more "attention to civic-function news, which may not attract the biggest audience but must be a public broadcaster's raison d'être in a digital age." As the report notes, this would have the added benefit of "freeing CBC from the traffic-maximizing, clickbait mentality that devalues serious journalism" (92). (It's not clear whether this move would reserve the clickbait market for the private sector.) It was also recommended that although it focused on "civic-function news," the CBC move to "publishing its news content under a Creative Commons licence." As the report noted, such a move "would go a long way toward moving the organization from a self-contained, public-broadcasting competitor to a universal public provider of quality journalism" (94). It went on to note that "such a move would also enrich digital-only and traditional news organizations and unleash new creative approaches to adding value to CBC News beyond what can possibly exist within a single organization" (94). Interestingly, while recommending that the CBC give away the news it creates to private news producers, the PPF also suggested that the federal government review the fair dealing provisions of the Copyright Act[7] and "tighten usage of copyrighted news material in favour of creators" (87).[8]

So, just as private broadcasters had for years argued that the CBC should be relegated to the commercial margins of the media system, the newspaper industry followed suit when the CBC began to bump up against their interests.

Changing of the Guard

As the Liberal government put its stamp on the regulatory system, the policy environment began to shift (Bradshaw and Dobby 2016; Houpt 2017). The terms of the Conservative appointees to both the CRTC and CBC ended in 2017. Ian Scott, the new chair of the CRTC, was a former telecommunications lobbyist and came to the job with a seemingly much more industry-friendly perspective than his predecessor. Catherine Tait took the helm of the CBC in July 2018. Although directly appointed by the Liberal government, she arrived with over thirty years of media experience, largely in the production industry (Yakabuski 2018).

Tait immediately took a much more visible role than Lacroix in navigating the shifting mediascape and defending the interests of the corporation. In September 2018, she announced a new English streaming service – Gem – fashioned after Radio-Canada's ICI TOU. She promised that it would carry "the crown jewels of Canadian content" and carry CBC content as well as feature films, children's programs, and National Film Board films (*CBC News* 2018). The following year, in a nod to the concerns of the newspaper industry voiced in *The Shattered Mirror,* the CBC began to explore content-sharing partnerships with newspapers. As Tait put it in an interview with the *Globe and Mail,* the purpose of this move was "to come up with solutions that would allow us to share and be more effective – and take responsibility, to ensure we have a diverse media ecosystem going forward" (Houpt 2019). Here the CBC appeared to move toward a more traditional role of directly supporting its private-sector counterparts, as it once did with radio and television.

While initially embracing co-productions with Netflix, Tait soon moved to break that relationship. As she noted in an interview with *Content Canada,* "a number of countries have done deals, as we did, with Netflix ... and over time we start to see that we're feeding the growth of Netflix ... rather than feeding our own domestic business and industry" (in Benzine 2019). She also compared Netflix's growing cultural influence to that of the British and French colonial empires (Canadian Press 2019a). Tait would soon stir up more controversy as she attempted to shield the corporation from the fickle character of government subsidy by developing new commercial revenue streams (Valiante 2019).

In May 2018, the CRTC issued a report on the future of programming distribution in Canada ([GD] CRTC 2018). While that report noted that government funding remained key to media content production, it also noted that in 2016 it was only half what it was in 1991. This decline was the product of a double squeeze: on the one hand, rising subscription revenues were primarily going to internet access rather than content; on the other hand, advertising income continued to shift away from content providers to digital platforms. Consequently, while the four largest Canadian media companies captured 80 percent of broadcast and BDU revenue, revenue was not flowing through to content production. Moreover, as the CRTC went on to note, with a growing number of streaming services based in the United States directly tapping Canadian broadcast markets, there was concern over how long a separate Canadian market for American audiovisual products might be maintained. Because the profits generated from this market by private broadcasters were a major driver of domestic production, the collapse of this market – and private broadcasters – could have a serious negative impact on domestic production as well.

In this context, deregulation was not seen as an option. As the commission noted: "With the removal of regulatory requirements that promote or provide support for Canadian producers and creators of all types of content, Canadians will see less of themselves and less of the content that reflects their values, needs and interests, not to mention the heavy negative impact on Canadian artists, creators and producers." However, the commission also recommended that "future legislative and regulatory" approaches be "adaptable and innovative" and "engage new players"; that they focus on "production and promotion"; that "all players [in the system] should participate"; and that elements of the system "be nimble, innovative and rapidly adapt to change." Perhaps the most important shift in the commission's position here was that "online international services" should be brought into the regulatory fold, although how exactly this might be accomplished was not addressed. The report did not make any recommendations regarding the CBC, preferring to leave those for a future discussion of the corporation's mandate. However, as they made their way into regulatory policy, the principles laid out here would influence the direction of the corporation.

Broadcasting and Telecommunications Legislative Review Panel

In June 2018, the minister of Canadian heritage and the minister of innovation, science and economic development jointly struck the Broadcasting and Telecommunications Legislative Review Panel (BTLR) to review Canada's communications legislative framework. The review centred on the Broadcasting Act, the Telecommunications Act, the Radiocommunication Act, and the linkages between them.[9] The focus was on "affordability, economic competitiveness, cultural sovereignty, accessibility, consumer rights, or privacy and online safety" ([GD] Innovation, Science and Economic Development Canada 2020). Over the course of its hearings, the panel received over 2,000 submissions from a wide range of interested parties, including public and private broadcasters and Google and Netflix.

Drawing upon a discourse of cultural nationalism, the CBC's submission framed the corporation as "the cultural institution that helps knit our vast and diverse society into something extraordinary in the world" ([GD] CBC 2019a, 2). The submission was built around three key actions (4):

A. Strengthen Public Broadcasting as a cornerstone of Canadian culture;
B. Strengthen the quality and access to trusted news and information for all Canadians;
C. Strengthen Canadian culture by ensuring that all companies who benefit from our market contribute to the sustainability of Canadian culture.

The submission was comprehensive in terms of specifying the place of the corporation within the larger media system and providing it with greater independence, in terms of both increasing its corporate powers and distancing it from government. For instance, the submission moved to deflect the ongoing criticism that the corporation unfairly competed with private broadcasters, declaring that "our competition is not Canadian companies, but the global digital giants flooding Canada with foreign content" (3). And while it stressed the corporation's commitment to digital and mobile services that had been key since at least the 2014 strategic plan, it also provided insights into research efforts to engage with different user profiles and reach and engage with younger people. The CBC's "important role and contribution in reflecting Indigenous people in its programming" was also highlighted (15), and specific recommendations for appointment processes that would "strengthen the governance and independence" of the corporation were made (22). To counter criticism that the CBC is a "state" broadcaster or somehow beholden to government, there was a recommendation that the Broadcasting Act clarify that "the Corporation has complete editorial freedom with respect to the content it broadcasts" (28). Broad policy recommendations toward affordable broadband, net neutrality, bringing digital services (like newspapers) under the jurisdiction of the Broadcasting Act, and "requiring digital media undertakings to provide Canadian rights holders with access to aggregate data about how their content is used" were also included, as well as recommendations to make ISPs, wireless providers, and OTT services contribute equitably to Canadian production (30–33).

Perhaps most interesting were recommendations for specific revisions to both the Broadcasting Act and the Telecommunications Act. Key here were additions to the CBC's mandate, as well as recommendations for what not to change in this regard. Among the points made were to retain the reference to the corporation as providing "a wide range of programming that informs, enlightens and entertains," and to add language that increases the scope of the corporation's activities in terms of technology, innovation, and service to Indigenous peoples (40). Language to increase the corporation's financial flexibility as well as help "ensure sufficient, predictable levels of funding for the public broadcaster to meet its mandate" was also recommended (42). And following up on the corporation's submission to Creative Canada, adding a clause to the mandate "to promote and make Canadian programming and content available internationally" was also recommended (41). Thus, just as it had done some sixty years earlier in the face of ongoing regulatory wrangling and uncertainty over its mandate, the CBC made its own suggestions for the form the new mandate might take. However, whether the BTLR or the government would take the corporation up on its suggestions remained to be seen.

The BTLR Panel's final report, titled *Canada's Communications Future: Time to Act*, was published in January 2020 ([GD] Innovation, Science and Economic Development Canada 2020). Calling on a discourse of nationalist purpose, the panel noted that its recommendations were rooted in an

> overarching vision [of] a legislative framework ... that reaffirms Canada's sovereignty, supports our democratic values and inclusivity, and aims to realize the promise of advanced technologies for the benefit of Canada's economy and future prosperity, and Canadians as citizens, users, and creators. All Canadians deserve to live a connected life: to connect with ideas, opinions, content, news and information, people, cultures, services and economic opportunities locally, nationally, and globally. (19)

Here, just as with radio almost 100 years earlier, the technology is envisioned to draw the disparate places and peoples of the country together by empowering them to connect both with each other and with the world outside Canada's borders. At the same time, these technological abilities implicitly legitimate state intervention. While there were some concerns that the panel might call for a merger of the Broadcasting and Telecommunications Acts – which in turn might result in a watering down of the cultural objectives of broadcasting – there were recommendations to maintain the separate acts and add stronger cultural language to the Telecommunications Act (28).

The panel's self-described "vision" for a revamped Canadian media system had several key dimensions: (1) to bring "all media and communication entities into the [Broadcasting] Act"; (2) to update the role of CBC/Radio-Canada; (3) a concern that users of the media system, whether individuals or institutions, have affordable, guaranteed, universal access to broadband "media content, including diverse, trusted and accurate sources of news content, safeguards against privacy breaches, Big Data, or harmful content"; (4) accelerated "roll-out of advanced wireline and wireless networks"; and (5) a "reimagined" CRTC that would have "much stronger research and analytic capabilities, as well as "greater participation by public interest groups" (11–18). There were ninety-seven individual recommendations, many of which were familiar from past committees and inquiries. However, as illustrated in the report's title, the panel underscored the fact that it was now time to address "pressing and urgent issues" that had long gone unaddressed (18–19). It recommended that "all media and communication entities [be brought] into the scope of the Broadcasting Act," that the act be extended "beyond audio and audiovisual content to include alphanumeric news content made available to the public by means of telecommunications," and that this field of content be "collectively known as media content" (29).

Traditional concerns of production and distribution were reframed as "Creation, Production and Discoverability of Canadian Content." As noted earlier, here the traditional concern of ensuring that Canadians simply have access to Canadian media products is replaced by the concern that Canadian media products be found in the ever-increasing sea of media products available to them. As the report clearly illustrates, Canada's media industries face increasing challenges from a number of directions. Declining revenues for both private broadcasters and BDUs threaten the media production funding regime (140–42). At the same time, simple discovery of Canadian media products is complicated by the abilities of foreign platforms "to collect and use consumer data ... to customize their offerings and ... creates a competitive challenge for existing Canadian companies" (116). In the face of these concerns, there were recommendations to have platforms both pay their share of content production and ensure that Canadian content was visible and easily discoverable (172–74).

Although the panel did not adopt all of the CBC's recommendations, in the face of conflicting opinions about the future role of the CBC within the system, it was supportive of the corporation's broad public purpose. Thus, the panel recommended that the Broadcasting Act "be amended to remove the specific reference to radio and television in the mandate of CBC/Radio-Canada" so that it "is able to provide a wide range of media content ... on multiple platforms and media" (163). It also recommended that the existing mandate "be amended to add the following elements" and powers (166):

- reflecting local communities and audiences;
- providing national, regional, and local news;
- reflecting Canadian perspectives on international news;

- reflecting Indigenous Peoples and promoting Indigenous cultures and languages;
- showcasing Canadian content to international audiences; and
- taking creative risks.

It also recommended "that the Act be amended to ensure that the national public broadcaster has the objects and powers it needs to deliver on its updated mandate" (166).

There is some overlap between these recommendations and those of the CBC, particularly in terms of increasing the corporation's focus on local, international, and Indigenous programming. Interestingly, however, while the CBC recommendations were framed as strengthening the media system in general ([GD] CBC 2019a, 35–46), the BTLR Panel's recommendations were largely framed as activities that would fall outside the purview of private broadcasters. The panel noted that "there may therefore be fewer and fewer incentives for commercial content providers to provide local content in a global marketplace. CBC has a role to play in addressing this situation" ([GD] Innovation, Science and Economic Development Canada 2020, 163). Here, once again, we can see that the regulatory recommendations for the focus of the CBC's activities have flipped from the national to the local as the focus of private capital has shifted.

The BTLR Panel's report also noted that the current environment was putting "significant pressure on the preservation of reliable news sources at the local, regional, national, and international level," and that "nowhere will the role of a well-resourced public media provider be more important than in the area of news and information content" (164). In terms of Indigenous content, it recommended that CBC/Radio-Canada help with "capacity building and nurturing this aspect of Canadian content" (165) – again, not activities that might be expected of the private sector. Also, as per the above list of additions to the mandate, "taking creative risks" is not something that Canadian private broadcasters are particularly well known for.

Here, then, we can see that while there was a deliberate effort to expand the general purview of the CBC to meet the exigencies of the shifting environment, that effort was focused on the margins of the reach of private capital.

Funding recommendations were similarly structured. The panel provided strong evidence that, by international standards, the CBC was chronically underfunded (166–69). However, it also noted that the ability of the corporation to "transform itself successfully into a public media institution … is somewhat compromised by its continuing reliance on advertising, which necessarily introduces a commercial imperative into its decision-making" and warps its ability "to pursue a diversity of media content to reflect Canada's own makeup" (168). Similarly, a "focus on advertising puts it directly on a collision course with private broadcasters and even print media, as all pursue a dwindling pot of traditional advertising revenues and compete with giant foreign operators for the online business." Consequently, "reducing CBC/Radio-Canada's reliance on this dwindling pot can provide some useful breathing space for the private broadcasters" (168–69). In this context, the panel recommended "that the Broadcasting Act be amended to require the federal government to enter into funding commitments of at least 5 years with CBC/Radio-Canada," and that the corporation "gradually eliminate advertising on all platforms over the next five years, starting with news content" (169).

The panel also made recommendations regarding CBC governance and accountability. In terms of the appointments process, it recommended "that the Broadcasting Act be amended to enshrine an open, transparent, and competency-based appointment process for Governor in Council appointments of CBC/Radio-Canada Chair, President, and Board of Directors" (170). In terms of oversight, it recommended that "the Broadcasting Act be amended to shift the CRTC's role from licensing individual services of CBC/Radio-Canada to overseeing all its content-related activities" (171). The CBC recommendation that it be granted "greater financial flexibility" was not included in the panel's recommendations ([GD] CBC 2019a, 42). Here, then, whereas the panel moved to give the CBC appointments process greater independence from the government, the financial management of the corporation did not receive the same treatment.

Consequently, while the panel's recommendations moved to better specify and increase the scope of the CBC activities within the system, they largely followed the traditional pattern of subordinating the interests of the corporation to those of private capital in terms of both the range of activities specified in the mandate and the relinquishment of advertising revenue. And while the panel advocated for more resources for the corporation, it did not seek to increase the CBC's financial independence.

Legislation

In response to the BTLR Panel's report, the government tabled Bill C-10, an Act to amend the Broadcasting Act, in November 2020. It was the first of three promised bills to address the recommendations made in the report. Bill C-10 moved to make OTT services like Netflix, Disney+, and Amazon Prime responsible to the larger cultural purposes of the Broadcasting Act. However, it did not encompass all of the panel's legislative recommendations. In particular, other than slightly shifting the CBC's technological focus in section 3(1)(l) from providing "radio and television services" to providing " broadcasting services" more broadly, no other changes were made to its mandate.[10]

Some changes to the Broadcasting Act were highly controversial. For instance, some critics were concerned that Bill C-10 gave the CRTC too much power to determine the kinds of online activities that might be subject to regulation (Winseck 2021a; Geist 2021a). Others thought that the imposition of new taxes "could lead to the costs of [some] digital services skyrocketing by nearly 50 per cent" (Geist 2021b). However, before the legislation was passed, a federal election was called and the bill died on the Order Paper.

The Liberals secured another minority government under Justin Trudeau in September 2021. As the new government was formed, the prime minister's mandate letter to Minister of Heritage Pablo Rodriguez included a number of the government's goals regarding new broadcasting legislation. It stated: "You will work to introduce legislation to reform the Broadcasting Act, ask web giants to pay their fair share." Building on the recommendations of the BTLR, a number of goals were also specified for the CBC, including (1) updating its mandate "with unique programming that distinguishes it from private broadcasters"; (2) increasing "the production of national, regional and local news"; (3) "ensuring that Indigenous voices and cultures are present on our screens and radios"; (4) "bringing Canada's television and film productions to the world stage"; and (5) "providing additional funding to make it less reliant on private advertising, with a goal of eliminating advertising during news and other public affairs shows." However, the letter made no mention of instituting a stable funding mechanism for the CBC ([GD] Prime Minister of Canada 2021).

The broadcast legislation was reintroduced in Parliament as the Online Streaming Act in February 2022. Rather than replacing the 1991 Broadcasting Act, Bill C-11 contained over 150 amendments to that act and related legislation, including some amendments designed to address issues that had been raised in its earlier incarnation. The contents of the Online Streaming Act are much too extensive to be fully reviewed here. Suffice it to say that they move to assert Canadian sovereignty over the system at large, including "foreign broadcasting undertakings that provide programming for Canadians" (section 3[1][a]), define "online undertaking[s]" as a specific class of broadcast undertaking (section 2[1]), and move to make those undertakings responsible to the larger cultural proposes of the system (section 3[1][f.1]). The larger national purposes of the system described in section 3(1)(d) are expanded to include "the development and export of Canadian programs globally" (section 3[1][d][ii]), and, in terms of diversity, the specified range of peoples/interests the system is dedicated to serve is greatly increased (section 3[1][d][iii]), and "news and current events – from the local and regional to national and international" – are specifically referenced as programming provided by the system. Online undertakings "that provide programming services of other broadcasting services" are also charged with ensuring the "discoverability of Canadian programming services and original Canadian programs" (section 3[1][q]), as well as promoting and recommending Canadian programming (section 3[1][r]). However, "programs" on social media are specifically excluded from regulation (section 4.1[1]).

The definition and responsibilities of community broadcasting are also enlarged. However, the community element is specified to be "innovative and complementary to the programming provided for mass audiences" and to "cater to tastes and interests not adequately provided for by the programming provided for mass audiences" (section 3[1][s][i] and [ii]). In other words, while the earlier version of the 1991 Broadcasting Act did not specify the relationship between community broadcasters and the other elements of the system, in this version community broadcasters are clearly subordinate to broadcasters providing "programming for mass audiences."

As anticipated, the powers of the CRTC were modified to meet the system's changing conditions and provide powers to regulate "online undertakings." While exempting online undertakings from licensing requirements, the bill provides the commission with a range of powers to impose conditions on those undertakings, including the proportion of Canadian programs offered on those services, and the discoverability of those programs (section 9.1[1][a]–[p]). Powers to impose monetary penalties on undertakings in violation of regulations are included (Part II.2), as is a mechanism for appealing disputes between the commission and the CBC to the minister of Canadian heritage (section 19, subsections 1–3). However, recommendations to increase the commission's research and public participation capacities were not addressed, raising the possibility that small independent online creators might find it difficult to have their voices heard as the CRTC moved to develop regulation from the legislation (McKelvey 2020).

As for the CBC, apart from carrying over the shift in technological focus from Bill C-10, no other changes to the mandate were included in the legislation. Despite efforts to address the problems critics highlighted in Bill C-10, some concerns about regulatory overreach remained. Debates were cut short, however, as the government pushed the bill to the Senate (Woolf 2022).

CBC Licence Renewal

As the amendments to the Broadcasting Act were being formulated and winding their way through the legislative process, the CBC underwent a licence renewal hearing. The corporation released a two-page strategic plan that outlined the principles and priorities that would underlie its corporate strategy over the next few years ([GD] CBC 2019c). Largely following the ideas outlined in the BTLR submission, there were five key priorities:

1. Customized digital services: personal, relevant, and engaging experiences ... to make sure all Canadians see themselves reflected in our digital services ...
2. Engaging with young audiences: ... bringing the best content to our children and youth ...
3. Prioritizing our local connections: ... strengthen this connection with significant local and regional content ...
4. Reflecting contemporary Canada: reflect the range and richness of this country's diversity, celebrating our different perspectives ... We will do this in our staffing, as well as our content choices.
5. Taking Canada to the world: ... If Canadian culture is going to be strong, it needs to be part of the global market ... We will ensure our country and Canadian creators are seen and heard the world over.

Specific proposals for regulatory changes were elaborated in a Supplementary Brief ([GD] CBC n.d.c). Key among them was establishing some flexibility in terms of calculating quotas such as exhibition goals and programming expenditures across conventional and digital services rather than tying them to specific platforms (6). This was similar to the regulatory changes granted to private ownership groups in Broadcasting Regulatory Policy 2010-167 ([GD] CRTC 2010a), where companies were allowed to calculate their expenditures across conventional and specialty channels. Exhibition quotas were proposed for local metropolitan and non-metropolitan markets in both English and French ([GD] CBC n.d.c, 7). Other proposals included new consultation on reporting requirements regarding "content created by and for Indigenous peoples," the reflection of diversity "on-screen, on-air, in content production, and within CBC/Radio-Canada's workforce," and for "gender parity in audio-visual content production" (1).

The licence renewal hearing was initially announced for May 2020, but was postponed to January 2021 because of COVID-19. A series of questions for public comment that somewhat followed up on the plan were posed in the initial announcement.

Meanwhile, in September 2020, the CBC announced the launch of Tandem, a new production service focused on creating sponsored and branded content. Critics saw this as blurring the lines between news and advertising, as well as extending rather than decreasing commercial activity, and the announcement drew the ire of both former and present CBC journalists, public interest groups, and commercial broadcasters (Gollom 2021). In the end, however, Tandem was only one of a number of contentious issues that would come to characterize the licence renewal hearing.

The CRTC handed down its licensing decision in June 2022 ([GD] CRTC 2022). Prefacing it with a quote from its May 2018 report "Harnessing Change" ([GD] CRTC 2018), the commission stated that the "future regulation of the broadcasting system must not only be flexible, but also nimble, innovative and continuously capable of rapidly adapting to change." It also noted that the structure of the CBC's operations had changed dramatically since the last licensing hearing in 2013, with much more emphasis now on digital media broadcasting. The commission then went on to grant the corporation more regulatory flexibility in a number of areas. For instance, while maintaining "minimum thresholds for local programming in Canada's non-metropolitan areas," "such requirements in metropolitan markets" were eliminated (against the CBC's recommendation). Reflecting the corporation's growing focus on digital services, the commission announced that it would grant the CBC's request to move from "exhibition requirements or broadcasting quotas" on specific stations to "a multiplatform expenditure approach for all of the CBC's English- and French-language licensed audiovisual services." Spending requirements for programs of national interest were also expanded to include expenditures on online platforms. At the same time, noting how the vast majority of PNI and other programming genres were contracted from independent producers, the commission found that it was not "necessary to impose any exhibition or expenditure requirements on the CBC in regard to independent productions." The CRTC also approved the CBC's operation of Tandem, finding the "initiative ... consistent with the context in which the CBC currently finances its operations."

In true historical form, however, much of this new-found "flexibility" was located on the economic margins of the system, and came with specific obligations. Eliminating local programming requirements in metropolitan markets focused the CBC on the less profitable non-metropolitan areas where private broadcasters were less likely to invest. Similarly, while allowing more flexibility in locating PNI investments, spending requirements in this category remained much higher for the CBC than for private broadcasters.[11] New obligations imposed by the CRTC also pushed the CBC toward a higher standard than the private sector in terms of both the diversity of broadcast content and monitoring progress toward meeting organizational goals. For instance, although the CBC expressed reluctance to "earmark specific amounts for specific communities," the commission required that "a fixed portion of independent programming expenditures [be] directed to programming produced by Indigenous Peoples, official language minority communities (OLMC), racialized Canadians, Canadians with disabilities, and Canadians who self-identify as LGBTQ2." For the private sector, these responsibilities remained voluntary, urged on by promises of extra Canadian programming expenditure (CPE) credits for such programming ([GD] CRTC 2017a). The CRTC also required the CBC "to submit multiple new reports to the Commission including ... a diversity of workforce report, and a report on parameters for self-identification and best practices surrounding privacy issues" ([GD] CRTC 2022). While not increasing programming requirements, the commission also underscored the CBC's commitment to increase its offerings for children and youth.

In large part, these new obligations met priorities that had been identified by the CBC in briefs and submissions to various inquiries since at least the Creative Canada consultations – once again illustrating that, led by what it perceives to be its mandate, the corporation is drawn to developing high standards for the system that generally push the boundaries of those met by the private sector.

Reaction to the licensing decision was fast and furious, as a wide range of groups took exception to the new flexibility the CRTC granted the CBC. L'Association québécoise de la production médiatique (AQPM) and the Canadian Media Producers Association sought to appeal the decision before the Federal Court of Appeal, and more than a dozen parties petitioned the Governor-in-Council (cabinet) to set aside or return the decision to the CRTC for reconsideration (Canadian Association of Broadcasters 2022; Thiessen 2022). Those organizations included the Canadian Association of Broadcasters, the Canadian Media Guild, Friends (formerly Friends of Canadian Broadcasting), the Public Interest Advocacy Centre, L'Alliance des producteurs francophones du Canada, the Quebec Ministry of Culture and Communications, and the International Alliance of Theatrical Stage Employees, Moving Picture Technicians, Artists and Allied Crafts of the United States, Its Territories and Canada (IATSE). Their concerns included the lack of expenditure requirements on independent production; mandatory thresholds of local programming in metropolitan areas; not shutting down Tandem or otherwise limiting the CBC's advertising practices; and allowing expenditures to be calculated across linear and online platforms. In other words, many of the major stakeholder groups and advocacy organizations associated with public broadcasting wanted reversed those elements of the decision that provided the CBC with more latitude in how it allocated its resources.

In September 2022, the Governor-in-Council referred the decision back to the CRTC. The order stated: "The CRTC will reconsider the matter and may rescind or confirm the decision either with or without change" ([GD] Governor-in-Council 2022).

While the CRTC was reconsidering the CBC licensing decision, the Senate sent Bill C-11 back to Parliament for final reading. The bill did not pass the Senate without amendments, including one aimed at Tandem that would stop the CBC from broadcasting or developing "an advertisement or announcement

on behalf of an advertiser that is designed to resemble journalistic programming" (Karadeglija 2022). But after more controversy, particularly over the reach
of the bill, it passed Parliament largely in its original form and received royal
assent at the end of April 2023 ([GD] Department of Canadian Heritage 2023).
Apart from the shift in the CBC's technological focus discussed above, there
was no substantive change to the CBC's mandate and no mention of a funding
formula for the corporation.[12]

On June 14, 2023, Bell Canada announced that it was laying off 1,300 workers,
closing or selling nine radio stations, and closing two foreign bureaus. On the
same day, the company filed a request with the CRTC to drop its spending
requirements on local news (Canadian Press 2023). If history is to be our guide,
these events will result in pressure on the CBC to fill these gaps in the system.

Conclusion

FRAMED BY A discourse of nationalism, the field of broadcasting was partially separated from larger market forces and a peculiarly Canadian broadcasting system took form. From the beginning, this field has been a site of social struggle as the Canadian state has worked to forge emergent broadcast technologies to ways of representing Canadian social life at the national, regional, and local levels.

In this context, public broadcasting was largely situated at the margins of private investment as first the Canadian Radio Broadcasting Commission (CRBC) and later the Canadian Broadcasting Corporation (CBC) assumed responsibility for elements of the national system that private, profit-oriented operators were loath to approach – namely, the construction of a national radio network and the production of programming to fill it. As the system developed and television was introduced, an independent regulatory board was instituted. Faced with a variety of pressures, both external and internal to the system, first the Board of Broadcast Governors (BBG) and later the Canadian Radio-television and Telecommunications Commission (CRTC) adjudicated further expansion of the broadcasting field. In this process, private capital was the favoured vehicle for expansion.[1] Not only was the perennially underfunded and legislatively constrained CBC without ready investment capital, but dominant, liberal economic assumptions concerning the benefits of competition, the flexibility of private capital, and the risk of investment also held sway over these decisions.

Inspired by nationalist and cultural purpose and led by both implicit and explicit mandate – as well as pushed by both regulators and private operators – the CBC has often worked as a kind of development vehicle, taking up elements of production and distribution that the private sector was unwilling or unable to undertake. The character of this role has shifted through time, as the organization has engaged with different technologies, across national, regional, and local levels, and between different language and cultural groups. But it is a position the CBC has occupied from the start.

In this position, the CBC has been a trailblazer in embracing and developing new media technologies and markets. It has been at the forefront of both AM and FM radio, television, microwave and satellite distribution, and online services. Despite the fact that digital media technologies were not explicitly mentioned in the 1991 Broadcasting Act, the CBC interpreted its mandate "as technologically neutral or platform agnostic" and continued this pioneering role by delivering internet-based services ([GD] Standing Committee on

Canadian Heritage 2008, 58). The CBC has also proven itself to be a mainstay for Canadian programming, supporting the independent production industry and providing a range of distinctively Canadian programs in the face of reluctance for this task on the part of the private sector. From news to drama to sports to comedy, and more recently with online content, the CBC has been a pioneer in almost all electronic media genres.

As online media moved to displace traditional media, the CBC was once again drawn to the economic margins of the system. Budget cuts through the 1990s and first decade of the new millennium forced the corporation to sharpen its focus. Faced with shrinking resources, it decided to begin shifting resources from conventional television and radio platforms to meeting Canadians on emerging digital platforms, particularly mobile digital platforms ([GD] CBC 2014b). While this decision was unpopular with many commentators, it did follow the organization's traditional developmental logic. More recently, the corporation has identified this area as a priority for future growth, once again raising the ire of critics and stakeholders (Woolf 2023).

The Public and the Private

One historical constant in the Canadian broadcasting system has been change, as first radio and then television, cable and satellite, and the internet have flooded the system with foreign content and regulators and the public broadcaster have struggled to develop and maintain a Canadian presence in broadcast media. In the current environment, even if regulators succeed in making streaming platforms responsible to the larger public purposes of the system, the business model upon which conventional private broadcasters are based is increasingly tenuous (Taras and Waddell 2020, 160–61). Not only does it appear that their advertising revenue is, as Dwayne Winseck (2021b, iii) points out, in "terminal decline" but in the face of an increasing number of transnational streaming services, their ability to secure the Canadian rights to popular American programs is seriously threatened. How private broadcasters and the organizations that own them will respond to this situation is not clear. However, given their histories, it is highly unlikely that the situation will result in the production of more distinctively Canadian programs. Rather, given the rigidities of the Canadian market, apart from content that is bound to specific geographic regions, such as news, it is likely that they will either produce or co-produce more programs designed for the international market or cease business altogether. As we have seen, in the case of the former, to improve their currency, such programs are often constructed to downplay or cleanse them of identifiable Canadian qualities (Tinic 2009, 6; 2015).

Broadcast distribution undertakings (BDUs) also face shrinking market opportunities. Cord cutting is accelerating, which means smaller audiences for the channels they carry and smaller contributions to the Canadian Media Fund (CMF) (Law 2022b). In other words, despite the fact that the converged media companies that dominate Canada's network media economy are well positioned to maintain their profitability, as with advertising-driven private broadcasters it is unlikely that BDUs will be maintaining, let alone increasing, their contributions to production funds (Winseck 2021b; Law 2022a).

Moreover, at the time of writing, Canadian content regulations are scheduled for review ([GD] CRTC n.d.). As noted in a Nordicity (2023, 22) study, "the Canadian broadcasting system support of CanCon is being compromised by its loss of market share and viewers to streaming services." Consequently, the review will probably focus on ways to have the program expenditures of the over-the-top (OTT) companies that Bill C-11 strives to have contribute to the system qualify as Canadian productions. Perhaps the major hurdle in this regard is the ownership of the intellectual property (IP) rights to these programs. Transnational streaming companies are loath to relinquish such rights, and in order to qualify as Canadian for the purposes of accessing production funds, IP must be in Canadian hands. But even if that were overcome, given the history of this issue it is hard to imagine that the review will result in regulation that yields content that represents the wide range of ideas, values, and ways of life of the peoples living in this country, rather than the "6 pointers" that have for so long been the hallmark of the productions supported by private broadcasters (Geist 2023; O'Byrne 2022).

From this perspective, the future of distinctive Canadian television programming is bleak. The CBC stands out as the key vehicle for producing programs and other media content that reflects Canadian ideas and perspectives. Focused by mandate to be "distinctively Canadian" and reflect a diversity of Canadian perspectives, the corporation's track record in this regard is unmatched. Consequently, as the representation and circulation of Canadian perspectives within the system are increasingly threatened, the CBC stands out as the best vehicle for countering that threat.

As the CRTC ([GD] CRTC 2018, 2022) has said, regulation needs to be "nimble" to respond to the shifting circumstances facing the system. And, as we have seen, in terms of developing services and programming under changing conditions, the CBC has proven to be one of the most nimble organizations. In the face of an uncertain political future, providing the corporation with the means to weather political storms is also important. Both Liberal and Conservative governments have demonstrated that support for the corporation is not guaranteed, and calls from the Conservative Party to "defund the CBC" have become increasingly pronounced (Thomson 2023). Given that the futures of both the Canadian broadcasting system and the CBC are highly uncertain, providing the CBC with the greatest latitude to deal with this environment is the best way to ensure the future of both. The following are some suggestions for doing this:

1   One of the first steps in this direction would be to establish predictable five-to-seven-year funding for the corporation. This has been a perennial recommendation of inquiries and studies but has never been implemented. Despite the Justin Trudeau government's apparent support of the CBC, it too stopped short of recommending or establishing a multi-year funding formula in Bill C-11. History clearly shows that the CBC is true to its legislative mandate and generally fiscally responsible. Legislating a funding formula might be one of the best ways to insulate the corporation from political uncertainties as well as ensure that it can effectively carry out its responsibilities.

2   The CBC should have priority in the licensing of new services and platforms that complement existing operations. Too often such licensing requests have been turned down by the CRTC. The result has been that the private sector has been able to develop economies of scale and scope in their operations that have eluded the CBC. In the world of digital platforms and streaming apps, the corporation may have found the ability to repurpose and cross-promote content. But while under the Digital Media Exemption Order the CBC has enjoyed more latitude in developing new services than it did with specialty channels, at this time exactly how the Online Streaming Act will impact its ability to develop such services is not clear. What is clear is that the CBC needs to have flexibility in this regard if it is to follow and develop audiences and users in the quickly changing mediascape. This is not to say the corporation should abandon audiences that access its services via traditional media. As a number of critics point out, audiences for "television and radio are not disappearing nearly as quickly as the CBC's push to digital might suggest" (Taylor 2016; Taras and Waddell 2020, 130). Addressing the diverse character of the country necessitates meeting Canadians on the diverse technologies that comprise the broadcasting system.

3   The CBC should have enough borrowing authority to provide flexibility in meeting the exigencies of its operations. Although the CBC is an "agent of the Crown" and the federal government is responsible for its debts and liabilities, the corporation should not be forced to sell assets to meet short-term obligations, as it was in 2009 ([GD] CBC 2022). Exactly what such a borrowing limit might be is a question for the federal government and the corporation's administration to decide. But like other powers of the corporation, the limit should be legislated as well as linked to inflation.

4   History shows that it is important to insulate the CBC from the shifting winds
of political change. Ensuring a non-partisan process for the appointment of
the corporation's board of directors and president and CEO at arm's length
from the government of the day is one way to accomplish this goal. While
the Department of Canadian Heritage established a non-partisan independent
advisory committee to recommend candidates for the board of directors in
December 2022, as outlined by Peter Miller and Brian Rogers in 2016, a comprehensive merit-based appointment process should be part of broadcast legislation (Friends of Canadian Broadcasting 2016).

5   On a more controversial note, while there is a long history of people, government committees, and organizations – including the CBC itself – calling
to make the CBC advertising-free, giving the corporation free rein to solicit
advertising and undertake commercial activity would provide it with both
stability and flexibility. As CBC president Catherine Tait has noted, having a
diversified funding model is important "because we [the CBC] don't want to
be vulnerable to shifts in the marketplace and government" (Valiante 2019).
Moreover, as pointed out by Leonard Brockington, the first chair of the CBC,
unlike the private sector, every cent that the corporation takes in is devoted to
developing programming and services for Canadians. Consequently, commercial revenue is deployed to a much different purpose by the public sector than
the private sector.

A common argument against carrying advertising is that it draws public
broadcasters away from their mandates by encouraging them to produce and
schedule programming that attracts large audiences – in other words, programming that is "popular." For instance, as the Broadcasting and Telecommunications Legislative Review Panel ([GD] BTLR 2020, 168) notes, the CBC
"is somewhat compromised by its continuing reliance on advertising, which
necessarily introduces a commercial imperative into its decision-making" and
warps its ability "to pursue a diversity of media content to reflect Canada's
own makeup." This argument is specious on at least two levels. First, as we
have seen, on linear television private broadcasters schedule very little Canadian programming in prime time. In most instances, the CBC is scheduling
commercial Canadian programming against the private sector's commercial
American programming. This hardly seems to run counter to the CBC's mandate. As for the concern that producing popular Canadian programming necessarily undermines the CBC's abilities to "reflect Canada's own make-up," it
would seem that reflecting diversity is exactly what popular CBC programs
such as *Little Mosque on the Prairie, Kim's Convenience, Schitt's Creek,* and
Run the Burbs have been designed to do (Stursberg 2023). As Richard Collins
and colleagues (2001, 10) argue, "public service broadcasting must be popular

if it is to be effective. That means it must reach the many, not just the few."[2] Besides, if programming is to contribute "to shared national consciousness and identity" as specified in the CBC's mandate, it must be popular to some degree. Moreover, in the post–linear broadcasting world, where programming is streamed at the convenience of audience members, the traditional concern about having popular programming edge out programming for more specialized audiences completely loses its currency, as both popular and specialized programming can be made available on the same platform at the same time. Similarly, if the goal is to produce programming for minority tastes, there are other broadcasters in the system, such as community and not-for-profit specialty broadcasters, that might be better suited to that task.

The CBC 2021–22 annual report recognizes the importance of advertising to the corporation's financial sustainability and states that it should "play a leadership role in driving the advertising industry transformation around audience measurement and automation, and reinforce the value and effectiveness of television advertising" ([GD] CBC 2022, 53). The federal government should ensure that the CBC has the flexibility required to achieve this goal.

6 The argument against the CBC's carrying of foreign programming is similarly flawed. Historically, as we have seen, in order to maximize profits the private sector has utilized as much foreign programming as possible, and then been compelled by regulation to devote a portion of air time and/or income to Canadian programming. But because there is simply not as much money to be made from Canadian programming as there is from imported programming, it has always been a struggle to get private broadcasters to invest in Canadian programming – particularly programming focused primarily on Canadian markets. Driven by mandate rather than profit, the CBC operates on a different logic. Foreign programming is scheduled to help draw audiences to Canadian programs and supplement the CBC's income – income that is directed to the cultural and national purposes of the system. Consequently, if the CBC can generate much-needed income from deploying foreign programming on either its linear or streaming services, why shouldn't it be allowed to? While further study of the economic efficiency of the CBC's versus private broadcaster's use of the income derived from foreign programming for producing Canadian programming may be in order, on the face of it, the CBC appears to be both more efficient and more committed to this task than its private counterparts.

7 The CBC should also be allowed to undertake sports coverage as it sees fit. As we have seen, the corporation has been at the forefront of developing such coverage for both radio and television. As the popularity and income potential of such programming has increased, however, the CBC has come under

increasing pressure from the private sector to forgo that business. In the past, limited channel capacity may have led to such programming undercutting the CBC's mandate by edging out other types of programs from the schedule, but in the online environment carriage capacity is much greater and there is no need to prioritize one type of programming over another. Sports programming might provide both important income and publicity opportunities for the CBC.

8 Despite calls from government, private news organizations, and others for the CBC to discontinue advertising on its television and online news services, the CBC should be allowed to carry advertising on its newscasts as it sees fit. The CBC's comprehensive journalistic code ensures that its news adheres to what is arguably the highest standards in the country ([GD] CBC n.d.a). Moreover, to a large degree, the CBC news services are also converged, meaning that news reported on radio and television often originates from the same source/reporter. Consequently, content that is commercial on television is non-commercial on radio. Hence, to a degree, CBC is already commercial-free.

Besides, because news production is by and large undertaken commercially in this country, curtailing the CBC's ability to develop revenue in this regard will not ensure any greater objectivity or reliability in the news business in general. Rather, it would simply be a cash transfer to the private sector, with no guarantee that the revenue would be put to more efficient or effective use. The CBC also maintains a much greater range of news services than the private sector,[3] and cutting back on the revenue generated from news might endanger the comprehensiveness of that news net. And, with ongoing cutbacks in private news organizations, maintaining CBC news facilities is increasingly important (Hudes 2023). Given the crisis in financing news, perhaps there are ways in which the CBC and private-sector news producers might work together to improve news coverage, particularly at the local and regional levels. Things like sharing news-gathering resources, a news co-op like Canadian Press in its early days, or co-operative advertising agreements such as the one between Gem and the *Winnipeg Free Press* might be options in this regard ([GD] CBC n.d.d).

9 The CBC should also be allowed to extend its commercial activity into areas that overlap with its existing expertise, such as Tandem, the corporation's branded content arm. As noted by Scott Stewart, general manager of the market agency Glassroom, "a team like Tandem is nothing new on either the publishing or the broadcast side of industry" (in Summerfield 2021). Media companies such as Corus, the *Globe and Mail,* and Bell Media have been producing such material for years, as has the CBC since 2017 (Summerfield 2021; Gollom 2021). In response to concerns that such material might undermine the corporation's

journalistic credibility, as Catherine Tait said, "we have very, very clear guidelines that are going well beyond anybody in the industry" (in Gollom 2021). As we have seen, the CBC has a long history of responsible commercial behaviour, and in the current political and economic environment, maintaining its commercial flexibility may be key to its survival.

10 In order to sharpen its focus on its mandate to provide "distinctively Canadian" content, the CBC should reinstate in-house production, at least for documentaries. Although historically program production was seen as one of the CBC's primary responsibilities, for a variety of reasons the corporation has shuttered almost all such production other than news and current affairs. Partnering with private sector producers may result in the CBC giving up some degree of creative control as the private partner works to hone the product to its best economic interests. With entertainment products such as drama and sitcoms, this might mean watering down of distinctively Canadian content to allow for wider appeal in international markets, and it might have even more profound consequences for documentary programs as producers weigh the potential impact of their subject matter against future funding possibilities and other political and economic consequences. Somewhat insulated from direct government and private corporate influence, the CBC is in a unique position to produce cutting-edge social and political documentaries. Fully grasping that opportunity would help distinguish the corporation from other media producers. Similarly, in-house production might help ensure that the CBC retains intellectual property rights as it moves to take on a more international role.

11 Taking on a larger role in "bringing Canada's television and film productions to the world stage" is in both the corporation's plan and the Trudeau government's plan for it. Moreover, the Online Streaming Act specifically tasks the Canadian broadcasting system with "foster[ing] an environment that encourages the development and export of Canadian programs globally" (section [1] [d][ii]). Such a role might play well to the CBC's strengths as a development vehicle for Canadian media producers as a whole, as well as open up new revenue possibilities for the corporation. As we have seen, the CBC has highlighted the idea of showcasing Canadian media products at this level since at least the mid-1980s, and it has a long history of developing international co-productions (Tinic 2009).

One of the key issues in this regard is ownership of intellectual property rights, particularly on the domestic front. Assumptions regarding how IP rights are assigned can differ widely between different players and jurisdictions, and transnational streaming companies generally require full rights to the properties they carry (Barrett 2022). As Catherine Tait notes, without ownership of domestic rights, Canadians "are simply renting our country's stories and talent" (in Public Media Alliance 2023). The corporation ended "the collection of both profit participation and retransmission royalties on all projects pre-licensed by CBC from Canadian independent producers" in 2017 ([GD] CBC 2017a). However, as the largest single commissioner of independent productions, the CBC can play an important role in helping negotiate the place of Canadian media producers in both domestic and international streaming markets. Thus, the CBC should be given a free hand as well as the support of the federal government and its agencies in developing strategies in this regard.

At the same time, however, the CBC's primary focus should be on domestic media products. In recent times commercial imperatives have pointed producers toward transnational markets. To increase their currency, the propensity is to downplay the cultural distinctiveness of such products. As a national broadcaster, the CBC should work to counter that tendency and help ensure that there is not a growing void of media products that represent a wide range of Canadian ideas, values, and perspectives. No matter what the programming category or genre, "distinctively Canadian" media products should be the corporation's primary focus.

12 Discoverability is another area where the CBC might take a leading role. Discoverability was a particularly contentious subject in the debates surrounding Bills C-10 and C-11, as critics voiced concerns that interfering with the way algorithms recommend content at the national level could have repercussions for how that content is treated at the international level (Geist, n.d.). These arguments are reminiscent of those advanced to deter the regulation of radio, television, and broadcast distribution technologies. For such critics, unencumbered "consumer choice" is always framed as the optimal regulatory scenario. However, what these critics overlook are the ways in which such choices are predetermined by a larger set of economic forces; in order for there to be a real choice, those forces must be countered to some degree. Just as intervention was necessary to ensure that network distribution was available to facilitate access to Canadian programming in the early days of radio and television, and carriage regulations were central in this regard with the development of cable and satellite technology, so too discoverability is of primary importance to accessing Canadian media products in the ever-growing sea of online content. As noted, the Online Streaming Act has several provisions for helping ensure the discoverability of Canadian media content on transnational services in the national context. While it will be up to the CRTC to decide exactly what regulations arising from the legislation will look like and how they will be implemented, backed by regulatory support from the commission the CBC could help ensure that both the digital infrastructure and data are available to support discoverability, not only for itself but also for other not-for-profit

media producers such as the National Film Board, community and Indigenous broadcasters, and provincial broadcasters at both the national and international levels.

The rationale for generally expanding support for community and Indigenous media producers is discussed below. The CBC's role in facilitating their discoverability might take several forms. At the national level, the corporation could help develop and host the online infrastructure needed to support the discoverability of these organizations' content on its apps and online platforms. Here, subject to privacy provisions similar to those that it already has in place, the CBC might also act as a broker for the data and analytics necessary for algorithmic recommendations in the national context ([GD] CBC n.d.b). Similarly, it could take the lead in developing and promoting an online equivalent of a not-for-profit "green zone" like the one proposed by Bill Roberts at the 2003 Standing Committee on Canadian Heritage ([GD] Standing Committee on Canadian Heritage 2003, 245). At the international level, as part of the project of "bringing Canada's television and film productions to the world stage," when brokering deals with streaming services and other online hosts and portals, the CBC could represent the interests of other not-for-profit media producers as well as its own. As David Taras and Christopher Waddell (2020, 97) point out, "the relationships that it [the CBC] carves out with these new portals and hosts will determine much of its future." The same might be said for other not-for-profit media and broadcasters.

13 The possible impacts of artificial intelligence (AI) are somewhat speculative but, as Mark Mayne (2022) points out, in the broadcast realm it is already being used to enhance viewer experience "by enabling faster access to relevant content and optimising advertising that boosts viewer engagement," as well as to "make better decisions through data-driven analytics." As a not-for-profit broadcaster, the CBC is in a unique position to explore and develop applications of this technology in ways that might further the goals of public broadcasting and facilitate the fulfillment of its mandate. Toward this end, the CBC should be given a free hand in exploring possible applications of this technology.

Other Not-for-Profit Broadcasters

In both anglophone and francophone Canada, publicly mandated not-for-profit broadcasters such as community television and radio, provincial broadcasters, and Indigenous broadcasters have demonstrated the ability to generate media content that is important and relevant to diverse communities, particularly at the local and regional levels (Raboy 1990; Roth 2005; Skinner 2014, 2015; Kozolanka, Mazepa, and Skinner 2012). However, such media producers have historically been subordinated to the interests of private capital in terms of their access to advertising, funding, and modes of distribution. Similarly, while sections 3(1)(i)(iv) and 3(1)(d)(iii.4) of the Online Streaming Act enhanced the scope of the 1991 Broadcasting Act in recognizing the role of community media in the system, sections 3(1)(s)(i) and (ii) specifically subordinate these services to those of private broadcasters by specifying that they should be "complementary to the programming provided for mass audiences" and cater "to tastes and interests not adequately provided for by the programming provided for mass audiences." To some extent, this latter language is redundant, as by virtue of their mandates community broadcasters are by definition not serving mass audiences. However, if by chance they should develop programs with broad appeal, they should not be prohibited from circulating or further developing such programming,

In the face of the growing inability of private capital to provide media alternatives at the local and regional levels, like the CBC these organizations should be given freer rein within the system, with increased access to production funds, priority carriage on BDUs, access to advertising revenue, and help in negotiating discoverability in the shifting context of the system at large. While some organizations may eschew advertising and other commercial activity, others might want to take advantage of such opportunities.

Karen Wirsig and Catherine Edwards (2018) point out that independent community media outlets could play an important role in reinvigorating the media content and community relationships lost with the closing of local TV, radio, and newspaper outlets. They propose establishing public/community partnerships between the CBC and local community media outlets – partnerships that recall the kinds of relationships that the CBC had with private affiliates in the early days of both radio and television. They show that internationally there are a number of precedents for this kind of operation and offer several different models that such collaborations might take. As we have seen, historically there have been a range of public/private partnerships between the CBC and private broadcasters whereby the CBC has worked to subsidize and help develop their operations. In many cases, these affiliation agreements were quite successful in helping establish private media outlets. Putting the CBC's resources and expertise to work in helping to establish not-for-profit mandate-driven community media outlets might be an ideal way to ensure that a comprehensive range of programming and perspectives is available within the system.

Indigenous Broadcasting

Historically the interests of Indigenous broadcasters have been subordinated to those of private broadcasters in similar ways to community and other not-for profit broadcasters. On another front, within the CBC the interests of

Indigenous peoples and cultures have at times been overshadowed by service to southern and settler cultures. In 1990, however, the CRTC ([GD CRTC 1990) introduced its first "Regulatory Framework for Aboriginal Broadcasting," and since then has slowly moved to offer Indigenous broadcasters more independence in how they operate their organizations (see [GD] CRTC 2001; Bannerman 2020). More recently, on the path to reconciliation, the CRTC has initiated a process for the "Co-development of the Indigenous Broadcasting Policy" (CRTC, n.d.b); the CBC has enhanced its commitment to Indigenous representation and participation ([GD] CBC 2019a); and the Online Streaming Act specifies that "programming that reflects the Indigenous cultures of Canada and programming that is in Indigenous languages should be provided" within the broadcasting system (section 3[1][o]). Despite these good intentions, as Glen Coulthard (2014, 3) argues, no matter how well-meaning such "politics of recognition" may be, it is important that the process guard against reproducing "the very configurations of colonialist, racist, patriarchical state power that Indigenous peoples demands for recognition have historically sought to transcend" (cf. Bannerman and Ahmed 2022). Describing the dimensions of such a process is beyond the scope of this book, but by illustrating how deeply infused ideas and values can be within particular institutional forms and processes, the analyses at hand might help point toward spaces and places that need to be interrogated in this regard.

The CRTC: Private and Public Purpose

In supervising the development of the broadcasting system, the CRTC has worked in the interests of private capital in myriad ways, including sanctioning escalating concentration of ownership, adjusting Canadian content regulations to favour capital accumulation, and subordinating the interests of the CBC and other not-for-profit broadcasters to those of private capital. But to say that the commission is "captured" by specific interests or blocks of capital is too simplistic. For instance, in the 1960s the interests of private television broadcasters were paramount in regulation. A decade or so later, cable was favoured. Through the 1980s and 1990s, the entry of independent program producers and satellite broadcasters complicated the scene as the commission moved to accommodate their interests and negotiate their contributions to the system. And, with convergence at the turn of the century, sorting through the ways in which regulatory decisions impacted the range of interests held under one roof by the handful of converged media companies dominating the broadcasting and telecommunications sectors became increasingly complicated. Similarly, the CRTC's attempts to shape the growth of the system – such as its refusal to simply rubber-stamp mergers and acquisitions, its creation of the benefits package, and its unsuccessful efforts to bring internet service providers (ISPs) into the regulatory fold – do not appear to have favoured any particular private interest. Although, given form by the Broadcasting Act, the commission has generally worked to promote and shape Canadian capital, the 1999 decision not to regulate the internet and the ensuing revisiting and renewal of the digital media exemption order increasingly appeared to be detrimental to that larger interest as well.[4] Consequently, faced with pressures and encroachments on the system, and lacking investment capital of its own, rather than being captured per se, as Liora Salter and Rick Salter (1997, 313–14) argue, the commission does appear to have established a system of "co-management" that fashioned compromise between competing interests to develop the broadcasting system.

Here it would appear that a number of forces have been influencing the commission to subordinate the interests of the CBC to those of private capital. Not only was the CBC perennially underfunded and legislatively constrained from acquiring investment capital but dominant, liberal economic assumptions concerning the benefits of competition, the flexibility of private capital, the risk of investment, and the seeming fairness of allowing the government-subsidized public broadcaster to compete with private interests all held sway over these decisions. Since at least 1980, a range of external pressures further moved the CRTC in that direction. The tenuous state of the CBC's finances, admonitions and directions from government to make the broadcast system more flexible and responsive to market forces, and studies like the 1991 report on the economic status of television ([GD] Task Force on the Economic Status of Television 1991), which pointed to the need to provide private capital more flexibility in the system, all oriented the commission toward enlisting private capital rather than public or not-for-profit media to the task of development.

And while critics have often pointed to the sometimes excessive profits of private broadcasters, claiming that these were the product of favouritism on the part of the regulator, from a market perspective, unless private operators are in a position to generate a large surplus from their operations they cannot be expected to undertake further responsibilities in the system. However, given the independent legal status of private broadcasters, harnessing that surplus to the broad public purposes of the system has proved to be another matter.

In this context, it is clear that "different methods of financing and organizing cultural production" have indeed had "traceable consequences for the range of discourses and representations" within that system (Golding and Murdock 1991, 15). More importantly, it is also clear that the most important determinant of whether broadcast programming reflects Canadian attitudes, opinions, ideas, and so on is the explicit or implicit mandate of the broadcast organizations involved in the production of that programming. For those organizations focused on creating a privately appropriated surplus or profit from their operations and/or improving private shareholder value, the general impetus is to undertake activities that yield as large a profit as possible – which, in the context of the rigidities of the Canadian system, apart from news and current affairs, generally points toward either importing foreign programming or producing programming designed for foreign markets. On the other hand, not-for-profit organizations, equipped with a mandate to produce specific types or kinds of programming, are able to focus specifically on those types of programming. Hence, if the goal is to create recognizably Canadian broadcast media products, mandated not-for-profit organizations such as the CBC appear to be best suited to the task. However, countering the forces that cause the regulator to favour private capital is not easily accomplished. Steps in this direction might include the following:

1 More firmly focus the CRTC's mandate on cultural objectives. As the 2003 Lincoln Report noted, the CRTC should not "micromanage the business of the system's trustees" and instead should "focus exclusively on supervision and regulation through a cultural lens" ([GD] Standing Committee on Canadian Heritage 2003, 592). While the Online Streaming Act updates the powers and focus of the CRTC, it does not explicitly prescribe a stronger cultural focus for it.

2 Restore the obligations of BDUs to fund community television broadcasters. Here the commission needs to recognize that different modes of financing broadcast production do have "traceable consequences for the range of discourses and representations" within the system, and regulate accordingly (Golding and Murdock 1991, 15). As we have seen, because their interests have almost always been subordinated to those of private, profit-oriented corporations, independent community television has never been given a real chance at building audiences and achieving its goals.

3 As recommended by the Standing Committee on Canadian Heritage, "the CRTC's regulatory supervision of the CBC should be limited to the approval of new licence applications" ([GD] Standing Committee on Canadian Heritage 2003, 595). For too long the CRTC has micromanaged the policies of the corporation and supplanted the role of its board of directors. This state of affairs has continued over the twenty years since the Standing Committee on Canadian Heritage's report. However, given the CRTC's history of turning down CBC licence applications, some other mechanism that ensures the corporation a stronger position in this regard is in order. For instance, legislating that the CBC should have priority in the licensing of new services and platforms that complement existing operations might be appropriate here.

4 To some extent prioritizing the interests of private capital over those of community, Indigenous, and other interests in the broadcasting system might be the product of a situation where CRTC commissioners and staff are not well versed in the needs and concerns of those interests. Consequently, both commissioners and commission staff should represent the range of interests recognized in broadcast regulation. Appointing and investing in personnel that balance the ways in which different interests are represented in policy outcomes might help promote diversity in this regard.

5 Similarly, not all the productive elements of the system have access to the production funds available within the system. As noted in section 3(2) of the Broadcasting Act, "the Canadian broadcasting system constitutes a single system" and, as such, all the constitutive elements of the system should have access to its resources. The CRTC should work in this direction.

Finally

As has been well documented in this work, private capital has never been adequate to the task of providing a comprehensive broadcasting system that represents the diverse interests and perspectives of the peoples of Canada. As Serra Tinic (2009, 68) points out, in the Canadian context "there is little incentive [for private capital] to develop innovative programs that speak to a culturally diverse population that will never be large enough to justify the cost-benefit ratio of production investment." Mandated, not-for-profit media offer a more focused, cost-effective means of producing such programming. Consequently, regulation should be reoriented to provide such organizations more latitude in serving the diverse needs and interests of Canadians. Part of this effort must be directed toward making the ideas and perspectives provided by these producers discoverable in the vast sea of media products available on the internet. Like the Canadian state itself, the media system it encompasses is the product of social struggle and imagination. As we ride shifting political, economic, and technological tides, regulation must continue to be focused on making both the public and private sectors responsible to the broad public purposes of Canada's media system.

Notes

Introduction

1 References to the CBC include the French service, Radio-Canada (CBC/Radio-Canada).
2 *Broadcasting Act,* SC 1991, c 11; *Online Streaming Act,* SC 2023, c 8.

Chapter 1: The Development Context of Canadian Communications Policy

1 As we shall see, it also led to the subjugation of some voices/peoples as it worked to help exclude them from larger political processes.
2 Indigenous peoples were one of the key constituencies subjugated to the emerging Canadian state in this context (Daschuk 2013; Coulthard 2014).
3 The enlargement of the tariff in the late 1850s marks a key point in this process. Not only did it encourage a closer relationship between the state and capital formation within the country, but it also had the effect of "developing manufactures, trade and traffic" along emerging trade routes between the northern colonies (Innis 1956, 71; see Easterbrook and Aitken 1956, 373–75).
4 Perhaps the most vivid illustration of this growth of a diversity of interests, and the emergence of the state as a "site of struggle" between these interests, is to be found in the election campaign of 1911 (Bashevkin 1991, 15–16; cf. Traves 1979, 4–8).
5 Undoubtedly the state has been an "unequal structure of representation" in this context, as political structure and process have favoured some interests over others (Mahon 1980).
6 As Breuilly (1993, 36) argues, in liberal democracies the political impetus to nationalism is generally commensurate with the rise of industrialism. In Canada's case, it would appear that the late rise of industrialism, combined with the slow emergence of a diversity of forceful political voices, delayed the formation and diffusion of a broad or popular Canadian nationalism until the late nineteenth and early twentieth centuries (Zeller 1987).
7 A site that Coulthard (2014) might find to be part of the problematic "politics of recognition" that he describes in his book *Red Skin, White Mask.*
8 In this way, the emergent logic of these development policies of the 1870s built upon what Innis (1956, 229–31) identifies as the mainstays of Canadian economic development – the importation of American technique, sustained by British investment capital. Only, in a twist encouraged by the British "free trade" policies and the rapid development of American industry after the Civil War, direct investment capital from the United States begins to take the traditional place of British finance capital. As Dallas Smythe (1981) illustrates, however, the path of American direct investment set the Canadian economy on a path of slow absorption into the American industrial infrastructure.
9 The discussion in this section is generally applicable to what Hodgetts (1973, 145) terms "semi-independent, 'quasi-judicial,' administrative agencies." These are boards that adjudicate between the competing private interests, or private interests and the "public interest" as defined by the board and its terms of reference.

10 Schultz (1982, 92) claims that initially regulatory agencies had a "negative policing function," but that their responsibilities have evolved "over the last eighty years to include additional positive, prescriptive functions" such as promoting and planning development as well.

11 As Robert Babe (1990) illustrates, this has certainly been the case with many federal and provincial Crown corporations in the telecommunications industry, which have served as publicly subsidized linkages in larger telecommunications networks.

12 Similar institutional forms developed in other countries, particularly Commonwealth countries such as Australia and New Zealand. See, for instance, Ng (2019).

Chapter 2: Market, State, Culture

1 It was not until the 1960s and 1970s that popular concern was raised over the connections between "culture" as a "way of life" and the larger political and economic relations that give it form. See, for instance, Crean (1976).

2 Original emphasis here taken from an advertisement on the back cover of the *Canadian Forum* (May 1922) by Vipond.

3 While concerns were raised over the foreign domination of the Canadian media as early as the mid-nineteenth century, these were generally motivated by British imperial interests that decried the growing presence, and supposed effects, of American media products in Canada. See Bashevkin (1991, 7–80).

4 See, for instance, Winseck (1998); Magder (1993, 13); Babe (1990, 35–44).

5 For background see Nichols (1948); Rutherford (1978, 7–8); Babe (1990, 35–44); Winseck (1998, 75–11).

6 As Samuel Moffett (1972, 60) illustrates, by 1904 "there were 37,481 miles of commercial telegraph line in Canada against 19,431 miles of railroad."

7 Because telephone systems were initially developed at the local level, municipal and provincial governments played a large role in their formation (C. Armstrong and Nelles 1986; Babe 1990).

8 Daniel Czitrom (1983, 27) shows that the terms of this charter followed a pattern established in the United States in the development of the telegraph industry – only, in that country, it would appear that the privilege of stringing lines along public rights-of-way was granted to all comers, whereas in Canada with telephone lines it was a federally granted monopoly bestowed upon Bell.

9 Czitrom (1983, 25–29) illustrates that there was a similar dispute over AP's apparent news monopoly in the United States between 1870 and 1900.

10 It is interesting to note how, in the face of scarce resources, CP's co-operative corporate structure, given form by an Act of Parliament, enabled a particular set of private, commercial interests to maximize the output of news copy that represented "Canadian" perspectives while at the same time minimizing the costs of its production. In other words, by deferring the realization of a surplus from the production process until a later (and possibly never materializing) moment in that process, the productive output of scarce resources was maximized. Moreover, within such a network of productive relationships, it is not *necessary* to realize a profit from the final distribution of the product to the market. Only enough revenue to sustain these relations of production needs to be realized. While, as we shall see, various networking arrangements have been employed by both the public and private sectors in television production, organizational relations following this pattern have never been instituted – despite the obvious advantages for maximizing resources they hold.

11 Both the theatrical and music industries in Canada were also heavily dominated by American companies through the first part of the twentieth century (Tippett 1990, 142–43).

12 The problems of incorporating francophone Canadians into this vision of Canada through an oral medium were seldom addressed and, as we shall see, would later become a vexing problem for government ownership (cf. Vipond 1992, 23; Raboy 1990).

13 Czitrom (1983, 75) notes that David Sarnoff, head of RCA, proposed a similar technical structure for US radio in 1924, in order to build an economy of scale in transmission and focus scarce funds on program production.

14 While there are no financial figures available to illustrate the problem here, it is interesting to note that what would later prove to be one of the most financially successful stations in the country (CFRB in Toronto) was vertically integrated with Rogers Majestic Corporation, the junior partner in the manufacturers' patent pool. In his appearance before the Aird Commission, the manager of the station explained that it was not built "to pay" in the short term (Nolan 1989, 503). The only other station in Canada owned by manufacturing interests was CFCF in Montreal, which was owned by the Canadian Marconi Company Ltd. Both these stations moved to affiliate with American networks as soon as it was technically feasible. The only other company with the ability to harness economies of scale through vertical integration was the CNR.

15 The CNR's network radio operations were an exception to this rule. And while in the early days of the Depression there were many politically motivated charges that the railway's radio operations were an unnecessary and wasteful expenditure of taxpayers' money, E.A. Weir (1965, 93–95) presents figures that illustrate the expense of these operations to be quite reasonable, compared with the advertising expenses of later major Canadian corporations.

16 Some exceptions to the commission's proposals were that "no real property could be acquired by the company without prior approval of the Governor in Council" and "no limitation on the type or length of advertising messages was mentioned" (Vipond 1992, 226). While the former consideration would have ensured the government some control over the corporation's incursions into the private sector, the latter would have bolstered the corporation's financial independence for, as Vipond (1992, 221) points out, the Aird Commission's proposed controls on advertising would have made it difficult to generate much advertising revenue. In effect, though, provisions that the corporation be ensured full receipt of licence fees, less administrative expenses, as well as a guaranteed government subsidy and the right to borrow money for capital expenditures, would have provided it with both wide latitude of action in the marketplace and the financial resources to exercise its responsibilities.

Chapter 3: The CRBC and the Making of the National Radio Broadcasting System

1 See J. O'Brien (1964); Prang (1965); Weir (1965, 117–36); Peers (1969, 64–102); Vipond (1992).

2 A pamphlet issued by the CRL illustrated the breadth of these aims (Canadian Radio League 1931).

3 As Donna Kaufman (1987) illustrates, the legal foundation of this decision is not clear. However, the legal question addressed was over control between "transmitter and receiver," not the assignment or appropriation of a property right in the radio spectrum.

4 John O'Brien (1964, 250–93) offers a thorough and detailed account of the CRL's representations to the parliamentary committee. As he illustrates, the forces against public ownership were both persistent and well organized, and they put up considerable opposition to the position advanced by the CRL.

5 Reportedly, the CRBC paid the railway $50,000 for its radio assets, but a letter from W.S. Thomson, director of publicity at the CNR, to Hector Charlesworth sets their value at $129,854 (Library and Archives Canada, RG 41, vol. 33, file 22-1; Weir 1965, 139–40).

6　The CRBC's carriage contract with the railways raised the ire of the Trans-Canada Telephone system, particularly among the publicly owned systems in the prairies. At the time, the contract was thought to be the product of backroom political dealing (Weir 1965, 163–64).

7　CRBC letter to CFC, in Library and Archives Canada, RG 41, vol. 33, file 2-2-4-2.

8　As Merrill Dennison (1935, 50), an accomplished Canadian writer and dramatist resident in New York, put it, given the commission's program budget, it "is not in a position to offer anyone who may be dignified by the name 'artist' a fee commensurate with his or her professional standing." As Dennison's place of residence illustrates, one of the perennial problems faced by the commission, as well as other Canadian media producers, is that given the underdevelopment of Canadian markets, there were greater financial benefits for such artists in foreign markets. However, given the American stranglehold on almost all fields of artistic and cultural endeavour at the time, it is not surprising that the CRBC was able to find people to work for much inferior compensation.

9　A memorandum from listeners in Moose Jaw delivered to the minister of marine and fisheries by C.E. Bothwell details a range of these and other complaints. Library and Archives Canada, RG 41, vol. 33, file 2-2-4.

10　A memo from the director of programming seems to indicate that production problems during the summer of 1933 resulted in these programs being broadcast in the west. See Library and Archives Canada, RG 41, vol. 33, file 2-2-4.

11　Early in its tenure, the CBC institutionalized this distinction between French and English programming, and with the introduction of FM radio and television services, a separate network for each of these linguistic groups was set up.

12　Library and Archives Canada, RG 41, vol. 39.

13　The problems of the CRBC were compounded by the often vague and tentative nature of the legislation that gave it form. For instance, in a September 30, 1935, letter to the minister of marine and fisheries the chairman complained that the executive encountered serious difficulty in securing employees as the legislation governing the commission did not allow for hiring permanent staff. Library and Archives Canada, RG 41 vol. 33, file 2-2-4-2.

14　In this vein, Rule 2 of the CRBC's "Rules and Regulations," dated April 15, 1933, stated (Bird 1988, 124):

> These regulations are intended to ensure that all broadcast facilities in Canada, whether privately or publicly owned, shall be so designed, installed and operated as to take full advantage of the latest scientific developments and improvements in physical plant and the methods of operation of broadcast systems, so that the maximum service will be obtained for each station, and the best possible service rendered for Canadian listeners.

15　Historically, neither the private profit-oriented broadcasters nor the public broadcaster have readily disclosed financial information for fear of undermining their competitive positions in the market. Hence, it is difficult to tell exactly what the financial position of the private stations was at this time. However, both Weir (1965) and Peers (1969) present anecdotal information to support the idea that many stations were on rocky economic ground during the early 1930s.

16　During its tenure, the CRBC phased out the "amateur" class of licence, thereby closing off one avenue of possible diversification.

17　As Anne MacLennan (2001) points out, there were some exceptions to this rule, such as radio station CKWX in Vancouver, where links with American networks were hard to come by.

Chapter 4: The CBC and the Entrenchment of Canadian Broadcasting

1 Advertising developed in distinctive stages, each based upon the development of techniques for reaching and segmenting different kinds of audience members (Leiss, Kline, and Jhally 2005, 123–60).

2 Financial information for the early operation of broadcast stations is extremely difficult to obtain. However, E. Austin Weir (1965, 182) compares the expenditures of the CRBC for fiscal year 1935–36 with those of the CBC for 1937–38 as a percentage of revenue: (1) for programs: CRBC 29.5 percent, CBC 52.5 percent; (2) for network facilities: CRBC 40 percent, CBC 25.8 percent; (3) for general administration and station operation: CRBC 30.5 percent, CBC 21.7 percent. Similar figures were reported to the 1938 parliamentary committee on broadcasting by the CBC's officers.

3 In 1938, for instance, in excess of 85 percent of the CBC's income was spent on programming and line rental charges for the networks ([GD] Standing Committee on Radio Broadcasting 1938, 11).

4 As William Malone (1962, 34) illustrates, "comparable payments to affiliates in the U.S. by C.B.S. and N.B.C. in 1935 were 24.09 and 22.02 percent respectively."

5 Interestingly, in the early years, this concern was tempered by an ongoing debate both within the CBC and between the corporation and the government over "controversial" programming. Religious broadcasts, some political broadcasts, and programs concerning issues of public morality, such as birth control, were often refused because of their controversial nature. In this way, the CBC moved to both promote and define a forum of public discussion free of commercial constraint. To some extent, this tradition continues today. However, the shifting, normative nature of the corporation's definition of "controversial" has kept the CBC embroiled in struggles over how the limits of public discussion are to be defined.

6 Despite extreme pressure from some members of the government, the CBC steadfastly refused to make its financial accounts public record during the 1938 committee proceedings lest this information be used against the corporation by its private sector "competitors" ([GD] Standing Committee on Radio Broadcasting 1938, 16–18).

7 In the United States, the "quiz show scandals" of the 1950s also provided impetus to the separation of advertising and program content.

8 Howard Fink (1981, 238) makes the point that this characterization is more appropriate to the American system than to its Canadian counterpart. As he points out, not only was the development of Canadian radio drama interrupted by the Second World War, but with slower adoption rates for television in Canada, as well as continued support by the CBC, radio programming remained stronger and more colourful in Canada much longer than in the United States.

9 As Raboy (1990, 68–72) notes, government censorship was particularly repressive in Quebec, where it was directed against both debates over conscription and critical discussion of the war effort.

10 For a discussion of how news was handled under the CRBC, see Vipond (1999).

11 As Eaman (1994, 105–23) illustrates, the CBC withdrew from the BBM's service in 1956. In 1959, the American A.C. Neilson Company launched a Canadian "diary"-based service to which the CBC subscribed. By the mid-1960s, however, the CBC again began purchasing BBM's information, and by 1970 it was making extensive use of both these services – thereby supporting both the Canadian service and the branch plant. For the most part, because the CBC's programming practices have varied considerably from those of private, profit-motivated broadcasters, the corporation has often had to rely on its own audience research. To this end, the CBC's audience research department has

constructed measures such as an "audience enjoyment index" in an attempt to measure what audiences like about their programs. However, as Eaman (1994) illustrates, such measures do not attempt to uncover the kind of programming that audiences might desire, only what they seem to enjoy, nor are they vigorously employed in the production process.

12 For more discussion of this topic, see Peers (1969, 366–67, 387–88), and Blakely (1979, 107–11).

13 While reliable statistics on the growth of radio advertising are difficult to come by prior to the 1960s, there is evidence to suggest that the dollar value of radio advertising in Canada more than doubled between 1948 and 1960, despite the introduction of television in 1952 (cf. Firestone 1966, 128–30; Leiss, Kline, and Jhally 1988, 92). This is in marked contrast to expenditures in the United States, where radio advertising suffered a sharp decline from 1948 to 1955 as advertisers migrated to television (Leiss, Kline, and Jhally 1988, 91).

14 Comparing statistics from a study done for the Royal Commission on National Development in the Arts, Letters and Sciences (Massey-Lévesque Commission) in 1949 with similar data compiled in 1956 for the Royal Commission on Broadcasting (Fowler Commission), it would appear that commercial time on CBC stations fell by approximately 30 percent between 1949 and 1956, while it increased by a similar amount on private stations affiliated with the CBC's networks. For unaffiliated private English stations, the amount of commercial time doubled (Royal Commission on Broadcasting 1957, 199). And, as Weir (1965, 319) notes, by 1963 sustaining features were no longer required by most private stations and attempts to increase network reserve time were met with strong resistance.

15 Raboy (1990) clearly documents the evolution of this "nationalist" focus in the evolution of broadcasting policy.

16 Perhaps driven by the hegemony of American capital in other venues of cultural expression, concern for the use of "Canadian talent" was a consistent theme in the discussion of broadcast productions throughout the 1930s and 1940s. This concern would later find expression in the "Canadian content rules" promulgated by the Board of Broadcast Governors.

Chapter 5: Television and Early Postwar Canadian Broadcasting Policy

1 Television production took form amid a mixture of different technologies. Prior to the introduction of videotape to the US market in 1956, much programming was produced live. However, there were several recording techniques in use. "Telefilm" involved shooting a program or series on film and then airing it on television. "Kinescope," another common recording technique, involved making a film of a live television image that could then later be taken on air. By the mid-1960s, both of these techniques had generally been replaced by relatively easily edited videotape.

2 While both the reliability and validity of broadcast audience measurement techniques have been vigorously disputed, they have had a very real effect on programs and programming decisions, largely because they have been accepted as fact by both advertisers and broadcasters (Eaman 1994, 140–59).

3 Canada, *Public Announcement No. 26* (Ottawa: CBC, April 11, 1949). See "Television – Statement of Government Policy," Canada, *House of Commons Debates,* 20th Parl, 1949, 1st sess, 2050–52.

4 As a number of writers argue, this "high" cultural vision has enjoyed some currency in both the discourse and institutions of Canadian cultural policy (Crean 1976; Collins

1990; Lee and Winn 1991). Yet, as this book illustrates, such critics often overplay their hands in the field of broadcasting policy and, to some degree, in other policy fields as well. However, vestiges of this perspective continued to haunt broadcasting regulation for decades.

5 The commission's lack of understanding of the commercial dynamics that drove television in the United States is illustrated in the fact that, on the one hand, it charged that advertising was "spoiling" television programs through commercial interruption of both teleplay "intermissions" and "the very material of the show" (47), while, on the other hand, it welcomed private capital's participation in the development of the system, and recommended the importation of "better quality" US programs. Consequently, it is questionable whether the commission understood the degree to which commercial imperatives permeated the American system.

6 Not all of the commissioners agreed with these broadcasting recommendations. Arthur Surveyer, the only one of the five commissioners without a direct affiliation to a university, filed a dissenting opinion on the question of the institution of an independent regulatory board, recommending "that as a matter of elemental equity their demand for an independent regulatory board should be granted" ([GD] Royal Commission on National Development in the Arts, Letters and Sciences 1951, 391).

7 Further to this point, somewhat ironically the Massey family fortune was built upon Massey-Ferguson, manufacturer of industrial farm machinery.

8 As Dallas Smythe (1981, 178) points out, the Massey-Lévesque Commission dismissed the television standard question "as a trivial technical issue [when] it blandly stated that standards do '... not constitute a problem on this continent where it may be assumed that all countries will adopt the established system of the United States'" ([GD] Royal Commission on National Development in the Arts, Letters and Sciences 1951, 46).

9 While Paul Rutherford (1990, 62) notes that there was some reluctance on the part of both sponsors and advertising agencies to accept this new arrangement, with the popularity of the medium "a modus vivendi was worked out," although some companies, such as Proctor and Gamble and Lever Brothers, refused to buy time under these circumstances.

10 The CBC did not only help capitalize broadcasters. As we have seen, it provided a ready source of income to telegraph companies and later telephone interests, to Canadian Press, and to the Bureau of Broadcast Measurement. Through the late 1950s and early 1960s, it would also play a large role in capitalizing the Trans-Canada Telephone systems microwave relay system, and through most of the 1970s it would be Telesat Canada's only broadcast satellite customer (cf. Weir 1965; Babe 1990).

Chapter 6: The Emergence of the Dual System

1 As Michael Storper and Allen Scott (1986, 3–5) illustrate, the growth of the American economy through the late 1950s and 1960s was hinged between two events: (1) the growth of the domestic market for consumer durables, and (2) growing US involvement in the Vietnam War, which was itself fuelled by the emerging "military industrial complex" and "cold war ideological climate." Both events had a strong impact on Canada's political economy: on the one hand, C.D. Howe's branch-plant policy issued an open invitation to American foreign direct investment capital as surpluses generated in the US domestic market sought profitable avenues of growth; on the other hand, this further integration of Canadian and American industrial infrastructure fuelled increasing political integration. Two examples of this process during this period are found in the

negotiation of a North American defence agreement and the Canada-US Automotive Products Agreement (the Auto Pact). In turn, these events fuelled the debate over Canadian sovereignty.

2 These shifting circumstances may have been instrumental in focusing Harold Innis's attention on the field of communication studies. As Easterbrook and Watkins (1980, 262) note, "it is likely that Innis' shift to communication studies reflected his awareness of the 'increasing fragmentation of knowledge' that these changes were bringing with them and led to his search for 'an integration of basic approaches' beyond the limited range of Canadian experience."

3 The struggle surrounding the recommendations of the 1961 report of the Royal Commission on Publications (O'Leary Commission) illustrates these tensions (cf. Bashevkin 1991, 61–82). The commission was originally struck by the Conservatives in an effort to find a solution to the escalating domination of the Canadian periodical market by American publishers through the postwar period. The Liberal government moved to adopt the commission's recommendations in 1965. The intervention focused on building an advertising market for Canadian publications and involved two measures to facilitate this. The first was an amendment to the Customs Act to prevent magazines with a high percentage of advertising by Canadian companies from entering the country. The second sought to put an end to "split-run" editions published inside the country by amending the Income Tax Act to stipulate that only advertising placed in Canadian-owned publications would qualify for tax deductions by the companies placing those ads. Although many Canadian newspapers opposed the latter because it "diminished their potential value as commercial properties, by excluding foreign bidders" for their properties, the government proceeded anyway. Thus, once again the national interest took precedence over a particular domestic economic interest. Amid threats of economic retaliation by the American government, *Time* and *Reader's Digest,* which together accounted for a major share of the Canadian advertising market, were exempt from the latter provision and allowed to continue business as usual. By the mid-1970s, however, the political climate had changed. In combination with an effort to win back television advertising from American border broadcasting stations, the terms of the income tax provision were extended to cover broadcasting and include these two magazines. This was not the end of the story, though. The legislation remained a major irritant to American interests and, in the early 1990s, a copyright agreement wound its way through a complex regulatory maze to in fact restore much of the revenue lost "to American program producers by this measure through a levy on Canadian cable-TV subscribers." And later, in January 1997, the United States won a judgment against Canada before the World Trade Organization under newly negotiated General Agreement on Tariffs and Trade (GATT) provisions, whereby the preferential tax treatment of Canadian-owned magazines was ruled illegal.

4 *Broadcasting Act,* SC 1958, c 22.

5 E. Austin Weir (1965, 366) illustrates that the CBC's "dependence on government advances" did indeed constrain its ability to participate in the ensuing expansion of the system.

6 Generally, because the technology of the time made dubbing the soundtrack of English programs with French almost impossible and importing French-language programming difficult, French-language stations had a much higher percentage of domestic content, with Radio-Canada airing a total of 87 percent Canadian programming, compared with 76 percent for the private stations (Romanow 1974, 38).

7 While there appears to be no historical record of the BBG's deliberations on this matter, the following provides an overview of some of the parameters of the decision provided by other writers in this area.

8 As Erik Barnouw (1990) illustrates, to some extent such efforts to differentiate commercials from programs were already becoming redundant, as performers were often incorporating sponsor's products in program content (see also Newell, Salmon, and Chang 2006).

9 Part of the problem in this respect was that the stations that comprised the private network failed to agree on almost every aspect of network operation, except extracting as much money as possible from the arrangement (cf. Rutherford 1990, 117).

10 In the radio realm, by 1965 private stations had already far outdistanced the CBC in terms of growth. Moreover, the CBC's radio advertising revenue had suffered a precipitous plunge, largely because the corporation refused the new advertising practices brought on by the move to musical formats and stuck to selling time in blocks (Special Senate Committee on the Mass Media 1970b, 292–93).

11 As Weir (1965, 363) notes, as the second stations came on stream, major advertisers tended to focus on and split their expenditures between the stations in the major centres, exacerbating this problem. Indeed, that the CTV affiliates' urban locations yielded a more efficient vehicle for advertisers is illustrated in the fact that in March 1963, the Bureau of Broadcast Measurement reported that CTV's newscast reached a weekly average of 320,000 households a night from nine stations, while the CBC network reached 707,000 on forty-four stations.

12 Interestingly, O.J. Firestone (1966, 294) notes that between 1962 and 1965 the CBC's cost-per-thousand was rising at a faster rate than that of the private broadcasters: 5.5 percent as opposed to 5 percent. However, whether this was a result of the CBC's ability to capitalize on its specialized audiences or simply the rising value of the rural audiences it constructed to advertisers is not known.

13 Behind the idea of program "balance" at the CBC resides an ogre of immense proportions. As the second Fowler Commission ([GD] Committee on Broadcasting [Fowler II] 1965, 124) noted, "balance" was illustrated in the range of programming the CBC presented to meet the needs of its diverse audiences, such as "news, public affairs, science and general information, sports, drama, music, ballet, opera, and light entertainment." However, as R. Bruce McKay (1976, 197–201) illustrates in a landmark participant-observational study of the internal workings of the corporation, balancing the diverse demands placed upon the organization so that they might be manifest in such program categories or formats put incredible pressure on both managerial and production practices as they were shifted to accommodate literally dozens of complex and contradictory objectives. Indeed, from McKay's observations, it seems miraculous that the organization was able to function at all.

14 Here, as had been the case with the creation of Canadian Press in the newspaper industry, the intensive capitalization of Canadian telecasts was facilitated by an agreement that sought to maximize the return to investors through a common ownership relationship.

15 Exactly how profitable this relationship was to the individual affiliates is not known because financial returns to the regulator were kept confidential (Hardin 1985, 180). It would appear that through the late 1960s and well into the 1980s, many were very profitable, particularly the larger stations. Herschel Hardin (1985: 180) claims that as a return on net assets, profits hovered around 55 percent, perhaps higher for CTV affiliates in major centres. However, despite the fact that many private stations may have generated high returns on investment for many years, the large expense of high-quality dramatic productions has always precluded their being undertaken by individual stations, and only the largest and most profitable – generally the CTV affiliates – would be in a position to make the cash contributions necessary to enable such productions. However,

given that these "investments" never had any real chance of producing a return for their investors during this period, there was little incentive to make them (cf. Audley 1983, 289).

16 As noted in the *Report of the Task Force on the Economic Status of Television* ([GD] Task Force on the Economic Status of Television 1991), over the next several decades there would be a variety of pressures upon private stations to consolidate their services. In this process, rising corporate debt often undermined the economies of scale that restructuring promised (21). However, patterns of investment often took a much broader scope than such industry studies account for, as these corporations also moved to invest in new services, such as satellite systems and pay-TV networks, as well as foreign broadcast holdings. Tracing the extent of these investments and the degree to which they were financed through income from Canadian television station holdings is beyond the scope of this work. However, public records hold many illustrations of how corporations such as WIC, Canwest/Global, Baton, and Rogers parlayed their ownership of both the CTV affiliates and a handful of cable systems into large corporate empires. These investments boldly illustrate the difficulties in imposing state control of private capital and attempting to deploy it to public purpose.

17 As Robert Babe (1990, 220–28) illustrates, the struggle over the ownership and control of Telesat between the federal government and Telecom Canada is one of intense corporate intrigue as the telephone companies basically blackmailed the government into handing them control of the company over a period of two decades.

18 *Broadcasting Act*, SC 1967–68, c. 28.

Chapter 7: The Capitalization of Canadian Communication and Culture

1 Despite the larger move to build Canadian ownership, the gaps in Canadian industrial infrastructure soon signalled difficulties with this strategy as, in 1971, federal money was allocated to "Spar Aerospace in Toronto and RCA's branchplant in Montreal" to seed the development of a commercial satellite industry (Babe 1990, 222). Thus, this nationalist project was immediately inscribed in transnational relations of production. As well, of course, placing the satellites in orbit would also be dependent upon American technique.

2 The problems encountered by the federal government in both these areas are exemplified in the stream of policy documents and proposals issued by the DOC through the 1970s and early 1980s, as well as in a number of studies done during this period ([GD] Department of Communications 1971, 1973a, 1973b, 1975, 1983a, 1983b, 1983c). Moreover, the report of the Restrictive Trade Practices Commission Part I ([GD] Restrictive Trade Practices Commission 1981) offers a detailed account of the stilted and self-interested structure of the Canadian telecommunications industry. Taken together, these sources illustrate that the "rigidities" of Canada's political economic infrastructure resulted in practically insurmountable problems for mounting a coordinated effort to meet challenges due to the larger shifts in the world's economy during this period.

3 To a large extent, these moves paralleled government actions in other industries as the federal government struggled to gain control over an increasingly fickle economy (Howlett and Ramesh 1992, 203, 219–21, 248–52).

4 George Streeter (1986) offers a good overview of the ways in which the emerging cable system was hailed as a panacea for almost all of North American society's ills through the late 1960s and 1970s.

5 Details of these disputes may be found in Robert Babe's (1990, 208–28) and Marc Raboy's (1990) studies.

6 *Broadcasting Act*, SC 1967–68, c 2; *Broadcasting Act*, SC 1991, c 11.

7 For instance, see Babe (1979); Audley (1983); Raboy (1990, 1996); Collins (1990); Ellis (1992); L. Jeffrey (1996); Magder (1996).

8 In this project, the CRTC deployed strategies similar to those that Vincent Mosco (1979) illustrates were deployed by the FCC in its efforts to simplify the increasing complexities of broadcast regulation as private capital took hold in the system.

9 As Paul Audley (1983) notes, the weakness of the Canadian television advertising market compared with the American market first noted in the 1960s continued to dog the system through the 1970s, eliciting concern from both broadcasters and regulators alike.

10 Apart from the carriage of American stations and the commercial substitution policy, these "Canadian" cable regulations were very similar to those enacted by the FCC in American markets a few years earlier (Head, Sterling, and Schofield 1994, 76). Thus, as the cable system was integrated into the broadcasting system, American technique was again adapted to Canadian purpose. And, just as in previous instances of such technology transfer, not only did the Canadian system follow the American system in both physical and regulatory outline but, as in both the radio and television systems before it, American programming ensured the adoption of this "Canadian" technology by Canadian audiences.

11 As the CBC set out to improve and extend its service to the North, lack of funding for local programming put into sharp relief the contradictions between the CBC's nationalist project and the programming needs of the communities it set out to serve (cf. McNulty 1988b). Inuit communities, in particular, were marginalized within the emerging system (Inuit Broadcasting Corporation, n.d.). These problems helped set these communities on the path to developing their own media (Roth 2005).

12 While it is sometimes suggested that this problem could have been, or could still be, avoided by auctioning licences to the highest bidder, this was not an effective solution, as under such an arrangement, the private sector would have been largely relieved of its public responsibilities of carrying Canadian programming.

13 Thus, it would appear that to the degree the CRTC is dependent on private capital to promote the growth of the system, Rianne Mahon's (1980) characterization of the CRTC as a component of the capitalist "hegemonic apparatus" of the Canadian state is indeed correct. However, as we have seen, the CRTC was also concerned that interests other than capital should be represented within the system, and took steps to ensure that they were. Consequently, there would not appear to be a necessary correspondence between the actions of the commission and the promotion of private capital. Rather, in combination with this "structural" constraint, the problem would seem to be more a combination of several social forces, such as (1) varying degrees of access to the regulator by different social interests; (2) ideology; and (3) a generally reigning perspective that private capital is the most efficient and effective way to promote economic growth.

Chapter 8: The Rise of the Transactional Audience

1 As noted by the Canadian Centre for Policy Alternatives (2003), as a result "between 1988 and 1994, Canada lost 334,000 manufacturing jobs, equivalent to 17% of total manufacturing employment."

2 *Broadcasting Act,* SC 1991, c 11.

3 Directions to the CRTC (Direct-to-Home (DTH) Satellite Distribution Undertakings) Order, SOR/95-319, https://laws.justice.gc.ca/eng/regulations/SOR-95-319/page-1.html.

4 *Telecommunications Act,* SC 1993, c 38.

5 As Joseph Jackson (1999) notes, the cabinet directive "allowed for exceptions in the 'public interest' in the course of its enactment and, until its withdrawal by the Mulroney government, this exception was applied to nearly every case heard by the Commission."

6 As Lydia Miljan, Tegan Hill, and Niels Veldhuis (2020) illustrate, some of the basic principles of what we have defined as neoliberalism at the opening of this chapter framed that budget. For instance, as Finance Minister Paul Martin is quoted as stating in his 1995 budget speech: "We are acting on a new vision of the role of government in the economy. In many cases that means smaller government." As the authors go on to point out, in preparing the budget six specific questions guided the assessment of government spending: (1) Does the program serve the public interest? (2) Is it affordable? (3) Is government intervention necessary? (4) What is the appropriateness of the federal government's involvement? (5) Is there potential for private/public sector cooperation? (6) Is it efficient? (13).

7 For instance, in February 1997, Baton Broadcasting – once the "flagship" of the CTV network and the epitome of profitability in the system – announced extensive layoffs, ostensibly because the regulator's long-standing program of protecting the revenues of private broadcasters in local markets was no longer working (*Globe and Mail* 1997).

8 Much of this programming would eventually be displaced by sensationalist fare focusing on such things as aliens and conspiracy theories (Lockwood 2011).

9 For an explanation of the CAVCO point system used by the CRTC, see CRTC (2016).

10 In fiscal 2000, the CBC had operating revenues for its main channels of about $1.2 billion. Approximately $800 million of this came from its parliamentary appropriation and about $350 million came from advertising and program sales. A further $116 million was from cable and satellite subscription fees for the corporation's specialty services ([GD] Standing Committee on Canadian Heritage 2003, 254).

Chapter 9: *Plus ça change*

1 As Stursberg went on to note, "a possible reason for the higher audiences is that the 'CBC is the only major English language broadcaster whose prime time schedule between 8 p.m. and 11 p.m. is available for Canadian programs.'" Hence, "the CBC can schedule Canadian programs when Canadians are watching television" ([GD] Standing Senate Committee on Transport and Communications 2007).

2 As Sylvia Blake (2018) illustrates, "while a multitude of stakeholders seem to agree that diversity is a laudable objective, they rarely agree about what precisely it means or what the role for policy should be to best support it."

3 See https://www.youtube.com/watch?v=NqSIgotE4Tw.

4 Stursberg (2012, 194–99) also details how the shifting technology impacted the CBC's news production, as what had previously been "news silos" in radio, television, and the internet were collapsed into a single news production "hub."

5 As Winseck (2021b, 44) notes, these funds "did not come close to off-setting the decline in advertising revenue."

6 As we have seen, this was also a role that the CBC had proposed for itself in the past.

7 *Copyright Act*, RSC 1985, c C-42.

8 In late 2018, the federal government announced a $600 million package of tax credits and incentives over five years to help struggling news producers (Canadian Press 2018). Still, criticism of the CBC's news operations continued (Hopper 2018).

9 *Broadcasting Act*, SC 1991, c 11; *Telecommunications Act*, SC 1993, c 38; *Radiocommunications Act*, RSC 1985, c R-2.

10   The full text of the amendment to section 3(1)(l) is: "The Canadian Broadcasting Corporation, as the national public broadcaster, should provide broadcasting services incorporating a wide range of programming that informs, enlightens and entertains."

11   PNI for private broadcasters was set at 5 percent of total program spending, while it was 42 percent for Radio-Canada and 55 percent for the CBC.

12   There was also a change in section 6.1, subparagraph 3(1)(m)(iv), from "be in English and in French, reflecting the different needs and circumstances of each official language community, including the particular needs and circumstances of English and French linguistic minorities" to "be in English and in French, reflecting the different needs and circumstances of each official language community, including the specific needs and interests of official language minority communities."

Conclusion

1   As noted in section 3(1)(n) of the 1991 Broadcasting Act, "where any conflict arises between the objectives of ... [CBC/Radio-Canada] ... and the interests of any other broadcasting undertaking of the Canadian broadcasting system, it shall be resolved in the public interest." Consequently, as we have seen, in regulatory practice by and large, "the public interest" would appear to be the interests of private capital.

2   Similarly, as Serra Tinic (2009, 69) notes, "the network has ... shown that it can achieve success in popular entertainment programming. Political sketch comedies, in particular, often rate well, drawing audiences away from imported programming on the private networks."

3   The following table compares five different news services in terms of Canadian bureaus, international bureaus/correspondents, and international bureaus in different countries.

News service	Canadian bureaus	International bureaus/ correspondents	International bureaus – countries
Canadian Press	12	1	US
CBC	40	5	China, UK, US(3)
CTV	7	3	UK, US(2)
Global News (Corus)	21	2 (correspondents)	UK, US
CityNews (Rogers)	1	0	–

*Sources:*https://www.cbc.ca/news/about-cbc-news-1.1294364;https://en.wikipedia.org/wiki/CTV_News;https://globalnews.ca/pages/about/;https://toronto.citynews.ca/about/;https://www.thecanadianpress.com/contact/our-newsrooms/; [GD] CBC 2022.

4   As we saw with the Supreme Court decisions that ISPs do not fall under the definition of "broadcasting undertaking" and the blocking of US Super Bowl advertising, the CRTC is also constrained by the legal system (R. Armstrong 2016, 185; Canadian Press 2019b).

Works Cited

Government Documents [GD]

Broadcasting Act, SC 1958, c 22.

Broadcasting Act, SC 1967–68, c 2.

Broadcasting Act, SC 1991, c 11.

CBC (Canadian Broadcasting Corporation). 1939a. *Annual Report.* Ottawa: CBC.

–. 1939b. Statement of Policy with Respect to Controversial Broadcasting, July 8. Library and Archives Canada, RG 41, vol. 33, file 191.

–. 1946. A Digest of Statements on the Policies, Administration, and Programs of the Canadian Broadcasting Corporation. Library and Archives Canada, RG 41, vol. 33, file 191.

–. 1959. *Annual Report, 1958–59.* Ottawa: CBC.

–. 1960. *Annual Report, 1959–60.* Ottawa: CBC.

–. 1961. *Annual Report, 1960–61.* Ottawa: CBC.

–. 1985. *Let's Do It!* Ottawa: CBC.

–. 1998. "CBC News Online Launches." November 16. https://www.cbc.ca/10th/timeline-Content/19981116_news.html.

–. 1999. *Unique, Essential, Connected: CBC Radio-Canada – Our Commitment to Canadians.* Toronto: CBC Radio-Canada.

–. 2010. "Avis de consultation de radiodiffusion CRTC 2010-488 – Examen de la politique sur la distribution par satellite de radiodiffusion directe." September 8. https://site-cbc.radio-canada.ca/documents/impact-and-accountability/regulatory/crtc-2010-488.pdf.

–. 2011a. *Annual Report, 2010–11.* Ottawa: CBC.

–. 2011b. *Strategy 2015.* Accessed July 14, 2021. http://cbc.radio-canada.ca/en/explore/strategies/strategy-2015/.

–. 2012a. "CBC Hamilton." May 10. https://cbc.radio-canada.ca/en/media-centre/cbc-hamilton.

–. 2012b. "Same Strategy, Different Path." https://site-cbc.radio-canada.ca/site/budget/en/index.html.

–. 2014a. *Final Comments; Let's Talk TV: Broadcasting Notice of Consultation 2014-190.* https://site-cbc.radio-canada.ca/documents/impact-and-accountability/regulatory/bnc-2014-190-cbcsrc-final-30ct2014.pdf.

–. 2014b. *Strategy 2020: A Space for Us All.* https://cbc.radio-canada.ca/en/vision/strategy/strategy-2020.

–. 2017a. "CBC to Eliminate Profit Participation and Retransmission Royalties from Its Deals with Canadian Independent Producers." Press release, September 11. https://www.cbc.ca/mediacentre/press-release/cbc-to-eliminate-profit-participation-and-retransmission-royalties-from-its.

–. 2017b. *A Creative Canada: Strengthening Canadian Culture in a Digital World.* https://cbc.radio-canada.ca/en/media-centre/a-creative-canada-strengthening-canadian-culture-in-digital-world.

–. 2019a. *Our Canada, Our Democracy: Canada in a Digital World*. Ottawa: CBC.

–. 2019b. "When the CRTC Decided the Internet Couldn't Be Regulated." CBC Archives, May 17. https://www.cbc.ca/archives/when-the-crtc-decided-the-internet -couldn-t-be-regulated-1.5119781.

–. 2019c. *Your Stories, Taken to Heart: Our New Three-Year Strategy*. https://site-cbc. radio-canada.ca/documents/vision/strategy/2019-strategic-plan-en.pdf.

–. 2022. *Annual Report, 2021–22*. Ottawa: CBC. https://cbc.radio-canada.ca/en/impact-and -accountability/finances/annual-reports.

–. n.d.a. "Journalistic Standards and Practices." https://cbc.radio-canada.ca/en/vision/ governance/journalistic-standards-and-practices.

–. n.d.b. "Privacy Notice for Digital Platforms." https://cbc.radio-canada.ca/en/ impact-and-accountability/privacy/privacy-notice.

–. n.d.c. "Supplementary Brief: Towards a 21st Century, Audience-First Regulatory Framework for Canada's Public Broadcaster." https://site-cbc.radio-canada.ca/ documents/impact-and-accountability/regulatory/2019/Supplementary%20brief.pdf.

–. n.d.d. "Winnipeg Free Press." https://cbchelp.cbc.ca/hc/en-ca/articles/360051804433 -Winnipeg-Free-Press.

Committee on Broadcasting. 1932. *Proceedings*.

–. 1934. *Proceedings*.

Committee on Broadcasting (Fowler II). 1965. *Report*. Ottawa: Queen's Printer.

Consultative Committee on the Implications of Telecommunications for Canadian Sovereignty (Clyne Committee). 1979. *Report*. Ottawa. Minister of Supply and Services.

CRBC (Canadian Radio Broadcasting Commission). 1932–36. *Annual Reports*. Ottawa: King's Printer.

–. 1933. "Rules and Regulations." In *Documents of Canadian Broadcasting*, edited by Roger. Bird, 124–32. Ottawa: Carleton University Press, 1988.

CRTC (Canadian Radio-television and Telecommunications Commission). 1974a. Public Announcement, September 18. Ottawa.

–. 1974b. "Radio Frequencies Are Public Property." Public Announcement and Decision on CBC License Renewals, March. Ottawa.

–. 1978. *A Report on Pay-Television*. Ottawa: Department of Supply and Services.

–. 1979. *Special Report on Broadcasting in Canada: 1968–1978*. Ottawa: Minister of Supply and Services.

–. 1980. *The 1980s: A Decade of Diversity*. Ottawa: Department of Supply and Services.

–. 1985a. Public Notice CRTC 1985-139: A Broadcasting Policy Reflecting Canada's Linguistic and Cultural Diversity. July 4. https://crtc.gc.ca/eng/archive/1985/PB85-139. htm.

–. 1985b. Public Notice CRTC 1985-194: The Review of Community Radio. August 26. https://crtc.gc.ca/eng/archive/1985/PB85-194.htm.

–. 1990. Public Notice CRTC 1990-89: Native Broadcasting Policy. September 20. https:// crtc.gc.ca/eng/archive/1990/pb90-89.htm.

–. 1991a. Decision CRTC 91-423: Canadian Broadcasting Corporation. June 28. https:// crtc.gc.ca/eng/archive/1991/db91-423.htm.

–. 1991b. Decision CRTC 91-826: Television Northern Canada Incorporated. October 28. https://crtc.gc.ca/eng/archive/1991/DB91-826.htm.

–. 1993. Public Notice CRTC 1993-74: Structural Hearing. June 3. https://crtc.gc.ca/eng/ archive/1993/PB93-74.htm.

–. 1995a. "Competition and Culture on Canada's Information Highway: Managing the Realities of Transition." https://publications.gc.ca/site/eng/9.657671/publication.html.

–. 1995b. Public Notice CRTC 1995-48: Introduction to Decisions Renewing the Licences of Privately-Owned English-Language Television Stations. March 24. https://crtc. gc.ca/eng/archive/1995/pb95-48.htm.

–. 1996. Public Notice CRTC 1996-69: Call for Comments on a Proposed Approach for the Regulation of Broadcast Distribution Undertakings. May 17. https://crtc.gc.ca/eng/ archive/1996/PB96-69.htm.

–. 1997. Public Notice CRTC 1997-25: New Regulatory Framework for Broadcast Distribution Undertakings. March 11. https://crtc.gc.ca/eng/archive/1997/PB97-25.htm.

–. 1998. Public Notice CRTC 1998-44: Canadian Television Policy Review: Call for Comments. May 6. https://crtc.gc.ca/eng/archive/1998/PB98-44.htm.

–. 1999a. Decision CRTC 99-42: Television Northern Canada Incorporated. February 22. https://crtc.gc.ca/eng/archive/1999/DB99-42.htm.

–. 1999b. Public Notice CRTC 1999-84: New Media. May 17. https://crtc.gc.ca/eng/ archive/1999/PB99-84.htm.

–. 1999c. Public Notice CRTC 1999-97: Building on Success: A Policy Framework for Canadian Television. June 11. https://crtc.gc.ca/eng/archive/1999/pb99-97.htm.

–. 2000a. Decision CRTC 2000-1: Licences for CBC English-Language Television and Radio Renewed for a Seven-Year Term. January 6. https://crtc.gc.ca/eng/archive/2000/ DB2000-1.htm.

–. 2000b. Public Notice CRTC 2000-13: Community Radio Policy. January 28. https:// crtc.gc.ca/eng/archive/2000/pb2000-13.htm.

–. 2001. Public Notice CRTC 2001-70: Changes to Conditions of Licence for Certain Native Radio Undertakings. June 15. https://crtc.gc.ca/eng/archive/2001/pb2001-70.htm.

–. 2004. "Broadcasting Policy Monitoring Report." https://publications.gc.ca/collections/ Collection/BC9-1-2004E.pdf.

–. 2007. Broadcasting Public Notice CRTC 2007-53: Determinations regarding Certain Aspects of the Regulatory Framework for Over-the-Air Television. May 17. https:// crtc.gc.ca/eng/archive/2007/pb2007-53.htm.

–. 2008a. Broadcasting Public Notice CRTC 2008-4: Diversity of Voices. January 15. https://crtc.gc.ca/eng/archive/2008/pb2008-4.htm.

–. 2008b. Broadcasting Public Notice CRTC 2008-100: Regulatory Frameworks for Broadcasting Distribution Undertakings and Discretionary Programming Services. October 30. https://crtc.gc.ca/eng/archive/2008/PB2008-100.htm.

–. 2008c. *CRTC Report to the Minister of Canadian Heritage on the Canadian Television Fund.* https://crtc.gc.ca/eng/publications/reports/ctf080605.htm.

–. 2009a. Broadcasting Regulatory Policy CRTC 2009-329: Review of Broadcasting in New Media. June 4. https://crtc.gc.ca/eng/archive/2009/2009-329.htm.

–. 2009b. *Compensation for Value of Signal: Discussion Paper on the CRTC Illustration.* May 14. https://crtc.gc.ca/eng/publications/p090514.htm.

–. 2010a. Broadcasting Regulatory Policy 2010-167: A Group-Based Approach to the Licensing of Private Television Services. March 22. https://crtc.gc.ca/eng/ archive/2010/2010-167.htm.

–. 2010b. *The Implications and Advisability of Implementing a Compensation Regime for the Value of Local Television Signals.* March 23. https://crtc.gc.ca/eng/publications/ reports/rp100323.htm.

–. 2011. *Results of the Fact-Finding Exercise on the Over-the-Top Programming Services.* October. https://crtc.gc.ca/eng/publications/reports/rp1110.htm.

–. 2013a. Broadcasting Decision CRTC 2013-263: Canadian Broadcasting Corporation – Licence Renewals. May 28. https://crtc.gc.ca/eng/archive/2013/2013-263.htm#bm.

–. 2013b. Broadcasting Notice of Invitation CRTC 2013-563: Let's Talk TV: A Conversation with Canadians about the Future of Television. October 24. https://crtc.gc.ca/eng/archive/2013/2013-563.htm.

–. 2014. *Maximizing the Ability of Canadian Consumers to Subscribe to Discretionary Services on a Service by Service Basis.* April 24. https://crtc.gc.ca/eng/publications/reports/rp140424e.htm.

–. 2015a. Broadcasting Regulatory Policy CRTC 2015-86: Let's Talk TV: The Way Forward – Creating Compelling and Diverse Canadian Programming. March 12. https://crtc.gc.ca/eng/archive/2015/2015-86.pdf.

–. 2015b. Broadcasting Regulatory Policy CRTC 2015-96: Let's Talk TV: A World of Choice – A Roadmap to Maximize Choice for TV Viewers and to Foster a Healthy, Dynamic TV Market. March 19. https://crtc.gc.ca/eng/archive/2015/2015-96.htm.

–. 2016. Broadcasting Regulatory Policy CRTC 2016-224: Policy Framework for Local and Community Television. June 15. https://crtc.gc.ca/eng/archive/2016/2016-224.htm.

–. 2017a. Broadcasting Decision CRTC 2017-148: Renewal of Licences for the Television Services of Large English-Language Ownership Groups. May 15. https://crtc.gc.ca/eng/archive/2017/2017-148.htm.

–. 2017b. "Types of TV Broadcasters." May 15. https://crtc.gc.ca/eng/television/services/types.htm.

–. 2018. "Harnessing Change: The Future of Programming Distribution in Canada." https://crtc.gc.ca/eng/publications/s15/.

–. 2022. Broadcasting Decision CRTC 2022-165: Canadian Broadcasting Corporation – Various Audio and Audiovisual Services – Licence Renewals. https://crtc.gc.ca/eng/archive/2022/2022-165.htm.

–. n.d. "Regulatory Plan to Modernize Canada's Broadcasting Framework." https://crtc.gc.ca/eng/industr/modern/plan.htm.

Department of Canadian Heritage. 1996. *Making Our Voices Heard: Report of the Mandate Review Committee.* Ottawa: Department of Supply and Services.

–. 2017. *Creative Canada: Policy Framework.* Ottawa. https://www.canada.ca/content/dam/pch/documents/campaigns/creative-canada/CCCadreFramework-EN.pdf.

–. 2023. "Online Streaming Act Receives Royal Assent." April 27. https://www.canada.ca/en/canadian-heritage/news/2023/04/online-streaming-act-receives-royal-assent.html.

Department of Communications. 1971. *Instant World: A Report on Telecommunications in Canada.* Ottawa: Information Canada.

–. 1973a. *Computer/Communications Policy: A Position Statement by the Government of Canada.* April. Ottawa: Information Canada.

–. 1973b. *Proposals for a Communications Policy for Canada.* March. Ottawa: Information Canada.

–. 1975. *Communications: Some Federal Proposals.* Ottawa: Information Canada.

–. 1983a. *Building for the Future: Towards a Distinctive CBC.* Ottawa: Deparment of Supply and Services.

–. 1983b. *Culture and Communications: Key Elements of Canada's Economic Future. Brief Submitted by the Hon. Francis Fox, Minister of Communications, to the Royal Commission on the Economic Union and Development Prospects for Canada.* Ottawa: Department of Supply and Services.

–. 1983c. *Towards a New Broadcasting Policy.* Ottawa: Department of Supply and Services.

–. 1987. *Vital Links: Canadian Cultural Industries.* Ottawa: Department of Supply and Services.

Department of Marine and Fisheries. 1923. "License to Use Radio." April 18. Library and Archives Canada, RG 97, vol. 149, 6206-72-1. In *Documents of Canadian Broadcasting*, edited by Roger Bird, 31–34. Ottawa: Carleton University Press, 1988.

Federal Cultural Policy Review Committee (Applebaum-Hébert Committee). 1982. *Report*. Ottawa: Department of Communications.

Governor-in-Council. 2022. "Order Referring Back to the CRTC Broadcasting Decision CRTC 2022-165: SI/2022-44." September. https://canadagazette.gc.ca/rp-pr/p2/2022/2022-09-28/html/si-tr44-eng.html.

House of Commons. 1934. *Debates*. Vol. 1.

–. 1935. *Debates*.

–. 1936. *Journals*.

IHAC (Information Highway Advisory Council). 1997. *Preparing Canada for a Digital World*. Ottawa: Industry Canada.

Industry Canada. 1996. "Convergence Policy Statement." Accessed May 12, 2005. http://strategis.ic.gc.ca/epic/internet/insmt-gst.nsf/en/sf05265e.html.

Innovation, Science and Economic Development Canada. 2020. *Canada's Communications Future: Time to Act*. Ottawa. https://ised-isde.canada.ca/site/broadcasting-telecommunications-legislative-review/en/canadas-communications-future-time-act.

Parliamentary Committee on Broadcasting. 1942. *Proceedings*.

–. 1943. *Proceedings*.

–. 1947a. *Proceedings*.

–. 1947b. *Report*.

–. 1961. *Proceedings*.

Prime Minister of Canada. 2021. "Minister of Canadian Heritage Mandate Letter." December 16. https://pm.gc.ca/en/mandate-letters/2021/12/16/minister-canadian-heritage-mandate-letter.

Privy Council. 1979. *Submissions to the Royal Commission on Financial Accountability – Responsibility in the Constitution: Part II, Non-Departmental Bodies*. Ottawa: Minster of Supply and Services.

Restrictive Trade Practices Commission. 1981. *Telecommunications in Canada: Part 1 – Interconnection*. Ottawa.

Royal Commission on Broadcasting. 1957. "Canadian Television and Sound Programmes, Appendix XIV." In *Report, Royal Commission on Broadcasting* (Fowler Report). Ottawa: Queen's Printer.

Royal Commission on National Development in the Arts, Letters and Sciences. 1951. *Report* (Massey Report). Ottawa: King's Printer.

Royal Commission on Newspapers. 1981. *Report* (Kent Report). Ottawa: Supply and Services Canada.

Royal Commission on Radio Broadcasting. 1929. "Report." In *Documents of Canadian Broadcasting*, edited by Roger Bird, 41–55. Ottawa: Carleton University Press, 1988.

Royal Commission on Railways and Transportation. 1917. Report of the Royal Commission to Inquire into Railways and Transportation in Canada (Smith Report). Ottawa: J. de L. Tache.

Royal Commission on the Economic Union and Development Prospects for Canada. 1985. *Report*, vol. 1. Ottawa: Minister of Supply and Services.

Senate Special Committee on Mass Media. 1970a. Davey Report. *Volume 1: The Uncertain Mirror*. Ottawa: Queen's Printer.

–. 1970b. Davey Report. *Volume 2: Words, Music, Dollars*. Ottawa: Queen's Printer.

Special Committee on Broadcasting. 1936. *Proceedings*.

Special Committee on Radio Broadcasting. 1946. *Report*.

Standing Committee on Canadian Heritage. 1995. *The Future of the Canadian Broadcasting Corporation in the Multi-Channel Universe*. Ottawa: Canada Communication Group.

–. 2003. *Our Cultural Sovereignty: The Second Century of Canadian Broadcasting* (Lincoln Report). Ottawa: Communication Canada.

–. 2005. *Reinforcing Our Cultural Sovereignty – Setting Priorities for the Canadian Broadcasting System: Second Response to the Report of the Standing Committee on Canadian Heritage*. Ottawa: Canadian Heritage. https://publications.gc.ca/site/eng/9.687381/publication.html.

–. 2008. *CBC/Radio-Canada – Defining Distinctiveness in the Changing Media Landscape: Report of the Standing Committee on Canadian Heritage*. Ottawa: Canadian Heritage. https://www.ourcommons.ca/Content/Committee/392/CHPC/Reports/RP3297009/chpcrp06/chpcrp06-e.pdf.

–. 2017. *Disruption – Change and Churning in Canada's Media Landscape: Report of the Standing Committee on Canadian Heritage*. Ottawa: Canadian Heritage. https://www.ourcommons.ca/documentviewer/en/42-1/CHPC/report-6/page-5.

Standing Committee on Radio Broadcasting. 1938. *Proceedings*.

Standing Senate Committee on Transport and Communications. 2006. *Final Report on the Canadian News Media*. June 6. https://sencanada.ca/content/sen/committee/391/tran/rep/repfinjun06vol1-e.htm.

–. 2007. *The Challenges Ahead for the Canadian Television Fund*. May. https://sencanada.ca/content/sen/committee/391/tran/rep/repmay07-e.htm.

Statistics Canada. 2008. *Television Broadcasting Industries 2007*. Ottawa: Statistics Canada.

–. 2010. "Television Broadcasting." July 12. https://www150.statcan.gc.ca/n1/daily-quotidien/100712/dq100712a-eng.htm.

Task Force on Broadcasting Policy. 1986. *Report*. Ottawa: Minister of Supply and Services.

Task Force on the Economic Status of Television. 1991. *Report of the Task Force on the Economic Status of Television* (Girard-Peters Report). Ottawa: Minister of Supply and Services.

Secondary Sources

Aitken, Hugh G.J. 1961. *American Capital and Canadian Resources*. Cambridge, MA: Harvard University Press.

–. 1967. "Defensive Expansionism: The State and Economic Growth in Canada." In *Approaches to Canadian Economic History*. edited by W.T. Easterbrook and M.H. Watkins. Toronto: McClelland and Stewart.

Albo, Greg, and Jane Jenson. 1997. "Remapping Canada: The State in the Era of Globalization." In *Understanding Canada: Building on the New Canadian Political Economy*, edited by Wallace Clement, 215–39. Montreal and Kingston: McGill-Queen's University Press.

Allard, Thomas J. 1979. *Straight Up: Private Broadcasting in Canada, 1918–58*. Ottawa: Canadian Communications Foundation.

Alzner, Belinda. 2012. "CBC Hamilton Digital Service Officially Launched." *J-Source*, May 10. https://j-source.ca/cbc-hamilton-digital-service-officially-launched/.

Anderson, B. 2006. *Imagined Communities: Reflections on the Origin and Spread of Nationalism*. London: Verso.

Anderson, John. 2016. *An Over-the-Top Exemption: It's Time to Fairly Tax and Regulate the New Internet Media Services.* Ottawa: Canadian Centre for Policy Alternatives. https://policyalternatives.ca/publications/reports/over-top-exemption.

Anderson, Peter S. 1976. "The CBC and Its Mandate." MA thesis, Simon Fraser University.

Armstrong, Christopher, and H.V. Nelles. 1986. *Monopoly's Moment: The Organization and Regulation of Canadian Utilities, 1830–1930.* Philadelphia: Temple University Press.

Armstrong, Robert. 2016. *Broadcasting Policy in Canada.* 2nd ed. Toronto: University of Toronto Press.

Audley, Paul. 1983. *Canada's Cultural Industries.* Toronto: James Lorimer.

Babe, Robert E. 1979. *Canadian Television Broadcasting Structure, Performance and Regulation.* Ottawa: Economic Council of Canada.

–. 1988. "Copyright and Culture." *Canadian Forum,* February/March. Also reproduced in *The Strategy of Canadian Culture in the 21st Century,* edited by Ian Parker, John Hutcheson, and Pat Crawley, 57–65. Toronto: TopCat Communications.

–. 1990. *Telecommunications in Canada: Technology, Industry, and Government.* Toronto: University of Toronto Press.

–. 1993. "Communication: Blindspot of Western Economics." In *Illuminating the Blindspots: Essays Honoring Dallas W. Smythe,* edited by Janet Wasko, Vincent Mosco, and Manjunath Pendakur, 15–39. Norwood, NJ: Ablex Publishing.

–. 2011. "'Life Is Information': The Communication Thought of Graham Spry." In *Media, Structures, and Power: The Robert E. Babe Collection,* edited by Edward Comor, 66–80. Toronto: University of Toronto Press.

Baggaley, Carman D. 1981. *The Emergence of the Regulatory State in Canada, 1867–1939.* Technical Report No. 15. Ottawa: Economic Council of Canada.

Bannerman, Sara. 2020. *Canadian Communication Law and Policy.* Toronto: Canadian Scholars.

Bannerman, Sara, and Nawshaba Ahmed. 2022. "Online Streaming Act Claims to Level the Playing Field ... but for Whom?" *The Conversation,* June 6. https://theconversation.com/online-streaming-act-claims-to-level-the-playing-field-but-for-whom-179051.

Barney, Darin. 2005. *Communication Technology.* Vancouver: UBC Press.

Barnouw, Erik. 1968. *The Golden Web: A History of Broadcasting in the United States: 1933–1953.* New York: Oxford University Press.

–. 1990. *Tube of Plenty: The Evolution of American Television.* 2nd rev. ed. New York: Oxford University Press.

Barrett, Douglas. 2022. "Commentary: The Importance of Canadian IP in Defining Canadian Content." *Cartt.ca,* May 4. https://cartt.ca/commentary-the-importance-of-canadian-ip-in-defining-canadian-content/.

Bashevkin, Sylvia B. 1991. *True Patriot Love: The Politics of Canadian Nationalism.* Toronto: Oxford University Press.

Baskerville, Peter. 1992. "Transportation, Social Change and State Formation, Upper Canada, 1841–1864." In *Colonial Leviathan: State Formation in Mid-Nineteenth Century Canada,* edited by Allan Greer and Ian Radforth, 230–56. Toronto: University of Toronto Press.

Beale, Alison. 1988. "The Question of Space: Transportation in Relation to Communication with Some Implications for Broadcasting." In *Communication Canada: Issues in Broadcasting and New Technologies,* edited by Rowland Lorimer and Donald Wilson, 42–57. Toronto: Kagan and Woo.

Beaty, Bart, and Rebecca Sullivan. 2006. *Canadian Television Today.* Calgary: University of Calgary Press.

Bell. 2010. "Bell to Acquire 100% of Canada's No.1 Media Company CTV." News release, September 10. https://www.bce.ca/news-and-media/releases/show/bell-to-acquire-100-of-canadas-no1-media-company-ctv#.

Beltrame, Julian. 2007. "CRTC Rejects TV Network Fees." *Toronto Star,* May 17. https://www.thestar.com/business/2007/05/17/crtc_rejects_tv_network_fees.html.

Benzine, Adam. 2019. "CBC Will No Longer Work with Netflix to Produce Shows, Says Catherine Tait." *Financial Post,* October 8. https://financialpost.com/telecom/media/cbc-will-no-longer-work-with-netflix-to-produce-shows-says-catherine-tait.

Berland, Jody. 1994. "Radio Space and Industrial Time: The Case of Music Formats." In *Canadian Music: Issues of Hegemony and Identity,* edited by Beverley Diamond and Robert Witmer, 173–87. Toronto: Canadian Scholars.

Berland, Jody, and Will Straw. 1994. "Getting Down to Business: Cultural Politics and Policies in Canada." In *Communications in Canadian Society,* edited by Benjamin D. Singer. Scarborough: Nelson Canada.

Berlin, Barry. 1990. *The American Trojan Horse: U.S. Television Confronts Canadian Economic and Cultural Nationalism.* Westport, CT: Greenwood Press.

Bird, Roger, ed. 1988. *Documents of Canadian Broadcasting.* Ottawa: Carleton University Press.

Blake, Raymond, ed. 2007. *Transforming the Nation: Canada and Brian Mulroney.* Montreal and Kingston: McGill-Queen's University Press.

Blake, Sylvia. 2018. "Diversity for Everyone? Mapping the Evolution of Broadcast Diversity Objectives in the CRTC's Let's Talk TV Proceedings." https://crtc.gc.ca/eng/acrtc/prx/2018blake.htm.

Blakeley, Stewart W. 1979. "Canadian Private Broadcasters and the Reestablishment of a Private Broadcasting Network." PhD dissertation, University of Michigan.

Bliss, Michael. 1970. "Canadianizing American Business: The Roots of the Branch Plant." In *Close the 49th Parallel: The Americanization of Canada,* edited by Ian Lumsden, 27–42. Toronto: University of Toronto Press.

–. 1982. "The Evolution of Industrial Policies in Canada: An Historical Survey." Discussion Paper No. 218. Ottawa: Economic Council of Canada.

Boddy, William. 1987. "Operation Frontal Lobes versus the Living Room Toy: The Battle over Programme Control in Early Television." *Media, Culture and Society* 9 (3): 347–68.

Bradshaw, James, and Christine Dobby. 2016. "'This Was Going to Be the Blais Show.'" *Globe and Mail,* September 9. https://www.theglobeandmail.com/report-on-business/blais-crtc-profile/article31797971/.

Bredin, Marian, Scott Henderson, and Sarah A. Matheson, eds. 2011. "Introduction." In *Canadian Television: Text and Context,* 3–20. Waterloo: Wilfrid Laurier University Press.

Breuilly, John. 1993. *Nationalism and the State.* 2nd ed. New York: Manchester University Press.

Brewis, T.N. 1968. *Growth and the Canadian Economy.* Toronto: McClelland and Stewart.

Brown, Craig. 1966. "The Nationalism of the National Policy." In *Nationalism in Canada,* edited by Peter Russell, 155–63. Toronto: McGraw-Hill.

Canadian Association of Broadcasters. 2022. "Petition by the Canadian Association of Broadcasters Requesting That the Governor in Council Set Aside and Refer Back to the Canadian Radio-television and Telecommunications Commission for Reconsideration Broadcasting Decision CRTC 2022-165." August. Accessed February 9, 2023. https://frpc.net/wp-content/uploads/2022/08/CAB-Petition-to-Cabinet-Concerning-the-CBC-SRC-Licence-Renewal-Final.pdf.

Canadian Centre for Policy Alternatives. 2003. *Lessons from NAFTA: The High Cost of "Free Trade."* Ottawa: CCPA. https://policyalternatives.ca/publications/reports/lessons-nafta.

Canadian Press. 2005. "CBC Seeks Another $75 Million to Reinstate Regional Programming." *Misener.org*, February 2. https://misener.org/cbc-seeks-another-75-million-to-reinstate-regional-programming/.

–. 2014. "Tory-Appointed CBC Chair Slams 'Wilfully Destructive' Tory Attacks in Newly Revealed Letter." *National Post*, May 29. https://nationalpost.com/news/politics/tory-appointed-cbc-chair-slams-wilfully-destructive-tory-attacks-in-newly-revealed-letter.

–. 2016. "As Prime Minister, Kellie Leitch Would Scrap CBC." *Marketing Magazine*, November 25. Accessed June 9, 2022. http://marketingmag.ca/media/as-prime-minister-kellie-leitch-would-scrap-cbc-187129/.

–. 2018. "Ottawa Bolsters Struggling Media with $600M in Tax Measures." *CTV News*, November 21. https://www.ctvnews.ca/politics/ottawa-bolsters-struggling-media-with-600m-in-tax-measures-1.4186881.

–. 2019a. "CBC President Catherine Tait Compares Netflix to Colonialism of the British and French Empires." *National Post*, January 31. https://nationalpost.com/news/canada/cbc-president-tait-warns-of-cultural-imperialism-danger-from-netflix.

–. 2019b. "Supreme Court Overturns Decision That Allowed U.S. Super Bowl Ads in Canadian Broadcast." *CBC News*, December 19. https://www.cbc.ca/news/business/super-bowl-ad-decision-overturned-1.5402138.

–. 2023. "Bell Asks CRTC to Drop Local News Requirements after Mass Layoffs." *Globe and Mail*, June 23. https://www.theglobeandmail.com/business/article-bell-asks-crtc-to-drop-local-news-requirements-after-mass-layoffs-2/.

Canadian Radio League. 1931. "The Canadian Radio League: Objects, Information, National Support." January. Library and Archives Canada, Spry Papers, RG 42, vol. 1076, file 158-1. See also RG 42(76).

Careless, Maurice. 1966. "Metropolitanism and Nationalism." In *Nationalism in Canada*, edited by Peter Russell, 271–83. Toronto: McGraw-Hill.

Carey, James. 1988. "Technology and Ideology: The Case of the Telegraph." In *Communication as Culture*, 201–30. Boston: Unwin Hyman.

Carey, James, and John Quirk. 1988. "The Mythos of the Electronic Revolution." In *Communication as Culture*, edited by James Carey, 113–41. Boston: Unwin Hyman.

Carr, David. 2013. "Giving Viewers What They Want." *New York Times*, February 24. https://www.nytimes.com/2013/02/25/business/media/for-house-of-cards-using-big-data-to-guarantee-its-popularity.html.

Carscallen, Helen. 1966. "Control in a Broadcasting System." MA thesis, University of Toronto.

Castells, Manuel. 2000. *The Rise of the Network Society*. 2nd ed. Malden, MA: Blackwell.

Cavanagh, Richard P. 1992. "The Development of Canadian Sports Broadcasting 1920–78." *Canadian Journal of Communication* 17, 3. https://cjc.utpjournals.press/author/Cavanagh%2C+Richard+P.

CBC News. 1984. "CBC Reports on Budget Cuts in 1984." https://www.cbc.ca/player/play/video/1.7056999.

–. 2006a. "Bell Globemedia Makes $1.7B Bid for CHUM." July 12. https://www.cbc.ca/news/business/bell-globemedia-makes-1-7b-bid-for-chum-1.583543.

–. 2006b. "Cuts Begin Right Away as Bell Globemedia Swallows CHUM." July 12. https://www.cbc.ca/news/entertainment/cuts-begin-right-away-as-bell-globemedia-swallows-chum-1.583542.

–. 2007a. "CanWest, Goldman Sachs Buy Alliance Atlantis for $2.3B." January 10. https://www.cbc.ca/news/business/canwest-goldman-sachs-buy-alliance-atlantis -for-2-3b-1.641207.

–. 2007b. "Oda Pledges $200M to Canadian Television Fund Social Sharing." January 26. https://www.cbc.ca/news/entertainment/oda-pledges-200m-to-canadian -television-fund-1.664341.

–. 2009a. "CBC to Cut Up to 800 Jobs, Sell Assets." March 25. https://www.cbc.ca/news/ entertainment/cbc-to-cut-up-to-800-jobs-sell-assets-1.793965.

–. 2009b. "Heritage Fund Consolidation Extends to TV, New Media." March 9. https://www.cbc.ca/news/entertainment/heritage-fund-consolidation-extends -to-tv-new-media-1.784989.

–. 2010. "CBC Blasts CRTC for TV Signals Decision." March 23. https://www.cbc.ca/ news/entertainment/cbc-blasts-crtc-for-tv-signals-decision-1.916370.

–. 2018. "Gem, CBC's Rebranded TV App, to Stream 'Crown Jewels of Canadian Content.'" September 12. https://www.cbc.ca/news/entertainment/cbc-catherine-tait- gem-tv-streaming-app-1.4820239.

CCAU (Coalition of Canadian Audiovisual Unions). 2002. "Rejuvenating Canadian Series Drama Production." https://www.actra.ca/actra/images/02sept/draftpaper31. pdf.

Chandler, Marsha A. 1983. "The Politics of Public Enterprise." In *Crown Corporations in Canada: The Calculus of Instrument Choice,* edited by J. Robert S. Prichard, 185–217. Toronto: Butterworths.

Charland, Maurice. 1986. "Technological Nationalism." *Canadian Journal of Political and Social Theory* 10 (1–2): 196–221.

Charlesworth, Hector. 1935. "Broadcasting in Canada." *Annals of the American Academy of Political and Social Science* 177: 42–48.

Collins, Richard. 1990. *Culture, Communication and National Identity: The Case of Canadian Television.* Toronto: University of Toronto Press.

Collins, Richard, Adam Finn, Stuart McFadyen, and Colin Hoskins. 2001. "Introduction." *Canadian Journal of Communication* 26 (1): 3–16.

Corry, J.A. 1939. *The Growth of Government Activities since Confederation: A Study Prepared for the Royal Commission on Dominion Provincial Relations.* Ottawa.

–. 1941. "The Genesis and Nature of Boards." In *Canadian Boards at Work.* Toronto: Macmillan.

Coulthard, Glen Sean. 2014. *Red Skin, White Masks: Rejecting the Colonial Politics of Recognition.* Minneapolis: University of Minnesota Press.

Craven, Paul, and Tom Traves. 1987. "Canadian Railways as Manufacturers." In *Perspectives on Canadian Economic History,* edited by Douglas McCalla, 118–43. Toronto: Copp Clark Pitman.

Crean, S.M. 1976. *Who's Afraid of Canadian Culture?* Don Mills, ON: General Publishing.

Croley, Steven P. 2007. *Regulation and Public Interests: The Possibility of Good Regulatory Government.* Princeton, NJ: Princeton University Press.

CRTC (Canadian Radio-television and Telecommunications Commission). 2016. "So What Makes It Canadian?" October 13. https://crtc.gc.ca/eng/cancon/c_cdn.htm.

Curtis, Bruce. 1992. "Class, Culture, and Administration: Education Inspection in Canada West." In *Colonial Leviathan: State Formation in Mid-Nineteenth Century Canada,* edited by Allan Greer and Ian Radforth. Toronto: University of Toronto Press.

Czitrom, Daniel J. 1983. *Media and the American Mind: From Morse to McLuhan.* Chapel Hill: University of North Carolina Press.

Dal Bó, Ernesto. 2006. "Regulatory Capture: A Review." *Oxford Review of Economic Policy* 22 (2): 203–25.

Danks, Brad. 2015. "The CRTC'S 'Let's Talk TV' Hearing." *Bar Talk*, February. https://www.cbabc.org/BarTalk/Articles/2015/February/Features/The-CRTC-Let%E2%80%99s-Talk-TV-Hearing.

Daschuck, James. 2013. *Clearing the Plains: Disease, Politics of Starvation and the Loss of Aboriginal Life*. Regina: University of Regina Press.

Davis, Charles, and Emilia King. 2017. "Transnational Over-the-Top Media Distribution as a Business and Policy Disruptor: The Case of Netflix in Canada." *The Journal of Media Innovations* 4 (1): 4. https://www.researchgate.net/publication/317280461_Transnational_over-the-top_media_distribution_as_a_business_and_policy_disruptor_The_case_of_Netflix_in_Canada.

Dennison, Merrill. 1935. "Radio in Canada." *Annals of the American Academy of Political and Social Science* 177: 49–54.

Dewar, Kenneth C. 1982. "The Origin of Public Broadcasting in Canada in Comparative Perspective." *Canadian Journal of Communication* 8 (2): 26–45.

Dixon, Guy. 2006. "CBC Wants Mandate Review Every 10 Years." *Globe and Mail*, September 29. https://www.theglobeandmail.com/arts/cbc-wants-mandate-review-every-10-years/article969239/.

Douglas, Susan. 1995. "Broadcasting Begins." In *Communication in History: Technology, Culture, Society*, 2nd ed., edited by David Crowley and Paul Heyer, 232–39. White Plains, NY: Longman Publishers.

Drache, Daniel. 1982. "Harold Innis and Canadian Capitalist Development." *Canadian Journal of Political and Social Theory* 6 (1–2): 35–60.

–, ed. 1995. *Staples, Markets, and Cultural Change: Selected Essays of Harold Innis*. Montreal and Kingston: McGill-Queen's University Press.

Drache, Daniel, and Meric S. Gertler. 1991. *The New Era of Global Competition: State Policy and Market Power*. Montreal: McGill-Queen's University Press.

Druick, Zoe, and Apa Kostopoulas, eds. 2008. *Programming Reality*. Waterloo: Wilfrid Laurier University Press.

Dygert, Warren B. 1939. *Radio as an Advertising Medium*. New York: McGraw-Hill.

Eaman, Ross. 1994. *Channels of Influence: CBC Audience Research and the Canadian Public*. Toronto: University of Toronto Press.

Easterbrook, W.T., and Hugh G.J. Aitken. 1956. *Canadian Economic History*. Toronto: Macmillan.

Easterbrook, W.T., and Mel Watkins. 1980. *Approaches to Canadian Economic History: A Selection of Essays*. Gage Publishing in association with the Institute of Canadian Studies at Carleton University.

Ellis, David. 1979. *Evolution of the Canadian Broadcasting System*. Ottawa: Department of Supply and Services.

–. 1992. *Split Screen: Home Entertainment and the New Technologies*. Toronto: Friends of Canadian Broadcasting.

Elmer, Greg, and Mike Gasher, eds. 2005. *Contracting Out Hollywood: Runaway Productions and Foreign Location Shooting*. Lanham, MD: Rowman and Littlefield.

Evans, Mark. 2000. "iCraveTV Waves White Flag in Web Rebroadcasting Battle." *Globe and Mail*, February 29. https://www.theglobeandmail.com/report-on-business/icrave-tv-waves-white-flag-in-web-rebroadcasting-battle/article25456936/.

Faguy, Steve. 2017. "How the CRTC Screwed Over Community Television to Save Local News." https://blog.fagstein.com/2017/09/03/community-tv-vs-local-news/.

Fink, Howard. 1981. "The Sponsor's v. the Nation's Choice: North American Radio Drama." In *Radio Drama,* edited by Peter Lewis, 185–243. New York: Longman.

Firestone, O.J. 1966. *Broadcast Advertising in Canada: Past and Future Growth.* Ottawa: University of Ottawa Press.

Foucault, Michel. 1972. *The Archaeology of Knowledge.* London: Tavistock Publications.

–. 1991. "Governmentality," translated by Rosi Braidotti, revised by Colin Gordon. In *The Foucault Effect: Studies in Governmentality,* edited by Graham Burchell, Colin Gordon, and Peter Miller, 87–104. Chicago: University of Chicago Press.

Fowke, Vernon. 1967. "The National Policy: Old and New." In *Approaches to Canadian Economic History,* edited by W.T. Easterbrook and M.H. Watkins, 237–58. Toronto: McClelland and Stewart.

Fraser, Blair. 1967. *The Search for Identity: Canada, 1945–1967.* Toronto: Doubleday.

Fraser, Fil. 1994. "The Participation of Aboriginal and Other Cultural Minorities in Cultural Development." *Canadian Journal of Communication* 19 (3–4). https://cjc.utpjournals. press/doi/full/10.22230/cjc.1994v19n3a829?.

Fraser, Matthew. 1999. *Free-for-All: The Struggle for Dominance on the Digital Frontier.* Toronto: Stoddart.

Friends of Canadian Broadcasting. 2014. "Broadcasting Notice of Consultation CRTC 2014-190, CRTC Let's Talk TV Proceeding – Final Submission." October 3. https://legacy.friends.ca/explore/article/broadcasting-notice-of-consultation-crtc -2014-190-crtc-lets-talk-tv-proceeding-final-submission/.

–. 2016. "Précis: Miller-Rogers Opinion on Options for a Merit-Based CBC Board of Directors Appointment Process." November 14. https://legacy.friends.ca/explore/ article/precis-miller-rogers-opinion-on-options-for-a-merit-based-cbc-board-o f-directors-appointment-process/.

Friends of Canadian Media. 2001. "Follow the Money: Who Paid for Canadian Television, 1990–2000." August. Accessed May 16, 2005. http://www.friends.ca/files/PDF/ publications/followthemoney.pdf.

Gagne, Wallace. 1976. "Technology and Canadian Politics." In *Nationalism, Technology and the Future of Canada.* edited by Wallace Gagne. Toronto: Macmillan Company of Canada.

Gasher, Mike. 1998. "Invoking Public Support for Public Broadcasting: The Aird Commission Revisited." *Canadian Journal of Communication* 23 (2). https://cjc.utpjournals .press/doi/full/10.22230/cjc.1998v23n2a1032.

Geist, Michael. 2021a. "Not Just Big Tech: Government Memo Shows Bill C-10 Targets News Sites, Podcast and Workout Apps, Adult Websites, Audiobooks, and Sports Streamers for CRTC Regulation." *Michael Geist* (blog), May 20. https://www.michaelgeist. ca/2021/05/not-just-big-techbillc10/.

–. 2021b. "The Bill C-10 Effect: Why Canadian Consumers Face a Future of Cancon Surcharges and Blocked Services." *Michael Geist* (blog), May 25. https://www. michaelgeist.ca/2021/05/the-bill-c-10-effect-why-canadian-consumers-face-a-future -of-cancon-surcharges-and-blocked-services/.

–. 2023. "Bill C-11 Estimates Revealed: Internal Government Documents Show No Impact on Net Employment, Admit Streamers Already Invest Millions in 'Unofficial Cancon.'" *Michael Geist* (blog), April 14. https://www.michaelgeist. ca/2023/04/bill-c-11-estimates-revealed-internal-government-documents-show -no-impact-on-net-employment-admit-streamers-already-invest-millions-in -unofficial-cancon/.

–. n.d. "Post Tagged with 'Discoverability.'" *Michael Geist* (blog). https://www.michaelgeist. ca/tag/discoverability/.

Gergin, Maria. 2011. "Silencing Dissent: The Conservative Record." Canadian Centre for Policy Alternatives, April 6. https://policyalternatives.ca/publications/commentary/silencing-dissent-conservative-record.

Giddens, Anthony. 1984. *The Constitution of Society: Outline of a Theory of Structuration.* Berkeley: University of California Press.

Gillies, Donald J. 1990. "Technological Determinism in Canadian Telecommunications: Telidon Technology, Industry and Government." *Canadian Journal of Communication* 15 (2): 1–15.

Gittens, Susan. 1999. *CTV: The Television Wars.* Toronto: Stoddart.

Globe and Mail. 1988. "CBC All-News Network Launch Put Off to August from February." December 23.

–. 1997. "Baton to Cut 154 Jobs at TV Stations in Ontario: Broadcaster Clears Decks for Competition." February 12, B2.

Globerman, Steven. 1983. *Cultural Regulation in Canada.* Montreal: Institute for Research on Public Policy.

Goldberg, Kim. 1989. *The Barefoot Channel: Community Television as a Tool for Social Change.* Vancouver: New Star Books.

Golding, Peter, and Graham Murdock. 1991. "Culture, Communication, and Political Economy." In *Mass Media and Society,* edited by James Curran and Michael Gurevitch, 15–32. London: Edward Arnold.

Gollom, Mark. 2021. "CRTC Peppers CBC with Questions about Plans for Controversial Branded Content." *CBC News,* January 15. https://www.cbc.ca/news/canada/crtc-cbc-tandem-hearing-branded-content-1.5875081.

Gonick, C.W. 1970. "Foreign Ownership and Political Decay." In *Close the 49th Parallel: The Americanization of Canada,* edited by Ian Lumsden, 43–74. Toronto: University of Toronto Press.

Gorbould, Paul. n.d. "CBC.ca Prehistory." https://www.cbc.ca/10th/columns/prehistory_gorbould.html.

Gracey, D.P. 1982. "Federal Crown Corporations in Canada." In *Public Administration in Canada,* edited by Kenneth Kernaghen. Toronto: Methuen.

Grant, George. 1965. *Lament for a Nation.* Toronto: McLelland and Stewart.

Greer, Allan, and Ian Radforth. 1992. "Introduction." In *Colonial Leviathan: State Formation in Mid-Nineteenth Century Canada,* edited by Allan Greer and Ian Radforth, 3–16. Toronto: University of Toronto Press.

Gruneau, R., and D. Whitson. 1993. *Hockey Night in Canada: Sport, Identities, and Cultural Politics.* Toronto: Garamond.

Hardin, Herschel. 1974. *A Nation Unaware: The Canadian Economic Culture.* Vancouver: J.J. Douglas.

–. 1985. *Closed Circuits: The Sellout of Canadian Television.* Vancouver: Douglas and McIntyre.

Harris, Sophia. 2016a. "$25 'Skinny' TV Packages Called a 'Ripoff' as Industry 'Stares Down' CRTC." *CBC News,* March 3. https://www.cbc.ca/news/business/crtc-skinny-basic-pick-and-pay-1.3472647.

–. 2016b. "'Ridiculous': Customers Disappointed by New Pick and Pay TV." *CBC News,* December 1. https://www.cbc.ca/news/business/pick-and-pay-tv-crtc-1.3875187.

Harvey, David. 1989. *The Condition of Postmodernity: An Enquiry into the Origins of Cultural Change.* Oxford: Basil Blackwell.

–. 2005. *A Brief History of Neoliberalism.* New York: Oxford.

Hatton, Steve. 2002. "The Death of Canada's Local TV Affiliate." *Channel Canada,* December 14. https://www.channelcanada.com/Editorial/the-death-of-canadas-local-tv-affiliate/.

Head, Sydney W., Christopher H. Sterling, and Lemuel B. Schofield. 1994. *Broadcasting in America: A Survey of Electronic Media.* 7th ed. Boston: Houghton Mifflin.

Hearst, Stephen. 1992. "Broadcasting Regulation in Britain." In *Television and the Public Interest: Vulnerable Values in West European Broadcasting,* edited by Jay G. Blumler, 61–78. London: Sage Publications.

Hodgetts, J.E. 1946. "Administration and Politics: The Case of the Canadian Broadcasting Corporation." In *Canadian Journal of Economics and Political Science* 12 (4): 454–69.

–. 1973. *The Canadian Public Service: A Physiology of Government 1867–1970.* Toronto: University of Toronto Press.

Hoover, Herbert. 1930. Address to the Association of National Advertisers. November 10. American Presidency Project. https://www.presidency.ucsb.edu/node/212347.

Hopper, Tristan. 2018. "Tristin Hopper: Really Want to Help Print Journalism, Ottawa? Stop CBC from Undercutting Us." *National Post,* November 30. https://nationalpost.com/opinion/tristin-hopper-really-want-to-help-print-journalism-ottawa-stop-cbc-from-undercutting-us.

Houpt, Simon. 2014. "CBC 'in Peril' If Funding Cuts Not Reversed, Former Board Members Say." *Globe and Mail,* July 15. https://www.theglobeandmail.com/arts/books-and-media/cbc-in-peril-if-funding-cuts-not-reversed-former-board-members-say/article19613536/.

–. 2017. "'I Think I Passed': CBC's Hubert Lacroix Reflects on His Time as President." *Globe and Mail,* December 1. https://www.theglobeandmail.com/arts/television/i-think-i-passed-cbcs-hubert-lacroix-reflects-on-his-time-as-president/article37168274/.

–. 2019. "CBC President Catherine Tait on the Netflix Flap and Why She Calls the Broadcaster One of the 'Custodians of Democracy.'" *Globe and Mail,* March 1. https://www.theglobeandmail.com/arts/article-cbc-president-catherine-tait-on-the-netflix-flap-and-why-she-calls-the/.

Howlett, Michael, and M. Ramesh. 1992. *The Political Economy of Canada: An Introduction.* Toronto: McClelland and Stewart.

Hudes, Sammy. 2023. "BCE Laying Off 1,300 People, Closing Foreign News Bureaus and 9 Radio Stations across Canada." *CBC News,* June 14. https://www.cbc.ca/news/business/bce-layoffs-radio-1.6876075.

Hull, W.H.N. 1962. "The Public Control of Broadcasting: The Canadian and Australian Experiences." *Canadian Journal of Economics and Political Science* 28 (1): 114–26.

Hunter, Lawson, Kenneth G. Engelhart, and Peter Miller. 2017. *Canadian Television Content: Creation, Discovery and Export in a Digital World.* Commentary No. 498, December. C.D. Howe Institute.

Iacobucci, Edward M., and Michael J. Trebilcock. 2012. *The Role of Crown Corporations in the Canadian Economy: An Analytic Framework.* Calgary: University of Calgary, School of Public Policy Research Papers.

Ibbitson, John. 2015. "How Harper Created a More Conservative Canada." *Globe and Mail,* February 6. https://www.theglobeandmail.com/news/politics/globe-politics-insider/how-harper-created-a-more-conservative-canada/article22829480/.

Innis, Harold A. 1933. *The Problems of Staple Production.* Toronto: Ryerson.

–. 1946. *Political Economy in the Modern State.* Toronto: Ryerson.

–. 1952. *Changing Concepts of Time.* Toronto: University of Toronto Press.

–. 1954. *The Cod Fisheries: The History of an International Economy.* Toronto: University of Toronto Press.

–. 1956. *Essays in Canadian Economic History.* Edited by Mary Q. Innis. Toronto: University of Toronto Press.

Inuit Broadcasting Corporation. n.d. "History of the Inuit Broadcasting Corporation." https://inuitbroadcasting.ca/about-us/history-of-the-inuit-broadcasting-corporation/.

Irving, John A. 1957. "The Fowler Commission Report on Broadcasting in Canada." In *Proceedings of the Ninth Annual Conference, the Institute of Public Administration of Canada,* edited by P.T. Clark and F.J. McGilly, 314–15. Toronto: University of Toronto Press.

Jackson, John D. 1995. "Broadcasting: Centralization, Regionalization, and Canadian Identity." In *Communications in Canadian Society,* edited by Benjamin D. Singer, 221–36. Scarborough, ON: Nelson Canada.

Jackson, Joseph. 1999. "Newspaper Ownership in Canada: An Overview of the Davey Committee and Kent Commission Studies." Political and Social Affairs Division, Parliamentary Research Bureau. December 17. https://publications.gc.ca/Pilot/LoPBdP/BP/prb9935-e.htm.

Jeffrey, Brooke. 1980. "Telecommunications: Towards a National Policy." *Canadian Regional Review,* September, 15–21.

Jeffrey, Liss. 1996. "Private Television and Cable." In *The Cultural Industries in Canada: Problems, Policies and Prospects,* edited by Michael Dorland, 203–56. Toronto: James Lorimer.

Jessop, Bob. 2021. "Poulantzas' Changing Views on Law and the State." In *Research Handbook on Law and Marxism,* edited by Paul O'Connell and Umut Özsu, 156–72. Northampton, UK: Edward Elgar Publishing.

Karadeglija, Anja. 2022. "Senators Amend Online Streaming Bill to Ban CBC Sponsored Content." *Saltwire,* December 13. https://www.saltwire.com/atlantic-canada/news/senators-amend-online-streaming-bill-to-ban-cbc-sponsored-content-100805340/.

Kaufman, Donna Soble. 1987. *Broadcasting Law in Canada.* Toronto: Carswell.

Kesterton, Wilfred, and Roger Bird. 1995. "The Press in Canada: A Historical Overview." In *Communications in Canadian Society,* edited by B. Singer, 30–50. Toronto: Nelson Canada.

Kiefel, Barry. 2014. "Hubert Lacroix Must Fight for CBC – or Resign." *Toronto Star,* July 21. https://www.thestar.com/opinion/commentary/2014/07/21/hubert_lacroix_must_fight_for_cbc_or_resign.html.

Kozolanka, Kirsten. 2012. "Public Service Educational Broadcasting: Between the Market and the Alternative Margins." In *Alternative Media in Canada,* edited by Kirsten Kozolanka, Patricia Mazepa, and David Skinner, 46–64. Vancouver: UBC Press.

Kozolanka, Kirsten, Patricia Mazepa, and David Skinner, eds. 2012. *Alternative Media in Canada.* Vancouver: UBC Press.

Kristoff, Nicholas D. 1984. "Canada-US Trade." *New York Times,* December 11, D24.

Law, Howard. 2022a. "Commentary: The Broadcasting Act Version 7.0 – Canada's Cultural Glue." *CARTT.ca,* April 25. https://cartt.ca/commentary-the-broadcasting-act-version-7-0-canadas-cultural-glue/.

–. 2022b. "Commentary (Part Three): Will C-11 Save Canadian Content?" *CARTT.ca,* May 2. https://cartt.ca/commentary-part-three-will-c-11-save-canadian-content/.

Laxer, Robert M. 1973. *Canada Ltd.: The Political Economy of Dependency.* Toronto: McClelland and Stewart.

Lee, Ian R., and Conrad Winn. 1991. "The Policy Elite Audience: Its Significance and Some Findings." In *Communications in Canadian Society,* edited by Benjamin D. Singer. Scarborough, ON: Nelson Canada.

Lefebvre, Henri. 1991. *The Production of Space,* translated by Donald Nicholson-Smith. Oxford: Basil Blackwell.

Leiss, William, Stephen Kline, and Sut Jhally. 1988. *Social Communication in Advertising: Persons, Products, and Images of Well-Being.* Scarborough, ON: Nelson Canada.

–. 2005. *Social Communication in Advertising: Persons, Products, and Images of Well-Being.* 3rd ed. Scarborough, ON: Nelson Canada.

Levitt, Kari. 1970. *Silent Surrender.* Toronto: Macmillan.

Lexpert. 2013. "Supreme Court of Canada Declares Proposed CRTC 'Value for Signal' Regime Ultra Vires." *Lexpert: Business of Law,* March 1. https://www.lexpert.ca/archive/supreme-court-of-canada-declares-proposed-crtc-value-for-signal-regime-ultra-vires/348915.

Linnitt, Carol. 2014. "Charities Bullied into Muting Their Messages: Researcher." *Narwhal,* July 21. https://thenarwhal.ca/charities-bullied-muting-their-messages-researcher/.

Litt, Paul. 1992. *The Muses, the Masses, and the Massey Commission.* Toronto: University of Toronto Press.

Litvak, Isaiah, and Christopher Maule. 1974. *Cultural Sovereignty: The Time and Reader's Digest Case in Canada.* New York: Praeger.

Lockwood, Brian. 2011. "High Ratings Aside, Where's the History on History?" *Forbes,* October 17. https://www.forbes.com/sites/bradlockwood/2011/10/17/high-ratings-aside-wheres-the-history-on-history/.

Lorimer, Rowland. 1996. "Book Publishing." In *The Cultural Industries in Canada: Problems, Policies and Prospects,* edited by Michael Dorland, 3–34. Toronto: James Lorimer.

Lower, Arthur R.M. 1946. *Colony to Nation: A History of Canada.* Toronto: Longmans, Green.

Lyman, Peter. 1983. *Canada's Video Revolution: Pay-TV, Home Video and Beyond.* Toronto: James Lorimer.

MacDonald, Gayle. 2002. "Dying a Dramatic Death." *Globe and Mail,* July 13, R.1–4.

–. 2007. "Film Library at Centre of Sale." *Globe and Mail,* June 25, R1–2.

Maclean's. 1990. "Cutting the CBC." December 17, 10.

MacLennan, Anne F. 2001. "Circumstances beyond Our Control: Canadian Radio Program Schedule Evolution during the 1930s." PhD dissertation, Concordia University.

–. 2005. "American Network Broadcasting, the CBC, and Canadian Radio Stations during the 1930s: A Content Analysis." *Journal of Radio Studies* 121: 85–103.

MacPherson, C.B. 1957. "The Social Sciences." In *The Culture of Contemporary Canada,* edited by Julian Park, 181–221. Ithaca, NY: Cornell University Press.

Magder, Ted. 1989. "Taking Culture Seriously: A Political Economy of Communications." In *The New Canadian Political Economy,* edited by Wallace Clement and Glen Williams, 278–96. Montreal and Kingston: McGill-Queen's University Press.

–. 1993. *Canada's Hollywood: The Canadian State and Feature Films.* Toronto: University of Toronto Press.

–. 1996. "Film and Video Production." In *The Cultural Industries in Canada: Problems, Policies and Prospects,* edited by Michael Dorland, 145–77. Toronto: James Lorimer.

Mahon, Rianne. 1980. "Regulatory Agencies: Captive Agencies or Hegemonic Apparatuses." In *Class, State, Ideology and Change,* edited by J. Paul Greyson, 154–69. Toronto: Holt Rinehart and Winston.

Malone, William. 1962. "Broadcast Regulation in Canada: A Legislative History." PhD dissertation, Harvard University.

Manera, Tony. 1996. *A Dream Betrayed: The Battle for the CBC.* Toronto: Stoddart.

Mann, Ruth. 2016. "The Harper Government's New Right Neoliberal Agenda and the Dismantling of Status of Women Canada and the Family Violence Initiative." *International Journal for Crime, Justice and Social Democracy* 5 (2): 50–64.

Mann, Susan. 2002. *The Dream of Nation: A Social and Intellectual History of Quebec*. 2nd ed. Montreal and Kingston: McGill-Queen's University Press.

Marx, Karl, and Friedrich Engels. (1848) 1985. *The Communist Manifesto*. Hammondsworth, UK: Penguin Books.

Marx, Leo. 1964. *The Machine in the Garden*. New York: Oxford University Press.

Matheson, Stuart L., and Philip M. Walker. 1970. *Computers and Telecommunications: Issues in Public Policy*. Englewood Cliffs, NJ: Prentice-Hall.

Mayne, Mark. 2022. "Top 10 Trends of 2022: FAST, AI, Virtual Production, and More." IBC, December 14. https://www.ibc.org/features/top-10-trends-of-2022-fast-ai-virtual-production-and-more/9346.article.

McCalla, Douglas. 1992. "Railways and the Development of Canada West." In *Colonial Leviathan: State Formation in Mid-Nineteenth Century Canada*, edited by Allan Greer and Ian Radforth, 192–229. Toronto: University of Toronto Press.

McChesney, Robert W. 1990. "The Battle for the U.S. Airwaves, 1928–1935." *Journal of Communication* 40 (4): 29–57.

–. 1993. *Telecommunications, Mass Media, and Democracy: The Battle for the Control of U.S. Broadcasting, 1928–1935*. New York: Oxford University Press.

McFadyen, Stuart, Colin Hoskins, and David Gillen. 1980. *Canadian Broadcasting: Market Structure and Economic Performance*. Montreal: Institute for Research on Public Policy.

McKay, R. Bruce. 1976. "The CBC and the Public: Management Decision-Making in the English Television Service of the Canadian Broadcasting Corporation, 1970–1974." PhD dissertation, Stanford University.

McKelvey, Fenwick. 2020. "Online Creators Left on the Outside of Broadcasting Act Reforms." *Policy Options*, December 1. https://policyoptions.irpp.org/magazines/december-2020/online-creators-left-on-the-outside-of-broadcasting-act-reforms/.

McMurdy, Deirdre. 2007. "CEO Tired of Subsidizing CBC." *Ottawa Citizen*, January 11. Accessed February 21, 2022. https://www.pressreader.com/canada/ottawacitizen/20070111/281522221608878.

McNulty, Jean. 1988a. "Technology and Nation-Building in Canadian Broadcasting." In *Communication Canada: Issues in Broadcasting and New Technologies*, edited by Rowland Lorimer and Donald Wilson, 176–98. Toronto: Kagan and Woo.

–. 1988b. "The Political Economy of Canadian Satellite Broadcasting." *Canadian Journal of Communication* 13 (2): 1–15.

Ménard, Marion. (2013) 2016. "CBC/Radio-Canada: Overview and Key Issues." Library of Parliament. Accessed August 3, 2022. https://publications.gc.ca/site/archivee-archived.html?url=https://publications.gc.ca/collections/collection_2016/bdp-lop/bp/YM32-2-2013-92-eng.pdf.

Miege, Bernard. 1989. *The Capitalization of Cultural Production*. London: International General.

Miljan, Lydia, Tegan Hill, and Niels Veldhuis. 2020. "Spending Reductions and Reform: Bases for the Success of the 1995 Budget." In *The Budget That Changed Canada: Essays on the 25th Anniversary of the 1995 Budget*, ed. William Watson and Jason Clemens. Vancouver: The Fraser Institute.

Miller, Mary Jane. 1987. *Turn Up the Contrast: CBC Television Drama since 1952*. Vancouver: UBC Press.

Mirrlees, Tanner, and Joseph Kispal-Kovacs, eds. 2013. *The Television Reader: Critical Perspectives in Canadian and US Television Studies.* Toronto: Oxford University Press.

Moffett, Samuel E. (1906) 1972. *The Americanization of Canada.* Toronto: University of Toronto Press.

Montagnes, James. 1941. "Profits Are in the Air: Broadcasting Has Turned a Corner: The Industry Is in the Black." *Canadian Business,* March.

Moogk, Edward B. 1975. *Roll Back the Years: History of Canadian Recorded Sound and Its Legacy Genesis to 1930.* Ottawa: National Library of Canada.

Moore, James. 2012. "Jean-Pierre Blais Mandate Letter from Minister James Moore." https://www.slideshare.net/friendscb/jeanpierre-blais-mandate-letter-from-james-moore.

Morin, Michel. 2017. "Commentary: The CRTC Is Adrift." *Cartt.ca,* July 8. https://cartt.ca/commentary-the-crtc-is-adrift/.

Morris, Peter. 1978. *Embattled Shadows; A History of Canadian Cinema: 1895–1939.* Montreal and Kingston: McGill-Queen's University Press.

Mosco, Vincent. 1979. *Broadcasting in the United States: Innovative Challenge and Organizational Control.* Norwood, NJ: Ablex Publishing.

–. 1989. *The Pay-per Society: Computers and Communication in the Information Age.* Toronto: Garamond Press.

–. 1990. "Toward a Transnational World Information Order: The Canada-U.S. Free Trade Agreement." *Canadian Journal of Communication* 15 (2): 46–63.

–, ed. 2009. *The Political Economy of Communication.* 2nd ed. Thousand Oaks, CA: Sage Publications.

Mundy, Greg. 1988. "'Free-Enterprise' or 'Public Service'? The Origins of Broadcasting in the U.S., U.K. and Australia." *Australia–New Zealand Journal of Sociology* 18 (3): 279–301.

Myers, Gustavus. 1972. *A History of Canadian Wealth.* Toronto: James Lorimer.

Nash, Knowlton. 1994. *The Microphone Wars.* Toronto: McClelland and Stewart.

Naylor, Dave. 2021. "CBC Gets to Keep Taxpayer Cash, but TV Department to Be Reviewed under O'Toole Government." *Western Standard,* August 16. Accessed June 13, 2022. https://www.westernstandard.news/news/cbc-gets-to-keep-taxpayer-cash-but-tv-department-to-be-reviewed-under-o-toole/article_645fbbf9-acod-5d98-8d8e-484329991345.html.

Neill, Robin. 1972. *A New Theory of Value: The Canadian Economics of H.A. Innis.* Toronto: University of Toronto Press.

–. 1991. *A History of Canadian Economic Thought.* London: Routledge.

Nelles, H.V. 2005. *The Politics of Development: Forests, Mines and Hydro-Electric Power in Ontario, 1849–1941.* 2nd ed. Montreal: McGill-Queen's University Press.

Nelson, Joyce. n.d. "A 'Catch-22' in Canadian Broadcasting." *In Search/En Quete* 8 (4): 4–34.

Newell, Jay, Charles T. Salmon, and Susan Chang. 2006. "The Hidden History of Product Placement." *Journal of Broadcasting and Electronic Media* 50 (4): 575–59.

News Media Canada. 2022. "Net Advertising Volume: Canada – Millions of Dollars (CDN Currency)." January 26. https://nmc-mic.ca/wp-content/uploads/2022/02/2020-Net-Ad-Volume-Report-01.26.2022.pdf.

Ng, Yee-Fui. 2019. "In the Moonlight: The Control and Accountability of Government Corporations." *Melbourne University Law Review* 43 (1): 303–36.

Nichols, M.E. 1948. *CP: The Story of the Canadian Press.* Toronto: Ryerson.

Noel, Alain, Gerard Boismenu, and Lizette Jalbert. 1993. "The Political Foundations of State Regulation in Canada." In *Production, Space, Identity,* edited by Jane Jenson, Manfred Bienefeld, and Rianne Mahon, 171–94. Toronto: Canadian Scholars.

Nolan, Michael. 1989. "An Infant Industry: Canadian Private Radio 1919–36." *Canadian Historical Review* 70 (4): 496–518.

Nordicity. 2006. "Analysis of Government Support for Public Broadcasting and Other Culture in Canada." https://site-cbc.radio-canada.ca/documents/impact-and -accountability/regulatory/bnph-2006-5-cbcrc-public-broadcaster-comparison.pdf.

–. 2011. "Analysis of Government Support for Public Broadcasting and Other Culture in Canada." https://www.nordicity.com/de/cache/work/85/CBC-Analysis%20of%20 Government%20Support%20for%20Public%20Broadcasting%20and%20Other%20 Culture%202011.pdf.

–. 2023. *The Digital Media Universe: Measuring the Revenues, the Audiences, and the Future Prospects.* https://www.nordicity.com/de/cache/work/178/Nordicity_DM_X%20 2023_FINAL%20REPORT_V2.pdf.

Nordicity, and Peter Miller. 2015. *Canadian Television 2020: Technological and Regulatory Impacts.* https://www.nordicity.com/de/cache/work/32/Canadian%20Television%20 2020_%20Technological%20and%20Regulatory%20Impacts%202015.pdf.

Nowak, Peter. 2022. "Three Telcos in a Trenchcoat: Industry Policy Sway Needs Attention." *TekSavvy,* January 19. https://blogs.teksavvy.com/three-telcos-in-a-trenchcoat -industry-policy-sway-needs-attention.

O'Brien, Greg. 2005. "Sports Networks to Air Some Drama and Comedy." *Cartt.ca,* October 7. https://cartt.ca/sports-networks-to-air-some-drama-and-comedy/.

O'Brien, John E. 1964. "A History of the Canadian Radio League, 1930–36." PhD dissertation, University of Southern California.

O'Byrne, Kyle. 2022. "(2/2) The Current Definition of Canadian Content, Explained." Canadian Media Fund, October 13. https://cmf-fmc.ca/now-next/articles/ cancondef-the-current-definition-of-canadian-content-explained-part-two/.

O'Neill, Brian. 2006. "CBC.ca – Broadcast Sovereignty in a Digital Age." *Convergence: The International Journal of Research into New Media Technologies* 12 (2): 179–97.

Panitch, Leo, ed. 1977. *The Canadian State.* Toronto: University of Toronto Press.

Patrick, Andrew S., Alex Black, and Thomas E. Whalen. 1996. "CBC Radio on the Internet: An Experiment in Convergence." *Canadian Journal of Communication* 21 (1): 125–40.

Pedwell, Terry. 2014. "CRTC to Netflix: Since You Won't Co-operate, We'll Ignore You." *CBC News,* September 29. https://www.cbc.ca/news/business/crtc-to-netflix-since -you-won-t-co-operate-we-ll-ignore-you-1.2781748.

Peers, Frank W. 1969. *The Politics of Canadian Broadcasting, 1920–51.* Toronto: University of Toronto Press.

–. 1979. *The Public Eye.* Toronto: University of Toronto Press.

Pendakur, Manjunath. 1990. *Canadian Dreams and American Control.* Toronto: Garamond.

Perl, Anthony. 1994. "Public Enterprise as an Expression of Sovereignty: Reconsidering the Origin of Canadian National Railways." *Canadian Journal of Political Science* 28 (1): 22–52.

Pikkety, Thomas. 2014. *Capital in the 21st Century.* Cambridge, MA: Belknap Press of Harvard University Press.

Pitsula, James M. 2007. "The Mulroney Government and Canadian Cultural Policy." In *Transforming the Nation: Canada and Brian Mulroney,* edited by Raymond Benjamin Blake, 357–80. Montreal and Kingston: McGill-Queen's University Press.

Piva, Michael J. 1992. "Government Finance and the Development of the Canadian State." In *Colonial Leviathan: State Formation in Mid-Nineteenth Century Canada,* edited by Allan Greer and Ian Radforth, 257–83. Toronto: University of Toronto Press.

Prang, Margaret. 1965. "The Origins of Public Broadcasting in Canada." *Canadian Historical Review* 461: 11–31.

Prichard, J. Robert S., ed. 1983. *Crown Corporations in Canada: The Calculus of Instrument Choice.* Toronto: Butterworths.

Public Media Alliance. 2023. "It's a Canada Thing: Standing Up for Our Industry and Our Stories." February 17. https://www.publicmediaalliance.org/cbc-radio-canada-president-its-a-canada-thing/.

Public Policy Forum. 2016. *Crown Corporation Governance: Three Ways to Manage the Tension between Autonomy and Control.* August 29. Ottawa: Public Policy Forum. https://issuu.com/ppforumca/docs/crown_corporation_governance_en_fin.

–. 2017. *The Shattered Mirror: News, Democracy and Trust in the Digital Age.* Ottawa: Public Policy Forum. https://shatteredmirror.ca/wp-content/uploads/theShattered-Mirror.pdf1.

Quebecor. 2007. "Videotron Suspends Contributions to Canadian Television Fund." Press release. *Marketwire,* January 23. https://archive.ph/20130119125432/http://www.ccnmatthews.com/news/releases/show.jsp?action=showRelease&searchText=false&showText=all&actionFor=632136.

Quill, Greg. 2009. "Reruns on Tap as CBC Cuts." *Toronto Star,* March 26. https://www.thestar.com/news/canada/2009/03/26/reruns_on_tap_as_cbc_cuts.html.

Raboy, Marc. 1990. *Missed Opportunities: The Story of Canada's Broadcasting Policy.* Montreal and Kingston: McGill-Queen's University Press.

–. 1995. *Public Broadcasting for the 21st Century.* Luton, UK: University of Luton Press.

–. 1996. "Public Television." In *The Cultural Industries in Canada: Problems, Policies and Prospects,* edited by Michael Dorland, 178–202. Toronto: James Lorimer.

Raj, Althia. 2013. "Jean-Pierre Blais Is on a Mission as CRTC Chief – But Whose Mission Is It?" *Huffington Post,* December 17. https://www.huffpost.com/archive/ca/entry/jean-pierre-blais-crtc_n_4454092.

Reinan, John. 2014. "How Craigslist Killed the Newspapers' Golden Goose." *MinnPost,* February 3. https://www.minnpost.com/business/2014/02/how-craigslist-killed-newspapers-golden-goose/.

Rens, Jean-Guy. 2001. *The Invisible Empire: A History of the Telecommunications Industry in Canada,* translated by Käthe Roth. Montreal and Kingston: McGill-Queen's University Press.

Resnick, Philip. 1990. "'Organized Capitalism' and the Canadian State." In *The Masks of Proteus: Canadian Reflections on the State,* edited by Philip Resnick, 153–78. Montreal and Kingston: McGill-Queen's University Press.

Rimock, Michael. 2013. "Regulatory Issues Concerning New Media Alternatives to Television." *Canadian Journal of Law and Technology* 11 (2): 335–42.

Roberts, Bill. 2001. "We Should Reserve Electronic Green Space for Public Service Broadcasters." *Policy Options,* September, 74–76.

Robertson, Grant. 2009. "CTV Closes Two Stations, Raising Fears for Local TV." *Globe and Mail,* February 26. https://www.theglobeandmail.com/report-on-business/ctv-closes-two-stations-raising-fears-for-local-tv/article20441227/.

Romanow, Walter I. 1974. "The Canadian Content Regulations in Canadian Broadcasting: An Historical and Critical Study." PhD thesis, Wayne State University.

Roth, Lorna. 2005. *Something New in the Air: The Story of First Peoples Television Broadcasting in Canada.* Montreal and Kingston: McGill-Queen's University Press.

Rowland, Wade. 2013. *Saving the CBC: Balancing Profit and Public Service.* Montreal: Linda Leith Publishing.

–. 2015. *Canada Lives Here: The Case for Public Broadcasting.* Montreal: Linda Leith Publishing.

Rutherford, Paul. 1978. *The Making of the Canadian Media.* Toronto: McGraw-Hill Ryerson.

–. 1990. *When Television Was Young: Primetime Canada 1952–1967.* Toronto: University of Toronto Press.

Salter, Liora. 1981. "'Public' and Mass Media in Canada: Dialectics in Innis' Communication Analysis." In *Culture, Communication and Dependency: The Tradition of H.A. Innis,* edited by William H. Melody, Liora Salter, and Paul Heyer, 193–207. Norwood, NJ: Ablex Publishing.

–. 1988. "Reconceptualizing the Public in Public Broadcasting." In *Communication Canada: Issues in Broadcasting and New Technologies,* edited by Rowland Lorimer and Donald Wilson, 232–48. Toronto: Kagan and Woo.

Salter, Liora, and Felix Odartey-Wellington. 2008. *The CRTC and Broadcasting Regulation in Canada.* Toronto: Thomson Carswell.

Salter, Liora, and Rick Salter. 1997. "Displacing the Welfare State." In *Understanding Canada: Building on the New Canadian Political Economy,* edited by Wallace Clement, 311–37. Montreal and Kingston: McGill-Queen's University Press.

Sandwell, B.K. 1951. "Present Day Influences on Canadian Society." In *Royal Commission Studies: A Selection of Essays Prepared for the Royal Commission on National Development in the Arts, Letters and Sciences,* 1–11. Ottawa: King's Printer.

Sassen, Saskia. 1991. *The Global City: New York, London, Tokyo.* Princeton, NJ: Princeton University Press.

Saulnier, A. 2015. *Losing Our Voice: Radio-Canada under Siege.* Translated by Pauline Couture. Toronto: Dundurn.

Saunders, D. 1999. "CBC Should Drop Its Expansion Plans, CRTC Hearing Told Network Advised to Stick to Public Service, Leave Commercials to Private Broadcasters." *Globe and Mail,* June 9, A4.

Saunderson, Hugh Lawrence. 1972. *Broadcasting and Regulation: The Growth of the Single System in Canadian Broadcasting.* Thesis. Ottawa: Carleton University.

Sauvageau, Florian. 1998. "Millennium Blues: The 1997 Southam Lecture." *Canadian Journal of Communication* 23 (2).

Schiller, Dan. 1988. "How to Think about Information." In *The Political Economy of Information,* edited by Vincent Mosco and Janet Wasko, 27–43. Madison: University of Wisconsin Press.

Schultz, Richard. 1982. "Regulatory Agencies and the Dilemmas of Delegation." In *The Administrative State in Canada: Essays in Honour of J.E. Hodgetts,* edited by O.P. Dwivedi, 89–106. Toronto: University of Toronto Press.

Sears, Val. 1990. "CBC Is About to Lose Its Power to Promote National Unity." *Toronto Star,* June 12.

Shea, Albert A. 1963. *Broadcasting the Canadian Way.* Montreal: Harvest House.

Shoalts, David. 2014. "Hockey Night in Canada: How CBC Lost It All." *Globe and Mail,* October 10. https://www.theglobeandmail.com/sports/hockey/hockey-night-in-canada -how-cbc-lost-it-all/article21072643/.

Skinner, David. 2012. "Sustaining Alternative Media." In *Alternative Media in Canada,* edited by Kirsten Kozolenko, Patricia Mazepa, and David Skinner, 25–45. Vancouver: UBC Press.

–. 2014. "Media on the Margins?" In *Mediascapes: New Patterns in Canadian Communication,* 4th ed., edited by Leslie Regan Shade, 344–63. Toronto: Thomson Nelson.

–. 2015. "Alternative and Community Media in Canada: Structure, Policy, and Prospects." In *The Routledge Companion to Alternative and Community Media,* 199–209. New York: Routledge.

Smulyan, Susan. 1994. *Selling Radio: The Commercialization of American Broadcasting 1920–1934.* Washington: Smithsonian Institution Press.

Smythe, Dallas. 1981. *Dependency Road: Communications, Capitalism, Consciousness and Canada.* Norwood, NJ: Ablex Publishing.

Snyder, Louis L. 1987. *The New Nationalism.* Ithaca, NY: Cornell University Press.

Sorensen, Chris. 2007. "TV Ad Limits Lifted." *Toronto Star,* May 18. https://www.thestar.com/business/2007/05/18/tv_ad_limits_lifted.html.

Sotiron, Minko. 1997. *From Politics to Profit: The Commercialization of Canadian Daily Newspapers, 1890–1920.* Montreal and Kingston: McGill-Queen's University Press.

Spiller, Frank, and Kim Smiley. 1986. *Multicultural Broadcasting in Canada.* Ottawa: Francis Spiller Associates.

Spry, Graham. 1931. "Canada's Broadcasting Issue." *Canadian Forum,* April.

–. 1961. "The Decline and Fall of Canadian Broadcasting." *Queen's Quarterly* 68 (2): 213–25.

Spry, Irene M. 1981. "Overhead Costs, Rigidities of Productive Capacity and the Price System." In *Culture, Communication and Dependency: The Tradition of H.A. Innis,* edited by William H. Melody, Liora Salter, and Paul Heyer, 155–66. Norwood, NJ: Ablex Publishing.

Starr, Paul. 2004. *The Creation of the Media: Political Origins of Modern Communications.* New York: Basic Books.

Statista. 2022. "Annual Advertising Revenue Generated by CBC/Radio-Canada from 2010 to 2020." *Statista.com,* February. https://www.statista.com/statistics/483006/cbc-radio-canada-annual-advertising-revenue/.

Stephenson, H.E., and Carlton McNaught. 1940. *The Story of Advertising in Canada: A Chronicle of Fifty Years.* Toronto: Ryerson Press.

Storper, Michael, and Allen J. Scott. 1986. "Production, Work, Territory: Contemporary Realities and Theoretical Tasks." In *Production, Work, Territory: The Geographical Anatomy of Industrial Capitalism,* edited by Allen J. Scott and Michael Storper. Boston: Allen and Unwin.

Straw, Will. 1996. "Sound Recording." In *The Cultural Industries in Canada: Problems, Policies and Prospects,* edited by Michael Dorland, 95–117. Toronto: James Lorimer.

Streeter, George Thomas. 1986. "Technocracy and Television: Discourse, Policy, Politics and the Making of Cable Television." PhD dissertation, University of Illinois at Urbana-Champaign.

Stursberg, Richard. 2012. *The Tower of Babble: Sins, Secrets and Successes inside the CBC.* Toronto: Douglas and McIntyre.

–. 2023. "Richard Stursberg: The Sad Truth Is That Pierre Poilievre May Be Right about the CBC." *The Hub,* February 27. https://thehub.ca/2023-02-27/richard-stursberg-the-sad-truth-is-that-pierre-poilievre-may-be-right-about-the-cbc/.

Stursberg, Richard, and Stephen Armstrong. 2019. *The Tangled Garden: A Canadian Cultural Manifesto for the Digital Age.* Toronto: James Lorimer and Company.

Summerfield, Patti. 2021. "The Buyer's Perspective on CBC's Branded Content Arm." *Media in Canada,* January 6. https://mediaincanada.com/2021/01/06/the-buyers-perspective-on-cbcs-branded-content-arm/.

Surridge, Grant. 2009. "Over-the-Air CTV Losses Predicted to Be Near $100 Million." *Vancouver Sun,* February 28. https://www.pressreader.com/canada/vancouver-sun/20090228/281547991798022.

Taras, David. 2015. *The Digital Mosaic: Media, Power, and Identity in Canada.* Toronto: University of Toronto Press.

Taras, David, and Christopher Waddell. 2020. *The End of the CBC.* Toronto: University of Toronto Press.

Taylor, Gregory. 2013. *Shut Off: The Canadian Digital Television Transition.* Montreal and Kingston: McGill-Queen's University Press.

–. 2016. "Dismantling the Public Airwaves: Shifting Canadian Public Broadcasting to an Online Service." *International Communication Gazette* 78 (4): 349–64.

Tencer, Daniel. 2015. "Unions Demand Resignation of CBC Execs, Say They're Planning Cuts Despite New Government." *Huffington Post,* October 30. https://www.huffpost.com/archive/ca/entry/unions-demand-resignation-of-cbc-execs-say-theyre-planning-cut_n_8434202.

Thiessen, Connie. 2022. "CBC/Radio-Canada Licence Renewal Decision Referred Back to CRTC for Re-evalution." In *Broadcast Dialogue,* September 22. https://broadcastdialogue.com/cbc-radio-canada-licence-renewal-decision-referred-back-to-crtc-for-re-evalution/.

Thomas, Eric. 1992. "Canadian Broadcasting and Multiculturalism: Attempts to Accommodate Ethnic Minorities." *Canadian Journal of Communication* 7 (2): 281–300.

Thomas, Paul G., and Orest W. Zajcew. 1993. "Structural Heretics: Crown Corporations and Regulatory Agencies." In *Governing Canada: Institutions and Public Policy,* edited by Michael Atkinson, 115–47. Toronto: Harcourt Brace Jovanovich Canada.

Thompson, John B. 1981. *Critical Hermeneutics: A Study in the Thought of Paul Ricoeur and Jürgen Habermas.* Cambridge: Cambridge University Press.

Thomson, Stuart. 2023. "Pierre Poilievre Wants to Defund the CBC." *The Hub,* January 9. https://thehub.ca/2023-01-09/pierre-poilievre-wants-to-defund-the-cbc-heres-what-that-may-look-like/.

Tinic, Serra. 2005. *On Location: Canada's Television Industry in a Global Market.* Toronto: University of Toronto Press.

–. 2009. "Between the Public and the Private: Television Drama and Global Partnerships in the Neo-Network Era." In *Television Studies after TV: Understanding Television in the Post-Broadcast Era,* edited by Graeme Turner and Jinna Tay. London: Routledge.

–. 2010. "The Global Economic Meltdown: A Crisotunity for Canada's Private Sector Broadcasters?" *Popular Communication* 8 (3): 193–97.

–. 2015. "Where in the World Is Orphan Black? Change and Continuity in Global TV Production and Distribution." *Media Industries Journal* 1 (3): 54–59.

Tippett, Maria. 1990. *Making Culture: English-Canadian Institutions and the Arts before the Massey Commission.* Toronto: University of Toronto Press.

Traves, Tom. 1979. *The State and Enterprise: Canadian Manufacturers and the Federal Government 1917–1931.* Toronto: University of Toronto Press.

Tuck, Simon. 2000. "Webcasting Ready for Takeoff." *Globe and Mail,* October 5. https://www.theglobeandmail.com/technology/webcasting-ready-for-takeoff/article4167973/.

Tucker, Gilbert Norman. 1936. *The Canadian Commercial Revolution 1845–1851.* New Haven, CT: Yale University Press.

Tupper, Allan, and G. Bruce Doern. 1981. "Public Corporations and Public Policy in Canada." In *Public Corporations and Public Policy in Canada,* edited by Allan Tupper and G. Bruce Doern, 1–50. Montreal: Institute for Research on Public Policy.

Underhill, Frank H. 1964. *The Image of Confederation.* Toronto: CBC.

Valiante, Giuseppe. 2019. "CBC Must Diversify Revenue to Protect It from Political Whims, President Says." *National Post,* May 3. https://nationalpost.com/pmn/news-pmn/canada-news-pmn/cbc-must-diversify-revenue-to-protect-it-from-political-whims-president-says.

Vipond, Mary. 1980. "The Nationalist Network: English Canada's Intellectuals and Artists in the 1920s." *Canadian Review of Studies in Nationalism* 7 (1): 32–52.

–. 1989. *The Mass Media in Canada.* Toronto: James Lorimer.

–. 1992. *Listening In: The First Decade of Canadian Broadcasting 1922–1932.* Montreal and Kingston: McGill-Queen's University Press.

–. 1994. "The Beginnings of Public Broadcasting in Canada: The CRBC, 1932–36." *Canadian Journal of Communication* 19: 151–71.

–. 1999. "The Continental Marketplace: Authority, Advertisers, and Audiences in Canadian News Broadcasting, 1932–1936." *Journal of Radio Studies* 6: 169–84.

Vlessing, Etan. 2014. "CBC's Hubert Lacroix: 'I Have No Intention of Resigning.'" *Media in Canada,* June 26. https://mediaincanada.com/2014/06/26/cbcs-hubert-lacroix-i-have-no-intention-of-resigning/.

Walters, David Wynn. 1960. "Broadcasting in Canada." MA thesis, Northwestern University.

Watkins, Mel. 1982. "The Innis Tradition in Political Economy." *Canadian Journal of Political and Social Theory* 6 (1–2): 12–34.

Watson, H.G. 2018. "Over 250 Canadian News Media Outlets Have Closed in the Last 10 Years." *J-Source,* October 4. https://j-source.ca/over-250-canadian-news-media-outlets-have-closed-in-the-last-ten-years/.

Weir, E. Austin. 1965. *The Struggle for National Broadcasting in Canada.* Toronto: McClelland and Stewart.

Whitaker, Reg. 1977. "Images of the State in Canada." In *The Canadian State: Political Economy and Political Power,* edited by Leo Panitch, 43–56. Toronto: University of Toronto Press.

Whitson, David, and Richard Gruneau. 1997. "The Real Integrated Circus: Political Economy, Popular Culture, and 'Major League' Sport." In *Understanding Canada: Building on the New Canadian Political Economy,* edited by Wallace Clement, 359–85. Montreal and Kingston: McGill-Queen's University Press.

Whyte, M. 1999. "A Leap into Cyberspace: The CBC Is Making a Firm Commitment to New Media in the Belief That the Internet Is the Future. Does the Public Broadcaster Have Any Idea What It's Doing?" *National Post,* May 26, B9.

Williams, Glen. 1989. "Canada in the International Political Economy." In *The New Canadian Political Economy,* edited by W. Clement and G. Williams, 116–37. Montreal and Kingston: McGill-Queen's University Press.

Williams, Raymond. 1976. *Keywords: A Vocabulary of Culture and Society.* London: Fontana.

–. 1979. *Television, Technology and Cultural Form.* Glasgow: Fontana/Collins.

Winseck, Dwayne. 1995. "Power Shift? Towards a Political Economy of Canadian Telecommunication and Regulation." *Canadian Journal of Communication* 20: 81–106.

–. 1998. *Reconvergence: A Political Economy of Telecommunications in Canada.* Cresskill, NJ: Hampton Press.

–. 2014. "Arm's Length or Strong Arming the CRTC? Minister Moore's 'Mandate Letter' to CRTC Head Jean-Pierre Blais." *Mediamorphis,* January 9. https://dwmw.wordpress.com/2014/01/09/arms-length-or-strong-arming-the-crtc-minister-moores-mandate-letter-to-crtc-head-jean-pierre-blais/.

–. 2021a. "Bill C-10 and the Future of Internet Regulation in Canada." Centre for International Governance Innovation, June 2. https://www.cigionline.org/articles/bill-c-10-and-the-future-of-internet-regulation-in-canada/.

–. 2021b. *Growth and Upheaval in the Network Media Economy in Canada, 1984–2020.* Global Media and Internet Concentration Project, Carleton University. https://doi.org/10.22215/gmicp/2021.1.

–. 2022. *Media and Internet Concentration in Canada, 1984–2021*. Ottawa: Global Media and Internet Concentration Project, Carleton University. https://doi.org/10.22215/gmicp/2022.02.

Wirsig, Karen, and Catherine Edwards. 2018. "Public Community Partnerships to Improve Local Media in Canada." In *Journalism in Crisis: Bridging Theory and Practice for Democratic Media Strategies in Canada*, edited by Mike Gasher, Colette Brin, Christine Crowther, Gretchen King, Errol Salamon, and Simon Thibault, 101–24. Toronto: University of Toronto Press.

Woodrow, R. Brian, and Kenneth B. Woodside. 1982. *The Introduction of Pay TV in Canada*. Montreal: Institute for Research on Public Policy.

Woolf, Marie. 2022. "MPs Rush over 150 Amendments to Streaming Bill, Senate Says It Won't Be Pressured." *CBC News,* June 15. https://www.cbc.ca/news/politics/streaming-bill-committee-amendments-1.6490285.

–. 2023. "CBC Signals Plans to Go Full Streaming, Ending Traditional TV and Radio Broadcasts." *Globe and Mail,* February 7. https://www.theglobeandmail.com/politics/article-cbc-digital-streaming/.

Yakabuski, Konrad. 2018. "Will the CBC Find Its Raison d'être? Not Likely." *Globe and Mail,* April 5. https://www.theglobeandmail.com/opinion/article-will-the-cbc-find-its-raison-detre-not-likely/.

Zeller, Suzanne. 1987. *Inventing Canada: Early Victorian Science and the Idea of a Transcontinental Nation*. Toronto: University of Toronto Press.

Zerbisias, Antonia. 2005. "Feds' Media Stance Is Good News for Moguls." *Toronto Star,* April 12, D7.

Index

Note: (t) after a page number indicates a table.

audience share, 177, 178, 204–5, 217, 223–24, 233, 289*n*1; beginnings, 86–88; Board of Broadcast Governors conflict, 147–48; board of directors, 138, 224, 227, 240, 244–45, 248, 256; broadcast centre, 240; broadcasting regulation report, 216–21; Canadian programming expenditure (CPE) credits, 260–61; capitalization, 133, 284*n*10; content-sharing partnerships, 99–100, 250; controversial programming, 92, 282*n*5; criticisms of, 222; cultural nationalism, 106–7, 263, 283*n*15; vs cultural purposes, 95; domestic vs international news bureaus, 290*n*3(t); dual vs single system, 148; foreign licensing agreements, 157–58; francophone prime-time viewing, 238; government control scandals and censorship, 99, 282*n*9; government policy responsibilities, 105; high cultural programs, 149; Indigenous language programming, 195–96; in-house production, 184, 244, 246, 270; intellectual property rights, 270–71; internal strife, 147, 150; labour disputes, 150; legislative review submission, 252–53; letter to (board of directors), 244–45; licence renewal, 175–77, 213, 217, 238, 239, 258–62, 276; local news programming, 242–43, 255; local programming, 238, 246, 247, 255, 260; mandate, 154, 159, 160, 196, 198, 246, 289*n*6 (chap.9); mandate as "distinctively Canadian," 206, 265, 270, 271; mandate review, 206–7, 224–25, 252–53, 254–55, 256, 290*n*10; as national vs public broadcaster, 160; news bureaus, 100, 204, 240; news silos vs single hub, 289*n*4; as nimble organization, 265; Northern and Native Access Program, 195; opinion polls, 222; ownership alternatives, 109; policy and practices, 94–99; presidents, 205, 209, 219, 224, 233, 240, 249, 250; principal contradiction, 104; vs private competition, 129, 130–31, 133, 248; private media complaints, 248–50; private partnerships, 126, 130–31, 132, 273; private vs public interest, 88–89,

120–21, 126, 130–31, 263, 284*n*7, 290*n*1; programming strategy, 176; purposes, 88–89, 145–46, 246; regulatory commission relationship (CRTC), 175–77, 205, 208, 213, 217, 224, 260–61, 276; regulatory criticisms of, 175–77; regulatory flexibility, 239, 260–61; two public elements, 128; as two systems, 146; unions, 245. *See also* Canadian content; Radio-Canada
—advertising: advertisement-free proposal, 247; branded content production service, 259, 260, 261–62, 269–70; commercial time, 108, 283*n*14; competition, 255–56; co-operative agreements, 269; cost-per-thousand rates, 149, 286*n*12; vs cultural purposes, 95; dependence, 149, 267; elimination recommendation, 256; flexibility, 267, 268, 269; local advertising for regional service, 208; practices, 93–94, 96–98; pressures, 94–95; revenue, 90, 127, 130, 176, 237, 247; social sanctions, 96–98; sponsorships, 100–101. *See also* advertising
—digital: advertising, 238, 248–50; audience views, 248; audio broadcasting, 208; beginnings, 208–9; budget, 209; cross-promotion, 266; digital-only news, 238, 240; media pioneer and trailblazer, 263–64; music services, 215, 239; platforms, 244, 264; policy consultation brief, 246–47; programs of national interest (PNI), 260, 290*n*11; resource allocation, 244; streaming service, 250; technology, 225; television, 220; website beginnings, 208–9. *See also* digital media broadcasting
—funding: borrowing authority, 266; branded content production service, 259, 260, 261–62, 269–70; budget cutbacks, 147, 194, 204, 205–6, 207, 214, 215, 224, 233, 239–40, 241, 289*n*6 (chap. 8); budget disclosure refusal, 147–48; Canadian talent expenditures, 152–53; cutbacks protests, 205–6; defunding, 199–200, 265–66; diversified funding model, 267–68; excise tax, 122–23; expenditures, 93, 148, 282*nn*2–3; financial flexibility

Directors Guild of Canada (DGC), 236, 242
direct-to-home (DTH) satellite
broadcasting, 200–201, 230
Drache, Daniel, 17, 110
Dunton, Davidson, 133

Eaman, Ross, 101, 282*n*11
Easterbrook, W.T., 136, 285*n*2
economic development. *See* Canada;
political economy of communication
Edwards, Catherine, 273

Facebook, 223, 235, 237, 241
Fecan, Ivan, 233, 236
Federal Combines Investigation Act, 40
Federal Communications Commission
(FCC): broadcast regulation, 73, 288*n*8,
288*n*10; cable and satellite partnership,
165; television licensing, 111
Federal Court of Appeal: broadcast
exemptions, 235–36; licence renewal,
261; regulatory powers, 234
Federal Cultural Policy Review
Committee (Applebaum-Hébert
Committee), 183–84
federal government: budget cutbacks,
204, 289*n*6 (chap. 8); department
restructuring, 204; federal provincial
relations, 57–58, 62, 280*n*3; nationalist
program, 137, 280*n*3
Federal Radio Commission (FRC), 45
fee for carriage (value-for-signal), 230,
231, 233, 234, 235, 237
film industry (Canada): American
influence, 38, 40–41, 279*n*11 (chap. 2);
development challenges, 38, 40–41, 56,
279*n*11 (chap. 2); foreign film quotas,
40; funding, 168; screen time, 204;
transnational relations of production,
40–41
film industry (United States): branch-
plant structure, 40–41; monopolies, 111;
telefilms, 112, 113, 123, 125
Fink, Howard, 106, 282*n*8
Firestone, O.J., 286*n*12
First World War, 37, 57
Fordist regime of production, 82, 163, 172
Fowler Commission (Royal Commission
on Broadcasting), 110, 126–31, 132–34,
135, 138, 140, 283*n*14

Fowler II (Committee on Broadcasting),
144, 147, 160, 286*n*13
free trade agreements: Canada-US Free
Trade Agreement (CUSFTA), 190,
191–92, 204; North American Free Trade
Agreement (NAFTA), 190, 192, 204
French-language broadcasting:
consolidation, 199; content quota levels,
285*n*6; francophone Canadians, 197,
280*n*12; on Indigenous network, 211;
licensing appeal, 261; official language
minority communities (OLMC), 260,
290*n*12; prime-time Canadian content
schedule, 208, 216–17; radio broadcasting,
49, 72, 88, 92; specialty channel (ICI
ARTV), 243; streaming service (ICI
TOU), 250; Tele-Canada, 196. *See also*
Quebec; Radio-Canada; television
broadcasting industry (Canada)
Friends (formerly Friends of Canadian
Broadcasting), 261
Friends of Canadian Broadcasting, 242, 245
Frontier Coverage Plan, 177, 288*n*11

Galaxie digital audio service, 209
Gasher, Mike, 51
General Agreement on Tariffs and Trade
(GATT), 285*n*3
General Electric (GE), 44, 121
Gertler, Meric, 110
Gillen, David, 177
Girard-Peters (Task Force on the Economic
Status of Television), 186, 198–200
Glassco Commission (Royal Commission
on Government Organization), 147
Global Television Network, 175, 202, 212,
228, 290*n*3(t)
Globe and Mail newspaper, 213, 228, 249, 269
Golding, Peter, 10
Goldman Sachs, 228
Google, 223, 237, 241, 252
Gordon Commission (Royal Commission
on Canada's Economic Prospects), 136
Gramsci, Antonio, 82
Grey Cup, 148
Grierson, John, 41

Hardin, Herschel, 286*n*15
Harper, Stephen, 222, 233, 238, 245
Harvey, David, 163, 190